Honduras

WORLD BIBLIOGRAPHICAL SERIES

General Editors:
Robert G. Neville (Executive Editor)
John J. Horton

Robert A. Myers   Ian Wallace
Hans H. Wellisch   Ralph Lee Woodward, Jr.

John J. Horton is Deputy Librarian of the University of Bradford and currently Chairman of its Academic Board of Studies in Social Sciences. He has maintained a longstanding interest in the discipline of area studies and its associated bibliographical problems, with special reference to European Studies. In particular he has published in the field of Icelandic and of Yugoslav studies, including the two relevant volumes in the World Bibliographical Series.

Robert A. Myers is Associate Professor of Anthropology in the Division of Social Sciences and Director of Study Abroad Programs at Alfred University, Alfred, New York. He has studied post-colonial island nations of the Caribbean and has spent two years in Nigeria on a Fulbright Lectureship. His interests include international public health, historical anthropology and developing societies. In addition to *Amerindians of the Lesser Antilles: a bibliography* (1981), *A Resource Guide to Dominica, 1493-1986* (1987) and numerous articles, he has compiled the World Bibliographical Series volumes on *Dominica* (1987), *Nigeria* (1989) and *Ghana* (1991).

Ian Wallace is Professor of German at the University of Bath. A graduate of Oxford in French and German, he also studied in Tübingen, Heidelberg and Lausanne before taking teaching posts at universities in the USA, Scotland and England. He specializes in contemporary German affairs, especially literature and culture, on which he has published numerous articles and books. In 1979 he founded the journal *GDR Monitor*, which he continues to edit under its new title *German Monitor*.

Hans H. Wellisch is Professor emeritus at the College of Library and Information Services, University of Maryland. He was President of the American Society of Indexers and was a member of the International Federation for Documentation. He is the author of numerous articles and several books on indexing and abstracting, and has published *The Conversion of Scripts* and *Indexing and Abstracting: an International Bibliography*. He also contributes frequently to *Journal of the American Society for Information Science, The Indexer* and other professional journals.

Ralph Lee Woodward, Jr. is Chairman of the Department of History at Tulane University, New Orleans, where he has been Professor of History since 1970. He is the author of *Central America, a Nation Divided*, 2nd ed. (1985), as well as several monographs and more than sixty scholarly articles on modern Latin America. He has also compiled volumes in the World Bibliographical Series on *Belize* (1980), *Nicaragua* (1983), and *El Salvador* (1988). Dr. Woodward edited the Central American section of the *Research Guide to Central America and the Caribbean* (1985) and is currently editor of the Central American history section of the *Handbook of Latin American Studies*.

VOLUME 139

Honduras

Pamela F. Howard-Reguindin

Compiler

With the assistance of Martha E. McPhail

CLIO PRESS

OXFORD, ENGLAND · SANTA BARBARA, CALIFORNIA
DENVER, COLORADO

British Library Cataloguing in Publication Data

Howard-Reguindin, Pamela F.
Honduras. – (World bibliographical series v. 139)
I. Title   II. Series
016.9728

ISBN 1-85109-137-8

Clio Press Ltd.,
55 St. Thomas' Street,
Oxford OX1 1JG, England.

ABC-CLIO,
130 Cremona Drive,
Santa Barbara,
CA 93117, USA.

Designed by Bernard Crossland.
Typeset by Columns Design and Production Services Ltd, Reading, England.
Printed and bound in Great Britain by
Billing and Sons Ltd., Worcester.

972.83' 0016

THE WORLD BIBLIOGRAPHICAL SERIES

This series, which is principally designed for the English speaker, will eventually cover every country (and many of the world's principal regions), each in a separate volume comprising annotated entries on works dealing with its history, geography, economy and politics; and with its people, their culture, customs, religion and social organization. Attention will also be paid to current living conditions – housing, education, newspapers, clothing, etc.– that are all too often ignored in standard bibliographies; and to those particular aspects relevant to individual countries. Each volume seeks to achieve, by use of careful selectivity and critical assessment of the literature, an expression of the country and an appreciation of its nature and national aspirations, to guide the reader towards an understanding of its importance. The keynote of the series is to provide, in a uniform format, an interpretation of each country that will express its culture, its place in the world, and the qualities and background that make it unique. The views expressed in individual volumes, however, are not necessarily those of the publisher.

VOLUMES IN THE SERIES

1 *Yugoslavia*, John J. Horton
2 *Lebanon*, C. H. Bleaney
3 *Lesotho*, Shelagh M. Willet and David Ambrose
4 *Rhodesia/Zimbabwe*, Oliver B. Pollack and Karen Pollack
5 *Saudi Arabia*, Frank A. Clements
6 *USSR*, Anthony Thompson
7 *South Africa*, Reuben Musiker
8 *Malawi*, Robert B. Boeder
9 *Guatemala*, Woodman B. Franklin
10 *Pakistan*, David Taylor
11 *Uganda*, Robert L. Collison
12 *Malaysia*, Ian Brown and Rajeswary Ampalavanar
13 *France*, Frances Chambers
14 *Panama*, Eleanor DeSelms Langstaff
15 *Hungary*, Thomas Kabdebo
16 *USA*, Sheila R. Herstein and Naomi Robbins
17 *Greece*, Richard Clogg and Mary Jo Clogg
18 *New Zealand*, R. F. Grover
19 *Algeria*, Richard I. Lawless
20 *Sri Lanka*, Vijaya Samaraweera
21 *Belize*, Ralph Lee Woodward, Jr.
23 *Luxembourg*, Carlo Hury and Jul Christophory
24 *Swaziland*, Balam Nyeko
25 *Kenya*, Robert L. Collison
26 *India*, Brijen K. Gupta and Datta S. Kharbas
27 *Turkey*, Merel Güçlü
28 *Cyprus*, P. M. Kitromilides and M. L. Evriviades
29 *Oman*, Frank A. Clements
31 *Finland*, J. E. O. Screen
32 *Poland*, Richard C. Lewański
33 *Tunisia*, Allan M. Findlay, Anne M. Findlay and Richard I. Lawless
34 *Scotland*, Eric G. Grant
35 *China*, Peter Cheng
36 *Qatar*, P. T. H. Unwin
37 *Iceland*, John J. Horton
38 *Nepal*, John Whelpton
39 *Haiti*, Frances Chambers
40 *Sudan*, M. W. Daly
41 *Vatican City State*, Michael J. Walsh
42 *Iraq*, A. J. Abdulrahman
43 *United Arab Emirates*, Frank A. Clements
44 *Nicaragua*, Ralph Lee Woodward, Jr.
45 *Jamaica*, K. E. Ingram
46 *Australia*, I. Kepars
47 *Morocco*, Anne M. Findlay, Allan M. Findlay and Richard I. Lawless

48 *Mexico*, Naomi Robbins
49 *Bahrain*, P. T. H. Unwin
50 *The Yemens*, G. Rex Smith
51 *Zambia*, Anne M. Bliss and J. A. Rigg
52 *Puerto Rico*, Elena E. Cevallos
53 *Namibia*, Stanley Schoeman and Elna Schoeman
54 *Tanzania*, Colin Darch
55 *Jordan*, Ian J. Seccombe
56 *Kuwait*, Frank A. Clements
57 *Brazil*, Solena V. Bryant
58 *Israel*, Esther M. Snyder (preliminary compilation E. Kreiner)
59 *Romania*, Andrea Deletant and Dennis Deletant
60 *Spain*, Graham J. Shields
61 *Atlantic Ocean*, H. G. R. King
62 *Canada*, Ernest Ingles
63 *Cameroon*, Mark W. DeLancey and Peter J. Schraeder
64 *Malta*, John Richard Thackrah
65 *Thailand*, Michael Watts
66 *Austria*, Denys Salt with the assistance of Arthur Farrand Radley
67 *Norway*, Leland B. Sather
68 *Czechoslovakia*, David Short
69 *Irish Republic*, Michael Owen Shannon
70 *Pacific Basin and Oceania*, Gerald W. Fry and Rufino Mauricio
71 *Portugal*, P. T. H. Unwin
72 *West Germany*, Donald S. Detwiler and Ilse E. Detwiler
73 *Syria*, Ian J. Seccombe
74 *Trinidad and Tobago*, Frances Chambers
76 *Barbados*, Robert B. Potter and Graham M. S. Dann
77 *East Germany*, Ian Wallace
78 *Mozambique*, Colin Darch
79 *Libya*, Richard I. Lawless
80 *Sweden*, Leland B. Sather and Alan Swanson
81 *Iran*, Reza Navabpour
82 *Dominica*, Robert A. Myers
83 *Denmark*, Kenneth E. Miller
84 *Paraguay*, R. Andrew Nickson
85 *Indian Ocean*, Julia J. Gotthold with the assistance of Donald W. Gotthold

86 *Egypt*, Ragai, N. Makar
87 *Gibraltar*, Graham J. Shields
88 *The Netherlands*, Peter King and Michael Wintle
89 *Bolivia*, Gertrude M. Yeager
90 *Papua New Guinea*, Fraiser McConnell
91 *The Gambia*, David P. Gamble
92 *Somalia*, Mark W. DeLancey, Sheila L. Elliott, December Green, Kenneth J. Menkhaus, Mohammad Haji Moqtar, Peter J. Schraeder
93 *Brunei*, Sylvia C. Engelen Krausse, Gerald H. Krausse
94 *Albania*, William B. Bland
95 *Singapore*, Stella R. Quah, Jon S. T. Quah
96 *Guyana*, Frances Chambers
97 *Chile*, Harold Blakemore
98 *El Salvador*, Ralph Lee Woodward, Jr.
99 *The Arctic*, H.G.R. King
100 *Nigeria*, Robert A. Myers
101 *Ecuador*, David Corkhill
102 *Uruguay*, Henry Finch with the assistance of Alicia Casas de Barrán
103 *Japan*, Frank Joseph Shulman
104 *Belgium*, R.C. Riley
105 *Macau*, Richard Louis Edmonds
106 *Philippines*, Jim Richardson
107 *Bulgaria*, Richard J. Crampton
108 *The Bahamas*, Paul G. Boultbee
109 *Peru*, John Robert Fisher
110 *Venezuela*, D. A. G. Waddell
111 *Dominican Republic*, Kai Schoenhals
112 *Colombia*, Robert H. Davis
113 *Taiwan*, Wei-chin Lee
114 *Switzerland*, Heinz K. Meier and Regula A. Meier
115 *Hong Kong*, Ian Scott
116 *Bhutan,* Ramesh C. Dogra
117 *Suriname*, Rosemarijn Hoefte
118 *Djibouti*, Peter J. Schraeder
119 *Grenada*, Kai Schoenhals
120 *Monaco*, Grace L. Hudson
121 *Guinea-Bissau*, Rosemary Galli
122 *Wales*, Gwilym Huws and D. Hywel E. Roberts
123 *Cape Verde*, Caroline S. Shaw
124 *Ghana*, Robert A. Myers
125 *Greenland*, Kenneth E. Miller

126 *Costa Rica*, Charles L. Stansifer
127 *Siberia*, David N. Collins
128 *Tibet*, John Pinfold
129 *Northern Ireland*, Michael Owen
     Shannon
130 *Argentina*, Alan Biggins
132 *Burma*, Patricia M. Herbert
133 *Laos*, Helen Cordell
134 *Monserrat*, Riva Berleant-Schiller

135 *Afghanistan*, Schuyler Jones
136 *Equatorial Guinea*, Randall Fegley
137 *Turks and Caicos Islands*, Paul G.
     Boultbee
138 *Virgin Islands*, Verna Penn Moll
139 *Honduras*, Pamela F. Howard-
     Reguindin
140 *Mauritius*, Pramila Ramgulam
     Bennett

*Dedicated to those who have
made life such a pleasure:
my family and close friends*

In memory of Donald Allen Howard

Contents

INTRODUCTION xv

THE COUNTRY AND ITS PEOPLE 1
General   1
Current events   4

GEOGRAPHY 6
General   6
Regional   8
Geology and natural resources   9
Maps, atlases and gazetteers   10

TOURISM 14
General   14
Sailing directions   16

TRAVELLERS' ACCOUNTS 17

FLORA AND FAUNA 25
General   25
Flora   26
Fauna   27

PREHISTORY AND ARCHAEOLOGY 32
General   32
Copán   40

HISTORY 47
Central America: general   47
Honduras: general   50
Local, urban, regional and departmental   53
Colonial   57
19th century   60
20th century   63

POPULATION 66

Contents

ETHNIC GROUPS AND REFUGEES 69
Black Caribs (Garífunas) 69
Native peoples 71
Refugees 74

FOLKLORE 77

RELIGION 80

SOCIAL CONDITIONS 84
General 84
Social structure 87
Social problems 90

SOCIAL SERVICES, HEALTH AND WELFARE 93

HUMAN RIGHTS 100

POLITICS 104
Central American region 104
Honduran characteristics 108
Political parties 113

MILITARY, ARMED FORCES AND DEFENCE 116

FOREIGN RELATIONS 121
General 121
With other Central American states 124
With USA 129

CONSTITUTION, LAWS AND JUDICIAL SYSTEM 136

ADMINISTRATION AND LOCAL GOVERNMENT 142

STATISTICS 144

ECONOMICS 146

INVESTMENT, FINANCE, BANKING AND CURRENCY 156

TRADE, COMMERCE, INDUSTRY AND MINING 160

FORESTRY 165

AGRICULTURE, LAND TENURE AND AGRARIAN REFORM ... 167

TRANSPORTATION AND COMMUNICATION 174

Contents

LABOUR AND TRADE UNIONS 177

ENVIRONMENT AND ECOLOGY 184

EDUCATION 186

SCIENCE AND TECHNOLOGY 192

LITERATURE 194

LANGUAGE 200

THE ARTS 203

LIBRARIES AND ARCHIVES 207

BOOKS, PUBLISHING, JOURNALISM AND MASS MEDIA 209

PROFESSIONAL PUBLICATIONS 211

ENCYCLOPAEDIAS AND DIRECTORIES 213

BIBLIOGRAPHIES 215

INDEX OF AUTHORS 221

INDEX OF TITLES 227

INDEX OF SUBJECTS 243

MAP OF HONDURAS 259

Introduction

On Christopher Columbus's fourth and final voyage in 1502, he landed on the island of Guanaja, one of the Bay Islands to the north of Honduras. Shortly afterwards he sailed to the mainland and took possession of the territory of Honduras on behalf of the King of Spain. The conquest of the territory known as 'the depths' began twenty years later.

The history of Honduras from conquest to 1821 exhibited numerous characteristics common to many of the other Spanish colonies: enslavement and or decimation of the native people, extractive mining, establishment of large haciendas, and the imposition of Catholicism. Independence was declared in 1821 and a popular federal government emerged. Honduras at that period formed part of the United Provinces of Central America. It was a tenuous union at best, subject to constant struggles and a civil war, and in spite of General Francisco Morazán's valiant efforts to hold it together, the union was dissolved in 1839. Since then a succession of elected presidents and military strongmen have ruled the nation. Currently the government is divided into three branches: legislative, executive and judicial.

When speaking about development in Latin America, there is a common adage which applies to any number of countries: 'Honduras (Brazil, Mexico, etc.) es el país que siempre será' (Honduras is the country that always will be . . .). The underlying message – that the country will never reach its full economic potential – is somewhat puzzling in the case of Honduras. The country is in what should have been a perfect location for trade (other than narcotics transhipments), it has people and fertile lands capable of producing large quantities of highly desirable commodities such as bananas and coffee, and when compared to its neighbours, has enjoyed a relatively democratic political system and a considerable amount of tranquillity. Yet, in spite of billions of dollars of foreign aid, it has remained one of the poorest nations in the world, characterized disparagingly and unfortunately as a 'rented republic only because it

Introduction

could not sell its sovereignty' (Selser, *Honduras: república aquilada*), a collection of nothing-to-do-but-stare villages, the quintessential banana republic, or even worse, a dump in the centre of the world.

Geography

The second largest country in Central America (only its neighbour to the south, Nicaragua, surpasses it in size), Honduras is roughly the size of Tennessee or England, encompassing an area of 112,088 square kilometres (43,277 square miles). The extremely mountainous terrain has caused it to be described as not unlike a neglected, crumpled piece of paper, a fact which has probably served as a deterrent or an obstacle to its progressive development. Its numerous narrow river valleys tend to attract the majority of the population. The long Caribbean coastline to the north stretches 644 kilometres (400 miles), offering many isolated, sandy beaches, reefs, the Bay Islands and the Honduran part of the Mosquito Coast. To the south, the very brief, 64-kilometre (40-mile) Pacific Ocean boundary lies on the Gulf of Fonseca, the waters of which are shared with El Salvador and Nicaragua (and which have been a constant source of disputation between the countries). Lowland savannas cover the eastern region, reaching from the Caribbean to the inland central mountains. Thanks to the numerous mountain ranges, the climate varies tremendously in the central region but in general, is temperate. To the north, the coast tends to be hot, humid and sticky. Precipitation varies, with the north coast and eastern lowlands getting the lion's share of rainfall. In the interior and on the Pacific Coast there are distinct wet and dry seasons with the months from May to November being the wettest.

Society

The population of Honduras was estimated to be 3.6 million in 1980, 4 million by 1983 and is now estimated at just over 5 million, with an annual growth rate of 3.1 per cent. Most of the people live in the central interior and on the northern coast, leaving the eastern savannas sparsely populated. Almost 60 per cent of the population live in rural areas. The largest cities are Tegucigalpa, the capital, with an estimated 608,100 inhabitants; San Pedro Sula with approximately 400,000; La Ceiba, 105,000 and Choluteca, 57,000. Over 90 per cent of the population is considered *mestizo*, with varying degrees of Spanish, African and native American backgrounds. The population

xvi

of the northern coast is the most diverse; there are *mestizos*, Black Caribs (Garífunas), West Indian blacks and, to a lesser extent, Chinese and Middle Eastern 'turcos' or 'arabes'. To the east there are large numbers of Miskito (native Americans), many of whom associate freely and regularly with the Miskito of Nicaragua. Although Spanish is the official language spoken as a primary or secondary language by everyone, English is commonly used by Bay Islanders and north coast residents. The Black Caribs, Miskito, Sumu and Lenca peoples each maintain their own language in addition to using Spanish. The vast majority of the population adheres to the Roman Catholic faith; however, to the east the Moravian Church has many converts and on the Bay Islands there are many Methodists. For most of the nation medical care ranges from minimal to non-existent; thus there are high rates of infant and childhood mortality and malnutrition. The life expectancy of males is 58 years, the lowest in Central America. The most persistent major diseases are malaria, enteric illnesses, typhoid and influenza. Literacy rates have improved somewhat since the 1950s, reaching 56 per cent of the population by 1990. Although there are over 8,000 primary schools, completion of studies is relatively rare; this is even more so at one of the four universities.

Economy

As with all of the Central American countries, the Honduran economy is largely agrarian. Once limited to the cultivation of bananas, crop diversification has evolved. Today the main products are sugar-cane, corn, bananas (still the principal crop), coffee, cattle, beans, cotton, sorghum and tobacco. Most manufacturing revolves around food processing and simple assembly operations of small consumer goods such as foods, beverages, fabrics and tobacco products.

The major trading partners of Honduras are the United States (not surprisingly), Japan, Venezuela, Mexico, the Central American Common Market, and the European Economic Community. Export products include bananas, coffee, wood, beef, sugar and silver. The major imported commodities include machinery, chemicals, manufactured equipment, and raw materials such as petroleum. Overall, the per capita income in Honduras ranks at the bottom, along with Haiti, for the Western hemisphere. In 1970, it was US$725 and in 1980, $886, but it slipped back to $850 in 1988, leaving the citizenry little better off than it was in the 1970s – or worse if inflation is taken into account. And this after over one billion dollars in foreign aid from the US alone between 1980 and 1987.

Introduction

Transportation and communication

Historically, the transportation system in Honduras was constructed primarily to benefit the banana plantation owners and facilitate the exportation of their 'green gold'. Consequently, access to, in and about the country is rather difficult. Virtually all of the 1,268 kilometres of railway lines are in the north, leading from inland valley plantations to the coastal ports of Puerto Cortés, Tela, La Ceiba, Puerto Castilla, Trujillo and Puerto Lempira. The 12,058 kilometres of roads also tend to be used more for transporting goods for export than for inter-urban convenience. Even the Pan-American highway, built during World War II, is several dozen kilometres distant from the capital, Tegucigalpa, and only briefly passes through southern Honduras. The country supports two international airports: one tucked into the mountains near Tegucigalpa and the other in San Pedro Sula. There are in addition around a dozen US military airstrips.

In the realm of communication, radios are still a major source of news and education with over five times as many radio as television transmitters. Computers *are* being used, but they are a long way from being common. There are four major daily newspapers: *La Tribuna* and *El Heraldo* in Tegucigalpa and *El Tiempo* and *La Prensa* in San Pedro Sula.

Government and politics

Honduran politics of the nineteenth and twentieth centuries borders on the surreal with a steady succession of 117 presidents taking office between 1824 and 1933, lasting no more than a year on average. North American power, influence and interference has been constant, and more often than not, uncompromising in the political and commercial spheres. Yet, throughout its turbulent history, the roots of a two-party political system emerged and developed, and today, politics revolve around the Liberal and Conservative parties, with a significant rôle being played by the armed forces. For most of the 1960s and up to 1981, the military was the principal force in politics, either governing directly, influencing general policy, or controlling national security affairs (see *Honduras: a country study*). But the military was finally forced to relinquish power when charges of ineptitude and corruption surfaced, and presidential elections were held in 1981, returning the country to civilian rule – at least officially so. For most of the 1980s, an uncomfortable and often controversial triumvirate – the Honduran president, the leader of the military and the Central American policies of the Ronald Reagan administration – ruled the nation.

About the bibliography

In view of the availability of CD-ROM products and online database searching, one can only consider bibliographies such as this to be a 'ready reference' first step towards initiating the research process. It is not a substitute for thorough research of published or online bibliographical resources and the personal guidance of librarians, professors or specialists. An attempt was made to keep within the English-language preference of the Series' guidelines; however, because of the paucity of research about Honduras in certain fields, it was necessary to include several hundred entries of Spanish-language materials. These have been given particularly detailed annotations to better inform the non-Spanish reader. The uneven coverage in some sections reflects the vagaries of the publishing field and the ebb and flow of scholarly interest in a given topic. Consequently, the chapters on archaeology, history and politics are rather full, while those on religion, local government and forestry are less so.

Book-length studies were given preference over journal articles; however, substantial, current articles of lasting value were also included. Articles of fewer than five pages were generally excluded as were those written prior to 1985, with a few exceptions. Several significant doctoral dissertations written after 1985 have been included, but one should not fail to consult University Microfilm International's (UMI) compact disk or online database service to ascertain the existence of a dissertation on a given Honduran topic before starting to write one's own. Many dissertations are available through normal inter-library loan channels, and those that are not can be obtained through the offices of UMI (300 N. Zeeb Road, Ann Arbor, MI 48106). Only a couple of readily available masters' theses have been included because of their uniqueness or potential usefulness. As for US government documents, a search of the Government Printing Office compact disk revealed over 70 unclassified items concerning Honduras; a selection of only the most recent and significant have been included.

The bulk of the materials included in the bibliography are readily available at Arizona State University, University of California at Los Angeles, or San Diego State University and are accessible via inter-library loan services. No effort was made to include more inaccessible materials such as manuscripts, rare books or special collections. Although there are excellent research collections of Honduran materials available at the University of California at Berkeley, Tulane University and the University of Texas at Austin, it was not possible to make trips to view those resources for this bibliography. In any case, it was the compiler's intention to include primarily mainstream publications which are to be found in mid- to large-sized libraries and which are easily accessible and available for review.

Introduction

Acknowledgements

A bibliography such as this represents the collective thoughts and labours of hundreds of scholars, writers, officials and others who have been motivated, inspired or impelled to share their insights on a country very dear to them. Without their endeavours and personal sacrifices, this bibliography would have been impossible to compile. It would also have been a difficult task without the support, advice, assistance and tolerance of many other generous people. First, I would like to express my sincere appreciation to Martha McPhail of San Diego State University who joined this project rather late in its genesis but gave it new life and contributed greatly to its content. She enthusiastically identified 150 new sources for the bibliography and wrote approximately 225 of the annotations. She brought to the project her personal insight and knowledge of Honduras, gained while working there as a Fulbright lecturer in library science, and offered many critical suggestions to improve its scope, content and format. In addition, I am grateful to the Professional Development Committee of the Arizona State University Library for two grants to offset expenses associated with the bibliography. Dennis Brunning, Doug Stewart and Anne Leibold of the Reference Department of Arizona State University provided valuable computer expertise at the start of the project for which I am indebted. Norma Corral of the Reference Department of the University Research Library, University of California at Los Angeles and Deborah Blouin of the Reference Department of Arizona State University were instrumental in obtaining massive inter-library loans and catalogue computer print-outs without which this work would have been greatly delayed. David Shepherd, of Southwestern College, deserves warm and heartfelt gratitude for recuperating the full database when I thought I had deleted and lost it for good. I am also grateful to Catherine Friedman of San Diego State University and Suzanne Ramirez for lending me their personal computers to complete the project. Throughout the task, my husband, Henry, and mother, Dorothy, have been good-natured pillars of strength and support in a variety of ways.

Pamela Howard-Reguindin
Washington, DC
January 1992

The Country and Its People

General

1 **Beautiful Honduras: experiences in a small town on the Caribbean.**
Hilda de Casteñada.   London: Stockwell, 1934. 47p. maps.
A collection of well-written essays portraying the lifestyle of the tropical Caribbean coastal zone, focusing on descriptions of the setting and the daily lives of the inhabitants. Contains illustrations of the countryside.

2 **Honduras.**
Boulogne, France: Editions Delroisse, [1975?]. 144p. maps.
An excellent source of contemporary colour photographs on Honduras, this coffee-table tome will delight young and older readers alike. Linguists will appreciate the text in Spanish, French, English and German which briefly covers Honduran culture, geography, and history. The lack of a table of contents or an index hinders its use.

3 **Honduras.**
Allan Carpenter, Tom Balow.   Chicago, Illinois: Children's Press, 1971. 95p. maps. (Enchantment of Central America).
Written for the young reader, this series explores the people and their lives, government, problems and international relations. In addition to social conditions this volume on Honduras highlights the many natural resources – islands, mahogany trees, silver and soil – that Columbus missed in his quest for treasures. One chapter relates the life stories of three children in three different areas of Honduras. The 'Handy Reference Section' contains a time line, pronunciation guide, instant facts and holidays. The text is followed by an index.

4 Honduras.

Luís Marinas Otero. Tegucigalpa: Universidad Nacional Autónoma de Honduras, 1983. 399p.

This basic textbook pays particular attention to the history, geography and social situation of contemporary Honduras. It is divided into two parts; the first provides a general survey of the country and the second deals with more specific aspects of Honduran history.

5 Honduras.

Noé Pineda Portillo. Madrid: Anaya, 1988. 126p. bibliog. (Biblioteca Iberoamericana, no. 89).

This excellent overview of Honduras depicts its land, people, economy and governmental organization. The geology and main physical features are aptly described as are the principal cities. All topics are illustrated with beautiful colour photographs.

6 Honduras: a country guide.

Tom Barry, Kent Norsworthy. Albuquerque, New Mexico: Inter-Hemispheric Education Resource Center, 1990. 160p. map. bibliog.

The Resource Center is a non-profit, private research and policy institute founded in 1979. It produces books, policy reports, and audio-visual materials about US foreign relations with Third World countries. Barry is senior analyst at the Center and he and Norsworthy have written several books on Central America. This is an excellent, concise alternative to the thorough yet conservative *Honduras: a country study* by the American University, Foreign Area Studies Department (q.v.). In addition to a solid analysis of recent political, economic and social events, the authors include hard-to-find information on women, guerrillas, para-military groups, quality of communications, media and the environment.

7 Honduras: a country study.

Edited by James D. Rudolph. Washington, DC: American University, 1984. 2nd ed. 294p. maps. bibliog. (Area Handbook Series; DA pam.; 550-151).

As described in the Foreword, 'this volume is one of a continuing series of books prepared by Foreign Area Studies, The American University, under the Country Studies/Area Handbook Program'. Written by a team of social scientists, the study focuses on historical antecedents and on the cultural, socio-economic and political characteristics of Honduras. Of particular value are the chapters on national security (military), the numerous tables and diagrams, the list of acronyms and the thorough index. It is probably the best, succinct general overview in English of contemporary Honduras and is a useful introduction for students, travellers and persons who might be relocating to the country. This volume supersedes the *Area handbook for Honduras* (Washington, DC: Foreign Area Studies of the American University, 1971).

8 Honduras: descriptive, historical, and statistical.

Ephraim George Squier. New York: Harper, 1858. Reprinted, New York: AMS, 1970. 278p. map.

A rewritten and slightly expanded version of the Honduran section from the author's earlier work entitled *The states of Central America* published in 1858 (q.v.). It includes supplementary material from secondary works to add to his own observations.

9 **Honduras: eye of the storm.**
   Mike Edwards. *National Geographic*, vol. 164 (Nov. 1983), p. 608-37.
   maps.

A National Geographic staff writer and photographer capture the essence of Honduran daily life and recount the sentiments of local élites and workers during their visit. Travelling mostly by land, the pair describe and show their encounters in Tegucigalpa, Tela, Copán, San Pedro Sula and border regions. As is usual with *National Geographic*, it is an excellent source of colour photographs depicting many aspects of Honduras. There is one map showing the distribution of Nicaraguan and Salvadoran refugees as of 1983, and another larger one of the road system, pinpointing the location of specific refugees camps, reception centres, agricultural and mineral resources.

10 **Honduras: general descriptive data.**
   Washington, DC: Pan American Union, 1924, 1946.

Interesting as a source of cursory views of Honduras in 1924 and 1946 – the only two issues available for review. Subjects include history, government, mining, exports, and education. Both contain many good black-and-white photographs. Earlier issues were published under the International Bureau of the American Republics.

11 **Honduras in pictures.**
   Prepared by the Geography Department of Lerner Publications
   Company. Minneapolis, Minnesota: Lerner Publications, 1987. 64p.
   (Visual Geography Series).

A revised edition of *Honduras in pictures* by Ken Weddle. 'Text and pictures provide a close look at the land, people, history, government, and economy of this Central American nation.' A good source of illustrations, but the text is rather dry and probably would not hold the attention of the children for whom it was written. It includes an index.

12 **Honduras: panorama y perspectivas.** (Honduras: panorama and
   perspectives.)
   Compiled by Leticia Salomón (et al.). Tegucigalpa: Centro de
   Documentación de Honduras, 1989. 244p.

Five essays by well-known university professors concerning the political system, armed forces and the Central American crisis, industrial concentration, economic, social and political issues and ethnic groups.

13 **Honduras: post report.**
   Washington, DC: Department of State, 1980- .

Irregularly published reports for the benefit of US personnel stationed at foreign posts or for the general tourist concerning living conditions at the various posts. They contain encapsulated information about history, politics and statistics for Honduras.

14 **Honduras: the making of a banana republic.**
Allison Acker. Boston, Massachusetts: South End Press, 1988. 250p.
maps.

Acker, a Canadian journalist, visited Honduras in 1984 and was inspired to probe more deeply into the historical and political aspects of the nation. She intentionally presents the little-explored Honduran perspective of national events by using Spanish-language sources and interviews with Hondurans. The result is a highly readable interpretation of Honduras from the days of conquest to the present. Following a brief yet titillating analysis of Honduras through foreign eyes as a primitive paradise or hell and Bananaland, Acker traces the national history from conquest through independence, civil war, the age of adventurism, the Banana empires (including 'Sam the Banana Man', Samuel Zemurray), party politics and the military connection. She concludes that the future of Honduras will be as full of exploitation and chaos as has its rocky past.

15 **The new Honduras: its situation, resources, opportunities, and prospects.**
Thomas R. Lombard. Chicago, Illinois; New York: Brentano's, 1887. 102p.

An account of the state of the nation as it was in 1886 emphasizing its new peace and stability and its prospects for the future, in contrast to the past. Brief historical outlines precede the description, which is based on the author's observations. Subjects considered include climate, agriculture, mining, and politics. The work is illustrated.

Current events

16 **Central America report.**
Guatemala: Inforpress Centroamericana, 1972- . weekly.

Informative, concise and objective reviews of Central American politics, economics, foreign relations and political–military matters. Each issue contains something about each country, including Honduras. The length varies from about 8 to 12 pages.

17 **Highlights: a confidential report, Central America and Panama.**
Miami, Florida: Centro Latinoamericano de Noticias, 1989- . monthly.

Up-to-date analyses of Central American politics and foreign relations by Latin American scholars and journalists. Issues tend to be about 20 pages in length with numerous photographs, tables and graphs.

18 **Honduras This Week: your Central American weekly review.**
Tegucigalpa: [n.p], [1988?]- . weekly.

An English-language newspaper presenting business, economic and diplomatic developments around Honduras. Deliberately selective in coverage, it does not print 'negative' news items. A weekly feature concerns commercial opportunities for import–export business. Its coverage reflects its membership: the Honduran Chamber of Tourism, the Honduran–American Chamber of Commerce, and the Chamber of

Commerce and Industry of Tegucigalpa. The name changed from *Tegucigalpa This Week* with volume four in 1991.

19 **Honduras Update.**
Cambridge, Massachusetts: Honduras Information Center, 1983- . monthly.
A newsletter concerning politics, government and human rights issues in Honduras.

20 **Mesoamérica.**
Fred B. Morris, Director.   San José, Costa Rica: Institute for Central American Studies, 1982- . monthly.
Reviews the current events of Central America on a monthly basis. Overall coverage includes political and economic issues with both factual reporting and commentaries.

21 **Update Latin America.**
Washington, DC: Washington Office on Latin America, 1976- . bi-monthly.
A very useful newsletter, usually 8-10 pages in length, with good coverage of the Central American republics. Since it is published by a non-governmental human rights organization chiefly supported by private foundations and religious organizations, human rights issues figure prominently in its reporting.

Geography

General

22 The geography of the savannas of interior Honduras.
Carl L. Johannessen.   Berkeley, California: University of California
Press, 1963. 283p. bibliog.

A preliminary report on the region, based on fieldwork done in 1954-56. Designed to emphasize the impact of human activity, it provides detailed reports on the vegetation, water, and economy. The report, which contains appropriate maps, tables and illustrations, discusses all aspects of agriculture, including native vegetation and cultivated plants, and their impact upon the geography.

23 High jungles and low.
Archie Fairly Carr.   Gainesville, Florida: University of Florida Press,
1953. 226p.

'A naturalist with a social conscience and a sense of humor' [Foreword, p. ix], and a University of Florida biology professor, Carr taught for five years at the Escuela Agrícola Panamericana (Panamerican Agricultural School) located south of Tegucigalpa, sixty miles from the Pacific coast. In his informative and amusing reminiscences of family life in Honduras in the late 1940s, he tells of the land, the people, geographical features and animals he encounters on a daily basis or on extended trips. Of particular note are his thoughts on north–south technology transfer, his description of the 'Penca' people, and a month-long diary of a trip to the 'wild country back of Pearl Lagoon on the Caribbean side of Nicaragua' with a United Fruit forester. The text is followed by sixteen pages of black-and-white photographs and an index.

24 **Honduras.**
Edward Wilkin Perry.   New York: Duffield, 1923. 395p.

A general description of Honduras with some historical commentary, but focusing on
physical features, agriculture, and mineral wealth, and including notes on the
conditions in 1921. Considerable attention is devoted to personal experiences,
inconveniences, and pests.

25 **Middle America: its lands and peoples.**
Robert Cooper West.   Englewood Cliffs, New Jersey: Prentice Hall,
1989. 3rd ed. 494p. maps. bibliog.

The revised, third edition of this cultural and historical geography of Central America,
Mexico and the West Indies has retained much of the historical material in the
previous editions, but the author has greatly updated the information on contemporary
Middle America and has added new maps and illustrations. Historical geographical
data on Honduras are spread throughout the text, but the principal characteristics of
the present-day land and people are given on pages 419 to 429.

26 **The new El Dorado: a short sketch of Honduras, C.A., its people,
climate, natural resources, and vast mineral wealth.**
J. B. Daniel.   Philadelphia, Pennsylvania: Dunlap & Clarke, 1888.
60p. maps.

This brief description written for the North American audience seeks to familarize its
readers with Honduras and to convince them that it is a civilized and cultured nation
with vast resources, and to encourage settlement and investment there. It includes a
report of the mineral deposits by Harvey Beckworth, identified as a mining expert.
Several illustrations reveal much about the era.

27 **Spanish Honduras: its rivers, lagoons, savannas, mountains, minerals,
forests, fish, game, agriculture, products, fruits, transportation and
natives.**
American–Honduras Company.   New York: W. R. Gillespie, 1906.
183p.

Another glowing description of the development possibilities in Honduras, particularly
in the areas of the company's concessions. Written for the express purpose of attracting
investors, it focuses on economic conditions and prospects, resources, and transportation potential, particularly regarding railroad and port facilities that the company
proposes to build. It includes engineering reports, as well as general description,
illustrations and data on the economy.

Regional

28 **Historical geography of the Bay Islands, Honduras: Anglo-Hispanic conflict in the western Caribbean.**
William V. Davidson. Birmingham, Alabama: Southern University Press, 1974. 199p. bibliog.

A most informative study of both the physical and the cultural geography of the Bay Islands off the north coast of Honduras in the Caribbean. The eight islands and sixty-five cays have a land area of ninety-two square miles. The author notes their physical features, rainfall, vegetation and other specific aspects of geography. An archaeological record suggests that the first residents were Paya. Buccaneering, common for years, helped create a strong British influence, present even today, although the culture is an admixture of Black Caribs, Spaniards, North Americans, Hondurans and others. The work is well illustrated and offers an excellent bibliography.

29 **Life and nature under the tropics: or, Sketches of travels among the Andes, and on the Orinoco, Río Negro, and Amazon.**
Henry Morris Myers, P. V. N. Myers. New York: D. Appleton, 1871. 330p. map.

The narrative of a scientific expedition sent out by the Lyceum of Natural History of Williams College in the summer of 1867. It is useful for its study of the flora and fauna of the Black River region, also known as the Río Tinto or Río Negro.

30 **Monografía del Departamento de Copán.** (Monograph of the Department of Copán.)
Jesus B. Y. Membreno. Tegucigalpa: Talleres Tipográficos Nacionales, 1942. 118p. maps. (Biblioteca de la Sociedad de Geografía e Historia de Honduras).

A geographical description of the westernmost department of Honduras and each of its five districts and sixteen municipalities. Contains an illustrated report on archaeological work conducted in 1939 at the Copán ruins by Gustav Stromsvik.

31 **Olancho: an account of the resources of the State of Honduras in Central America, especially of the Department of Olancho.**
New York Navigation and Colonization Company. New York: Wynkoop & Hallenbeck, 1865. 65p.

A description of the Company's 1859 concession to send settlers to the region. A glowing account of its physical features, resources and potential, data about Honduran products, and regulations regarding immigration, are all designed to interest potential colonists.

32 **Savannas of interior Honduras.**
Carl L. Johannessen. Berkeley, California: University of California
Press, 1963. 160p. maps. bibliog. (Ibero-Americana, 46).
Based on observations made during two field surveys, one in the rainy season (1954)
and the other at the beginning of the dry season (1955-56). The first visit included
Tegucigalpa, Zamorano, the Río Guayape Valley, the North Coast and the Bay
Islands. The second trip covered Danlí, Choluteca, Comayagua, Siguatepeque, Yoro,
Olanchito, San Esteban, Catacamas, Juticalpa and Talanga. Johannessen traces
historical shifts in plant associations in order to better understand the distribution of
the vegetation as it is today, and concludes that the existing vegetation is a product of
human activity as much as the result of physical environment. Chapters deal with the
physical setting, human settlement, modification of the savannas, and potential
influences on changes in vegetation and soils.

Geology and natural resources

33 **Coral reefs of the world.**
Prepared by the IUCN Conservation Monitoring Centre in collaboration
with the United Nations Environment Programme (UNEP), edited by
Susan M. Wells. Nairobi, Kenya: United Nations Environment
Programme and International Union for Conservation of Nature and
Natural Resources, 1988. 3 vols. maps. bibliog.
As many data as could be located on Honduran coral reefs are presented in volume 2,
pages 169-73, but, as the compiler notes, no information exists for mainland reefs. The
proposed marine park for Roatán in the Bay Islands is physically described, with notes
on its reef structure and corals, flora and fauna, economic and social value,
disturbances it has faced, its legal protection and management. Several recommendations for its protection are suggested. The same categories of information are provided
for the Swan Islands, but no information was available about their legal protection or
management.

34 **Curiosidades y bellezas de Honduras.** (Curiosities and beautiful sights of
Honduras.)
Eduardo Hernández Chévez. Tegucigalpa: Editorial Universitaria,
Universidad Autónoma de Honduras, 1985. 215p. maps. (Colección
Letras Hondureñas, no. 24).
Each of the eighteen departments of Honduras is briefly studied from the historical
and political points of view, and then the respective geographical attributes are
described. Most interesting however, are the descriptions of natural curiosities and of
the especially beautiful spots of each department. For instance, the annual crab
invasion of Atlántida is noted, as is the painted rock of La Ceiba. Caves, hot springs,
lakes, and other geographical features of interest are recorded. This source would be
of particular use to travellers interested in the unusual natural features of the country.

35 **Geochemistry at Honduran geothermal sites.**
Fraser Goff (et al.). *Los Alamos Science*, vol. 14 (Fall 1986), p. 90-3.

A scientific report from the Los Alamos National Laboratory concerning the exploration of several Honduran geothermal sites. The report focuses on the geochemical aspects of each site and includes findings on mineral deposits, water analysis and geophysical characteristics.

36 **Geology of Honduran geothermal sites.**
Dean B. Eppler. *Los Alamos Science*, vol. 14 (Fall 1986), p. 86-9.
maps. bibliog.

Discusses a joint Los Alamos National Laboratory and Honduran-sponsored project which aimed to document the location and geology of several geothermal sites in Honduras.

37 **South of the border: hot springs and hissing steam vents at an old mining town may fuel electrical power in Honduras.**
Robert Gannon. *Earth Science*, vol. 41 (Summer 1988), p. 12-13.

Discusses the possibility of harnessing geothermal heat beneath Plantanares, near the Guatemalan border. The hot springs and gas vents – twenty-eight groups over 0.2 square kilometres – lie along north–south faults. Mention is made of the rock formations of the area and the text is accompanied by several photographs.

38 **Volcanic history of Honduras.**
Howel Williams, Alexander R. McBirney. Berkeley, California: University of California, 1969. 101p. bibliog. (University of California Publications in Geological Sciences, vol. 85).

A major source for the geological and volcanic history of Honduras, this volume is based on sixteen weeks of fieldwork conducted between 1964 and 1967 by these recognized scholars in the field. Detailed, scientific information about the geological make-up of the land and the many maps and tables of numerical data enhance the scientific value of the study. An appendix entitled 'Microscopic petrography' provides descriptions of rock formations and their locations along the roads of various regions.

Maps, atlases and gazetteers

39 **Atlas of Central America.**
Stanley A. Arbingast (et. al.), cartography by William L. Hezlep. Austin, Texas: Bureau of Business Research, University of Texas, 1979. 62p. maps. bibliog.

The atlas treats each of the seven Central American republics separately, and also together as a region. For individual countries there are colour maps (on varying scales) delineating administration, population, economic activity, transportation and geology. The dates of the maps range from 1961 to 1974.

40   **The atlas of Central America and the Caribbean.**
     Diagram Group.   New York: Macmillan; London: Collier Macmillan,
     1985. maps.

This attractively illustrated atlas 'integrates maps, charts, diagrams, tables and text to
provide a unique, up-to-date reference guide to two-thirds of all Western Hemisphere
countries' [Foreword]. Part one summarizes the natural aspects of both the Caribbean
and Central America: climate, topography, vegetation, wildlife, waters, and prehistory
and history from 12,000 years ago to 1985. Part two covers Guatemala to Panamá with
profiles of each country in geographical order. Maps highlight towns, transportation
systems, tourist centres and national parks. It is particularly useful for the identification
of the national coats of arms and flags. Honduras appears on pages 44-7. Part three
concerns the Caribbean islands.

41   **Cartografía de la América Central: publicaciones de la Comisión de
     Límites.** (Cartography of Central America: publications of the Boundary
     Commission.)
     Comisión de Límites.   Guatemala: Tipografía Nacional, 1929. c. 126p.
     maps.

This work, with its text in Spanish and English, contains a series of hitherto forgotten
maps presenting the Guatemalan perspective of the boundary between Honduras and
Guatemala as presented during the 1918 mediation, and the refutations made by the
Guatemalan delegation regarding the Honduran perspective.

42   **A catalogue of Latin American flat maps, 1926-1964.**
     Palmyra V. M. Monteiro.   Austin, Texas: Institute of Latin American
     Studies, University of Texas, 1967-69. 2 vols. (Guides and
     Bibliographies Series, no. 2).

Maps published from 1926 to 1964 are listed under a heading for each nation. Maps of
Honduras are found in volume one (on pages 119 to 137) under the categories of
topographical, transportation and communications, population and language, instrumental, hydrographic, general and political, and maps depicting agriculture,
vegetation, soil and land use. Maps of the entire Central American region are listed on
pages 329 to 346. In addition to the categories above, maps are catalogued as:
economic, climate, mining and minerals, archaeological, and military. Listings of Latin
American maps and general sets also include Honduras.

43   **A catalogue of maps of Hispanic America.**
     New York: American Geographical Society, 1930-33. 4 vols. maps.
     (American Geographical Society, Maps of Hispanic America,
     Publication no. 3).

The work of compiling the catalogue was begun in 1920 under the direction of F. J.
Teggart. The set comprises an examination of the map collections in seven North
American libraries with those representing Honduras found in volume one of the set.
It includes maps appearing in scientific periodicals and books, and sheet and atlas
maps. There are also articles on the cartography of several countries.

Geography. Maps, atlases and gazetteers

44 **Diccionario histórico–geográfico de las poblaciones de Honduras.**
(Historical–geographical dictionary of Honduran settlements.)
Marcelina Bonilla. Tegucigalpa: Talleres Tipolitográficos 'Aristón',
1945. 256p. bibliog.

Contains some 5,000 entries, alphabetically arranged, of settlements, towns and
communities in Honduras. Some entries name famous sons and daughters born there.
For departments and larger towns, population statistics and important buildings such as
post offices or schools are designated.

45 **Gazetteer of Honduras: names approved by the United States Board on
Geographic Names.**
Washington, DC: Defense Mapping Agency, 1983. 2nd ed. 478p. maps.

An expanded, updated revision of the gazetteer of Honduras published in 1956. This
newer edition contains 22,000 entries for places and features approved by the US
Board on Geographic Names with cross-references from unapproved names. There are
six principal sources of US and Honduran map sets which can be used to locate the
approved names. As in the older edition, each entry includes the name, topographical
designation, latitude and longitude, administrative division, and locational reference.
In addition, the new edition provides Universal Transverse Mercator grid references
and the Joint Operations Graphic (JOG) sheet number.

46 **Guía para investigadores de Honduras.** (Research guide for Honduras.)
Tegucigalpa: Instituto Geográfico Nacional, 1986. 2nd ed. 104p. maps.
bibliog.

Prepared by the National Geographic Institute, Panamerican Institute of Geography
and History (IPGH) and the General Secretariat for Urban Studies, this compilation of
forty-six detailed black-and-white maps covers many aspects of Honduran geography.
It is especially useful for the study of natural resources. Each map is accompanied by a
lengthy description, legend, date, scale, sponsoring agency and a reference where more
information is available. The maps date from the 1950s to the early 1980s and range in
scale from 1:2,000,000 to 1:20,000.

47 **Honduras.**
Washington, DC: Central Intelligence Agency, 1983. map.

Relief is shown by shading and spot heights, depths shown by contours. Includes a
location map with radial distance, comparative area map, subject maps of population,
land utilizations, and economic activity, and graphs of population, educational levels,
population growth from 1925 to 1975, land use, occupation, principal trade
commodities for 1980, and per capita gross domestic product for 1945-80.

12

48 **Honduras: índice anotado de los trabajos aerofotográficos y los mapas topográficos y de recursos naturales.** (Annotated index of aerial photographic coverage and mapping of topography and natural resources.) Washington, DC: Pan American Union, Department of Economic Affairs, 1965. 11p. maps.

A guide to the available aerial photographic maps for the topography and natural resources of Honduras. The text is in English and Spanish, supplemented by several colour maps.

49 **Honduras: official standard names approved by the United States Board on Geographic Names.** United States Board on Geographic Names. Washington, DC: Division of Geography, Department of the Interior, 1956. 235p. (Gazetteer, no. 27).

This gazetteer contains around 19,000 entries for places and features in Honduras. The entries include approved standard names and unapproved variant names, the latter cross-referenced to the standard names. Each entry consists of the name, topographical designation (e.g. cave, populated area or lagoon), latitude and longitude, administrative division, and locational reference to one of three map sets produced by Honduran and US agencies.

50 **Latin American history: a teaching atlas.** Cathryn L. Lombardi, John V. Lombardi, K. Lynn Stoner. Madison, Wisconsin: Published for the Conference on Latin American History by the University of Wisconsin Press, 1983. 144p. maps. bibliog.

A useful atlas, emphasizing themes and topics appropriate for undergraduate courses in Latin American history. It is organized chronologically with maps representing the important divisions of the area. These may be denoted by boundary disputes, archaeological sites, ecclesiastical divisions, sea or land routes of explorers, battles and campaigns, foreign relations or other factors. There is much about Honduras scattered throughout the volume and use of the thorough index is advised. The scales of the maps differ.

51 **Research guide to Honduras.** Prepared by Fernando Lanza Sandoval, in collaboration with Rigoberto Granados Garay, Leticia Bustillo de Young. Mexico: Pan American Institute of Geography and History, 1977. 45p. maps.

An invaluable tool for geographers, this work offers index maps with explanatory text, a guide to the sources of basic, contemporary maps and documents for the study of territorial development. It also contains lists of publications and topographical maps available from the National Geographic Institute of Honduras.

Tourism

General

52 **Anthony's Key Resort: unspoiled tropical charm in the Bay Islands.**
Rick Frehsee. *Skin Diver*, vol. 39 (Jan. 1990), p. 62-6.
Known as the pillar coral capital of the Caribbean, Roatán and the Bay Islands offer spectacular skin-diving and underwater photography opportunities. A perfect vacation spot for families and singles, the resort offers horse-riding, picnics and a weekly pig roast in addition to diving. The author also describes the nearby reefs with sponges, corals and deep underwater clefts. The article contains several illustrations. A similar article by this author appeared on p. 104ff in vol. 37 (Jan. 1988), of the same magazine.

53 **Central America: Guatemala, Honduras, Belize, El Salvador, Nicaragua, Costa Rica, Panama.**
Prepared by L. Langlais (et. al). Geneva, Switzerland: Nagel, 1980. 319p. maps.
The descriptions of Honduran geography, resources, history, and people contained in this somewhat dated travel guide are still useful. Tours and features of interest are also given, with a detailed description of Copán site. The section on Honduras is found on pages 73 to 105 of this (1980) edition.

54 **Fodor's Central America.**
New York: Fodor's Travel Publications, 1988. 4th ed. 349p. maps.
The 1988 edition of this travel guide to Central America, which includes Belize and Panamá, contains an excellent chapter on Honduras written by John Chater, coordinator of the Honduras/Vermont Partners of the Americas programme. Characteristics and highlights of cities and towns are succinctly noted, accommmodation and restaurants accurately recorded, transportation information is given for all modes of travel, and opportunities for shopping, nightlife and sports duly included.

This is an essential companion to the chapter on Honduras in the *South American handbook* editions prior to 1991.

55 **Motoring in Central America and Panama: a compilation of information on the Pan American Highway from the Mexico–Guatemala border to the border between Panama and Colombia.**
Washington, DC: Organization of American States, 1977. 4th ed., revised and updated. 34p. maps. bibliog.
This pamphlet gives very useful information on the status of roads and highways, primarily the Inter-American Highway, places to stop along the route, and regulations concerning motor vehicle use (some of which have no doubt been superseded). A route description and maps of Honduras are provided on pages 22 to 24.

56 **Pan-American highway guide: a comprehensive travel guide to Mexico, Central America [and] South America, by road-rail-sea-air, 1968-1969.**
Ernst A. Jahn. New York: Compsco, 1968. 144p. maps.
Out-of-date information for the traveller on the Pan-American Highway, but interesting for the light it sheds on transportation in the mid-1960s in Latin America. Schedule and fare information are provided for planes, buses, ships, and trains. Charts show the average daily food expenses, petrol prices, average driving time between points, and mileage tables with road conditions. On page 94, a profile and graph of the highway shows that the 152 miles of the highway in Honduras are paved, ranging from a low elevation of 13 feet at Choluteca to 4,500 feet at San Marcos de Colón.

57 **South American handbook.**
London: Rand McNally, 1989. 65th annual ed.
The title of this work is misleading since it covers Mexico, Central America, and the Caribbean with comparable depth. Although a scant 28 pages are dedicated to Honduras, it is crammed full of detailed information about local transportation, hotels, restaurants and visitor sites. The maps are useful, giving sufficient detail to orient any tourist. It is the best guide available for both low- and high-budget travellers. An editorial note informs readers that future volumes will segregate Mexico and Central America into a separate volume.

58 **Your Central America guide.**
Henry F. Godfrey. New York: Funk and Wagnalls, 1970. 295p. maps. bibliog.
A dated but interesting section on Honduras and its people is found on pages 173-214 in this travel guide. Tegucigalpa, San Pedro Sula and Copán are given special treatment.

Sailing directions

59 **Catalogue of Admiralty charts and other hydrographic publications, 1983.**

Taunton, England: Hydrographer of the Navy, 1983. maps.

A catalogue of British maritime charts, guides and similar resources useful to navigators and pilots. The index can be used to locate charts of waters on both the Pacific and Gulf of Mexico sides of Honduras.

60 **Cruising guide to the Bay Islands.**

Julius M. Wilensky, edited by John R. Van Ost, with sketch charts by Jo Haight. Stamford, Connecticut: Wescott Cove, 1979. 144p. maps.

An avid yachtsman, skilled sailor, and author of cruising guides to other regions, Wilensky has written an interesting guidebook to the islands for any seafaring explorer of the northern coast of Honduras, scuba-divers, snorkellers or fishermen. He includes very detailed sketch charts based on soundings and bearings (elevations and soundings in feet) by navigators, and augmented by local knowledge. Specific charts include the Cayos Cochinos, the northern coast of Honduras nearest to the islands, as well as Morat, Barbareta, Utila, and Guanaja. Colour aerial photographs reveal settlement sizes and reef formations. Supplies and services, weather, itinerary planning, chartering information and other travel tips make it a must for seafaring travellers to the area. The work includes an index.

61 **Pacific coasts of Central America and United States pilot.**

Taunton, England: Hydrographer of the Navy, 1975. 8th ed., with supplements. (Publication no. 8).

A valuable source of sailing directions for anyone sailing the Pacific Ocean from the US–Canadian border to Panamá, or vice versa.

62 **Sailing directions enroute for the west coasts of Mexico and Central America.**

Washington, DC: Defense Mapping Agency, Hydrographic/Topographic Center, 1980. 2nd ed. 171p. maps. (Publication no. 153).

Updated periodically, this guide to the Pacific coast of Honduras and other Central American countries offers information about signals, cautions, climate, regulations and other pertinent tips for successfully navigating the waters.

Travellers' Accounts

63 **Adventures in the far interior of South Africa.**
J. Leyland. Cape Town, South Africa: Struik, 1972. (Africana collectanea, vol. 40).

On pages 243-65 the author describes his travels around Omoa, Honduras and Lake Petén in what was then known as British Honduras. As a naturalist, he was primarily in pursuit of rare birds, monkeys, reptiles, waterfowl and other small creatures. He was especially proud of capturing a pair of oscillated turkeys near Lake Petén. This is a reprint of the 1866 edition.

64 **Blue blaze: danger and delight in strange islands of Honduras.**
Jane Harvey Houlson. Indianapolis, Indiana: Bobbs-Merrill, 1934.
305p. maps.

Written by the assistant to F. A. Mitchell-Hedges, an archaeologist, the work tells of a 1932 expedition to gather indigenous artefacts. Sponsored by the British Museum and the Museum of the American Indian, a small group explored the Honduran islands by boat while looking for archaeological sites. The tone of the narrative is quite enthusiastic and topics range from fauna to geography, but although it is pleasant reading, it is not to be considered a major source of reliable data for the period.

65 **Cabbages and kings.**
O. Henry (pseud. for William Sydney Porter). [n.p.]: Doubleday, Page for *Review of Reviews*, 1904. 312p.

The setting for William Sydney Porter's novel is Trujillo on the Caribbean coast of Honduras where the author lived in exile for several months in 1896. His biographer notes Porter's contentment in the balmy, beautiful, languid, historic city, which he referred to as a paradise and where he had intended to make his home. Incidents of life in Honduras were the subject of some of O. Henry's short stories as well as of this novel.

66 **Central America: describing each of the states of Guatemala, Honduras, Salvador, Nicaragua, and Costa Rica; their natural features, products, population, and remarkable capacity for colonization.**
John Baily. London: T. Saunders, 1850. 164p.

Based on twenty years of residence and visits to the region, Baily favourably describes five Central American republics as they were in the early nineteenth century. The book was written for the purpose of attracting would-be European settlers to Central America. The author also published a detailed *Map of Central America* (London: T. Saunders, 1850) to accompany the volume.

67 **Central America: how to get there and back in one piece with a minimum of hassle.**
Doug Richmond. Tucson, Arizona: H. P. Books, 1974. 176p.

This photo-essay of a trip through the five Central American nations was intended as an alternative travel guide for adventuresome tourists, with practical advice on how to avoid, if possible, less satisfying adventures and mishaps. The author's trip to Honduras is recounted on pages 109-27, with more anecdotal than practical information. Nevertheless, this is an interesting glimpse at Honduras by one of the many intrepid young North American wayfarers who explored Central America by bus, van or on foot in the late 1960s and early 1970s.

68 **The Central Americans: adventures and impressions between Mexico and Panama.**
Arthur Brown Ruhl. New York; London: C. Scribner's Sons, 1928. 284p. map.

A highly personalized travel account which includes the author's impressions of Honduras on pages 135-69. One anecdote of interest concerns his meeting with Froylán Turcios during which the poetry of Walt Whitman was discussed. Five photographs accompanying the text are of historical interest.

69 **Explorations and adventures in Honduras, comprising sketches of travel in the gold regions of Olancho, and a review of the history and general resources of Central America.**
William Vincent Wells. New York: Harper & Brothers, 1857. 588p. maps.

Wells's one-year exploration of Honduras was motivated by a search for the new El Dorado and the desire to work gold placers ['placer mining' is to extract gold in alluvial or glacial deposits by washing]. Fortunately for us, he decided to keep a diary while he searched. He took copious notes relating all of his activities and his impressions of the persons and places he visited. With wit, charm and not a little bias, he describes his travels throughout Olancho and other regions with specific chapters on commerce, currency, silver mining and Central American history. He also provides very detailed information concerning the climate, flora and fauna, society, and political matters. Although the focus is on Olancho, it is one of the most comprehensive descriptions extant of nineteenth-century Honduras. When Wells predicted that Honduras would 'become a highway of nations across the continent' it is unlikely that he would have imagined its role as a refuelling point for drug-laden aeroplanes or a staging post for the US military and the Contras. The text is accompanied by very good illustrations and several maps. Also published in Spanish as *Exploraciones y aventuras en Honduras, 1857* (San José, Costa Rica: Editorial Universitaria Centroamericana, 1978. 2nd ed.).

70 **Guatemala and her people of today; being an account of the land, its history and development; the people, their customs and characteristics; to which are added chapters on British Honduras and the republic of Honduras, with references to the other countries of Central America, Salvador, Nicaragua, and Costa Rica.**
Nevin Otto Winter. Boston: L. C. Page and Company, 1909. 307p.
Pages 245 to 279 deal with Honduras and give a cursory, but useful description of that country at the turn of the century. The work contains illustrations and photographs by the author.

71 **Honduras: the land of great depths.**
Cecil Charles. Chicago; New York: Rand-McNally, 1890. 216p. maps.
A travel account by an observant Yankee, written for the benefit of North Americans who may want to seek their fortune in Honduras. Filled with helpful hints of what to take and expect, it provides his impressions of the nation and its remoteness, particularly with respect to the modes and difficulties of travel, in addition to descriptions of its physical setting, people, social conditions, food, clothing, and housing, and a discussion of the economy. More information about people and lifestyles is offered than is usual in such accounts, but it does reflect the North American biases of the era and the author's problems with respect to the local customs and conditions. The book contains an index, illustrations and tables.

72 **Honduras: the reply of Colonel José M. Aguirre to some unjust strictures published against that republic by the *New York Times*.**
José M. Aguirre. New York: G. F. Ilsley, 1884. 54p.
A resident of Trujillo, Honduras, took offence at an article he happened to see in the *New York Times*. A voyager on a boat that called at the port of Trujillo described his recollections of it in condescending terms that reflected Yankee biases and a lack of familiarity with the region. The resident's reply refutes the article point by point and offers a more accurate description of the city, its people, facilities, and customs.

73 **A hoosier in Honduras.**
Albert E. Morlan. Indianapolis, Indiana: El Dorado, 1897. 215p.
The observations of a trader and traveller from Indiana on a voyage that took him to Belize, Honduras, and Nicaragua. The bulk of the volume deals with Honduras. The emphasis is on description in a spicy style, with the author recounting personal observations of physical setting, flora and fauna, and particularly of the towns he visited and the people with whom he dealt. Entertaining reading, but the information is disorganized and must be extracted carefully. The author later served as US consul in Belize. The book is illustrated with drawings.

74   **Incidents of travel in Central America, Chiapas and Yucatán.**
John Lloyd Stephens.   New York: Dover, 1969. 2 vols.

First published in 1841 by Harper, and many times since, this facsimile of the first edition faithfully reproduces the observations and experiences of an official American envoy sent to locate the crumbling Central American government in 1839. Although he was unsuccessful in that apparently impossible task, he did succeed in publishing a remarkable and entertaining account of his journey in the region. A keen observer and skilled raconteur he offers comments on a wide variety of topics such as archaeology (including much about Copán), people, politics, history, geography, economics, and society in general.

75   **Journey in Honduras and jottings by the way.**
R. G. Huston.   Cincinnati, Ohio: Robert Clarke, 1875. 39p. maps.

An account of a railway surveying mission, emphasizing the physical description of the tropical jungle.

76   **Jungle in the clouds: a naturalist's explorations in the Republic of Honduras.**
Victor Wolfgang Von Hagen.   New York: Duell, Sloan, & Pearce, 1940. 260p. maps. bibliog.

An early effort by a respected anthropologist, this is a travelogue, written for a general audience, of an expedition to trap and tame the elegant quetzal bird of the highland jungles of Honduras – a bright green bird with a blood-red breast. As much of the world prepared for war, the Von Hagens sought to change the legend of the beautiful creature. At the time of their quest no specimen of the quetzal had ever been captured, exhibited, photographed or successfully removed live from its natural jungle habitat. In this narration of their exciting trip to the cloud-covered jungles of northeastern Honduras the author tells of the difficulties in locating, capturing and caring for the birds, and of their discovery of a remote settlement of Jicaque people in Turrupán, with asides about the sloth and anteater. Always respectful of the local population and appreciative of the beautiful countryside, the adventure ends with a hair-raising encounter with the poisonous *Barba amarilla* snake in the ruins of Copán. A very enjoyable read with many striking black-and-white photographs of scenery, people and fauna. An index is included.

77   **A lady's ride across Spanish Honduras.**
Mary Lester.   Gainesville, Florida: University of Florida, 1964. 319p.
(A facsimile reproduction of the 1884 edition. Edinburgh; London: Blackwood and Sons). (Latin American Gateway Series).

Using the *nom de plume* María Soltera, the writer gives us an autobiographical account of the travels and observations of a well-bred, refined but adventurous English school-teacher who traversed Honduras by mule in 1881. Her trek began in Amapala, and after several weeks of perseverence ended, in disappointment, in San Pedro Sula. The book was originally published as a serial in *Blackwood's Magazine*.

78 **Letter to the King of Spain: being a description of the ancient provinces of Guazacapán, Izalco, Cuscatlán, and Chiquimula, in the Audiencia of Guatemala, with an account of the languages, customs and religion of their aboriginal inhabitants, and a description of the ruins of Copán.**
Diego García de Palacio, translated and with notes by Ephraim G. Squier; with additional notes by Alexander von Frantzuis and Frank E. Comparato, editor. Culver City, California: Labyrinthos, 1985. 66p. bibliog.
An account by the Auditor of the Audiencia of Guatemala to the King of Spain giving an excellent description of physical features of the Central American provinces and their inhabitants shortly after the Conquest. This memoir relates primarily to Cuscatlán, present-day El Salvador, but also records his impressions of the ruins at Copán, the first such account written by a European. A translation of *Carta dirijida al Rey de España*.

79 **Mosquito Coast; an account of a journey through the jungles of Honduras.**
Peter Keenagh. Boston, Massachusetts: Houghton Mifflin, 1938. 286p. map.
Disclaiming 'scientific knowledge of any kind', the author recounts his 1935 expedition into the Mosquito Coast jungles and the Bay Islands. Although the expedition was 'no more than an unjustified piece of elaborate and protracted inquisitiveness', it documents much about the Zambu and other local inhabitants. The text is supplemented by lovely sepia-toned photographs and a detailed map.

80 **Narrative of a residence on the Mosquito Shore: with an account of Truxillo, and the adjacent islands of Bonacca and Roatán, and a vocabulary of the Mosquitian language.**
Thomas Young. New York: Kraus Reprint, 1971. 2nd ed. 172p.
The account of an attempted settlement by English people on the Río Tinto (Negro) in Honduras from 1839 to 1841 written by an agent of the British Central American Land Company. It contains general information on the country, indigenous tribes, and aspects of labour. This is a reprint of the 1847 edition published by Smith, Elder and Company in London. The same firm also published the first edition in 1842.

81 **Notes on Central America: particularly the states of Honduras and San [sic] Salvador: their geography, topography, climate, population, resources, productions, etc., and the proposed Honduras Interoceanic Railway.**
Ephraim George Squier. New York: Harper & Brothers, 1855. 397p. Reprinted, New York: AMS, 1971. 397p. maps. bibliog.
Despite its title, this descriptive volume by the US chargé deals mainly with Honduras, providing detailed descriptions of the physical features, climate, resources, economy, society, and people, and offering accurate data on the conditions of the region in the mid-nineteenth century. He includes comment on the Interoceanic Railway, of which

Travellers' Accounts

he was one of the promoters. The portions dealing with El Salvador are quite limited, offering far less detail. The work is indexed.

82 **Rainbow countries of Central America.**
Wallace Thompson. New York: E. P. Dutton, 1926. 284p. maps.
This traveller's impressions of Honduras in the 1920s are contained in a chapter on pages 66 to 86. Other impressions are included under sections concerning agriculture, trade, education, highways, and politics. The book contains thirty wonderful photographs of the people and places in the region.

83 **The rainbow republics, Central America.**
Ralph Hancock. New York: Coward-McCann, 1947. 305p. maps.
(Invitation to Travel Series).
Although a somewhat dated travel guide, it provides insight into the country during World War II. Tegucigalpa appears on pages 107-10; interesting villages on pages 145-50; lodging on pages 178-9; holidays celebrated in Honduras on pages 222-4; and a guide to Copán on pages 255-61.

84 **Search for the Maya: the story of Stephens and Catherwood.**
Victor Wolfgang Von Hagen. Farnborough, England: Saxon House, 1973. 365p.
The fascinating personal history of the adventurous twosome, John Lloyd Stephens and Frederick Catherwood, who effectively gave birth to American archaeology. From 1839 to 1843 the travellers discovered and/or documented over forty archaeological sites in Mexico and Central America and produced several beautifully written and illustrated books which have stimulated the interests of historians, archaeologists and mayaologists for many generations (*Incidents of travel in Yucatán* and *Incidents of travel in Central America* being the most relevant for this part of the world). On pages 114-62, the story of Copán unfolds in a blend of Stephens's carefully scripted words and Von Hagen's more popularized version. The volume contains excellent reproductions of Catherwood's beautiful illustrations.

85 **The states of Central America; their geography, topography, climate, population, resources, productions, commerce, political organization, aborigines, etc., etc., comprising chapters on Honduras, San Salvador, Nicaragua, Costa Rica, Guatemala, Belize, the Bay Islands, the Mosquito shore, and the Honduras Inter-Oceanic Railway.**
Ephraim George Squier. New York: Harper & Brothers, 1858. 782p. maps. (Reprinted in 1970).
Squier's *Notes on Central America*, published in 1855, is incorporated into this more extensive work. This work includes a chapter on the Bay Islands (pages 603-28) and one on the Mosquito Shore (pages 629-63). Squier's proposal for an inter-oceanic railway route through Honduras is thoroughly detailed on pages 676 to 730. The text includes excellent geographical data for the region, especially along the proposed route.

86 **A student in Central America, 1914-1916.**
Dana Gardner Munro, edited by Jennifer S. H. Brown, E. Wyllys
Andrews, V. New Orleans, Louisiana: Middle American Research
Institute, Tulane University, 1983. 75p. map. (Publication no. 51).

A delightful memoir of an important Latin Americanist who maintained a special
interest and a significant role in Central American–US relations for much of the
twentieth century. Written some sixty-five years after the fact, this little book contains
Munro's vivid recollections of his first visit as a 'footloose student' to Central America.
In the chapter on Honduras, pages 52-62, the author describes (among other things),
his mule trip from Puerto Cortés to Tegucigalpa, Holy Week in Comayagua, and the
local political scene.

87 **Tangweera: life and adventures among gentle savages.**
Charles Napier Bell. Austin: University of Texas Press, 1989. 318p.

A facsimile edition of the 1899 first edition, long out of print, with a short introductory
essay emphasizing the continuing usefulness of Bell's ethnohistory of the Miskito
people. The work is crucial in understanding the distinctions between Miskito residents
along the eastern Honduran and Nicaraguan coasts and the Spanish-speaking central
and western residents. Bell's recollections of his boyhood in Mosquitia document the
diminishing British influence, the growing Moravian missionary presence, and the
changing economic and cultural practices of the region. His vivid descriptions of the
natural environment are also notable. Bell provides extraordinary insight into this
unique area and its inhabitants in the mid-nineteenth century.

88 **Through the volcanoes: a Central American journey.**
Jeremy Paxman. London: Joseph, 1985. 264p. maps.

In a chapter entitled 'Whispers of Vietnam', the English author relates his experiences
while passing through Honduras where he observes the obvious US military presence
and its influence on Honduran people and culture. The author's use of dialogue and his
vivid descriptions create an entertaining impressionistic narrative, not always flattering
to Hondurans or their American military partners. Nevertheless, the charm of
individual people and places does occasionally manage to emerge. The book includes
an index.

89 **Tramping through Mexico, Guatemala and Honduras: being the random
notes of an incurable vagabond.**
Harry Alverson Franck. New York: Century, 1916. (Also published,
London: T. Fisher Unwin, 1916). 378p. maps.

A self-described 'incurable vagabond', Franck spent four unbroken years travelling
overland by foot and steamer in Latin America. Pages 284 to 378 of the present
volume deal with his wanderings through Honduras. He tells of his trek through the
backwoods and rural sectors from Guatemala City to Tegucigalpa to the island port of
Amapala to catch a steamer to Panamá. His trials and tribulations – consisting of lack
of food, getting lost on many occasions, aching feet, poor lodgings in 'nothing-to-do-
but-stare' hamlets – tend to dominate his narrative and he seems to harbour such
acerbic contempt for the people and places he encountered that one wonders why he
bothered to make the journey in the first place. The Honduras segment of his trek
culminates in a chance encounter with the colourful character of Lee Christmas, a
mercenary soldier. If you can see through and tolerate all the pejorative, ethnocentric

and disparaging comments about the native Hondurans, there is much to glean about the living conditions of rural Honduras at the turn of the century.

90   **Travels in the free states of Central America: Nicaragua, Honduras, and San Salvador.**
Karl Scherzer, Ritter von.   London: Longman, Brown, Green, Longmans, & Roberts, 1857. Reprinted, New York: AMS, 1970. 2 vols.

This translation of *Wanderungen durch die mittel-amerikanischen Freistaaten* is a pleasantly written, detailed account by a keen observer and his scientist companion, Dr Moritz Wagner, of their travels through three Central American countries in the 1850s. Pages 262-320 of volume one and the first 119 pages of volume two are dedicated to Honduras. The survey of the population, geography, and social climate is highlighted by an eye-witness account of the disastrous earthquake that levelled San Salvador.

91   **A trip to British Honduras, and to San Pedro, Republic of Honduras.**
Charles Swett.   New Orleans, Louisiana: Price Current Print, 1868. 125p.

After the US Civil War, many US Southerners were so disenchanted with the reconstruction policies of the North that they sought to resettle in other countries. Swett was one such Southerner yet he felt it his 'Christian duty' to warn his fellow man against emigration to the British and Spanish Honduras after his three-month exploratory trip with friends. In his diary he tells of the trip by rail, ship and saddle to the two countries. In the chapter on British Honduras he focuses on information of interest to farmers; in that of Spanish Honduras, he focuses on documents about the settlement of Medina.

92   **Violent neighbors: El Salvador, Central America and the United States.**
Tom Buckley.   New York: Times Books, 1984. 358p. maps.

The *New York Times* reporter presents a panoramic overview of Central American political and social conditions, drawn from his years covering the region's turmoil. His account primarily concerns events and noted individuals in El Salvador, but anecdotal stories about Honduran involvement in the region's conflict are scattered throughout the narrative, particularly on pages 225-38. An index is included.

Flora and Fauna

General

93 **Aquatic biota of Mexico, Central America and the West Indies.**
Edited by Stuart H. Hurlbert, Alejandro Villalobos-Figueroa. San
Diego, California: San Diego State University, 1982. 529p. bibliog.
A most useful taxonomic bibliography for the fauna and flora of inland waters of
Mesoamerica and the Caribbean region. Each group has a summary of information on
its taxonomy, bio-geography and natural history and is written in both English and
Spanish. Some distributions of species are broken down by country, including
Honduras.

94 **Biologia centrali-americana, zoology, botany and archaeology.**
Edited by Frederick Ducane Goodman, Osbert Salvin. London: R. H.
Porter and Dulau, 1879-1915. 63 vols. maps. bibliog.
A monumental collective study of the flora and fauna of Central America containing a
great deal of information about Honduras interspersed throughout the text. The first
volume comprises an introduction to the set and an outline of the contents. Volumes
2-52, with contributions from a number of scholars, identify over 38,000 species of
fauna with over 1,000 plates of illustrations. Volumes 53-57 are concerned with botany
and describe over 11,000 species with maps and illustrations. Volumes 58-63 were
prepared by Alfred P. Maudslay and treat the archaeology of the region, including
reference to Copán. Although published at the turn of the century, it is still a most
valuable source of information and illustrations of the rich natural life of the tropical
region.

95 **Guía de los parques nacionales, refugios de vida silvestre, reservas biológicas y monumentos naturales de Honduras.** (Guide to the national parks, wildlife refuges, biological reserves and natural monuments of Honduras.)
Gustavo Adolfo Cruz. Tegucigalpa: Asociación Hondureña de Ecología, 1986. 49p. map.

As the title indicates, this is a guidebook to the natural life indigenous to Honduras. It is useful for identification and location of flora and fauna. The one colour map shows where the reserves and parks are located. It is a very good source for those wishing to get off the beaten path. The cover title is: *Areas silvestres de Honduras.*

Flora

96 **The *Eragrostis pectinacea–pilosa* complex in North and Central America (Gramineae: Eragrostoideae).**
Stephen D. Koch. Urbana, Illinois: University of Illinois Press, 1974. 74p. bibliog. maps. (Illinois Biological Monographs, no. 48).

Distribution maps show growth of some species of these grasses in Honduras.

97 **Ethnobotany of the Jicaque of Honduras.**
David Lewis Lentz. *Economic Botany*, vol. 40, no. 2 (1986), p. 210-19. maps.

Describes the medicinal uses of herbs and plants by the Jicaque people of northern Honduras.

98 **Los pinares de Honduras.** (The pine forests of Honduras.)
A. Wolffsohn. [Siguatepeque?]: Administración de Desarrollo Ultramar del Reino Unido en colaboración con la Escuela Nacional de Ciencias Forestales de Honduras, 1982. 22p. maps. bibliog.

Sponsored by the British Office for Overseas Development and the Honduran National School of Forestry Sciences, this study analyses the status and uses of local pine forests in Honduras.

99 **Plantas comunes de Honduras.** (Common plants of Honduras.)
Cyril Hardy Nelson Sutherland. Tegucigalpa: Editorial Universitaria, 1986. 2 vols. (Colección Docencia, nos 37, 40).

With rainforests, mountains, valleys, swamps, savannas and a tropical climate, the Honduran geography provides fertile grounds for thousands of vegetational varieties. In these two large volumes, the author, a professor of systemic botany and co-founder of the herbarium of the National Autonomous University of Honduras, has classified and documented thousands of plants with hundreds of cross-references from Latin and common names. Most illustrations, if not all, come from other cited sources and are of very good quality. Much of the value of this work is based on the incomplete or limited

26

work of others, but here it is carefully re-collated and reorganized into one useful source. The order is strictly alphabetical by common name. Each entry has the scientific name, family, plant habitat, characteristics and medicinal, esoteric or industrial uses. An earlier work by this author, *Nociones de taxonomía vegetal* (Tegucigalpa: Editorial Universitaria, 1982. 223p.; Colección Docencia, no. 7) is available but is less comprehensive than this one.

100 **Trees of Honduras.**
      S. J. Record, C. D. Mell.   *Tropical Woods*, no. 10 (1927), p. 10-47.
Two botanists describe dozens of trees indigenous to Honduras. The articles contains several black-and-white illustrations of the more common trees.

101 **Tropical trees found in the Caribbean, South America, Central**
      America, Mexico.
      Dorothy Hargreaves, Bob Hargreaves.   Portland, Oregon: Hargreaves
      Industrial, 1965. 64p.
A colourful booklet depicting the many trees – with close-ups of their blossoms – indigenous or imported to the tropical regions. Because there is no index, the entire volume must be perused to pick out those of Central America. Descriptions are rather brief but they do include major characteristics, uses, domains and nomenclature in English, Spanish, French and Dutch.

Fauna

102 **The bark and ambrosia beetles of North and Central America**
      (Coleoptera, Scolytidae): a taxonomic monograph.
      Stephen L. Wood.   Provo, Utah: Brigham Young University, 1982.
      1359p. bibliog. (Great Basin Naturalist Memoirs, no. 6)
The tropical climate and verdant plants of Central America support over 630 species of bark beetles, some of which are unique to Honduras. This exhaustive tome, with many illustrations and a vast amount of information (considering the topic), notes distribution by place where specimens were collected.

103 **Birds of tropical America.**
      Alexander Frank Skutch.   Austin, Texas: University of Texas Press,
      1983. 305p. maps. bibliog.
Central American birds are photographed by the author or sketched by Dana Gardner for identification. Their natural history and daily habits are also detailed in a lively fashion.

Flora and Fauna. Fauna

104 **The blennioid fishes of Belize and Honduras, Central America, with comments on their systematics, ecology, and distribution (Blenniidae, Chaenopsidae, Labrisomidae, Tripterygiidae).**
David W. Greenfield, Robert Karl Johnson. Chicago, Illinois: Field Museum of Natural History, 1981. 106p. bibliog. (Fieldiana. Zoology, new series, no. 8).
An annotated checklist of the blennioid fishes from Belize and Honduras, this study records 20 new species for Belize and 40 new ones from Honduras. Information on habitat association, depth distribution, co-occurrence and geographical distribution is conveyed with supplementary descriptions for lesser-known species. Unfortunately, the researchers do not tell us whether or not these fish would be good to eat, but judging from the illustrations they look mean and spiney.

105 **A distributional survey of the birds of Honduras.**
Burt Leavelle Monroe. [New York?]: American Ornithologists' Union, 1968. 458p. 28 maps. bibliog.
Spurred on by the long neglect of the subject by other ornithologists, Monroe undertook in 1958 to study the distribution of birds in Honduras. He asserts that Honduras serves as a major avenue of flight for North American migrants to and from their winter grounds to the south. He attributes at least 710 species to the country and describes 74 families in the volume. Although the descriptions and maps are good, the absence of photographs or drawings limits the value of the work to the non-specialist. Introductory chapters include physiography, geology, soils, climate and habitats in addition to an interesting chapter on the history of Honduran ornithology. The detailed index provides access via the common bird names. The bibliography is quite extensive.

106 **The ecology of the freshwater fishes of central Honduras: neotropical, reservoirs, food partitioning, reproduction.**
Peter David Vaux. PhD dissertation, University of California, Davis, 1985. 271p. (DAI 46/07B, p. 2182).
The objectives of this study were to document fish distribution in the Humuya, Sulaco and Yure drainages of central Honduras, and to investigate the tropic and reproductive ecology of the more common species. Collections were made over a two-year period from twenty-two riverine stations, and from Lake Yure, a small, recently constructed headwater impoundment. A total of thirty-two species, including four exotics, was collected from the area. [Author's abstract].

107 **A field guide to dangerous animals of North America, including Central America.**
Charles K. Levy. Brattleboro, Vermont: Stephen Greene, 1983. 164p. bibliog. maps.
Fish, bugs, reptiles, arthropods, and animals that bite, sting or poison humans or are dangerous to eat, are the subject of this field guide. Drawings of each animal accompany the text and some of the more interesting creatures are highlighted in colour plates. Type of attack, geographical distribution, prevention, and first-aid indications are stressed for each offender. Although there is no geographical index, many of the animals do inhabit Honduras and its waters. Recommended for anyone

planning to snorkel, hike, camp, scuba-dive or otherwise explore the less populated areas of Central America.

108   **A field guide to the birds of Mexico and Central America.**
Irby L. Davis.   Austin, Texas: University of Texas Press, 1972. 282p.
Another very comprehensive guide arranged by systematic order of families using the popular name of species. When known, data are provided for field marks, voice and range. Most species have a colour illustration by F. P. Bennett, Jr for assistance in visual identification. There is no specific listing of birds whose range is primarily in Honduras. The introduction notes that annotated checklists had been prepared in booklet form for regional use. but these were not reviewed by this bibliographer.

109   **The ground-beetles of Central America (Carabidae).**
Terry L. Erwin.   Washington, DC: Smithsonian Institution Press, 1990. 30p. bibliog. (Smithsonian Contributions to Zoology, no. 50).
Thorough coverage for the identification of the ground-beetles of Central America including the subfamilies Carabinae, Notiophilini, Loricerini and Carabini. The natural history and ecological and geographical ranges are depicted on maps and there are twenty-two figures and five tables of other illustrations in the study. This work comprises the second part of a planned series. The first part, to be published later, will include an introduction, analysis and methodology.

110   **A guide to the birds of Panama: with Costa Rica, Nicaragua, and Honduras.**
Robert S. Ridgely, John A. Gwynne, Jr.   Princeton, New Jersey: Princeton University Press, 1989. 2nd ed. 534p., 96p. of plates. maps. bibliog.
The second edition of this comprehensive book contains a chapter identifying the 162 species of birds occurring in Honduras, Costa Rica and Nicaragua that have not been sighted in Panamá. Most of these are illustrated on beautiful plates and have complete physical descriptions with range distributions indicated. The main text concerns birds known in Panamá but whose range may include Honduras. This is an essential reference work for bird identification and information.

111   **Life histories of Central American birds.**
Alexander Frank Skutch.   Berkeley, California: Cooper Ornithological Society, 1954-69. 3 vols. maps. bibliog. (Pacific Coast Avifauna, nos 31, 34, 35).
Based on observations taken from 1929 to 1956 on the Pacific side of southern Costa Rica, the author has amassed an incredible amount of detail on Central American birds and arranges it here in familial order. For each species he provides facts about the life history, eggs, nest, incubation, nestlings, natural enemies, voice, food gathering and arrival and departure times in Central America. Either black-and-white sketches by Don R. Eckelberry or photographs accompany each species description.

112 **Mamíferos silvestres de Honduras.** (Wild mammals of Honduras.)
Leonel Marineros, Francisco Martínez Gallegos.   Tegucigalpa:
Asociación Hondureña de Ecología, 1988. 2nd ed. 129p. bibliog.
Two biologists record descriptions of common, non-domesticated mammals found in
Honduras. The work includes several colour photographs of the more common
animals. It was published by the Honduran Ecology Association.

113 **Noteworthy records of bats from El Salvador, Honduras, and
Nicaragua.**
Ira F. Greenbaum, J. Knox Jones, Jr.   Lubbock, Texas: Museum,
Texas Tech University, 1978. 7p. bibliog. (Occasional Papers of the
Museum, Texas Tech University, no. 55).
Describes ten kinds of bats native to Middle America, one of which had never been
reported in Honduras. The reports present the karyotype of the *Centronycteris
maximiliani* for the first time. The report includes twenty citations to other studies.

114 **Ocean gallery: whale shark encounter.**
Mandy Wagner.   *Skin Diver*, vol. 37, no. 11 (1988), p. 48-9.
The world's largest fish, the whale shark, is the topic of this exciting report detailing
the encounter of the great fish and a skin-diver near the Bay Islands. Photographs
accompany the text.

115 **Phenetics and ecology of hybridization in buckeye butterflies
(Lepidoptera: Nymphalidae).**
John E. Hafernik.   Berkeley, California: University of California
Press, 1982. 109p. bibliog.
Buckeye butterflies are members of the pantropical nymphalid genus, *Junonia*. This
paper analyses interrelationships among the North and Central American repre-
sentatives. Samples used in phenetic analyses were collected in La Ceiba.

116 **Records of bats from Honduras and El Salvador.**
R. K. La Val.   *Journal of Mammology*, vol. 50, no. 4 (1969),
p. 819-22. bibliog.
Records fifteen bats found in Honduras with place sighted, gender and size of bat.

117 **Records of bats from Honduras and Nicaragua.**
R. Valdez, R. K. La Val.   *Journal of Mammology*, vol. 52, no. 1
(1971), p. 247-50.
Records sightings and measurements of a dozen bats from Honduras and one from
Nicaragua.

118 A revision of the Mexican and Central American spider wasps of the
     subfamily Pompilinae (Hymenoptera, Pompilidae).
     Howard Ensign Evans. Philadelphia, Pennsylvania: American
     Entomological Society, 1966. 442p. maps. (Memoirs of the American
     Entomological Society, no. 20).
A taxonomic study of Pompilinae, popularly known as spider wasps, with thirty-nine
genera or subgenera distributed in Central America. Great detail is given for genus,
with places of specimen collection noted. Distribution maps accompany each genus.

119 Serpientes venenosas de Honduras. (Poisonous snakes of Honduras.)
     Gustavo Adolfo Cruz. Tegucigalpa: Editorial Universitaria, 1987.
     160p. maps. bibliog.
Everything you would ever want to know about the poisonous snakes of Honduras,
and more. A descriptive catalogue of snakes, a glossary, medical treatments and many
black-and-white and colour illustrations make this a useful source for anyone straying
off the beaten paths of Honduras.

120 The snakes of Honduras.
     Larry David Wilson, John R. Meyer. Milwaukee, Wisconsin:
     Milwaukee Public Museum, 1982. 159p. bibliog. (Publications in
     Biology and Geology, no. 6).
There are ninety-one known species of snakes slithering about in Honduras. For each
species the authors, herpetologists from the US midwest, provide a partial synonymy, a
statement of the geographical range, dorsal patterns, ecological distribution, locality
records and distributional maps. There are also keys for familial identification, genera
and species. A major drawback of the book is its lack of information about whether or
not the snakes are poisonous. If I were bitten by a snake in Honduras, I would rather
have *Serpientes venenosas* (q.v.) readily available.

Prehistory and Archaeology

General

121 **Agricultural ecology and prehistoric settlement in the El Cajón region of Honduras.**
William M. Loker. PhD dissertation, University of Colorado at Boulder, 1986. 496p. (DAI 47/06A, p. 2210).
This dissertation reports the results of an ecological analysis of agricultural production and productivity among small farmers in the lower Sulaco and Humuya river valleys of central-western Honduras. Loker attempts to understand which elements of the physical and social environment are the principal determinants of variation in agricultural yield and practices. This information forms the basis of a settlement pattern analysis of archaeological remains found in this same area. In particular this study tests two hypotheses regarding prehistoric settlement: the first contends that prehistoric settlements were located to maximize access to prime agricultural land; the second states that sites with access to more and better agricultural land were larger and more politically powerful than sites with less prime agricultural land. The author successfully defines three agricultural resource zones of varying agricultural potential based on environmental characteristics such as slope, soil type, and vegetation. [Based on the author's abstract].

122 **Análisis arqueológico de la cerámica de Piedra Blanca.** (Archaeological analysis of Piedra Blanca pottery.)
Vito Veliz. Tegucigalpa: Instituto Hondureño de Antropología e Historia, 1978. 63p. bibliog.
The author is a well-qualified archaeologist who has held positions at the Honduran Institute of Anthropology and History and the Archaeological Project of Copán. In six chapters, he examines the geographical and historical–cultural context of this

northeastern site using a variety of previous studies and his personal observations. He then proceeds to establish an archaeological sequence from the formative to the post-classical periods of northeastern Honduras using ceramic fragments from the region and comparing them with those of other Central American sites. Many charts, tables and illustrations enhance the study.

123 **An archaeological investigation of intra-community social organizations at La Ceiba, Comayagua, Honduras.**
Julie Christina Benyo.   PhD dissertation, State University of New York at Albany, 1986. 697p. (DAI 47/04A, p. 1379).

The purpose of this investigation is the description and explanation of the spatial patterning of the community at La Ceiba in terms of intra-site social organization. This dissertation describes an intensive study of the residential architecture and the distribution of artefacts at the site of La Ceiba (ca. AD 650-900) located in west-central Honduras. Data pertaining to architectural form, range of variation, differential intra-site distribution content and social separation are used to define the exact nature of population aggregates within the community. The social units so defined are then investigated in terms of the various operative integrative features which served to unite these separate social organizations into a single community system. [From the author's abstract].

124 **An archaeological reconnaissance of northwestern Honduras; a report of the work of the Tulane University–Danish National Museum Expedition to Central America, 1935.**
Jens Yde.   Copenhagen: Levin & Munksgaard, 1938. 101p. maps. (Middle American Research Series, Middle American Research Institute, Tulane University, New Orleans, Louisiana, Publication no. 9). Reprint of *Acta archaeologica*, vol. IX.

A thorough report of this joint expedition into northwestern Honduras which provided a basis for the numerous archaeological investigations subsequently undertaken by the Middle American Research Institute. The archaeological sites in the Humuya, Ulúa and Copán–Chamelecón valleys, some of which had never before been visited by archaeologists, are well documented. The fifty-nine illustrations include maps of sites and artefacts discovered. An appendix lists all of the known archaeological sites in Honduras up to 1935.

125 **Archaeology in northwestern Honduras: interim reports of the Proyecto Arqueológico Sula.**
Edited by John S. Henderson.   Ithaca, New York: Archaeology Program, Latin American Studies Program, Cornell University, 1984- . maps. bibliog. (Volumes still being published).

Known for decades as rich in archaeological resources, the Sula Valley is the subject of this archaeological project sponsored jointly by Cornell University and the Honduran Institute of Anthropology and History. These interim reports reflect the progress made in the initial stages of the project. The first one (and the only one this reviewer could locate) contains three reports by Anthony Wonderley: land of Ulúa at the conquest, Naco phase (late post-classical) test excavations, and Rancho Ires phase (colonial) test excavation, and one report by Kevin Pope: recent geological history of the Sula Valley.

126 **Archaeology of central and southern Honduras.**
Doris Stone. Cambridge, Massachusetts: Peabody Museum, 1957.
135p. maps. bibliog. (Papers of the Peabody Museum of Archaeology
and Ethnology, Harvard University, vol. 49, no. 3).

The objective of this study is to offer a general survey of pre-Spanish, non-Mayan
Honduras (central and southern areas) which had previously been mostly neglected by
archaeologists. Being the daughter of Samuel Zemurray, Mrs Stone has the good
fortune to have many valuable contacts all over Honduras and utilized them to the full
for her archaeological studies. This detailed study provides a wealth of information on
sites in the Comayagua, central, eastern-central and southern regions concerning
geography, customs, dress, and artefacts of the ancient and contemporary inhabitants.
Several plates of pottery ware, sketches of sherds, and maps of the Tenampua site and
the Comayagua region are included.

127 **The archaeology of lower Central America.**
Edited by Frederick W. Lange, Doris Z. Stone. Albuquerque, New
Mexico: University of New Mexico Press, 1984. 476p. bibliog.

Papers presented at the Advanced Seminar on Lower Central American Archaeology
in 1980 are compiled here under the editorship of noted anthropologists. Doris Stone
provides a useful history of archaeological investigation, noting efforts and results at
various Honduran sites on pages 18-20. Lange contributes an excellent physical and
cultural geography for the fundamental understanding of regional development. A
most important synthesis of the archaeology of Honduras is reviewed by Paul Healey
on pages 113-61. He concludes that contemporary Honduran archaeology may be
twenty years behind work done in other places and suggests areas lacking in
documentation or investigation for future researchers. An appendix on page 382 lists
radiocarbon samples from Honduras. The work includes an index.

128 **Archaeology of the north coast of Honduras.**
Doris Stone. Cambridge, Massachusetts: Peabody Museum of
Archaeology and Ethnology, 1941. 103p. maps. bibliog. (Memoirs of
the Peabody Museum of Archaeology and Ethnology, Harvard
University, vol. IX, no. 1). Reprinted by Kraus.

The culmination of two years of field work, Stone attempts to 'place certain cultural
facts in the archaeological history of Honduras'. She also intends to link contemporary
local inhabitants with archaeological remains from various regions of the country,
particularly Colón, Olancho, Atlántida, Yoro, Cortés, Comayagua and Santa Bárbara.
Special emphasis is given to the Paya and Ulúa regions which are the subjects of in-
depth historical and archaeological analyses. There are numerous black-and-white
photographs of artefacts.

129 **Archaeology on the Mosquito Coast: a reconnaissance of the pre-Columbian and historic settlement along the Río Tinto.**
Catherine M. Clark, Frank G. Dawson, Jonathan C. Drake.
Cambridge, England: Centre of Latin American Studies,
University of Cambridge, [1982?]. 96p. maps. bibliog. (Centre
of Latin American Studies, University of Cambridge,
Occasional Publication no. 4).

Published in association with the Ministry of Culture and Tourism of Honduras and the
Honduran Institute of Anthropology and History, the archaeological excavation
project focuses on the examination of the remains of Paya and Miskito people, and the
permanent European settlement located at the delta of the Río Tinto (Black River).
One important finding of the excavation was evidence that indicated the English
settlers of the 1730s were not really pirates and buccaneers as the Spaniards claimed,
but were instead farmers and merchants. Artefacts recovered at the Black River
Colony site indicate the existence of mechanical sugar-processing, associated domestic
activity, a furnace for working iron and some military installations. The text includes
many maps and drawings of artefacts recovered.

130 **Cerro Palenque, Valle del Ulúa, Honduras: terminal classic interaction on the southern Mesoamerican periphery.**
Rosemary Alexandria Joyce. PhD dissertation, University of Illinois
at Urbana-Champaign, 1985. 564p. (DAI 46/07A, p. 1986).

The archaeological site zone of Cerro Palenque includes two distinct temporal foci. A
small public centre of Late Classical age (AD 450-850) previously reported was
replaced by an expanded settlement in the succeeding Terminal Classical and Early
Post-classical (AD 850-1050). The later site, the sole population centre for the area at
this period, includes a series of clusters of residential compounds and public
architectural zones including a ball court. Analysis of materials excavated at the site
indicate that the Terminal Classical occupants had distinctive ties with the Boca
ceramic sphere of the Maya Lowlands. Direct contact with the Maya Lowlands was
probably established via the Caribbean Coastal Lowlands of Belize, a pattern
suggested also for earlier periods. [From the author's abstract].

131 **The complete visitor's guide to Mesoamerican ruins.**
Joyce Kelly. Norman, Oklahoma: University of Oklahoma Press,
1982. 527p. maps. bibliog.

An 'obsessive ruin buff', Kelly has visited each and every one of the 119 sites and 41
museums included in this extensive guide to ruins in Mexico, Guatemala, Belize,
Honduras and El Salvador. The text is arranged by country, then in a logical
geographical sequence. The section on Honduras (pages 479-97) offers a detailed
description with many black-and-white photographs of the Copán site, in addition to
brief histories and descriptions of the National Museum of Honduras (in Tegucigalpa)
and the Regional Museum of Copán. Kelly recommends the minimum amount of time
necessary to fully enjoy or photograph sites and museums, gives distances and time
required to arrive at a given site and the best means of access to remoter areas. This is
an excellent site-by-site introduction to the wealth of archaeological ruins; however,
due to its considerable weight, it is a guidebook from which one should photocopy the
essentials and leave the volume at home.

132 **Copantl, jardín maya 'La Concordia'.** (Copantl, the Mayan garden 'La Concordia'.)
Augusto Morales y Sánchez. Tegucigalpa: Aristón, 1947. 122p.

An illustrated in-depth enquiry into the Mayan hieroglyphics and pottery remains at La Concordia national park.

133 **Elephants and ethnologists.**
Sir Grafton Elliot Smith. London: K. Paul, Trench, Trubner & Co.; New York: E. P. Dutton & Co., 1924. 135p., 51 plates on 32p. map.

A proponent of pre-historical, trans-Pacific human contact between Asia and the New World, Smith supports that theory using the design on Stela B at Copán as evidence. Stela B depicts what appears to be an Indian elephant with a turbanned *mahout* driver modelled by a sculptor who, the author suggests, copied an imported design and not a native tapir, as suggested by A. Maudslay. Feature by feature, he makes numerous comparisons between the stela designs and many other examples of antique Indian, Chinese and Cambodian art. Other representations of the elephant, the makara, the spiral ornament, the date of the diffusion of culture to America, and the significance of Indo-China are among the topics also discussed. Great use of woodcut illustrations by A. H. Gerrard is made to exemplify the author's points.

134 **Excavations at Guarabuqui, El Cajón, Honduras: frontiers, culture areas, and the southern Mesoamerican periphery.**
Lewis Clement Messenger, Jr. PhD dissertation, University of Minnesota, 1984. 328p. (DAI 45/12A, p. 3676).

Excavation at Guarabuqui, a Late Classical (AD 550-1000) village in the Cajón region of central Honduras, took place in 1981. Located on the first river terrace above the Sulaco River, the site was composed of 209 mounds, ramps, and retaining terraces buttressed by mud-mortared river-cobble walls. Platforms supported wattle-and-daub superstructures. The settlement was divided into three groups that were inhabited contemporaneously. Information on intra-site artefactual, burial, architectural, and settlement variability allowed for settlement, subsistence, economy, and exchange inferences for Guarabuqui and the Cajón region. [Based on the author's abstract]. The lengthy report offers substantial detail and illustrations of the site.

135 **A guide to ancient Maya ruins.**
C. Bruce Hunter. Norman, Oaklahoma: University of Oklahoma Press, 1986. 2nd ed., revised and enlarged. 342p. maps. bibliog.

This excellent guide for the traveller to numerous archaeological zones was written by a frequent leader of field-study tours for the American Museum of Natural History. The site at Copán is extensively described on pages 75-110 with more than twenty photographs and a map accompanying the text. The work is indexed.

136 **An historical analysis of the tropical forest tribes of the southern border of Mesoamerica.**
Anne MacKaye Chapman. PhD dissertation, Columbia University, .
1958. 183p. maps. bibliog.
Chapman reconstructs the lowland culture of the Conquest period by analysing historical documents. Her most important conclusion is the identification of these people as an 'ancient, unstratified tropical forest culture' not an elaborate 'circum-caribbean culture', as had formerly been assumed. She is specifically concerned with the Jicaque, Paya, Miskito, Sumu and Matagalpa peoples and provides in-depth descriptions of their society at the time of contact with the Spanish explorers.

137 **Interaction on the southeast Mesoamerican frontier: prehistoric and historic Honduras and El Salvador.**
Edited by Eugenia J. Robinson. Oxford, England: B.A.R., 1987.
2 vols. 462p. bibliog. (BAR International Series, no. 327).
A two-volume set of papers presented at a symposium during the 1985 American Anthropological Association conference. Seven regions in Honduras with ongoing archaeological projects are represented: the Sula Valley, Copán Valley, Naco Valley, Comayagua Valley, El Cajón region, La Entrada region and Santa Bárbara region. The papers are grouped by theme: architecture and settlement patterns, artefact distribution patterns, ceramics as a means of communication, ethnicity and the concept of the frontier. This work presents substantial coverage of a large part of Honduras, and most papers are amply illustrated with maps, pictures and graphs, and contain bibliographies, thus providing excellent access to many of the numerous separate ongoing archaeological projects in Honduras.

138 **Interregional interaction in the SE Maya periphery: the Santa Bárbara Archaeological Project 1983-1984 seasons.**
Edward Schortman, Patricia Urban, Wendy Ashmore.
Journal of Field Archaeology, vol. 13 (Fall 1986), p. 259-72.
bibliog.
Analyses human interaction in the Santa Bárbara region of central-western Honduras by relating artefacts found to their source of origin.

139 **Late ceramic horizons in northeastern Honduras.**
Jeremiah F. Epstein. PhD dissertation, University of Pennsylvania,
1957. 313p. bibliog.
Epstein uses two separate sherd collections from the Bay Islands and northeast coast of Honduras that pertain to the American Museum of Natural History to investigate the sequence of culture and temporal limits of the Ulúa polychromes in northeastern Honduras and the Coast Appliqué style.

Prehistory and Archaeology. General

140 **Material symbolics in pre-Columbian households: the painted pottery of Naco, Honduras.**
Anthony Wonderley. *Journal of Anthropological Research*, vol. 42, no. 4 (1986), p. 497-534.

A cultural and historical study of a non-élite ceramic type characteristic of northwestern Honduras just prior to the Spanish Conquest. The analysis illustrates how some commonplace artefacts may offer an unsuspected and untapped resource for the study of non-élite cognitive systems in pre-Columbian Mesoamerica. [Based on the author's abstract].

141 **Maya ruins in Central America in color: Tikal, Copán and Quirigua.**
William M. Ferguson, John Q. Royce. Albuquerque, New Mexico: University of New Mexico Press, 1984. 387p. maps. bibliog.

Exquisite photographic documentation of three very important classic Mayan centres unequalled in architectural grandeur and tropical beauty. Calling Copán the 'Athens of the classic Mayan cities' the authors provide detailed descriptions and histories (pages 186-293) for each of the many significant monuments at the site. The colour photographs are of excellent quality and many sketches of the monuments include iconographic and hieroglyphic interpretations. Many drawings are from Maudslay's *Biologia centrali-americana*, volume 1 (q.v.).

142 **Los mayas en Honduras: visión de un mundo extinguido.** (The Maya in Honduras: vision of an extinguished world.)
Pedro Aplicano Mendieta. Tegucigalpa: Imprenta y Papelería Calderón, 1969. 161p. bibliog.

An overview of Mayan civilization in Honduras up to the arrival of Hernán Cortés. The book touches upon all aspects of daily life and includes brief chapters about the Lencas, Chorotegas, and Chortís, but the lack of an index hampers use.

143 **The new archaeology and the ancient Maya.**
Jeremy A. Sabloff. New York: Scientific American Library, 1990. 193p. bibliog.

The transformation in methodology of Maya archaeologists is ably conveyed by a practitioner of the 'new archaeology' which examines cultural processes and changes through scientific research procedures. The author first presents the traditional model of Maya civilization, then explores new views as researched through settlement patterns, technology, agriculture, trade and daily life of the common people. Recent research of noted scholars concerning Copán is presented on pages 158-63. The work is beautifully illustrated.

144 **Obsidian sources and elemental analyses of artifacts in southern Mesoamerica and the northern intermediate area.**
Payson Sheets, (et. al). *American Antiquity*, vol. 55, no. 1 (1990), p. 144-58.

Several students of archaeology look at the sources of obsidian used to make stone implements and weapons in Honduras and Nicaragua.

Prehistory and Archaeology. General

145   **Palaeoecology of the Ulúa Valley, Honduras: an archaeological perspective.**
Kevin Odell Pope.   PhD dissertation, Stanford University, 1986. 224p. (DAI 47/02B, p. 550).

The Ulúa Valley is a large tropical floodplain in northwestern Honduras. This study takes a geoarchaeological approach in examining human palaeoecology against the backdrop of environmental diversity and change. Palaeoenvironmental reconstructions are based on geomorphic and soil data, and on the Late Holocene history of river channel changes. The Proyecto Arqueológico Sula surveyed 15 per cent of the valley and found over 500 prehistoric sites. Several hypotheses regarding human palaeoecology are formulated after considering sampling and preservation problems. For the Formative period, the ecologies of large alluvial fan villages and small riverbank villages are compared by examining access to resources and environmental risks. For the Classical period, relationships between settlement density and soil quality are examined in nine habitats. No correlation between settlement location and access to quality soils could be demonstrated, except for an apparent avoidance of marginal soils. An explanation for this lack of correlation based on evidence for trade with the Maya Lowlands, is that commercial agriculture along the river levees, clustering of settlements near large commercial centres and risks from floods and attack, were major factors governing settlement location. [Author's abstract].

146   **Pre-Columbian man finds Central America: the archaeological bridge.**
Doris Stone.   Cambridge, Massachusetts: Peabody Museum Press, 1972. 231p. maps. bibliog.

In this popular presentation of Central American prehistory, the noted archaeologist describes the mingling of Mesoamerican peoples, the life of the earliest villagers, notes the influence of outside tribes during the Classical era and provides details about the empire and trade during the Post-classical period. The work is richly illustrated with photographs of artefacts found throughout the regions. Ulúa polychrome ware found in Honduras is prominent, as are other examples from Honduran sites such as Playa de los Muertos, Lake Yojoa, La Paleta, Travesía, Tigre Island, Copán and other Honduran sites.

147   **Precolumbian population history in the Maya lowlands.**
Edited by T. Patrick Culbert, Don S. Rice.   Albuquerque, New Mexico: University of New Mexico Press, 1990. 395p. maps. bibliog.

Scholarly reports on the historical demography of lowland Maya by twenty-one contributors. The focus is limited to quantitative data and methodology; settlement patterns and ecological adaptation are omitted. Sixteen chapters give the population estimates for sites such as Quirigua, Seibal, Tikal and others. One chapter by David Webster and Anncorinne Freter specifically concerns the demography of Late Classical Copán (p. 37-61). They offer a preliminary synthesis of Phase II project data, carefully describing their methodology for demographic reconstruction. They conclude that at its peak maturity, between 700 and 850 AD, Copán's population ranged from 20,000 to 25,000 souls with 38 per cent concentrated in the urban core, an area of 1.19 square kilometres. An endnote reporting further fieldwork revises the estimate to 18,000 to 20,000 residents. The chapter includes two maps and ten tables of supporting data.

39

Prehistory and Archaeology. Copán

148 **A preliminary settlement pattern study of a prehistoric cultural corridor: the Comayagua Valley, Honduras.**
Boyd Dixon. *Journal of Field Archaeology*, vol. 16 (Fall 1988), p. 257-71. bibliog.
An archaeological survey of land settlement patterns in the Comayagua Valley in prehistoric times.

149 **Researches in the Uloa Valley, Honduras. Report on explorations by the Museum, 1896-97.**
George Byron Gordon. Cambridge, Massachusetts: Peabody Museum of American Archaeology and Ethnology, Harvard University, 1898. 44p. map. (Memoirs, vol. 1, no. 4). Reprinted by Kraus.
Gordon reports on a number of archaeological sites and ruins in the Ulúa Valley which had been occupied by several distinct populations in ancient times. His preliminary research on stone-covered mounds and other surface remains appeared not to be directly connected with the underground relics he analysed. The text is followed by excellent photographs of the river valley and of recovered relics.

150 **Systems of settlement in the precolombian Naco Valley, northwestern Honduras.**
Patricia Ann Urban. PhD dissertation, University of Pennsylvania, 1986. 835p. (DAI 47/05A, p. 1788).
The Naco Valley is the last intermontane valley along the middle Chamelecón River before it enters Honduras' extensive coastal plain, the Sula Valley. Known as a centre of Indian occupation at the Conquest, the area remained uninvestigated between the work in the 1930s carried out by a joint Harvard–Smithsonian project (W. D. Strong, director) and the project initiated in 1974 by J. S. Henderson (Cornell University). The Naco Valley Survey Project began in 1977 with the goals of locating and mapping prehistoric sites and determining their periods of occupation. The project continued to survey in 1978 and 1979 and initiated an excavation programme in 1979. [Author's abstract].

Copán

151 **Die Architektur von Copán (Honduras): Vermessung, Plandarstellung, Untersuchung der baulichen Elemente und des raumlichen Konzepts.**
(The architecture of Copán [Honduras]: survey, representation, investigation of architectural elements and spatial concepts.)
Hasso Hohmann, Annegrete Vogrin. Graz, Austria: Akademische Druck- u. Verlagsanstalt, 1982. 182p., [63]p. of plates. bibliog.
This is most certainly the definitive survey and analysis of monumental architecture at Copán. Using triangulation, polar and tachymetrical surveys, plus photogrammetry, the researchers produce a comprehensive compositional map for Copán, even reconstructing exactly the structures lost to earthquakes and erosion. Copiously

illustrated with over 300 photographs, charts and sketches, the work is accompanied by thirteen folded plans. The detailed text is in German but is included here because of its summaries in English and Spanish.

152 **The ball courts at Copán: with notes on courts at La Unión, Quirigua, San Pedro Pinula, and Asunción Mita.**
Gustav Stromsvik. Washington DC: Carnegie Institution of Washington, 1952. 214p. bibliog. (Carnegie Institution of Washington, Publication no. 596).
An in-depth study of the architecture and social uses of ball courts in Mayan society. Emphasis is on the court of Copán, but comparative information is given for the other courts mentioned in the title.

153 **Caverns of Copán, Honduras. Report on explorations by the Museum, 1896-97.**
George Byron Gordon. Cambridge, Massachusetts: Peabody Museum of American Archaeology and Ethnology, Harvard University, 1898. 12p. map. (Memoirs, vol. 1, no. 5).
An illustrated report documenting the exploration of several caves located in the mountains surrounding the Copán Valley. Some of the chambers were used for depositing partly cremated human remains; others had no apparent long-term use although remains or relics were found. Mention is made of cave cults. The author concludes that there was not sufficient evidence to determine whether the users of the caves lived before the construction of the Copán site, were contemporaneous with the people of Copán, or came after the decline of the Copán Maya.

154 **The classic Maya collapse at Copán, Honduras: a regional settlement perspective.**
Anncorinne Freter. PhD dissertation, Pennsylvania State University, 1988. 351p. (DAI 49/07A, p. 1861).
As part of the Proyecto Arqueológico Copán, this thesis focuses on the Classical Maya collapse as it was manifested at the site of Copán, located in the southeast periphery of the Maya Lowlands. The author uses data from five years of rural settlement survey and test pit excavations in conjunction with the data produced from extensive excavations conducted in the Main Group, the Residential Core Zone surrounding it, and the eleven rural sites that have been extensively excavated within the Copán valley region. She concludes that the royal ruling structure of the Copán polity could not be supported when the population nucleation and the agricultural stresses it caused exceeded the technology and abilities of élite management. The result was that the political structure of the centre was undercut and the population which had supported it fragmented into smaller, lineage-based settlement units. [Based on the author's abstract].

155 **Copán ayer y hoy: guía breve.** (Copán yesterday and today: a brief
   guide.)
   Tegucigalpa: Instituto Hondureño de Antropología e Historia, 1984.
   41p. maps. bibliog.

Much more than a tourist guide to the magnificent ruins of the Late Classical Maya site
at Copán, this slim work contains data on the ongoing investigation of the Copán
Archaeological Project, conducted under the auspices of the publisher. This guide
provides a general description of the site, with maps showing its location, the
breakdown of land-use zones and the distribution of monuments in the principal zone.
Previous interpretations of Copán society are described and contrasted with present-
day interpretations; that is, it is now known that the hieroglyphic monuments referred
to governmental administrations rather than to deities. An outstanding example, Altar
Q, shows sixteen governors of Copán. A chart lists the numerous stelae and altars,
gives their Maya and Christian dates and names the governors from 613 to 800 AD.
This most informative and helpful guide concludes with a code of conduct for visitors.

156 **Copán ceramics: a study of southeastern Maya pottery.**
   John M. Longyear, III.   Washington, DC: Carnegie Institution of
   Washington, 1952. 114p. bibliog.

Based on pottery excavations conducted at Copán during the years 1938, 1939 and
1946. The book is divided into two parts: Part I contains a general summary of the
ceramic sequence at Copán, a description of special deposits such as graves, tombs and
caches, and concludes with remarks about archaeological and historical problems in the
southeastern Maya area. Part II is for the motivated student and consists of detailed
text and illustrations of Copán pottery and artefacts.

157 **Copán: city of kings and commoners.**
   George E. Stuart, Kenneth Garrett.   *National Geographic*, vol. 176
   (Oct. 1989), p. 488-505.

A highly readable and beautifully illustrated account of the exploration and
reconstruction of one of the most remarkable Mayan settlements. Each group of ruins
is examined superficially along with the royal lineage and common folk responsible for
its construction. Especially noteworthy are the photographs and description of the
exceedingly rare 'eccentric flints' discovered by David Stuart: three painstakingly
flaked silhouettes of translucent chert each of which depicts seven Mayan profiles.

158 **Copán, home of the Mayan gods.**
   Francis Robicsek.   New York: Museum of the American Indian, Heye
   Foundation, 1972. 166p. bibliog.

An authority on Mayan civilization and archaeology, Robicsek presents theories and
artefacts pertaining to the history of Copán and its inhabitants. The excellent
photographs (some in colour) and sketches are by the author.

159 **Copán: tierra de hombres y dioses.** (Copán: land of men and gods.)
   Longino Becerra.   Tegucigalpa: Baktun Editorial, 1984. 292p. bibliog.

An extensive history of Copán replete with many black-and-white photographs and
detailed sketches. The author has incorporated material from standard sources and
contemporary interpretations (up to 1983). Divided into three parts, the first deals with

the history of the Mayan people. This is followed by a section devoted to Copán's place in Mayan history. Lastly, each of the important monuments is described in great detail. The explicit table of contents serves well as an index. An excellent, well-written source for the study of this fascinating archaeological site.

160 **Copán: una nueva visión del mundo maya.** (Copán: a new vision of the Mayan world.)
Ricardo Agurcía Fasquelle, William L. Fash, Jr. *Mesoamérica* (Guatemala), vol. 9 (Dec. 1985), p. 451-8.

In 1978, several Honduran cultural agencies initiated a coordinated project to encourage and support the study of this most treasured archaeological zone. Thus the Copán Archaeological Project was born. Agurcía Fasquelle, director of the Honduran Institute of Anthropology and Archaeology, and Fash, supervising archaeologist of the Project, here report on research that has shed new light on the original purpose of the magnificent site. Up until the early 1970s it was thought that the numerous stelae at Copán were representations of deities. It is now surmised that the stelae represent important statesmen and leaders of the people. This along with other new evidence led specialists to believe that the society of Copán was not of a theocractic government, but of a secular one; that it was not a ceremonial centre, but an urban centre of 15,000 inhabitants; not a conglomeration of temples, but one of residences for the nobility; from sculptures of gods to those of kings; and from hieroglyphics representing devinations to historical dates.

161 **Economic specialization and construction personnel in classic period Copán, Honduras.**
Elliott M. Abrams. *American Antiquity,* vol. 52, no. 3 (1987), p. 485-99. bibliog.

The degree of development of specialist positions associated with large-scale construction at the Maya site of Copán is evaluated. The methodology used involves the quantification of the energy in human labour which was expended in the construction of a major palace in the Main Centre of Copán. The results suggest that few specialists were required and that the vast majority of construction personnel were unspecialized conscripts. [Author's abstract].

162 **Excavaciones en el área urbana Copán.** (Excavations in the urban area of Copán.)
William T. Sanders. Tegucigalpa: Instituto Hondureño de Antropología e Historia, 1986- . rev. ed. maps. bibliog. (Further volumes are still being published).

There have been three distinct periods of research and exploration of the Copán archaeological zone: they started in the 1890s with the Peabody Museum expeditions, followed by intense interest in the 1930s financed by the Carnegie Institution, and the latest started in 1975 by the Proyecto Arqueológico Copán, an agency of the Honduran Institute of Anthropology and History. In this summary of years of research, Sanders's conclusions on the Maya social structure differ dramatically from theories presented by earlier archaeologists. The text is supplemented extensively by diagrams, charts, photographs, and maps.

163 **Guía de las ruinas de Copán.** (Guide to the Copán ruins.)
     Gustav Stromsvik. Tegucigalpa: Talleres Tipolito Aristón, 1946. 90p.
     A handy little guidebook to the ruins of Copán with several folding maps showing the
     layout of the site. Many of the principle stelae and buildings are briefly described.

164 **The hieroglyphic stairway, ruins of Copán: report on explorations by the
     Museum.**
     George Byron Gordon. Cambridge, Massachusetts: Peabody Museum
     of American Archaeology and Ethnology, Harvard University, 1902.
     38p. (Memoirs, vol. 1, no. 6). Reprinted by Kraus.
     Provides copious notes on and several hundred photographs of the hieroglyphic
     inscriptions on the most important stairway at Copán. As part of Mound 26, the
     stairway has mystified many an archaeologist. The reason for its demise is unknown
     and it has defied reconstruction attempts although the remaining pieces are quite
     impressive. Gordon attempts to decipher the remaining hierglyphs and concludes that
     the inscriptions contain considerable chronological matter, embracing long periods of
     time. The work is paged continuously with the other numbers of the volume and
     includes the index to volume 1 of the Memoirs.

165 **The House of the Bacabs, Copán, Honduras.**
     Edited by David Webster. Washington, DC: Dumbarton Oaks
     Research Library and Collection, 1989. 116p. bibliog.
     Excavated under the auspices of the Honduran Institute of Anthropology and History,
     phase II of the Copán Archaeological Project investigated the Mayan socio-political
     structure during the Late Classical period between AD 700 and 900. The investigation
     evaluates the significance of the élite Structure 9N-82 centre by synthesizing an
     epigraphic/iconographic method with a behavioural/anthropological approach. The
     descriptive text is illustrated by eighty-three detailed photographs, diagrams and
     sketches.

166 **The inscriptions at Copán.**
     Sylvanus Griswold Morley. Washington, DC: Carnegie Institution of
     Washington, 1920. 643p. maps. bibliog. (Carnegie Institution of
     Washington, Publication no. 219).
     This weighty tome represents an analysis of the date glyphs appearing on all known
     inscriptions at the site of Copán and incorporates data from earlier interpretations and
     site reports by Maudslay, Gordon, Spinden, Stephens and others, as well as newer
     information. Following an overview of the site location, description and history,
     Morley examines each inscription in periodic groupings: early, middle and great
     periods. Although this is a classic study of these particular Mayan inscriptions,
     subsequent investigators, using more modern dating methods, have come to different
     conclusions regarding the site's chronology. This valuable work is still a must for
     anyone doing research on Mayan glyph interpretation. The many reproductions of
     inscriptions, maps, charts and sketches enhance its value as a research tool, as does the
     detailed index. The text is accompanied by several appendices, including the English
     translation of a hitherto lost report by Juan Galindo, *A description of the ruins of
     Copán* written in 1834, and *The distribution of the several branches of Mayance
     linguistic stock* by William Gates.

167 **Late classic Maya economic specialization: evidence from the Copán obsidian assemblage.**

John Kenneth Mallory, III.   PhD dissertation, Pennsylvania State University, 1984. 370p. (DAI 45/09A, p. 2908).

In recent archaeological debates, one topic has been the complexity of the Late Classical Period. Mallory's dissertation considers this issue in a study of the organization of production at the major Maya centre of Copán. More specifically, his research concerns the degree to which economic specialization in the production and use of obsidian tools existed, and the effects such specialization had on other cultural subsystems. [Based on the author's abstract].

168 **Marvels of Copán: a handy illustrated guide.**

Joaquín Muñóz.   Guatemala: Unión Tipográfica Muñóz Plaza, 1941. 33p., [20]p. of plates. maps.

Described in the Preface as: 'Condensed from the accounts of John L. Stephens, A. P. Maudslay, Herbert J. Spinden and Gustav Stromsvik to whom all credit is due.' No doubt, much of the information contained within is in need of up-dating since more excavation work has been done since 1941, but this would still be a useful tourist guide to the ruins with its brief descriptions and numerous black-and-white photographs.

169 **Maya–Lenca ethnic relations in late classic period Copán, Honduras.**

Andrea Irene Gerstle.   PhD dissertation, University of California, Santa Barbara, 1988. 363p. (DAI 49/11A, p. 3405).

An attempt is made to evaluate the importance of external relations in the rise and fall of the Maya state of Copán. Copán represents an ideal case for the study of such relations because it is located in the boundary zone between distinct ethnic groups. Based on the literature of ethnic relations in modern and historical times, an approach suitable for use with archaeological data was developed and applied to the Copán data set. The analysis included artefactual, architectural and burial data from the complete excavation of three Late Classical Period élite residential sites located near the civic/ceremonial centre of Copán. [From the author's abstract].

170 **Metates as socioeconomic indicators during the Classic Period at Copán, Honduras.**

Mary Louise Spink.   PhD dissertation, Pennsylvania State University, 1983. 225p. (DAI 45/01A, p. 227)

The nature of intraregional procurement and circulation at the Maya site of Copán, Honduras, during the Classical period was studied focusing on a basic utilitarian item. Metates, or grinding stones, were found in every residence type sampled, regardless of the household's projected status. Attributes of the metates were compared among residences of various types to see if any of them served as indices of socio-economic position. One of the attributes tested was the origin of the most common material used, rhyolite. [Author's abstract].

171 **A new look at Maya statecraft from Copán, Honduras.**
William L. Fash, Jr. *Antiquity*, vol. 62, no. 3 (1988), p. 157-69.
bibliog.

The chief archaeologist of the Copán site interprets the stelae to be sculptures of the statesmen and rulers of the ancient city, not gods as previously thought.

172 **Scribes, warriors, and kings: the lives of the Copán Maya.**
William L. Fash, Barbara W. Fash. *Archaeology*, vol. 43
(May–June 1990), p. 26-35.

A lavishly illustrated account of research conducted at Copán to determine how its rulers responded to changing political and economic conditions. By analysing archaeological structures, such as fills beneath stairways or numbers of warrior and sacrifice imagery, the authors attempt to determine the relative strength, wealth or weakness of a given dynasty or ruler.

173 **Systems of labor organization in Late Classic Copán, Honduras: the energetics of construction.**
Elliot Marc Abrams. PhD dissertation, Pennsylvania State University, 1984. 362p. (DAI 45/06A, p. 1800).

A primary research goal in New World archaeology is assessing the complexity of cultural development of the Late Classical Mayan Indians of Mexico and Central America. In this analysis, the quantification of the energetic investment in residential structures serves as the basis for such assessment, the basic hypothesis being that social status is reflected in the differential energetic investment in these structures. A range of structures from the Mayan site of Copán, Honduras, was selected and the rates of work for each operation in construction were obtained through a variety of techniques, primarily replicative experimentation. Applied to each structure, these work rates yielded comparable investment figures, expressed in person-days. Using these figures, many questions concerning Late Classical Mayan society can be answered. [Author's abstract].

History

Central America: general

174 **A brief history of Central America.**
Hector Pérez Brignoli. Berkeley, California: University of California
Press, 1989. 223p. bibliog.
'The first interpretive history of Central America by a Central American historian to
be published in English'. Pérez Brignoli, a history professor at the University of Costa
Rica, has prepared an insightful and concise survey of Central America's history from
the early sixteenth century to the mid-1980s, starting with cultural geography and
finishing with the present crises. He treats many fundamental themes and challenges to
the area, and examines in depth the characteristics of colonial heritage, independence
and federation, the formation of nation-states and the development of export
economies based on coffee and bananas. Scrutinizing the 20th century, he highlights
the growing inequalities and impoverishment of the region, giving special attention
given to Costa Rica, but with references to Honduras throughout.

175 **The Cádiz experiment in Central America, 1808 to 1826.**
Mario Rodríguez. Berkeley, California: University of California
Press, 1978. 316p. maps. bibliog.
After briefly examining the Bourbon legacy in Central America, the author fully
explores the revolutionary changes in Spain wrought by the Constitution of Cádiz in
1812 and the impact of this liberal transformation upon Central America. He shows
that after an initial welcome and attempts at confederation, Central American unity is
fractured. Examples abound of rivalries between Honduras and Guatemala, and
between Tegucigalpa and Comayagua. This is a most insightful study of Central
American and Honduran political manoeuvring before, during and after gaining
independence from Spain. The work includes an index.

176 **Central America, a nation divided.**
Ralph Lee Woodward, Jr.   New York: Oxford University Press, 1985.
2nd ed. 390p. map. bibliog. (Latin American Histories Series).
Woodward, a leading North American expert on Central American history, offers an
in-depth socio-economic history of Central America. Although he treats the nations as
a single entity, he does provide a significant amount of data on Honduras throughout.

177 **The failure of union: Central America, 1824-1975.**
Thomas L. Karnes.   Tempe, Arizona: Center for Latin American
Studies, Arizona State University, 1976. 236p. map. bibliog.
The several unsuccessful efforts at creating a confederation of Central American states
since independence from Spain are analysed. The author attributes failure of union to
the growing nationalism of each country, weak representative governments, and the
uniqueness and isolation of Costa Rica from the other nations. The central role played
by Francisco Morazán is well developed; his efforts in the 1830s to create and cement a
confederation show how he has become a symbol for Central American unity and a
national hero for Honduras. The book includes an index.

178 **Forced native labor in sixteenth-century Central America.**
William L. Sherman.   Lincoln, Nebraska: University of Nebraska
Press, 1979. 496p. bibliog.
This exemplary ethnohistory of Central American society during the first century of
Spanish colonialism contains copious data on the natives of Honduras. The forced
labour, removal, treatment, and uses of natives are thoroughly documented. An
especially illuminating section on pages 41-53 recounts the central role of Honduras in
slave shipment; numerous grim incidents of abuses are related. This is an essential
work for comprehending the clash of cultures wherever they came into contact. It
contains an extensive bibliography and is indexed.

179 **Government and society in Central America, 1680-1840.**
Miles L. Wortman.   New York: Columbia University Press, 1982.
374p. maps. bibliog.
This fundamental study of politics, economics and society during and just after the
Colonial period provides an excellent overview of Central American history and social
structure. Wortman examines the region under Habsburg rule with Guatemala as the
central seat of power. The transformation of the colony under the Bourbon reforms is
thoroughly explored and well illustrated by statistical tables, as is the collapsing
economy at the end of the 18th century and the resulting crisis in the colonial
government. The achievement of independence from Spain and the Republican
experiment in liberal unity and federation is considered. The disappearance of central
rule as the Central American states became nations is the final subject of the study.
References to Honduras abound, from the rivalry between Tegucigalpa and
Comayagua to the role played by prominent individuals such as Francisco Morazán.
Most useful, perhaps, are the analyses of population composition and of the social
classes of Honduras during this period of change.

180 **Historia de las ideas en Centroamérica.** (History of ideas in Central America.)
Constantino Lascaris Comneno. San José, Costa Rica: Editorial Universitaria Centroamericana, 1982. 485p. bibliog.
A presentation of lines of thought that have influenced the historical evolution of Central America, arranged in chronological order from pre-Columbian times to the mid-nineteenth century. Both institutional philosophies and those of individuals are included. Honduran thinkers include José del Valle, Dionisio Herrera, and Francisco Morazán.

181 **The historiography of modern Central America since 1960.**
Ralph Lee Woodward, Jr. *Hispanic American Historical Review*, vol. 67, no. 3 (1987), p. 461-96.
An extensive bibliographical essay and historiography on sources related to nineteenth- and twentieth-century Central America published since 1960. Serves well to update an earlier work by William J. Griffith, 'The historiography of Central America since 1830', in the *Hispanic American Historical Review* (vol. 40, no. 4 [1960], p. 548-69).

182 **Morazán, defensor de la unión de Centroamérica.** (Morazán, defender of the Central American union.)
Rafael Bardales B. Tegucigalpa: Editorial Universitaria, 1983. 178p. bibliog.
The author gives his assessment of Morazán's central role in the creation of a Central American union in order to defend his reputation, which had been called into question in a book by Marroquín Rojas. The latter book exalted the role of Rafael Carrera, defended Manuel José Arce, and denigrated Morazán. Bardales strongly defends Morazán's efforts in the first part of this book; in part two he reproduces the texts of the 1824 and 1835 constitutions of the Central American confederation.

183 **Power in the isthmus: a political history of modern Central America.**
James Dunkerley. London: Verso, 1988. 691p. bibliog.
A comprehensive, orthodox narrative of the political history of Nicaragua, Guatemala, Honduras, El Salvador and Costa Rica, from independence through to 1985. The author intentionally focuses on local national events and trends, rather than on the US role in Central American politics as many other authors have done in the past. The first part of the work covers general historical developments up to 1950, followed by a chapter on post-war economy. The second part is dedicated to analyses of modern politics for the individual nations. The text is heavily footnoted and supplemented by many maps, tables, and an index.

184 **Spanish Central America: a socioeconomic history, 1520-1720.**
Murdo J. MacLeod. Berkeley, California: University of California Press, 1984, [c.1973]. 554p. maps. bibliog. (California Library Reprint Series).
This examination of Spanish dominion during the 16th and 17th centuries provides an essential foundation for understanding the colonial period in Honduras. Although MacLeod covers social and economic developments for the entire region, Honduras is prominent throughout. Some of the major themes explored include the use of natives

for forced labour, the establishment of gold and silver mines, the effect of epidemics on populations; the booms and busts caused by dependence on monoculture. One chapter (on pages 253-63) specifically examines the development of Honduran mining and its role in the settlement of central Honduras. The bibliography is extensive and an index is included.

185 **The works of Hubert Howe Bancroft: History of Central America.**
Hubert Howe Bancroft. San Francisco, California: A. L. Bancroft and Co., 1882-90. Vols 6, 7, 8 of the 39-volume set. (Also published separately in 1886-87 under the title *History of Central America*).

Although he was 'with but one lifetime at [his] disposal', and a mere 600 unacknowledged assistants, Mr Bancroft produced an awe-inspiring body of historical literature based on the organization and interpretation of thousands upon thousands of original documents, manuscripts and miscellanea, most, if not all, of which are now housed in the Bancroft Library of the University of California. The volumes concerning the history of Central America are divided chronologically: 1501-30 in volume 6; 1530-1800 in volume 7; and 1801-87 in volume 8. All imaginable facets of history, social life and customs, politics, intellectual trends and the Church are minutely and meticulously recounted. Each volume is crammed with details about the era concerned, but the rather poor indexing at the end of volume 8 necessitates creative and heavy use of the table of contents. Honduras is treated throughout all three volumes, both separately and in the Central American context. The text would probably overwhelm the less erudite reader on account of its heavy content and style, and frustrate the scholar because of its lack of bibliographical references for quotations. It is nevertheless a very important source of information for Central American history.

Honduras: general

186 **Diccionario histórico-biográfico hondureño.** (Honduran historico-biographical dictionary.)
Mario Argueta. Tegucigalpa: Editorial Universitaria, 1990. 205p. (Colección Realidad Nacional, no. 29).

An alphabetical listing of 164 notable persons in Honduran history, politics and culture. Each entry contains biographical data, major accomplishments and any publications.

187 **Enciclopedia histórica de Honduras: obra fundamental de información y consulta e imprescindible auxiliar pedagógico para maestros. . .** (Historical encyclopaedia of Honduras: a fundamental work of information and reference and an indispensible teaching aide for teachers. . .) Ramiro Colindres Ortega. Tegucigalpa: Graficentro Editores, 1988- . (Still being published).
The first volume of a planned multi-volume history of Honduras concerns the pre-Columbian and colonial periods. A well-illustrated work, written for students and intermediate readers, it accomplishes its aim of providing fundamental data on Honduran people, culture and history in an entertaining style. Emphasis is given to the accomplishments of the Maya, in particular at the important Copán site, but ethnographic sketches of other native Hondurans are provided. The challenges that native people faced and endured during the Conquest and colonization are addressed, and the uglier side of Spanish colonialism is not lightly glossed over. This is not really an encyclopaedia and access to its contents is difficult for lack of an index.

188 **Estampas de Honduras.** (Impressions of Honduras.) Doris Zemurray Stone. Mexico: [n.p.], 1954. 252p. bibliog.
An enjoyable overview of Honduran historical events, people and places from 1500 to 1900, written by the prominent anthropologist. The prologue is by Rafael Heliodoro Valle. Of particular note are the pieces on Chorotega Malalaca, Choluteca, and Comayagua. It includes an index, maps, illustrations, extensive footnotes and a bibliography.

189 **Evolución histórica de Honduras.** (Historical evolution of Honduras.) Longino Becerra. Tegucigalpa: Baktun Editorial, 1983. 227p. bibliog.
A very interesting history of Honduras developed from the author's presentations and classes for students and workers. He focuses upon class distinctions as determinants of society's structure and development. He proposes that Honduras has passed through four historical epochs where one class or a group of classes has played a dominating role. The primitive community, from 6000 BC to AD 1524, was without antagonistic social classes; property was held in common. As a Spanish colony from 1524 to 1821, Honduras was a feudal slave state, rigidly class-divided with the 'peninsulares' firmly in control. After independence in 1821, came the Anglo-US imperial rivalry; thus semi-feudalism lasted till 1876. Since 1876, Honduras has been a dependent capitalist state with bourgeoisie, proletariat and peasant classes. The author follows this class-based motive force of history analysis with different perspectives on famous events and people. For example, he notes that Francisco Morazán represented the emerging national bourgeoisie while Carrera represented the feudal aristocracy; their confrontation was not only of personalities but primarily between two antagonistic social classes. Popular rebellions against the dominant class, such as that of Lempira in 1537, are included to further enhance this account of the historic evolution of Honduras.

190 **Fechas de la historia de Honduras.** (Dates in Honduran history.)
Victor Cáceres Lara. Tegucigalpa: Tipografía Nacional, 1964. 402p.
bibliog.

Sixty-four important events in Honduran history are the subjects of brief essays, listed by the month in which they occurred. Most events included took place in the 19th century, but dates range from the first contact by Columbus with the island of Guanaja in 1502 to the execution of William Walker in Trujillo to a 1915 earthquake which destroyed the city of Gracias. An actual chronological listing by year would have made the work more useful.

191 **Historia de Honduras.** (History of Honduras.)
Medardo Mejía. Tegucigalpa: Universidad Nacional Autónoma de
Honduras, Editorial Universitaria, 1983-[89?]. 5 vols. bibliog.
(Colección Realidad Nacional, nos 8, 12, 14, 19, 23).

A comprehensive survey of nineteenth- and twentieth-century Honduran history that compares social and economic events to political ebbs and flows. Volume 1 was not available to this compiler, but one might deduce that it concerns the period from around 1800 to 1822. Volume two covers the period 1823-26, the Federal, feudal state of Central America; volume three, the Morazán decade (roughly from 1829 to 1840); volume four, the government of General Trinidad Cabañas; volume five, covers 1871-1910 and includes reproductions of relevant documents for the era. It is not known whether or not volume five is the last, but it appears to be.

192 **Historia de Honduras.** (History of Honduras.)
Mario Argueta, Edgardo Quiñónez. Tegucigalpa: Escuela Superior
del Profesorado 'Francisco Morazán', 1978. 251p. maps. bibliog.

A straightforward panorama of the 'battles, antagonisms and hopes' of Honduran society. In this textbook (perhaps for first-year college students) based on secondary sources, Argueta and Quiñónez cover Honduran history from pre-Columbian times to the late 1960s. Especially useful for information on the damage caused by Hurricane Fifi and the El Salvador–Honduras conflict of 1969. Contains many illustrations, but use is hindered by the lack of an index.

193 **Historical dictionary of Honduras.**
Harvey K. Meyer. Metuchen, New Jersey: Scarecrow Press, 1976.
399p. bibliog. (Latin American Historical Dictionaries, no. 13).

An interesting compilation of Honduran data and miscellanea written for both the scholar and the traveller. The compiler successfully conveys the feel or mood of events, discusses geographical features and provides statistics in order to enhance the facts. The book's coverage ranges from history to culture, people and geography and is arranged in alphabetical order by subject and with cross-references. Useful for quick verification of the major figures, places and events in Honduran history. The text is followed by an unannotated bibliography and a list of maps.

194 **Honduras confronts its future: contending perspectives on critical issues.**
Edited by Mark B. Rosenberg, Philip L. Shepherd. Boulder,
Colorado: L. Rienner, 1986. 268p. bibliog.
A collection of highly readable essays concerning democracy, human rights and social
justice, economic development, agricultural policy, foreign policy and national
security. This work is the result of a conference held in 1984, the objective of which
was to bring together scholars studying Honduras, policy-makers and leaders from all
sectors of Honduran life. The introduction provides succinct background information
and the final chapter indicates areas in need of further research.

195 **Honduras: portrait of a captive nation.**
Edited by Nancy Peckenham, Annie Street. New York: Praeger,
1985. 350p. bibliog.
A collection of essays, documents and reports that describe the country's individual
history and development in an effort to 'dispel the image of a "banana republic" or of a
mere location for U.S. military exercises'. The many contributions were prepared by
Central American and US statesmen, scholars and think-tanks, thus providing a broad
range of opinions and perspectives. The chapters range over a number of subjects and
consider, for example, Honduran history from the Spanish Conquest up to the 1980s,
rural politics, the Church, militarism, repression, the economy and the overwhelming
US presence since 1821.

196 **Los símbolos nacionales de Honduras.** (The national symbols of
Honduras.)
Hernán Carcamo Tercero. Tegucigalpa: Tipografía Nacional, 1983.
51p.
An illustrated guide to the national symbols of Honduras, including the flag and
regional emblems. A brief bibliography of sources is given on page 47.

Local, urban, regional and departmental

197 **The Anglo-Spanish struggle for Mosquitia.**
Troy S. Floyd. Albuquerque, New Mexico: University of New Mexico
Press, 1967. 235p. maps. bibliog.
The contention between Great Britain and Spain for hegemony over the Honduran
and Nicaraguan Mosquito Coast is the focus of this interesting historical interpretation.
This state of affairs lasted from their first contact in the sixteenth century through to
the late eighteenth century. Spanish efforts to defend the long coastline and offset the
English and their Sambo-Miskito allies are well documented. The work depicts the
importance of Trujillo and Fort Omoa in Honduran colonial development, and
illuminates the continuing distinctions between the English-speaking Caribbean people
and the Spanish-speaking mainlanders.

History. Local, urban, regional and departmental

198 **Apuntamientos para una historia colonial de Tegucigalpa y su alcaldía mayor.** (Notes on the colonial history of Tegucigalpa and its municipality.)
Mario Felipe Martínez. Tegucigalpa: Editorial Universitaria, 1982. 171p.

A history of the present-day capital city from its founding in 1578 until independence from Spain in 1821, this study details the city's political organization, urban development, religious and artistic life, education of its children, and its economic history. Primary sources in the archives of Seville, Guatemala, Tegucigalpa and Comayagua were examined, and some of these are reproduced. The work is especially useful for the names of mining operators and landowners.

199 **Comayagua antañona, 1537-1821.** (Comayagua of yesteryear, 1537-1821.)
José Reina Valenzuela. Tegucigalpa: Biblioteca de la Academia Hondureña de Geografía e Historia, 1968. 151p.

This is a comprehensive historical account of the former capital of Honduras which was also an important colonial centre from the date of its founding through to independence from Spain. Particularly noteworthy and well documented is the pervasive role of the Church. A listing of bishops and Spanish governors resident in Comayagua during the colonial period is provided. Numerous photographic plates depict the city's religious art and architecture.

200 **Comayagua durante la centuria de Fernández de Oviedo.** (Comayagua during Fernández de Oviedo's century.)
Mario Felipe Martínez Castillo, Gabriel Ureña Morales. In: *Memoria del Congreso sobre el Mundo Centroamericano de su Tiempo: V Centenario de Gonzalo Fernández de Oviedo.* Nicoya, Costa Rica: Comisión Nacional Organizadora, 1980, p. 387-401.

In 1539, Comayagua was founded for the second time by Alonso de Cáceres, a captain of Francisco de Montejo from Yucatán. The settlement did not gain importance until silver mines were discovered nearby, but by 1560 it had become an important Central American city – on a par with Guatemala and León – and the political, economic, religious, and administrative capital of Honduras. In 1599, governor Jorge de Alvarado was appointed and the city was declared the *de facto* capital of Honduras.

201 **El dominio insular de Honduras, estudio histórico-geográfico.** (The island territories of Honduras, a historico-geographical study.)
Gustavo A. Casteñada S. San Pedro Sula, Honduras: Tipografía Pérez Estrada, 1939. 271p.

The smallest department of the republic, that of the Bay Islands, was created under special circumstances and still does not meet the legal conditions for such status. This detailed history of the islands explains why that is so and provides a wealth of information for each island, reef and cay. Photographs, statistical tables and reprints of decrees and letters enhance the usefulness of this work.

54

202 **La fundación de la ciudad de Gracias a Dios y de las primeras villas y ciudades de Honduras en los documentos y erradas narraciones de los historiadores. (Nacimiento de la nacionalidad de Honduras). No fué fundada por Juan de Chávez.** (The founding of Gracias a Dios and the early Honduran towns and cities in the documents and erroneous narratives of historians. Birth of the Honduran nationality. It was not founded by Juan de Chávez.)
Federico Lunardi. Tegucigalpa: [n.p.], 1946. 267p. bibliog.
Commencing with Gracias a Dios and San Pedro Sula, Monsignor Lunardi relates the early history of twelve Honduran towns and cities, pointing out where and why errors had been made in the accounts of other historians. In part four of his work, he has reprinted lengthy excerpts from important historical documents, Cortés' letters and those of other explorers, concerning their discoveries in Honduras. The text is heavily footnoted and reveals a wealth of information concerning sixteenth-century Honduras.

203 **Homenaje a la ciudad de Gracias a Dios en el CD aniversario de su fundación, 1536-1936.** (Homage to the city of Gracias a Dios on the 400th anniversary of its founding, 1536-1936.)
Alvaro Pérez Estrada, Tito Pérez Estrada. San Pedro Sula, Honduras: Tipografía Pérez Estrada, 1936. 178p.
Historical data and biographical sketches of noteworthy events and people in this city which was founded by Spaniards in 1536 and currently the capital of Lempira Department. The work includes a brief anthology of poetry by local writers, several portraits of outstanding citizens and a chapter on Lempira.

204 **Memorias de un sampedrano.** (Memoirs of San Pedro Sula.)
Chalo Luque. San Pedro Sula, Honduras: G. R. Luque, 1979. 145p.
This is a self-published, personal narrative of life in the second-largest city of Honduras in the early decades of the 20th century, before its explosive industrial and population development. Popular customs are related, important persons and events are noted, and the city itself is evocatively described. An important glimpse at primary education is provided through the author's anecdotes. Personal photographs depict San Pedro Sula in marked contrast to its present-day bustling appearance.

205 **Merchants and industrialists in northern Honduras: the making of a national bourgeoisie in peripheral capitalism, 1870s-1972.**
Darío Aquiles Euraque. PhD dissertation, University of Wisconsin, Madison, 1990. (DAI vol. 51/09-A, p. 3194).
'This study has two parts: the first presents the economic structure of the San Pedro Sula bourgeoisie between the 1870s and the 1960s; the second part presents the politics of San Pedro Sula capitalists trying to make a regional bourgeoisie "national" in the 1960s. Chapters one to three detail capital accumulation in San Pedro Sula, Cortés and élite class formation there between the 1870s and the mid-1950s. [He] then characterize[s] post-World War II economic growth and offer[s] a comparative analysis of development in Tegucigalpa and San Pedro Sula before the industrialization of the 1960s.' [Author's abstract].

206 **Merchants, miners and monetary structures: the revival of the Honduran import trade, 1880-1900.**
Kenneth V. Finney. Secolas Annual (Southeastern Conference on Latin American Studies), vol. 12 (1981), p. 27-38.
Discusses the increasing level of imports (types of imports and their sources) through the Honduran Pacific port at Amapala from the 1880s to 1900.

207 **Penny ante imperialism: the Mosquito Shore and the Bay of Honduras, 1600-1914.**
Robert A. Naylor. Rutherford, New Jersey: Fairleigh Dickinson University Press; London: Associated University Presses, 1989. 315p. maps. bibliog.
This historical investigation focuses on the adventurers and entrepreneurs of British origin operating on the Caribbean coast who frequently obliged the British government to become involved in the area. The sporadic presence of British officialdom over the span of 250 years contributes to this case-study in British informal imperialism. The author shows that the Mosquito Coast received no long-range policy planning and insufficient attention, for the British would respond to particular events in a haphazardly, 'muddling through' fashion. The author studied numerous primary sources, and his extensive notes add immeasurably to knowledge about the history of this understudied region. His bibliography may be the most complete compilation of primary and secondary sources concerning the Mosquito Coast. The work is indexed.

208 **Santa María del Carbón: un expediente de tierras payas.** (Santa María del Carbón: a historical file on Paya lands.)
Sucelinda Zelaya Carranza. *América Indígena* (Mexico), vol. 44, no. 3 (1984), p. 461-6. bibliog.
Succinctly describes the concession of lands by the Honduran government to the Paya people at the behest of the missionary Manuel de Jesús Subirana. The file concerns the lands at El Carbón in the Agalta Valley of Olancho.

209 **Tegucigalpa de mis recuerdos; La Galería de los indispensables; Gobernantes de Honduras desde 1824 hasta 1978.** (My memories of Tegucigalpa; Gallery of Misfits; Honduran heads of state from 1824 to 1978.)
Marco Antonio Rosa. Tegucigalpa: Centro Técnico Tipo-Litográfico Nacional, 1978. 205p.
A native of Tegucigalpa reminisces fondly about his life from 1910 to 1978 in the capital city. Most interesting are his accounts of the social life and customs in the early part of the century, local celebrations, neighbourhood pharmacies, bookstores and barber-shops. Also included is a chapter on the history of Comayaguela by Salvador Turcios Ramírez and there are unusual portraits of the local misfits who roamed the streets of the capital.

210 **Tegucigalpa: a taste of colonial times.**
Adelfa G. Fernández. *Américas*, vol. 39 (Nov.–Dec. 1987), p. 38-43.
Once a centre for silver mining, the present-day capital of Honduras, nestling in a mountain valley, retains much of its charm of bygone days. Fernández provides a very brief history of the present capital of Honduras and describes many of its principle architectural features. The article contains many attractive photographs.

211 **Tradiciones tegucigalpenses.** (Traditions of Tegucigalpa.)
Gonzalo Guardiola. Tegucigalpa: Ministerio de Educación Pública, 1978. 125p.
Anecdotes and sketches of manners, customs, and characters of the capital city in the *costumbrista* literary style.

212 **El Valle de Comayagua, documentos para la historia.** (Comayagua Valley, historical documents.)
Federico Lunardi. Tegucigalpa: Sociedad de Antropología y Arqueológica de Honduras, 1946. 3 vols.
A carefully constructed and illustrated early history of this important city and valley from the first Spanish contact in 1537 – by conquistador Pedro Navarro – through to the establishment of the first convent and cathedral by the Order of Mercy. Only volume 1 of this set was available for review.

Colonial

213 **The conquest and colonization of Honduras, 1502-1550.**
Robert Stoner Chamberlain. Washington, DC: Carnegie Institution of Washington, 1953. 264p. maps. bibliog. (Carnegie Institution of Washington, Publication no. 598).
The complex history of the first half-century of Spanish discovery, influence, dominance and administration of the Province of Honduras is explored and documented with scholarly attention to detail. Using a wealth of official documents from the Archives of the Indies, the General Archives of the Government (Guatemala) and early published works, Chamberlain focuses on the career of the Spanish administrator, Francisco de Montejo and his conquest of Honduras and Higueras (now a part of western Honduras). Political intrigue and intervention, Indian revolts and relations, commercial endeavours, jurisdictional problems, the role of the Church and the military, and administrative and economic developments are all considered in this thorough study.

214 **The cost of conquest: Indian decline in Honduras under Spanish rule.**
Linda Newson. Boulder, Colorado: Westview Press, 1986. 375p.
bibliog. (Dellpain Latin American Studies, no. 20).
A well-documented analysis of the two indigenous Honduran social systems in effect at
the time of the Spanish Conquest. The author studies the nature of the chiefdoms and
indigenous groups extant before the arrival of the Spanish, their demographics, and the
method of colonization used by the conquistadors. In particular, Dr Newson minutely
examines the Spanish economic activities and institutions that had a major impact on
the lifestyle of the indigenous population. Many tables, a glossary, an extensive
bibliography and a detailed index enhance this scholarly text.

215 **Cristóbal de Olid, conquistador de México y Honduras.** (Cristóbal de
Olid, conquerer of Mexico and Honduras.)
Rafael Heliodoro Valle. Mexico: Editorial Jus, 1950. 316p. bibliog.
(Publicaciones de la Sociedad de Estudios Cortesianos, no. 5).
Sent by Hernán Cortés to establish order in part of his Central American fiefdom,
Olid's force of several hundred soldiers and archers first conquered Honduras for the
Spanish Crown. He established a settlement he called El Triunfo de la Cruz (Triumph
of the Cross), but things did not turn out well for him. He was accused of trying to
usurp authority for his own interests and was eventually convicted and beheaded.

216 **Documentos, historia de Honduras.** (Documents, history of Honduras.)
Compiled by Mario Felipe Martínez. Tegucigalpa: Editorial
Universitaria, 1983. 307p.
Sixty-three documents primarily written in the sixteenth century are reproduced
unedited. The originals of these documents are located in archives in Seville,
Guatemala and Comayagua. Many of the documents concern religious practices and
finances; several inventories of possessions provide insight into the colonialists'
material wealth. One document specifies the subject matter for several oil paintings.
Petitions, titles, *diezmos*, and tithes are frequent subjects. A subject index would have
made this work much more useful, but nevertheless, it does make available primary
sources for the study of Spanish administration and early colonial life in Honduras.

217 **Honduras.**
Luís Marinas Otero. Tegucigalpa: Universidad Nacional Autónoma
de Honduras, Editorial Universitaria, 1983. 2nd ed. 399p. bibliog.
(Colección Realidad Nacional, no. 6).
First published in Madrid in 1963, this history is notable primarily for its concentration
on Honduras during the colonial period. Spain's administration of its colony is fully
explored, and the interpenetration of the Crown and the Church in commerce, social
customs, religious practices and governmental policies is clearly evident. This work
also provides substantial data on Honduran economics and commerce during the 1950s
when the author apparently served as the Spanish envoy to Honduras.

218 **Hondureños en la independencia de Centroamérica.** (Hondurans in the Central American Independence movement.)
José Reina Valenzuela. Tegucigalpa: Esso Standard Oil, 1978. 173p. bibliog.
Focuses on the colonial and independence era of Honduran history through 1823. Some of the main topics featured are: the position of Honduras in the General Captaincy of Guatemala; events with Spain, the revolutionary stage, Honduras and the Cortes de Cádiz; differences between Comayagua and Tegucigalpa; empire and secession. Pages 24-9 contain the ecclesiastical divisions of Honduras as of 1806. There is no index or table of contents.

219 **El Padre Subirana y las tierras concedidas a los índios hondureños en el siglo XIX.** (Father Subirana and the lands conceded to Honduran Indians in the nineteenth century.)
William V. Davidson. *América Indígena* (Mexico), vol. 44, no. 3 (1984), p. 447-59. map. bibliog.
The efforts of missionary Manuel de Jesús Subirana to achieve the legal concession of lands to the Paya and Jicaque peoples are examined. In addition to presenting a biographical sketch of the missionary, there is a detailed analysis of the characteristics of the lands to be allocated and of the legal process: the paperwork and measurement processes; the agrarian measurement units; legal precedents; the lands' dimensions and locations; and their shape and suitability for native settlement patterns. Finally, Davidson considers the manner in which Father Subirana was able to obtain land titles, given the conditions of the time, and the impact that the event had on descendants of the native peoples who benefited from it.

220 **La provincia de Tegucigalpa bajo el gobierno de Mallol, 1817-1821: estudio histórico.** (The province of Tegucigalpa under the government of Mallol, 1817-21: an historical study.)
Rómulo E. Durón. Ciudad Universitaria Rodrigo Facio, Costa Rica: Editorial Universitaria Centroamericana, 1978. 225p.
A leading historian of his time, Durón assesses the last Spanish administration of Narciso Mallol just prior to independence. Originally published in Tegucigalpa by Tipografía Nacional in 1904.

221 **A statistical and commercial history of the Kingdom of Guatemala, in Spanish America: containing important particulars relative to its productions, manufactures, customs, &c, an account of its conquest by the Spaniards, and a narrative of the principal events down to the present time: from original records in the archives, actual observations and other authentic sources.**
Domingo Juarros, translated by John Baily. London: J. Hearne, 1823. Reprinted, New York: AMS, 1971. 520p.
Although this is not a complete translation of the *Compendio de la historia de la ciudad de Guatemala* (2 vols, Guatemala: Beteta, 1808-10), it contains a wealth of statistical and general information about the demographic, business and economic affairs of the Captaincy-General in Middle America as it was at the close of the colonial period.

222 **Tráfico de esclavos negros a Honduras.** (Black slave traffic to Honduras.)
Rafael Leiva Vivas. Tegucigalpa: Editorial Guaymuras, 1982. 157p. bibliog.

Although not solely about slavery in Honduras, this slim history does provide information on the slave trade of Africans brought to Honduras and of native peoples taken from Honduras, including their working and social conditions within the colonies on sugar plantations and in gold-mines. The author tells of how slaves were used to defend the Spanish forts at Omoa and Trujillo. The decree abolishing slavery issued by the United Provinces of Central America in 1824 concludes the work. Illustrations and tables are included.

223 **William Pitt's settlement at Black River on the Mosquito shore: a challenge to Spain in Central America, 1732-87.**
Frank Griffith Dawson. *Hispanic American Historical Review*, vol. 63, no. 4 (1983), p. 677-706. map. bibliog.

Using primary and secondary sources, Dawson relates the story of William Pitt, a distant relative of the renowned William Pitt, Earl of Chatham, pre-eminent in English political life. The former Pitt established an unofficial English colony in 1732 on the Honduran Mosquito Coast. The settlement of Black River, located 80 miles from the Spanish frontier town of Trujillo, became the area's administrative centre and a significant irritant to Spanish colonial administrators. They were particularly antagonized when, after 1740, Jamaican governors encouraged Pitt to develop his settlement into a crossroads for contraband trade and a staging-post for attacks on Spain's Central American possessions.

19th century

224 **1862.**
Ramón Oquelí. Tegucigalpa: Editorial Universitaria, 1989. 152p. bibliog. (Colección Realidad Nacional, no. 22).

The author has chosen the device of examining events chronologically throughout one year, to provide a frame of reference for understanding Honduras at a specific period of its past. Events chronicled focus primarily on political debates, events and persons; however, some information on social life and customs, trade, transportation and foreign relations can be gleaned. Honduran views on Mexico's war with France and the US Civil War are included.

225 **4 [cuatro] aproximaciones a Ramón Rosa.** (Four approaches to Ramón Rosa.)
Rafael Heliodoro Valle (et al.). Tegucigalpa: Oficina Central de Información, Secretaría de Cultura, Turismo e Información, 1976. 65p.

A collection of four essays in homage to Ramón Rosa, an important figure in 19th-century Honduran politics and intellectual circles. Authors of the essays are Rafael Heliodoro, Medardo Mejía, Pompeyo del Valle and Ramón Oquelí.

226 **Central America, 1821-c.1879.**
Ralph Lee Woodward, Jr. In: *Cambridge History of Latin America*,
vol. 3. Cambridge: Cambridge University Press, 1985, p. 471-506.
Offers an in-depth discussion and analysis of the first fifty years of Central American
independence, including the disintegration of the Central American federation and the
emergence of the nation-states. Woodward's article is followed by a lengthy, detailed
bibliographical essay, on pages 874 to 879.

227 **Francisco Morazán y sus relaciones con Francia.** (Francisco Morazán
and his relations with France.)
Rafael Leiva Vivas. Tegucigalpa: Editorial Universitaria, 1988. 178p.
bibliog.
Based on research conducted in French archives, Leiva Vivas provides new insight into
a little-known aspect of the political life of this Honduran hero. He analyses
correspondence between French officials and Morazán and presents 'irrefutable'
evidence that the controversial statue of Morazán erected in Tegucigalpa is actually a
faithful representation of the man. The work includes several illustrations.

228 **Francisco Morazán.**
Lorenzo Montúfar. Ciudad Universitaria Rodrigo Facio, Costa Rica:
Editorial Universitaria Centroamericana, 1982. 2nd ed. 196p.
This reprint of the author's essays examining and defending Francisco Morazán first
appeared in 1896 in a Guatemalan newspaper. The essays were written over a period
of months to commemorate the centenary of Morazán's birth. The author responds to
anonymous contemporary critiques, vigorously upholding the role played by Morazán
in the creation of a federalist union of Central American states.

229 **Gobernantes de Honduras en el siglo 19.** (Honduran rulers in the
nineteenth century.)
Victor Cáceres Lara. Tegucigalpa: Banco Central de Honduras, [1978
or 1979]. 390p. bibliog.
A political history of Honduras after independence in 1824 to the end of the 19th
century, as related through the policies, accomplishments and failures of the heads of
state, beginning with Dionisio de Herrera and ending with Terencio Sierra. The author
has served as an educator, journalist, ambassador and high-level government
administrator.

230 **Historia de la Federación de la América Central, 1823-1849.** (History of
the Central American Federation, 1823-49.)
Pedro Joaquín Chamorro Zelaya. Madrid: Ediciones Cultura
Hispánica, 1951. 644p.
The author, a noted Nicaraguan historian, recounts the history of the doomed
federation of Central American states: the political events that lead to its declaration
and demise. The book is based primarily on secondary sources.

231 **Honduras.**
Pablo Yankelevich.   Mexico: Instituto de Investigaciones Dr José
María Luís Mora; Guadalajara: Universidad de Guadalajara,
[1989-90]. 2 vols. bibliog.

Nineteenth-century Honduras is the focus of this set of separately published volumes.
In the first volume (published in 1989), an anthology of previously published
documents, journal and newspaper articles, and book chapters provides a structure for
understanding and interpreting Honduran history and national characteristics. Items
are grouped under two periods: disorganization and anarchy, 1840-76 and the liberal
reform, 1876-1930. Authors include William Wells, Rafael Heliodoro Valle, Ephraim
Squier and Jorge Morales in the first section; the second includes Ramón Rosa, José
Reina Valenzuela, Mario Argueta, and Victor Meza among others. The companion
volume (published in 1990), consists of a chronological history, a list of governments,
and biographical sketches of the authors anthologized in the first volume.

232 **The incredible yanqui: the career of Lee Christmas.**
Hermann B. Deutsch.   London; New York: Longmans, Green and
Company, 1931. 242p. 2 maps.

A rousing account of a remarkable 'gringo' soldier of fortune who spent over twenty
years in Central America – fighting, carousing, building up governments and helping to
topple others. Although the author destroys the myths that surrounded Christmas at
the turn of the century, one cannot help being impressed by the many exploits and
adventures the man provoked and endured during Central America's national period.

233 **José Cecilio del Valle: sabio centroamericano.** (José Cecilio del Valle:
a Central American intellectual.)
Carlos Meléndez Chaverrí.   San José, Costa Rica: Libro Libre, 1985.
231p. bibliog.

This biography was written to commemorate the bicentenary of Valle's birth in
Choluteca, Honduras and examines the life and contributions of this prominent
participant in the Central American independence and union movements. Numerous
excerpts of Valle's thoughts on topics such as education, economics, culture are
included in the text.

234 **Marco Aurelio Soto: reforma liberal de 1876.** (Marco Aurelio Soto:
liberal reform of 1876.)
José Reina Valenzuela, Mario Argueta.   Tegucigalpa: Banco Central
de Honduras, 1978. 250p. bibliog.

An important study of the reforms promoted by President Soto. These included secular
marriages, the separation of Church and state, expansion of the school system, and
improved public services. He also moved the capital from Comayagua to Tegucigalpa
in 1880.

235 **Movimientos populares en la historia hondureña del siglo XIX: período nacional.** (Nineteenth-century popular movements in Honduran history: national period.)
Mario R. Argueta. Tegucigalpa: Editorial Universitaria, 1986. 27p.

The noted historian succinctly asserts that 19th-century Honduras was far from static or free from conflict and tensions in the social and political spheres, although its economic development was stable or immobile. He classifies the conflicts as either élitist rebellions (palace revolutions) or popular insurrections. He examines the uprising by the Garífunas in 1832 along the Caribbean coast, the rebellions in Olancho in the 1830s and 1860s and several lesser ones. While not a detailed investigation, this brief work does provide an overview of the dissenting social forces about which little else has been written.

236 **Presencia de Máximo Gómez en Honduras.** (The presence of Máximo Gómez in Honduras.)
Rafael Leiva Vivas. Santo Domingo: Ediciones Fundación García-Arévalo, 1977. 35p. bibliog.

A Dominican soldier and *guerrillero*, Máximo Gómez fought for Cuban independence alongside José Martí and Antonio Maceo. He also spent five difficult years in Honduras (1879-84) and that is the subject of this brief biography.

237 **Ramón Rosa y el positivismo en Honduras.** (Ramón Rosa and positivism in Honduras.)
Hilario René Vallejo H. Tegucigalpa: Universidad Nacional Autónoma de Honduras, Departmento de Filosofía, 1978. 148p. bibliog.

A leading Central American intellectual of the 19th century, Rosa was a proponent of positivist theories.

20th century

238 **1954 en nuestra historia.** (1954 in our history.)
Mario Argueta. Tegucigalpa: Universidad Nacional Autónoma de Honduras, Editorial Universitaria, 1987. 28p. bibliog.

The author succinctly summarizes the momentous events which occurred in Honduran political, economic and social conditions in 1954 – he posits this year as a singular moment in Honduran history which greatly contributed to the republic's subsequent evolution. He examines the banana workers' strike, the resulting codification of labour laws, the establishment of a social security institute, and he investigates the convention signed for US military assistance which later allowed for a substantial presence of US military troops on Honduran soil for the training of Salvadoran soldiers and Nicaraguan counter-revolutionaries. Argueta also notes the confusion of that year's presidential election which allowed the vice-president to declare himself head of state.

239 **Boletín de la Defensa Nacional.** (Bulletin of National Defence.)
Director, Froylán Turcios. Tegucigalpa: Editorial Guaymuras, 1980.
225p. (Colección Talanquera).

A compilation of reprinted articles selected from the daily bulletin published in 1924.
Froylán Turcios was then director and editor of the bulletin. Selections focus on the
politics and government of the era and on military affairs. It includes bibliographical
references.

240 **Carías, el último caudillo frutero.** (Carías, the last fruit boss.)
Filander Díaz Chávez. Tegucigalpa: Editorial Guaymuras, 1982.
153p. bibliog.

The period known as the 'cariata', when Tiburcio Carías Andino served as dictator of
Honduras from 1933 to 1948, is examined. However, the author does not write a
traditional political biography of the man and his times; he analyses the class forces
and the structural underdevelopment of the country by using the methodology of
dependency theory to reveal the manipulation of Carías by the multinational banana
companies which turned Honduras into a neocolonial state.

241 **Carías: el caudillo de Zambrano, 1933-1948.** (Carías: the boss of
Zambrano, 1933-48).
Alejandro Salomón Sagástume F. Tegucigalpa: Graficentro, 1988.
127p. bibliog.

An illustrated biography of one of the most important Honduran politicians of the 20th
century. Characterized in this work as the 'gendarme of North American capital',
Carías managed for fifteen crucial years to keep a tight grip on Honduran politics and
serve US banana interests to the detriment of his own people.

242 **Conflict in Central America.**
Helen Schooley. Harlow, England: Longman, 1987. 326p. maps.
bibliog. (Keesing's International Studies).

This is a substantial examination of the economic and political conditions of the
Central American region during the past two decades which includes a chapter on the
political history of Honduras. Contains data on Honduras in sections documenting the
region or under topics such as land reform, Church–state relations, armed forces,
guerrilla movements, human rights and foreign involvement in Central America. It
includes an index.

243 **Five republics of Central America, their political and economic
development and their relations with the United States.**
Dana G. Munro, edited by David Kinley. New York: Russell &
Russell, 1967. 348p.

Munro served as an official of the US Department of State in Central America for
most of the first twenty years of this century. This work is especially useful for his
comments and observations of the region's development during the years he resided in
the area, although he does also offer historical surveys of earlier periods.

244 **Honduras: state for sale.**
Richard Lapper, James Painter.   London: Latin American Bureau,
1985. 132p. maps. bibliog.

Honduran history of the twentieth century and the dominant role of the US during this
time is the major focus of this book. After a few words about colonial history, Lapper
launches into the on-again/off-again relations between the US and Honduran
governments and the large US agricultural companies. The text is supplemented by
many useful charts and illustrations in addition to highlighted 'asides' relevant to
understanding the more complicated aspects of Honduran history (i.e., testimonials by
torture victims, descriptions of organizations, and excerpts from primary documents).
It also contains handy compendia of US–Honduran manoeuvres, limited statistical
data, and a chronology of important dates.

245 **Las revoluciones en Honduras.** (Revolutions in Honduras.)
Chalo Luque.   San Pedro Sula, Honduras: C. R. Luque, 1982. 222p.
(Memorias de un Soldado Hondureño, tomo 2).

The personal narrative of a soldier in the Honduran army during the 1920s and 1930s
in which he recounts many instances of skirmishes and battles against his fellow
Hondurans. He notes that he fought both for and against several officers and
politicians depending on the political climate at the moment. Particularly vivid is the
depiction of the battle in Tegucigalpa following the 1922 presidential election when
Carías was denied the office and a civil conflict erupted in the capital.

Population

246 **Demographic Yearbook.**
United Nations Department of Economic and Social Affairs, Statistical
Office. New York: United Nations, 1948- . annual
A bilingual publication in English and French, this annual compilation of statistical
information on all aspects of population for UN member nations is a most useful
source for anyone doing demographic research on Honduras. Categories include birth,
mortality, migration, marriage, divorce and annulment, household composition, and
the like.

247 **Fertility and mortality changes in Honduras, 1950-1974.**
Kenneth Hill, Committee on Population and Demography, Assembly
of Behavioral and Social Sciences, National Research Council.
Washington, DC: National Academy of Sciences, 1980. 56p. bibliog.
(Committee on Population and Demography, Report no. 3).
Provides statistics, time-series analyses and detailed interpretation of census data over
a twenty-five-year period. Numerous tables and charts assist the reader to understand
the changes that have occurred over the period. The non-specialist will find the five-
page glossary of demographic terminology following the text useful.

248 **The handbook of national population censuses: Latin America and the
Caribbean, North America and Oceania.**
Doreen Goyer, Eliane Domschke. Westport, Connecticut; London:
Greenwood Press, 1983. 711p. maps. bibliog.
For a description of the 14 censuses taken in Honduras from 1791 to 1974, see pages
212-21. It appears that four censuses were undertaken in the nineteenth century,
followed by ten in the twentieth century. The reviews of each census vary in length and
depth, but all include the government agency responsible, definitions and concepts,
special features, scope and quality.

249 **Populating a green desert: population policy and development: their effect on population redistribution, Honduras, 1876-1980.**
José Rafael del Cid. PhD dissertation, University of Texas, Austin, 1988. (DAI 50/02A, p. 407).
Describes changes in population distribution at different stages of the history of Honduras from 1876 to 1980, and explains why population redistribution occurs. In this sense, population policy and the style of development are considered to be independent variables in accounting for changes in population distribution. Population policy is defined as an explicit governmental statement that certain measures will be implemented in order to influence fertility, mortality and migration. Regarding the style of development, this dissertation identifies two extreme types within a continuum of development options: the enclave, and a more integrated way of development. The work shows that government development policy faces different structural constraints, from the particular topographic features of the country to the economic and political interests of organized groups. [Based on the author's abstract].

250 **Population and urban trends in Central America and Panama.**
Robert W. Fox, Jerrold W. Huguet. Washington, DC: Inter-American Development Bank, 1977. 224p. maps. bibliog.
The Inter-American Development Bank investigates the dimensions, patterns, and characteristics of population growth in Central America, projecting each country's increase to the year 2000. Honduran demographic data are presented on pages 136-54. Its 1975 population estimate of 3 million was noted as increasing at 3.47 per cent annual growth, which would double its population within 20 years. Birth rate, death rate, migration, age distribution and urban growth are given. Each department and urbanized area is enumerated and projected from 1940 to 2000. Twelve statistical tables and four charts graphically illustrate the demographic data. Population for Honduras in the year 2000 is projected at 6,881,000 with the size of Tegucigalpa at 974,000 and San Pedro Sula at 658,000 inhabitants.

251 **Primer Encuentro Nacional sobre Desarrollo Urbano: cuarto centenario de Tegucigalpa.** (First National Conference on Urban Development: fourth centenary of Tegucigalpa.)
Tegucigalpa: UNAH, Instituto de Investigaciones Económicas y Sociales, 1978. 257p. bibliog.
Nine scholarly papers presented at the first conference convened to investigate rapid urbanization and its attendant problems of infrastructural and housing needs primarily in Tegucigalpa, San Pedro Sula, and San Salvador. Most papers include excellent statistical tables representing data from the 1960s to the mid-1970s; these contribute to its value as a source for demographic studies.

252 **Scarcity and survival in Central America: ecological origins of the Soccer War.**
William H. Durham. Stanford, California: Stanford University Press, 1979. 209p. bibliog.
A scholarly, demographic analysis of the root causes of the 1969 Honduras-El Salvador conflict, emphasizing the interrelationship of population and land tenure. It

Population

addresses the scarcity of resources in El Salvador which caused migration to the relative abundance of resources in Honduras and the adverse effects of economies based on agricultural exportation. There are many black-and-white illustrations in addition to tables and graphs, and the work also includes a detailed index.

253   **Social classes, accumulation, and the crisis of 'overpopulation' in El Salvador.**
      Ernesto Richter.   *Latin American Perspectives*, vol. 7, no. 2-3 (1980), p. 45-56.

The author presents the opinion that both Honduras and El Salvador used the popularly named Soccer War of 1969 to influence the domestic problems that continue to plague the two countries. In Honduras, the war resulted from the lack of integration into the Central American Common Market, and served to strengthen the existing political establishment. In El Salvador, the war masked the problem of population growth and was used to justify repressive control measures. As an aside, the interests of the United States were not adversely affected in either country.

254   **Vital registration systems in five developing countries: Honduras, Mexico, Philippines, Thailand, and Jamaica.**
      Hyattsville, Maryland: US Department of Health and Human Services, 1980. c.150p. (Vital and Health Statistics, series 2: Data Evaluation and Methods Research, no. 79).

This volume is one of the results of an agreement between the National Center for Health Statistics and the Agency for International Development (AID) to conduct a project designed to improve civil registration and vital statistics in selected AID-assisted countries. Pages 1-29 are devoted to Honduras. Following a succinct survey of the vital and health statistics system, there are examples of the forms (translated into English) used to collect data.

Ethnic Groups and Refugees

Black Caribs (Garífunas)

255 **The Blacks of Central America.**
Kris DiLorenzo. *Crisis*, vol. 93, no. 6 (1986), p. 28-31.
Surveys and compares the treatment of blacks in Panamá, Costa Rica, Honduras, Belize, and Mexico. Particularly emphasizes Spanish and Mexican repression; the 1500s to 1787; and the exploitation of Barbadians, Jamaicans, and Costa Ricans recruited to work for the construction of the Panama Canal.

256 **The ethnomedicine of the Garífuna (Black Caribs) of Río Tinto, Honduras.**
Milton Cohen. *Anthropological Quarterly*, vol. 57, no. 1 (1984), p. 16-27. bibliog.
Based on fieldwork conducted in Honduras in 1978, the author surveys the medical beliefs and practices of the Garífuna. He concludes that although the Garífuna have knowledge of modern medicine, its limitations and the lack of social, economic and physical access to it discourage their use of it.

257 *Gubida* **illness and religious ritual among the Garífuna of Santa Fé, Honduras: an ethnopsychiatric analysis.**
Cynthia Chamberlain Bianchi. PhD dissertation, Ohio State University, 1988. 402p. (DAI 49/08A, p. 2287).
The Garífuna of Honduras are an Afro-Amerindian group inhabiting the shorelands of the Bay of Honduras. Their religious and ethnomedical practices reflect syncretism between West African, West-Central African, Island Carib Amerindian, Caribbean and Hispanic-American cultural patterns. This study focuses on an illness called *hasandigubida*, a condition believed to be caused by the spirits of dead relatives. The physical and behavioural symptoms of *hasandigubida* are related to similar phenomena in West and West-Central Africa attributed to the vengeance of angry ancestral spirits.

Ethnic Groups and Refugees. Black Caribs (Garífunas)

The *hasandigubida* complex, including therapeutic placation rituals, may be interpreted as a traditional ethnomedical system for dealing with emotional and physical distress. A related article by the author was published in Spanish as 'La enfermedad de gubida y el sincretismo religioso entre los garífunas: un análisis etnosiquiátrico', in *América Indígena*, vol. 44, no. 3 (1984), p. 519-42.

258 **Negros caribes de Honduras.** (Black Caribs of Honduras.)
     Ruy Galvão de Andrade Coelho.   Tegucigalpa: Editorial Guaymuras,
     1981. 208p. bibliog.
The Spanish translation of the doctoral dissertation (Northwestern University, 1955) of a Brazilian who later became a professor of social sciences and also worked in Unesco's Division of Racial Relations. Based on first-hand research conducted in 1947-48, primarily in the Trujillo region, the capital of the Black Caribs. The author methodically and thoroughly documents the arrival, settlement and sociology of the Black Caribs (Garífunas) in Honduras, the Bay Islands, and from Puerto Barrios to Iriona on the Mosquito Coast, from 1492 to the late 1940s. The work is particularly noteworthy for its in-depth treatment of social organization and spiritual beliefs and practices. There is a glossary of approximately 200 Carib terms used in the text.

259 **Sex roles and social change in native lower Central American societies.**
     Edited by Christine A. Loveland, Franklin O. Loveland.   Urbana,
     Illinois: University of Illinois Press, 1982. 185p. bibliog.
The interrelationship between male and female roles in the indigenous societies of lower Central America are examined by anthropologists studying the Rama, Garífuna, and Cuna peoples. The labour-force participation and domestic work of the Black Carib are investigated by Virginia Kerns. While her case-study is set in Belize, the results are applicable to Garífuna residents in Honduras. The text is indexed.

260 **Sojourners of the Caribbean: ethnogenesis and ethnohistory of the
     Garífuna.**
     Nancie L. Solien González.   Urbana, Illinois: University of Illinois
     Press, 1988. bibliog.
This in-depth study of the Garífuna (better known as Black Caribs) is based on nearly a quarter of a century of anthropological research by one who has spent extended periods of time living with them in Livingston, Guatemala and several Honduran villages. The three parts of the book review the historical circumstances and events giving rise to Garífuna ethnic identity, describe the cultural traits that serve as ethnic markers for the Garífuna, and investigate the processes and institutions which have contributed to the evolution of their culture.

Native peoples

261 **Apuntes sobre la afiliación cultural de los pobladores indígenas de los valles de Comayagua y Sulaco.** (Notes on the cultural affiliation between the indigenous settlers of the Comayagua and Sulaco valleys.) Gloria Lara Pinto. *Mesoamérica*, vol. 6, no. 9 (1985), p. 45-57. maps. bibliog.
A cultural anthropologist, Lara Pinto presents a bibliographical essay on the two valleys at the time of the Conquest. She attempts to determine the main indigenous geopolitical units of the era.

262 **Demographic catastrophe in sixteenth-century Honduras.**
Linda Newson. In: *Studies in Spanish-American Population History*, edited by David J. Robinson. Boulder, Colorado: Westview, 1981, p. 217-41. bibliog.
Newson attempts to analyse previously published figures and examine the causes of the dramatic decline of the Honduran indigenous population at the time of Spanish contact and thereafter. She presents documentary evidence combed from a variety of original sources located in the Archivo General de las Indias (General Archive of the Indies) and the Audiencia de Guatemala, among others, and concludes that the major reasons for the population decline are the Indian slave trade, conquest and disease. In addition, she proposes that overwork, ill-treatment, miscegenation and severe disruption of indigenous economies and societies as a result of conquest and colonization contributed to the decline of the native peoples.

263 **Ethnographical survey of the Miskito and Sumu Indians of Honduras and Nicaragua.**
Eduard Conzemius. Washington, DC: Smithsonian Institution, Bureau of American Ethnology, 1932. 191p. bibliog. (Bulletin no. 106).
Together the Miskito and Sumu inhabit the larger part of the vast region called the Mosquito Coast which extends from Cabo Honduras to Río San Juan on the border with Costa Rica. In his straightforward study, Conzemius describes, compares and contrasts many aspects of the two cultures. He covers practically every facet of daily life including time reckoning, hygiene and adornment, linguistic features, warfare, manufactured products, crime and punishment, and magic. The text is supplemented by a glossary and an index.

264 **Geografía de los indígenas toles (jicaques) de Honduras en el siglo XVIII.** (Geography of the Tol (Jicaque) Indians of Honduras in the 18th century.)
William Van Davidson. *Mesoamérica*, vol. 9 (June 1985), p. 58-90. maps. bibliog.
Davidson studies the impact of Spanish colonization on the Tol people in the 1700s. The early years were not productive for either group: many lives were lost and their society was disrupted, while many Spanish activities resulted in little success. The native people were not really incorporated into the national Honduran mainstream

until the 1860s with the work of Father Subirana. The author also traces the nomenclature of the indigenous people from Jicaque and variations to Tol and variations. Distribution, censuses, and settlements are documented, using original Central American archival sources.

265 **Handbook of Middle American Indians.**
Edited by Robert Wauchope. Austin, Texas: University of Texas Press, 1964-76. 16 vols plus supplement.

An absolute treasure chest of research on the native peoples of Mesoamerica and a standard reference tool. A 'definitive encyclopedia of the environment, archaeology, ethnology, linguistics, social anthropology, ethnohistory, linguistics and physical anthropology of the native peoples of Mexico and Central America'. One must be very creative to extract information about Honduras from this extensive set of volumes, but persistence and tenacity will have their rewards. Unfortunately, there is not one index to the set. Each volume, or part of a volume, has its own respective index that must be consulted under a variety of terms. For example, in volume 1, 'Natural environment and early cultures', there are index entries for Honduras, Lake Yojoa, Ulúa River, Copán and other physical features. In volume 3, 'Archaeology of Southern Mesoamerica', one must look under the names of archaeological sites or artefacts. All contributors are recognized scholars in the field and document their studies with ample bibliographical notes, illustrations and maps.

266 **Los hijos de la muerte: el universo mítico de los Tolupán-Jicaques, Honduras.** (Children of death: the mythical universe of the Tolupán-Jicaques, Honduras.)
Anne MacKaye Chapman. Mexico: Instituto Nacional de Antropología e Historia, 1982. 2nd enlarged ed. 324p. bibliog.

Long ago, the Jicaque people numbered at least 8,000. Today there are fewer than four hundred living in small groups isolated in mountain valleys lying to the north of Tegucigalpa. In the mid-1950s, Chapman periodically interviewed an elderly man to record and collect his oral interpretations of the myths of his people. These appear in this volume. The work also includes a survey of Tolupán-Jicaque history, individual myths, classification of these myths, many photographs, a glossary and indexes. This work was also published in French under the title: *Les enfants de la mort: univers mythique des indiens Tolupán (Jicaque)* (Mexico: Mission archéologique et ethnologique au Mexique, 1978).

267 **Los hijos del copal y la candela.** (The children of copal and candles.)
Anne Mackaye Chapman. Mexico: Universidad Nacional Autónoma de México, Instituto de Investigaciones Antropológicas, 1985-86. 2 vols. maps. bibliog. (Serie Antropológica: Etnología, nos 64, 86).

The subtitle of volume one is *Ritos agrários y tradición oral de los lencas de Honduras* (Agrarian rites and oral tradition of the Honduran Lenca people) and that of volume two is *Tradición católica de los lencas de Honduras* (The Catholic tradition of the Honduran Lenca people). Both volumes are based on original research by a well known ethnologist who interviewed dozens of Lenca people over a period of 21 years. In the first volume she documents the rituals related to the *composturas* (special ceremonies) and healing, in addition to a summary of the history of the people. In volume two she concentrates on the origins of the Catholic faith as adopted by the

Lenca and their respect for various saints and virgins, and ceremonies. A map depicts their territory in the departments of Intibucá, La Paz and Lempira. This is a very thorough study documenting this important indigenous culture in Honduras.

268   **The Jicaque (Torrupán) Indians of Honduras.**
      Victor Wolfgang Von Hagen.   New York: Museum of the American
      Indian, 1943. 112p. maps. bibliog.

A description of the lifestyle of the last remaining portion of these people to maintain their ancient customs, in the interior of Honduras. The text provides details of all aspects of life, economy, and society, and includes historical background, tables and illustrations.

269   **Los lencas de Honduras en el siglo XVI.** (The Lencas of Honduras in the
      sixteenth century.)
      Anne MacKaye Chapman.   Tegucigalpa: Instituto Hondureño de
      Antropología e Historia, 1978. 58p. map. bibliog.

Chapman documents the dismal history of the Lenca at the time they encountered the conquistadors. The topics investigated include the penurious condition of forced labour and slavery; missionaries; ethnic (mis)identification; cultural traits as considered by chroniclers and missionaries; and linguistic features.

270   **Matrilocality and the maintenance of ethnic identity: the Miskito of
      eastern Nicaragua and Honduras.**
      Mary W. Helms.   In: *Proceedings of the XXXVIIIth International
      Congress of Americanists*, vol. 2, p. 459-64. bibliog.   Munich,
      Germany: Kommissionverlag Klaus Renner, [1970?].

Helms proposes that the tendency toward matrilocality among the Miskito people is a positive adaptation to prevailing economic and social demands. The conference took place in Stuttgart and Munich from 12 to 18 August 1968.

271   **The Sumus in Nicaragua and Honduras: an endangered people.**
      Joseph Eldridge, Donald R. Strome, Jr., Anne Manuel.   New York:
      Americas Watch Committee, 1987. 43p.

Documents the plight of the Sumu people caught in the middle of the Contra-Sandinista conflict. It includes bibliographical references.

272   **With the Miskitos in Honduras.**
      New York: Americas Watch Committee, 1986. 29p.

A report of the delicate situation of the Miskito people in Honduran refugee camps and their difficult relations with the Nicaraguan and Honduran governments. It includes bibliographical references.

Refugees

273 **Forced to move.**
Renato Camarda. San Francisco, California: Solidarity Publications, 1985. 98p.

A moving documentation of the plight of Salvadoran refugees relocated to camps in Honduras. Through eye-witness accounts of refugees, personal testimonies of relief workers and priests, photographs and children's drawings, the editors portray the tenuous circumstances of these victims of the civil war that plagues El Salvador. Most refugees were residing at the UN High Commission for Refugees-sponsored La Virtud Refugee Camp located near the Honduran–El Salvadoran border. The refugees tell of the horror and tragedy of the Lempa River crossing massacre on 17 March 1981 and the serious problems they have in dealing with both the Salvadoran and Honduran military while they must stay in the camps. In addition, there is a chapter dedicated to Salvadoran refugees throughout the Americas, a chronology of the crisis from May 1980 to September 1983, appendices of US and Honduran military involvement, international visitors to camps, and other related statistics.

274 **A Hobson's choice for Miskito refugees.**
Margaret D. Wilde. *Christian Century*, vol. 106, no. 23 (1989), p. 726-8.

On a visit to refugee communities in Honduras, editor-at-large Margaret Wilde recounts the dilemmas facing the Sumu and Miskito who fled Nicaragua. Early on the Hondurans were hospitable, but after international agencies seemed to provide a higher standard of living for the refugees than their hosts enjoyed, the hospitality wore thin. Hondurans accused the Sumu and Miskito of laziness and of depleting their natural resources; on the other hand, the native peoples complained of being limited in the things they could do because of the many restraints put on them for not being legal Honduran residents.

275 **Honduras, a crisis on the border.**
Prepared by Iain Guest, Diane Orentlicher. New York: Lawyers Committee for International Human Rights, 1985. 117p. bibliog.

Examines the proposed repatriation by the Honduran government of 19,000 Salvadorans in refugee camps. The authors contend that the accusation that the camps were safe havens for guerrillas who were causing instability in Honduras was unverified and created a dangerous climate for those residing in the camps. They argue for increased protection through the United Nations High Commissioner for Refugees (UNHCR), and for less interference by the Honduran government and military forces.

276 **In need of safety: Salvadoran refugees in Honduras.**
Arthur Schmidt. *Migration Today*, vol. 12, no. 1 (1984), p. 21-6.

Documents the plight of Salvadoran refugees who crossed over the Honduran border between 1980 and 1984 and faced persecution from both the Salvadoran and Honduran militaries. Since both militaries regarded them as rebel sympathizers, they were poorly treated by Salvadoran officials and feared mistreatment by the Honduran government were they to be resettled in the rural Honduran interior as proposed by the UNHCR. Revised from a paper given at the XIth International Congress of the Latin American Studies Association in Mexico, 30 September 1983.

277 **In search of refuge.**
Yvonne Dilling, Ingrid Rodgers. Scottdale, Pennsylvania: Herald
Press, 1984. 288p. bibliog.

As a Witness for Peace, Dilling does what she can to alleviate the human suffering of Salvadoran refugees who fled to Honduras in the wake of military repression and war. She spent 15 months – from February 1981 to April 1982 – working as an education coordinator in refugee camps along the El Salvador–Honduras border. In her diary she attempts to take the perspective of the refugees: their fears, health and shelter problems, and the violence to which they are subjected. The text is particularly useful for her comments about the national and international agencies involved in relief work. It contains a glossary of Spanish words and acronyms, and illustrations of camp sites.

278 **Pacifying Rosemary's baby: Honduras left to push Contra pram.**
Joseph T. Eldridge. *The Nation*, vol. 248 (29 May 1989), p. 734-8.

Tackles the problems created by Contra activity in Honduras and the eventual resettlement of Nicaraguan Contras after the February 1990 presidential election. Eldridge was director of the Washington Office on Latin America from 1974 to 1986 and later spent 2½ years in Honduras as a private development consultant until he was requested to depart by Honduran authorities.

279 **Refugees and immigrants: a human rights dilemma.**
Animesh Ghoshal, Thomas M. Crowley. *Human Rights Quarterly*,
vol. 5, no. 3 (1983), p. 327-47.

Compares US policy regarding refugees and immigrants with that of Canada, Honduras, Somalia, Pakistan, and Thailand. In addition, there is discussion about the external and internal pressures that affect national policy-making as regards refugee issues.

280 **Los refugiados en Honduras, 1980-1986.** (Refugees in Honduras,
1980-86.)
Tegucigalpa: Centro de Documentación de Honduras, 1986. 35p. (Série
Cronológias, no. 6).

A month-by-month accounting of the Salvadoran and Nicaraguan refugee situation in Honduras from 1980 to 1986. Statistics, camp conditions, international activism, and impact on Honduran society are among the topics set forth.

281 **Los refugiados salvadoreños en Honduras.** (Salvadoran refugees in
Honduras.)
Tegucigalpa: Centro de Documentación de Honduras, [1982 or 1983].
42p. bibliog.

The situation of refugees from the conflict in El Salvador who are exiled in Honduran camps is investigated, with most attention given to those in the Mesa Grande camp. Help and hindrances by Honduran military, governmental, and non-governmental agencies are noted. The private relief agency World Vision is suspected of cooperating with those searching the camps for possible harbouring of guerrillas. The 1980 massacre of nearly 600 refugees near Santa Rosa de Copán is deplored in an appended text by the Catholic Diocese there; the text of the military's refutation of this massacre concludes the work.

282 **La reubicación de los refugiados salvadoreños en Honduras: un paso hacia la intervención.** (The relocation of Salvadoran refugees in Honduras: one step towards intervention.) Demetrio Paredes. *Estudios Centroamericanos: ECA*, vol. 39, no. 4 (1984), p. 515-32.

More than a million Salvadoran refugees, twenty per cent of the total population, fled the country in the early 1980s. Many of them relocated to Honduras. This article deals with the resettlement of the refugees from the La Virtud-Guarita camp to Mesa Grande camp between November 1981 and April 1982. The author claims that US foreign policies in El Salvador and Honduras generated so many refugees and displaced persons and forced them to move away from the border for military purposes. The UNHCR is seen as playing into the militaristic interests of the US instead of protecting the rights and security of the refugees. The article contains several photographs of camp conditions and three statistical charts.

283 **Undocumented Central Americans in Houston: diverse populations.** Nestor P. Rodríguez. *International Migration Review*, vol. 21, no. 1 (1987), p. 4-26. bibliog.

Since the late 1970s, Central Americans have sought asylum in the US while fleeing political conflict or economic decline in their own countries. Many of these undocumented migrants have settled in urban areas of the country. The author observed and interviewed 150 persons, many of whom were Hondurans, who have settled in Houston, Texas and constitute a new Latin element in the city. Four tables accompany the text.

Folklore

284 **According to our ancestors: folk texts from Guatemala and Honduras.**
Edited by Mary Shaw. Norman, Oklahoma: Summer Institute of
Linguistics of the University of Oklahoma, 1971. 510p. bibliog.
(Summer Institute of Linguistics, Publications in Linguistics and
Related Fields, no. 32).

Already well known for its linguistic, language and folklore studies, the Summer
Institute of Linguistics has produced another well-documented collection of folklore
touching upon the many themes and motifs of importance to native peoples. Focusing
primarily on the folklore of Guatemala, but including tales from the Black Caribs and
Jicaque Indians of Honduras, the editor presents story texts in the original languages
with free and literal translations. There is a section of comparative notes which
highlights the prominent themes, motifs, natural phenomena and ideal behaviours
evident in the stories. The tales from Honduras include *The Gorrilla and Monkey Co-
Godfathers, Carib History, How an Indian Saved the World, The Giant, The Creation
of Certain Birds*, and *The Creation*. Illustrations accompany many stories.

285 **Comizahual: leyendas, tradiciones y relatos de Honduras.** (Comizahual:
legends, traditions and stories from Honduras.)
Medardo Mejía. Tegucigalpa: Universidad Nacional Autónoma de
Honduras, Editorial Universitaria, 1981. 446p. bibliog.

Forty legends, poems, short plays, and tales make up this compilation of Honduran
folklore. A prologue attributes the origins of most Honduran folklore to the Toltecs
who arrived around 1000 AD after the collapse of the Maya. Some tales, the compiler
notes, derive from the Honduran colonial period, some from contemporary times.
Glossaries, maxims and complete ceremonies are reproduced.

Folklore

286 **Danlí en el recuerdo.** (Danlí in reminiscences.)
Darío González C. Tegucigalpa: Unidad de Artes Gráficas de la
Secretaría de Recursos Naturales, 1988. 101p. bibliog.
This is a potpourri of facts and legends about the city of Danlí, capital of El Paraíso, in
southern Honduras near the Nicaraguan border. Social life and customs are recounted,
as well as nine folktales. Brief biographies of some noted citizens are included.

287 **Escama de oro y otra de plata: figuras y ficciones de la tradición oral
hondureña.** (A flake of gold and another of silver: people and stories of
the Honduran oral tradition.)
Pompeyo del Valle. Tegucigalpa: Graficentro, 1989. 74p.
Collected by a well-known poet, the ten stories about mythological creatures and
places that make up this volume have been recounted for generations by Hondurans. It
also contains many charming illustrations.

288 **El folklore en la tierra de los pinos.** (Folklore in the land of pine trees.)
Sebastián Martínez. Tegucigalpa: [n.p.], 1963. 110p.
A rather strange mixture of international mythology and Honduran folklore, fiestas,
superstitions, belief, children's games and folk dances. It is especially useful for its
illustrations of national dances and musical instruments.

289 **El folklore en los tiempos coloniales.** (Folklore in colonial times.)
Sebastián Martínez. Tegucigalpa: [n.p.], 1969. 61p.
Similar to his earlier work (q.v.), this volume presents the legends of *La tetona* (The
large-breasted woman), *El sin cabeza* (The headless man), *La sucia (The nasty
woman)*, *El duende* (The goblin), in addition to brief sections on music and dance.

290 **Folklore hondureño; tradiciones, leyendas, relatos y cuentos populares
de la ciudad de Comayagua.** (Honduran folklore: traditions, legends,
accounts and popular stories from the city of Comayagua.)
Fernando P. Cevallos. Comayagua, Honduras: [n.p.], 1947. 2nd ed.
119p.
Twenty-eight legends and popular stories of colonial Comayagua, many of which
revolve around the Catholic Church. The editor also provides vignettes of seventeenth-
and eighteenth-century culture in the town, focusing on architecture, art, sculpture,
metalwork, music, the university, and church life. His information is based on sources
found in local archives.

291 **Mayangna yulnina kulna balna = Tradiciones orales de los índios
Sumus.** (Oral traditions of the Sumu Indians.)
Gotz von Houwald, Francisco Rener. Bonn: Seminar für
Völkerkunde, Universität Bonn, 1984. 213p. bibliog. (Bonner
amerikanistische Studien = Estudios americanistas de Bonn, 11).
Their habitat of forest and river on the Mosquito Coast is full of dangers yet beautiful;
it is an enemy that can also provide food, shelter, and a source of fabulous stories and
tales. For the Sumus, all natural phenomena have a unique character and personality

worthy of a folktale. In this selection of thirty-six tales about animals, rivers, floods, human experiences and other themes, one is introduced to their mythology and spiritual world. Each tale is transcribed in Sumu, Spanish and German and there are several interesting photographs of Sumus and their ambience. A glossary of Sumu terms translated into Spanish follows the text. The work also has the German title of *Mündliche Überlieferungen der Sumu-Indianer.*

292 **Pátrios lares: leyendas, tradiciones, consejas.** (Home fires: legends, traditions, advice.)
Pompilio Ortega. Tegucigalpa: Imprenta Caledrón, 1951. 2nd enlarged ed. 191p.

A curious collection of colourful legends and oral stories including *El Misionero* (The missionary), *La Biblia y el Popol Vuh* (The Bible and the Popol Vuh), *El Grito de Chicuaz* (Chicuaz' Shout), and others. Simple sketches serve to illustrate the more imaginative stories.

293 **Por las sendas del folklore.** (Down the paths of folklore.)
Rafael Manzaneras A. Tegucigalpa: [n.p.], 1960. 89p. bibliog.

After a brief treatise on the meaning and subdivisions of folklore, Manzanares recounts many folkloristic stories and legends of Honduras, describes dances and musical instruments, folk cuisine and holidays. The book contains several illustrations of marginal quality. On pages 86-9 he lists the national, school and folkloric holidays.

294 **Tradición oral indígena de Yamaranguila.** (Indigenous oral tradition of Yamaranguila.)
Claudia Marcela Carías (et al.). Tegucigalpa: Editorial Guaymuras, 1988. 208p. bibliog.

Folktales and legends of the Lenca people are presented in written form. Compiled by university students, this collection affords valuable insight into Lenca social life, customs, and religion. A lengthy introduction details the history and culture of this indigenous people whose numbers continue to diminish and who now reside primarily in the area of Yamaranguila.

Religion

295 **Acontecimientos sobresalientes de la Iglesia de Honduras, 1900-1962: primeros pasos para la elaboración de una historia de la Iglesia hondureña.** (Outstanding events of the Catholic Church in Honduras, 1900-62: first steps towards a history of the Honduran Church.) Rodolfo Cardenal. Tegucigalpa: Instituto Socioreligioso Juan XXIII, 1979. 74p.

An cursory outline of the major religious and political events in Church history of the 20th century in Honduras. A good source for Church politics as reflected in Honduras.

296 **Directorio geográfico de las congregaciones protestantes de Honduras por departamentos, municipios y áreas urbanas.** (Geographical directory of Protestant congregations in Honduras by department, municipality and urban areas.) Proyecto Centroamericano de Estudios Socio-Religiosos (PROCADES). San Francisco de Dos Ríos, Costa Rica: Instituto Internacional de Evangelización a Fondo, 1982. 146p. maps.

A directory of Protestant churches, organizations and ministries in the various departments, municipalities and urban areas of Honduras as of 1979.

297 **Home in Honduras: the Blumenscheins pioneer in La Suiza.** Marian Blumenschein. Independence, Missouri: Herald, 1975. 159p. bibliog.

In the late 1950s, Dr John Blumenschein, an obstetrician, sold his maternity hospital in Kentucky and moved his family with five children to a sparsely settled valley, La Suiza, near Lake Yojoa, Honduras with the intention of establishing a Protestant medical mission. This memoir of the experience, written by his wife, recounts the many trials, tribulations, surprises and adjustments of this hitherto middle-class family as they built a new life and new medical centre in rural Honduras.

298 **Honduras: Iglesia y cambio social.** (Honduras: the Church and social
     change.)
     Gustavo Blanco, Jaime Valverde. San José, Costa Rica: DEI, 1987.
     228p. (Colección Sociología de la Religión).
A substantial investigation of the dynamics of the Honduran Catholic Church during
the past thirty years from a sociological perspective. Documents and analyses the rôle
of the Catholic Church in fostering economic and social development in Honduras
starting with the 1950s and working through to the 1980s. The authors include some
material relating to the struggle for land reform and describe three models of Church
practice: the hierarchical or institutional church, the developmentalist church and the
prophetic church. A seminal source for understanding the historic importance the
Church has played in Honduran life, and how the Church is responding to changes in
Honduras and the world at large.

299 **The Moravians in Honduras.**
     Werner G. Marx. *Transactions of the Moravian Historical Society,*
     vol. 23, no. 3-4 (1984), p. 1-15.
Based on a paper presented at the vesper of the Moravian Historical Society,
9 October 1980. Marx relates the history of the Moravian Church in Honduras from its
introduction in 1930 to the early 1980s. He particularly emphasizes the spiritual,
educational, and medical mission efforts by the Church among the Miskito.

300 **Panorama histórico de la Iglesia en Honduras.** (Historical panorama of
     the Church in Honduras.)
     José María Tojeira. Tegucigalpa: Centro de Documentación de
     Honduras, 1986. 255p. bibliog.
A Jesuit priest relates the history of the Catholic Church in Honduras from its
inception during the time of the Conquest to the challenges confronting the Church
and the nation at present. The author examines the growth, development, policies, and
results of the Church for each century and includes biographical sketches of notable
clerics. Numerous statistical tables help to illustrate the analytical text with data
difficult to locate through normal channels. This work contributes to an understanding
of the social and historical reality of Honduras through its investigation of the rôle
played by this very important institution.

301 **Pioneer Protestant missionaries in Honduras.**
     Wilkins B. Winn. Cuernavaca, Mexico: Centro Intercultural de
     Documentación, 1973. [var. pag.]. maps. bibliog.
A brief summary of the work of A. E. Bishop and J. G. Cassel in the department of
Copán. It covers their services from 1896 to 1901, then reproduces the personal diaries
of each in which they recount their experiences in cryptic entries emphasizing the
travels and hardships they endured.

Religion

302 **Reflexión sobre la formación de la conciencia política: de la diocesis de Santa Rosa de Copán: para las comunidades cristianas.** (Reflection on the formation of a political conscience: the Santa Rosa of Copán diocese: for Christian communities.)
Honduras: [n.p.], [1980?]. 65p. bibliog.
Calls for political action and voting to benefit poor and marginalized Hondurans. It appears to be sympathetic to the tenets of liberation theology.

303 **El reformismo estatal y la Iglesia en Honduras, 1949-1982.** (State Reformism and the Church in Honduras, 1949-82.)
Rosa María Pochet Coronado. *Estudios Sociales Centroamericanos* (Costa Rica), vol. 11, no. 33 (1982), p. 155-87. bibliog.
Discusses the changes in Church–state relations starting in the late 1940s. By the 1960s and early 1970s, a Social Christian movement developed in Honduras but it had fallen apart by the mid-1970s as a result of the pressures of class conflict. However, it did serve to give rise to a popular, peasant movement, which in turn led to the development of Christian Democracy in the 1970s. The Christian Democrats soon began to support the bourgeoisie and in so doing lost their grassroots support. There ensued repression against the popular Christian liberation factions, and internal strife within the Catholic Church left Honduras with a leadership less interested in popular movements.

304 **Relación verdadera de la reducción de los índios infieles de la provincia de la Tagusigalpa, llamados Xicaques.** (A true account of the conversion of heathen Indians, called Xicaques, from the province of Tagusigalpa.)
Fernando Espino, introduction and notes by Jorge Eduardo Arellano. Managua, Nicaragua: Banco de América, 1977. 110p. bibliog. (Série Ciencias Humanas, no. 8).
Well into his seventies, the Franciscan friar Fernando Espino travelled to the then-called Province of Tagusigalpa in the 1660s-1670s to convert the Jicaque people to Catholicism. Since he was fluent in the Lenca and Jicaque languages he was requested to go and save as many souls as possible and send a report to his superior, the General Secretary of the Provinces of New Spain, MRPFr Francisco Calderón. In his report he tells of his successes – with many baptisms, catechisms and conversions in the San Buenaventura area – provides anthropological notes on the native peoples of the region and recounts the tragic demise of the missionaries who preceded him. The text is accompanied by interpretations and analyses of Espino's original report and copies of his work, biographical and bibliographical notes, and an index of names and places. It includes a facsimile reproduction of the title page of the original edition, published in Guatemala in 1674.

305 **Seed sowing in Honduras.**
Edith Moulton Melick. St. Louis, Missouri: Eden, 1927. 166p. maps.
A former missionary's description of the evangelical missions in Honduras, particularly those in San Pedro Sula, providing details on the activities and facilities, as well as on the local needs as she sees them. The work was prepared for use by evangelical

congregations in the US in order to encourage support of the missions. It contains illustrations.

306   **To be a revolutionary: an autobiography.**
      J. Guadelupe Carney, edited by Joseph Connolly, Eileen Connolly.
      San Francisco, California: Harper & Row, 1985. 473p. maps.
A moving autobiography of an Irish-American Jesuit missionary assigned to Honduras. He mysteriously disappeared as a result of his involvement in revolutionary Christian Socialism. He describes the plight of the poor *campesinos* [rural population] of Honduras and how he became committed to assisting them. The text is supplemented by an extensive index.

Social Conditions

General

307 **Bananas, gold and silver; oro y plata.**
David Saavedra.   Tegucigalpa: Talleres Tipográficos Nacionales, 1955.
436p. maps.

The prologue claims: 'Here you have a real book. This book is useful and emotive, in whose pages you will find the reflection of the natural wealth of our tropical lands and the enchantment that they constitute for the tourist, the paradisiacal panoramas of our exuberant jungles, of our virgin mountains, of our cristaline [sic] rivers. . .of our humble but peaceful and labouring inhabitants, even the old customs of our aborigines, which are slowly disappearing with the advances of civilization'. An amusing read for the casual investigator wanting 1950s-era information, and chock-full of tidbits designed to attract potential investors to Honduras. A handy compendium of scarce data, though the accuracy varies and the items are viewed through the eyes of the régime, which seeks to accentuate the positive and the recent development impact of its actions. Particularly notable for the chapters on agriculture, farming and statistics dating from 1920-35, and it also contains many tables and portraits of Carías régime members. The text is in both Spanish and English, the advertising matter of the time is interesting and the work is indexed.

308 **Bibliografía sociopolítica de Honduras.** (Socio-political
bibliography of Honduras.)
Ramón Oquelí.   Tegucigalpa: Editorial Universitaria, 1988.
2nd ed. 192p.

An unannotated listing by author of 2,020 items (books and journal articles) relating to a broad range of the socio-political experiences of Honduras.

309 **Characteristics of rural life and the agrarian reform in Honduras.**
George W. Hill, Marion T. Loftin. Tegucigalpa: OEA Misión de
Asistencia Técnica, 1961. 206p.
A study of rural development and land tenure in Honduras, emphasizing the needs of
the peasants and their poor living conditions. It calls for accelerated land reform, citing
the desperate needs of the people and the urgency of the situation.

310 **Cultural surveys of Panama – Nicaragua – Guatemala – El Salvador –
Honduras.**
Richard Newbold Adams with an appendix by Doris Stone.
Washington, DC: Pan American Sanitary Bureau, Regional Office of
the World Health Organization (WHO), 1957. 669p. maps. bibliog
(Pan American Sanitary Bureau Scientific Publications, no. 33).
Based on fieldwork done in 1955, this work emphasizes Ladino culture with only brief
mention of the native peoples, Black Caribs and Antilleans of the Bay Islands. Adams
provides a fairly detailed account of the daily lifestyle and working habits of urban and
rural Hondurans including religious activities, health beliefs and practices, and familial
relationships. The appendix by Doris Stone treats the Torrupán or Jicaque peoples of
Montana de la Flor. The book contains many useful statistical tables.

311 **Estudio sobre la participación de la mujer en el desarrollo económico y
social de Honduras.** (Study on the participation of women in the
economic and social development of Honduras.)
Bufete Acosta Bonilla (et al.). Tegucigalpa: Agencia para el
Desarrollo Internacional, 1977. 195p. bibliog.
The report of study sponsored by the US Agency for International Development which
aimed at investigating the roles of women in the economic and social services sectors.

312 **In over my head: a reporter's travels through the US proxy state of
Honduras.**
Jeff Gillenkirk. *America*, vol. 157 (4-11 July 1987), p. 9-15.
A critical analysis by a freelance writer of the US military rôle in Honduras from 1979
to 1987. In his argument he supports the notion that 'our current military buildup,
rather than protecting Honduras from Communism, appeared to be creating the
conditions that led to insurgencies in neighboring Nicaragua and El Salvador'.

313 **Level of living and participation in the informal market sector among
rural Honduran women.**
Sharon M. Danes, Mary Winter, Michael B. Whiteford. *Journal of
Marriage and the Family*, vol. 49, no. 3 (1987), p. 631-9. bibliog.
The team analyses factors that affect the market-sector participation of Honduran
women and the impact it has on the family's standard of living. The study is based on
data collected from approximately 130 household interviews in Moroceli, Honduras, in
1981. The study shows that the Honduran women in the informal sector are unlikely to
have formal education, are part of a female-headed household, older, single, part of a
free conjugal union arrangement, part of an extended family, and caring for a greater
number of young children. The participant in the formal sector is younger, part of an

extended family, and most probably married with fewer young children. A woman's participation in either sector improved the standard of living for the entire household.

314 **El machismo en Honduras.** (Masculinity in Honduras.)
A. León Padilla H.   Tegucigalpa: Editorial Universitaria, 1981. 40p. bibliog.

The author sets forth the characteristics of the male psychology and behaviour universal in Latin America, then delineates the peculiarities practised in Honduras. Noting the historical, cultural relations with its near-neighbour Mexico, the author cites the similarities of Honduran *machismo* with that of Mexican males which has been thoroughly studied. He predicts that the growing influence of US popular culture upon Honduran youth will modify *macho* behaviour as young females become more educated and assertive and young males conduct themselves in a less traditionally dominant way.

315 **Memories of a Central American: El Salvador, Honduras, Nicaragua (Contras), et cetera.**
Judá Guzmán.   New York: Vantage, 1988. c.90p.

An eclectic collection of anecdotes and reminiscences by a Honduran about life in Central America. Although this bibliographer was unable to obtain information about the author or his profession, the book offers a Honduran perspective on the first Jewish business, the banana companies, and the SOS Children's Village, among other miscellaneous topics.

316 **Monografía de la mujer hondureña.** (Monograph about the Honduran woman.)
María Luisa de Bertrand Anduray.   Tegucigalpa: Imprenta Offset/ Cultura de la Secretaría de Cultura y Turismo de la República de Honduras, Comisión Interamericana de Mujeres, 1980. 95p.

A compilation of several documents concerning the rights of women in Honduras. It includes a directory of the Inter-American Commission of Women, political and civil rights of Honduran citizens, labour laws, women and social security, as well as other issues of relevance to Honduran women.

317 **Notas sobre la evolución histórica de la mujer en Honduras.** (Notes about the historical evolution of women in Honduras.)
Leticia de Oyuela.   Tegucigalpa: Editorial Guaymuras, 1989. 45p.

A brief study of women in Honduran society from pre-Columbian times to the present. Chapters treat the woman of the distant past; Hispanic woman, seventeenth-century woman and family, the Independence movement; education and the modern state. The author cites the need for more work in this fertile area of research.

318 **Resumen del plan nacional de desarrollo, 1974-1978.** (Summary of the
national development plan, 1974-78.)
Tegucigalpa: Consejo Superior de Planificación Económica, [1973?].
165p.
A comprehensive development plan for the years 1974 to 1978, encompassing all
sectors of the economy, transportation, communication, energy, education, health,
nutrition and housing. For each sector treated, the objectives, goals, financing and
policies are set forth. Development plans of this sort are useful to verify what may be
considered important to a particular government or bureaucacy; however, one should
not be swayed by statistical estimates or assume without collaborating evidence that
the plans were actually implemented.

Social structure

319 **Campesinos: between carrot and stick.**
Medea Benjamin. *Nacla: Report on the Americas*, vol. 22, no. 1
(1988), p. 22-30.
Discusses the ramifications of the 1972 Agrarian Reform Act indicating that some
peasants have benefited, but over 8,000 new families become landless every year. The
author implies that the armed forces alone consider the reform to have been successful.

320 **Don't be afraid, Gringo: a Honduran woman speaks from the heart: the
story of Elvia Alvarado.**
Elvia Alvarado, translated and edited by Medea Benjamin. San
Francisco, California: Institute for Food and Development Policy,
1987. 171p. maps. bibliog. (Also published, New York: Harper and
Row, 1989).
The inspiring story of Elvia Alvarado, a remarkable *campesina* [peasant] activist in
Honduras. She tells of her growing political awareness, travels by foot through the
backlands of her country and shares her insight into the internal workings of rural
Honduras. As an organizer, she has worked towards land recovery for small farmers –
mandated by land reform laws – and suffered the consequences at the hands of the
Honduran military. Her voice is that of the common Honduran farmworker and
worthy of attention. The numerous excellent black-and-white photographs give the
reader even more insight into the character of the protaganist and the people she tries
to assist. The appendices list political parties and armed opposition, major *campesino*
organizations, US–Honduran military establishments and a resource centres guide.

321 **Familia, trabajo y reproducción social: campesinos en Honduras.**
(Family, work and social reproduction: Honduran peasants.)
Mario J. Torres Adrián. Mexico City: PISPAL, Colegio de México,
1985. 294p. bibliog.
An in-depth investigation of Honduran agrarian society through the author's micro-
level analysis of the *campesino* family. Valuable socio-demographic and economic data

Social Conditions. Social structure

are presented, using numerous statistical tables which amply illustrate and verify the textual analysis. Differentiation of roles within the family is clearly presented by charting their daily activities. This work presents a wealth of detailed information on the social structure of the majority of Hondurans who continue to live in rural communities.

322 **The heritage of the conquistadors: ruling classes in Central America from the Conquest to the Sandinistas.**
Samuel Z. Stone. Lincoln, Nebraska: University of Nebraska Press, 1990. 241p. bibliog.

This fascinating study written by a grandson of Samuel Zemurray (very much the North American élite of Central America) establishes the kinship ties among the political and economic élites of the five Central American nations, with primary emphasis on Costa Rica, but including data on Honduran first families. An extensive appendix presents genealogical trees depicting the continued influence of the conquistadors and colonial nobility. Contains many illustrations, a lengthy bibliography, and an index.

323 **Income levels, income distribution, and levels of living in rural Honduras: a summary and evaluation of quantitative and qualitative data.**
James F. Torres. Washington, DC: Rural Development Division, Bureau for Latin America and the Caribbean, Agency for International Development, 1979. 73p. bibliog.

Beginning with a look at the overall picture of national income and product, Torres then concentrates on the rural sector, analysing income and wealth distribution, expenditures, housing, life expectancy, nutrition, and infant mortality. He concludes with case-studies of individual rural communities. The time-frame analysed is from 1967 to 1978 and the case-studies focus on San Lorenzo, the southern zone, Comayagua, Yarumela, and Monjaras.

324 **Land, power, and poverty: agrarian transformations and political conflict in Central America.**
Charles D. Brockett. Boston, Massachusetts: Allen & Unwin, 1988. 229p. bibliog. (Thematic Studies in Latin America).

Analysing the relationship between political turmoil and agrarian structures throughout Central America, this work examines unequal land tenure, challenges to the élite landholders by the peasantry, and the role of governments in suppressing land reform movements. The limitations of agrarian policy as practised in Honduras are covered specifically on pages 123-42. The author notes that landlessness and rural unemployment has worsened in Honduras even after agrarian policy reforms; this is on account of population growth and commercial agricultural expansion.

325 **Loose structure of family in Honduras.**
Carl Kendall. *Journal of Comparative Family Studies*, vol. 14, no. 2
(1983), p. 257-72.
Kendall examines the structure of rural Ladino families from the municipality of
Yuscarán, near the Nicaraguan border and challenges the findings of S. Gudeman's
Relationships, residence and the individual: a rural Panamanian community (Minneapolis: University of Minnesota Press, 1976). His data reveal that kinship is a major
component of rural domestic life and that the presence of adoption and foster
parentage implies the importance of kin ties outside of the home.

326 **Market incorporation and out-migration of the peasants of Western
Honduras.**
Frank Kramer. PhD dissertation, University of California, 1986.
248p. (DAI 47/07A, p. 2673).
This work describes a process of structural change among peasant farmers of Western
Honduras during the period 1940 to 1970, in response to the opening and expansion of
an external market for beef in nearby El Salvador. Occurring before the current
involvement of foreign capital in the beef trade, this case-study allows us to evaluate
the impact of market incorporation on peasant agriculture under conditions of
relatively free trade, and to consider theories of trade-induced economic development
in this light. Assessing the overall benefits of market incorporation, it appears that,
contrary to conventional theory, new markets under free trade were not beneficial to
Western Honduras. [Author's abstract].

327 **Perceptions of selected goals in village development for Honduras by
three levels in the development chain.**
Darryl Vernon Mortensen. PhD dissertation, Oklahoma State
University, 1984. 131p. (DAI 45/12A, p. 3521).
The major purpose of this study was to ascertain perceptions relative to village
concepts and programmes as held by individuals categorized in one of the three levels
of programme involvement in the development chain as it is presently operating in
Honduras. Level one comprised US Administrators; level two, Middle Management
Administrators and Supervisors; and level three, Village Level personnel. A
questionnaire was developed with 46 questions pertaining to the village development
process. These questions were in four broad development areas: agriculture, health,
education, and administrative/developmental. From the findings of the study it is
evident that villagers are receptive, eager and able to recognize their needs and appear
equally willing to participate in planning and carrying to completion programmes which
will improve the quality of life in their respective villages. [Based on the author's
abstract].

Social problems

328 **Adult education community projects and planned parenthood.**
Margaret H. Davies. New York: International Planned Parenthood
Federation, 1981. 110p.
Assesses an inter-agency project which integrated literacy and adult education with
family planning in Honduras.

329 **Capitalism, campesinos and calories in southern Honduras.**
Jefferson C. Boyer. *Urban Anthropology*, vol. 15, no. 1-2 (1986),
p. 3-24. bibliog.
The post-1950 expansion of exports of beef, cotton, and sugar production in southern
Honduras has alienated peasants from working the land and has resulted in a restricted
regional food production. Data from interviews conducted in 1978 with 71 household
heads in seven highland communities (and a 1979 follow-up with twenty respondents),
family budget records (nine cases), and participant observation, revealed that
throughout the 1976-78 harvests, 45 to 70 per cent of small landholder households
failed to achieve even minimal caloric intake of their agricultural production.
Employment opportunities for the many landless and near-landless has not been
generated by what little capitalist growth there has been. Consequently, there has been
significant malnourishment and out-migration.

330 **Children of the volcano.**
Alison Acker. Westport, Connecticut: Between the Lines, 1986.
168p.
A fascinating first-hand account of the difficult and precarious lives of Central
American youths and children. Based on five months of travel to El Salvador,
Nicaragua, Guatemala and Honduras, Acker's book recounts the individual stories of
street vendors, refugees, guerrillas and other marginalized persons, the whole
interspersed with insightful commentary. A touching book that penetrates the human
roots of underdevelopment in Central America.

331 **The comforts of 10 Lemp Alley.**
Marci McDonald. *Maclean's*, vol. 100 (23 Feb. 1987), p. 221-4.
Relates the plight of the *desplazados* [displaced persons] forced to move as a result of
the Contra–Sandinista conflict, prostitution in Comayagua, and US military build-up in
Honduras. The article contains several photographs.

332 **Honduran women: the marginalized majority.**
New York: Women's International Resource Exchange, 1986. 20p.
bibliog.
This is a compilation of brief, previously published articles focusing on the economic
and social conditions of women, the great majority of whom live in dire poverty and in
an unhealthy environment under male domination. Three organizations working to
effect improvements are the Honduran Federation of Campesina Women; the
Federation of Honduran Women's Associations, mainly middle-class women working
on social legislative issues; and the Visitación Padilla Committee, an activist group
working on peace and justice issues. The latter group organizes an alternative

Honduran Women's Day, celebrated each January 25, in recognition of the date in 1958 when women won certain legal rights, including suffrage.

333 **Housing in Honduras; La vivienda en Honduras.**
Walter D. Harris (et al.). Washington, DC: Pan American Union, 1964. 316, 295p.

A thorough study of the characteristics of Honduran housing in the early 1960s. The report was prepared by a team under the sponsorship of the Alliance for Progress. It describes and analyses housing types, plans, construction materials, availability, cost, and construction methods. Sources used range from UN statistical compilations, Alliance for Progress reports and the like. Both urban and rural housing problems, policies, land control and planning are considered. Most data are from 1949-64 with some projections made to 1980. Recommendations are given for future needs and appropriate housing types, in addition to considerations about the most logical building types and construction methods. In addition, an extensive glossary was prepared that lists major housing terms in English and Spanish. This volume, which contains charts, tables and maps, would be useful to anyone conducting a historical study of housing problems and challenges in Latin America. The text is in English and Spanish.

334 **Los irresponsables: ensayo sobre la niñéz abandonada en Honduras.**
(The irresponsible ones: an essay on abandoned children in Honduras.)
René Canterero. Tegucigalpa: Talleres Litográficos de López y Cía, 1978. 56p.

Discusses the social and economic factors that give rise to the severe social problem of abandoned children, and notes the lack of orphanages and miserable conditions of the few that do exist. The book contains several illustrations.

335 **Lito the shoeshine boy.**
Lito Chirinos, as told to and translated by David Mangurian. New York: Four Winds, 1975. 64p.

Eleven-year-old Lito works as a shoeshine boy in Honduras. Here he recounts his daily life with its frustrations and diversions. Although it is a book for children, it is a good source of information about street children and visual scenes of Tegucigalpa. It is illustrated with photographs by the author.

336 **A sister for Jayme.**
William Valdéz. *Nuestro*, vol. 10 (Jan.–Feb. 1986), p. 36-43.

This is a report on the situation of adoption in Honduras. It contains box features on the dos and don'ts of international adoption and on how to overcome barriers to adoption.

337 **The social and cultural roots of political violence in Central America.**
Thomas P. Anderson. *Aggressive Behavior*, vol. 2, no. 4 (1976), p. 249-55. bibliog.

Anderson suggests that there are specific features of violence, personal and organized, that are rooted in the societal and cultural formation of the Central American peoples. Taking the neighbouring countries of Guatemala, Honduras, and El Salvador and the ideological violence of the twentieth century, he relates it to the social character of the

Social Conditions. Social problems

Spanish Americans of this area. The concepts of manliness, religion, and the contrasts between these features and the attitudes of the indigenous community, are established.

338 **A task that cannot wait.**
Edmund S. Nadolny. *Commonweal*, vol. 113 (9 May 1986), p. 274-7.
The author discusses the shortage of orphanages in a country with an estimated 100,000 orphans. Roaming the streets of Tegucigalpa, many waifs are abducted for illicit purposes and never heard of again. The Casa Temporal (Temporary House) shelter constantly runs out of supplies and the government cuts back on social services while at the same time it builds a military airfield for US forces.

339 **Youth: a solution to the crisis in Central America.**
Raúl Benítez Manaut. *International Social Science Journal*, vol. 37, no. 4 (1985), p. 519-29.
Young people worldwide are subjected to many challenges, including unemployment and the generation gap. Overthrown dictatorships, the militarization of societies and bloody wars are added problems that Latin American youths face. Benítez Manaut presents the debate among social scientists about the Central American conflict and argues that the social struggles in Central America result from intolerant dictatorial governments that have existed in Guatemala, Honduras, El Salvador, and Nicaragua. The only solutions, according to the author, are to involve youth in the fight against major social ills, stop the arms race, and sign the Contadora Act.

Social Services, Health and Welfare

340 **Acute respiratory infection control program pilot study in Honduras.**
Peter Hanson Boddy.   MA thesis (Public Health), San Diego State
University, 1988. 114 leaves. bibliog.
The thesis reports the results of a pilot study of an acute respiratory control
programme for children under five years of age in Honduras. Ethnographic surveys,
questionnaires and interviews provided the basis for determining the effectiveness of
health education and promotion. This study provides excellent recent data on infant
mortality, social conditions, and health-care training in Honduras.

341 **Anthropology, communications, and health: the Mass Media and Health
Practices Program in Honduras.**
Carl Kendall, Dennis Foote, Reynaldo Martorell.   *Human
Organization*, vol. 42, no. 4 (1983), p. 353-60. bibliog.
The authors deal with the specific problem of controlling diarrhoeal diseases in
Honduras. The Mass Media and Health Practices Project described here encouraged a
three-pronged approach to controlling the diseases, incorporating a communications
model, concern for health behaviour, and anthropology to foster oral rehydration
therapy in the home. Other preventative and curative components for controlling
diarrhoeal diseases were also included.

342 **Assessment of the public health sector in Honduras (1975-1985).**
Tegucigalpa: United States Agency for International Development,
1980. 147p.
Evaluates the growth, or lack thereof, of various facets of public health, including
hospitals, clinics, personnel, family planning and the other related subjects for the
decade indicated.

343 **The baby trade.**
Mary Jo McConahay. *Los Angeles Times Magazine*, 16 Dec. 1990, p. 13-18.
Many developing countries intentionally or unintentionally serve as baby suppliers to infertile couples of the developed world. Honduran mothers supply over 200 babies per year to such couples. This article documents the sad plight of poor Honduran women who view adoption to foreigners as the only viable option for their children's future. The article loosely explains the ins and outs of the adoption procedure and paints a profile of typical adoptive parents – not necessarily a flattering one.

344 **Breastfeeding, infant health, and socioeconomic status.**
Reynaldo Martorell, Chloe O'Gara. *Medical Anthropology*, vol. 9, no. 2 (1985), p. 173-81. (Special issue: Biocultural factors affecting infant feeding and growth).
In 1982, personnel from the Stanford University Food Research Institute conducted a survey of 758 mothers of infants who lived in low-income neighbourhoods of Tegucigalpa. They wanted to assess the relationship between breast-feeding, infant health and socio-economic status. It was concluded that breast-feeding had a positive influence on infant health and bottle-feeding a strong negative impact.

345 **Bridging the communication gap: how mothers in Honduras perceive immunization.**
José E. Zelaya Bonilla, José I. Mata Gamarra, Elizabeth M. Booth. *Assignment Children*, vol. 69-72 (1985), p. 443-54.
A survey was conducted of 275 rural mothers to determine their attitudes, knowledge and practices with regard to immunization. After it was discovered that the concept of immunization and the vaccination cards were not fully understood by the mothers, a multi-media educational campaign was developed and tested for a two-year period.

346 **Can we return to the régime for comparative policy analysis? or, the state and health policy in Central America.**
Thomas John Bossert. *Comparative Politics*, vol. 15, no. 4 (1983), p. 419-41.
Analyses the need for primary health-care services in rural areas and the impact of programmes in place on the general health status of the populations of Costa Rica, Guatemala, Honduras, and Nicaragua. The political characteristics of the régimes (power, stability, ideological orientation and democracy) and their respective adoption and implementation process in the area of health care are examined.

347 **Comparación transcultural de las costumbres y actitudes asociadas al uso de alcohol en dos zonas rurales de Honduras y México.** (Patterns of alcohol consumption in two semi-rural areas between Honduras and Mexico.) Guillermina Natera (et al.). *Acta Psiquiátrica y Psicológica de América Latina*, vol. 29, no. 2 (1983), p. 116-27.

A comparison of the pattern of alcohol consumption in two semi-rural areas between Honduras and Mexico using the 'informant' method. The results indicated that in Honduras less tolerance was evident toward excessive consumption of alcohol than in Mexico, where moderate consumption of alcohol was considered acceptable by the subjects interviewed. Honduran women were more apt than were Mexican women to refuse a marriage proposal from men who were known to drink excessively.

348 **Consumers of oral contraceptives in a social marketing program in Honduras.** P. E. Bailey (et al.). *Studies in Family Planning*, vol. 20, no. 1 (1989), p. 53-61.

Presents the results of a point-of-purchase survey conducted in Honduran pharmacies in 1986, and describes types of contraceptive purchases and buyers.

349 **Contraceptive availability and use in five developing countries.** Richard M. Cornelius, John A. Novak. *Studies in Family Planning*, vol. 14, no. 12 (1983), p. 302-17.

Many developing countries have experienced reductions in fertility, but how much of this is due to family planning is not known. The authors review recent research on contraceptive availability, and data from the Contraceptive Prevalence Surveys of Westinghouse Health Systems are used to examine fertility rates and family planning in five countries: Colombia, Costa Rica, Honduras (3,594 females), Nepal, and Thailand. Factors examined are: method and source awareness or use; socio-demographic and urban or rural differences; travel time to preferred outlet; accessibility and use; availability and use among intended users; and preferred methods of users and non-users. Suggestions for further research are given, along with eleven tables and two figures.

350 **Contraceptive use and fertility in Honduras, 1981-84.** Barbara Janowitz (et al.). *Studies in Family Planning*, vol. 18, no. 5 (1987), p. 291-301.

Presents data on contraceptive use and fertility in Honduras obtained from a household survey conducted in 1984, and compares these data with similar information obtained from surveys carried out in 1981 and 1983. Specific issues examined are the use of sterilization as a contraceptive; places of purchase; price and brand of oral contraceptive; differing rates of fertility for rural and urban women; and duration of breast-feeding.

Social Services, Health and Welfare

351 **Dengue epidemic in Honduras, 1978-1°**
M. Figueroa (et al.). *Bulletin of th.*
Organization, vol. 16, no. 2 (1982), p. 130-7.

A health survey of a dengue epidemic which broke out in 1978. It looks at the immunology, microbiology, isolation and purification of the virus, and its effect on the Honduran population from infants to adults.

352 **The ecology of malnutrition in Mexico and Central America: Mexico, Guatemala, British Honduras, Honduras, El Salvador, Nicargua, Costa Rica and Panama.**
Jacques Meyer May, Donna L. McLellan. New York: Hafner, 1972. 395p. maps. bibliog. (Studies in Medical Geography, no. 11).

An exemplary study of malnutrition and ecological damage for each of the Central American countries. It is especially valuable for its detailed dietary, population, and economic statistics.

353 **Epidemias del siglo XIX en Honduras.** (Nineteenth-century epidemics in Honduras.)
Victor C. Cruz Reyes. *Mesoamérica*, vol. 6, no. 9 (1985), p. 371-90. bibliog.

Smallpox and cholera epidemics were not uncommon to Hondurans of the nineteenth century. Using original government documents and secondary sources, Cruz Reyes offers a cogent study detailing both how the epidemics were controlled and their devastating effects on the public in general. The article includes a table showing death rates from a cholera epidemic in 1858.

354 **Ethnomedicine and oral rehydration therapy: a case study of ethnomedical investigation and program planning.**
Carl Kendall, Dennis Foote, Reynaldo Martorell. *Social Science and Medicine*, vol. 19, no. 3 (1984), p. 253-60. bibliog.

Diarrhoeal disease prevention and control with oral rehydration therapy are among the goals of the World Health Organization. The authors support the use of ethnographic research in the disease prevention and control programme in Honduras and show how local beliefs and practices contributed to the programme's effectiveness. The sample population included 750 to 800 families living in over twenty communities.

355 **Exposure to the modern health service system as a predictor of the duration of breast feeding: a cross-cultural study.**
Nancy B. Mock (et al.). *Medical Anthropology*, vol. 9, no. 2 (1985), p. 123-38. (Special issue: Biocultural factors affecting infant feeding and growth).

A comparative study of mothers from Honduras, Bolivia, and the Philippines, their exposure to health service systems and its influence on the duration of breast-feeding. The multiple analysis of variance studies included demographic and socio-economic variables in addition to breast-feeding, other feeding practices and exposure to health services.

366 **The unintended consequences of disaster assistance.**
D. Neil Snarr, E. Leonard Brown. *Proceedings of the North Central Sociological Association Conference, 1983.* (Copies available from University Microfilms International).

After Hurricane Fifi (1974), a US$ 2 million disaster relief project to help rural peasants was initiated. The purpose of the assistance was to help motivate peasant farmers to take up farming once again. Five years after the hurricane, 270 persons were interviewed to assess the relief effort. It was concluded that the project was not completely successful because need was greater than expected and resources were spread too thin, and also because the distribution system was fraught with corruption and, consequently, dissatisfaction.

367 **User satisfaction with permanent post-disaster housing: two years after Hurricane Fifi in Honduras.**
D. Neil Snarr. *Disasters*, vol. 4, no. 1 (1980), p. 83-91.

Snarr conducted a survey of Hondurans who had received new housing after Hurricane Fifi. Almost 400 wood or cinderblock houses were constructed at three sites and approximately one-third of the recipients were interviewed. Questions regarding materials, location, neighbourhood, institutional services, availability of work, facilities, site characteristics and social environment were considered. In general, satisfaction among respondents was found to be very high.

368 **Why women don't get sterilized: a followup of women in Honduras.**
Barbara Janowitz (et al.). *Studies in Family Planning*, vol. 16, no. 2 (1985), p. 106-12.

In 1980, a study to determine interest in and access to sterilization for females was initiated at two Ministry of Health hospitals in Honduras. The initial study revealed that 42 per cent of women wanting sterilization from the Tegucigalpa hospital and 21 per cent from the San Pedro Sula hospital had had a tubal ligation. A follow-up study conducted two years later, with interested but unsterilized women from the initial study showed that 33 per cent of women in the Tegucigalpa group, compared to 15 per cent in the San Pedro Sula group, had later been sterilized.

Human Rights

369 **Cuando las tarántulas atacan.** (When the tarantulas attack).
Longino Becerra. Tegucigalpa: Baktun, 1987. c.250p.
Becerra recounts the tragic story of his brother's disappearance, torture and murder, allegedly at the hands of Nicaraguan Contras.

370 **Death squads go on trial.**
Anne Manuel. *The Nation*, vol. 246 (Feb. 1988), p. 224-6.
Reports on the trial of the Honduran government before the Inter-American Court of Human Rights, the judicial branch of the Organization of American States. The government was tried for the abduction and disappearance of four persons, a tactic frequently used by other countries but never brought to trial.

371 **Governmental liability for "disappearances": a landmark ruling by the Inter-American Court of Human Rights.**
Linda Drucker. *Stanford Journal of International Law*, vol. 25 (Fall 1988), p. 289-322. bibliog.
The Introduction explains that: 'On July 29, 1988, the Inter-American Court of Human Rights (the Court) issued an unprecedented ruling. The Court held the government of Honduras liable for the disappearance of student activist Manfredo Velásquez Rodríguez and ordered the Honduran government to compensate Velásquez Rodríguez' family. The case has received widespread publicity in the international news media both because it marks the first time that a Latin American government has been brought to trial for alleged death squad activities and because of the brutal assassinations of two witnesses while the case was still pending.' This fascinating article presents the procedural history of the case, the Court's finding that the Honduran government violated several articles of the American Convention on Human Rights, evidence submitted to the court, and the establishment of procedural mechanisms and evidentiary standards for future adjudication of disappearance cases.

372 **Honduras: civilian authority–military power: human rights violations in the 1980s.**
London: Amnesty International Publications, 1988. 54p. maps. (AI index: AMR/37/02/88).
This is a very thorough, well-documented report summarizing human rights abuses from 1980 to 1987. It notes that most victims are activists of trade unions, universities, peasant associations, political organizations, and human rights workers. Victims are detained without acknowledgment for longer than the legal time limits. Some torture and other degrading treatments are documented. The report sets forth several conclusions and recommendations for compliance by the government to ensure that the military and police operate within the law and are held accountable for their actions.

373 **Honduras: without the will.**
Anne Manuel. New York: Americas Watch, 1989. 83p. maps.
The Human Rights Watch consists of five regional committees that document, survey and report on human rights abuses around the world. The Americas Watch periodically reports on such abuses in North, Central and South America and publishes national overviews of 'extrajudicial executions', disappearances, torture, arbitrary detention, failure to prosecute, censorship and persecution, and monitors the worst, most flagrant perpetrators. This volume, written by the director of Americas Watch, contains all of the above as well as information about the US role in human rights abuse: military and police financial support and State Department and Embassy denial of abuses. The exploits of Battalion 3-16, death squads and the decision of the Inter-American Court of Human Rights in the Velásquez Rodríguez case are also discussed. Earlier reports issued by the committee for Honduras are: *Honduras on the brink: a report on human rights based on a mission of inquiry* (1984), *Human rights in Honduras: Central America's sideshow* (1987), *Human rights in Central America: a report on El Salvador, Guatemala, Honduras and Nicaragua* (1984).

374 **How holocausts happen: the United States in Central America.**
Douglas V. Porpora. Philadelphia, Pennsylvania: Temple University Press, 1990. 224p. bibliog.
Porpora challenges American citizens to shake off their apathy and heighten their awareness of the actions of the US government which is substantially responsible for what he refers to as a 'holocaust-like' genocide of Central Americans. He compares the atrocities committed by the Nazis and the German citizens' collective silence to the horrifying deaths of tens of thousands of Nicaraguans, Salvadorans and Guatemalans while the American people are kept quiescent through government lies and media distortion. Those US citizens propelled to defend the Central American people, such as Witness for Peace and the Sanctuary Movement, are praised for their righteous actions and all US citizens are urged to act on their moral principles. Honduras is mentioned in an examination of the inequitable land distribution of the region. The work includes an index.

375 **Human rights in Central America: a report on El Salvador, Guatemala, Honduras and Nicaragua.**
New York: Americas Watch, 1983. 39p. bibliog.

The information contained in this summary report of human rights abuses had been published previously in reports of each individual country. The section on Honduras – on pages 24-30 – notes the rising incidence of extrajudicial killings, naming among the victims in 1983 an economist, an agricultural union president and students. The past president of the university employees' association was listed as missing. Lack of investigation about these abuses is decried and General Gustavo Alvarez Martínez is described as the virtual head of state.

376 **Human rights in Honduras, 1984.**
Lucila Funes de Torres. Washington, DC: Washington Office on Latin America, Committee for the Defense of Human Rights in Honduras, 1985. c. 200p. bibliog.

This report thoroughly documents the numerous violations of human rights in a very critical year. General Alvarez Martínez, the main perpetrator behind disappearances, torture and the murder of hundreds of nationals and refugees, was removed from his office in mid-1984. Nevertheless, the statistics collected after his departure indicate continued violations, although not as numerous as before. Under categories of violation type, victims are listed by name and by the circumstances surrounding their violation. The appendix includes a communiqué issued by the Honduran Armed Forces on 29 December 1984 and the response to it by the Committee of Relatives of Missing Detainees in Honduras and by Ramón Custodio López, director of the Committee for the Defense of Human Rights in Honduras. Originally published in Spanish under the title *Los derechos humanos en Honduras* (Tegucigalpa: Centro de Documentación de Honduras, 1984. 194p.).

377 **Human rights in Honduras: signs of "the Argentine method".**
Juan E. Méndez. New York: Americas Watch Committee, 1982. 39p. bibliog.

This is the first report of the Americas Watch Committee on human rights violations in Honduras. It expresses concern about the possible connection between General Alvarez Martínez and the Argentine military, infamous for its innumerable cases of human rights abuses. These links were later verified in a subsequent report (1986). The 1982 report notes that disappearances and the treatment of refugees were the most pressing issues. An appendix lists 33 Hondurans who disappeared between January 1981 and October 1982 and 50 Salvadoran refugees who disappeared.

378 **Human rights in Honduras after General Alvarez.**
Anne Nelson. New York: Americas Watch Committee, 1986. 59p. bibliog.

Nelson's report notes a dramatic improvement in the human rights situation since General Alvarez Martínez was forced from power in early 1984. The three years under his charge produced unprecedented, systematic human rights violations of Honduran citizens and also some Salvadorans and Nicaraguans residing there as refugees. The report offers details on the status of the various refugee camps throughout the country, noting that some 20,000 Salvadorans lived in three camps with restricted liberty of movement; 13,000 Miskito refugees were relatively unrestricted in Gracias a Dios

Department; and some 10,000 to 20,000 Nicaraguans in the El Paraíso–Choluteca area
were living unrestricted.

379 **Human rights – compliance of Honduras with American convention –
exhaustion of domestic legal remedies – proof of disappearances – proof
of government liability, etc.**
Samuel M. Witten. *American Journal of International Law*, vol. 83
(April 1989), p. 361-7. bibliog.
An opinion paper and summary issued by an attorney/adviser to the US Department of
State concerning the case of the disappearance of Manfredo Velásquez Rodríguez and
the decision against the Honduran government handed down by the Inter-American
Court of Human Rights.

380 **The situation of human rights in Honduras, 1989.**
Tegucigalpa: CODEH, 1990. 19p.
This yearly report by the Committee for the Defence of Human Rights in Honduras
notes that during the last year of Azcona Hoyo's presidency, significant violations have
continued in areas of political, civil, economic and social rights, the majority having
been committed by the military. The statistics report 1,291 illegal detentions, 241 cases
of torture, 39 'extrajudicial executions' (i.e., murders), and 8 political assassinations
among other violations. An eight-page report dated March 1990 is tipped in; this
responds to the US State Department's 1989 human rights report for Honduras, which
'tries to soften the reality of Honduras' human rights situation'. The US report
presents only 7 extrajudicial executions, 39 cases of torture and gives no specified
number of detentions.

381 **Testifying to torture.**
James LeMoyne. *New York Times Magazine* (5 June 1988), p. 44-7,
62.
The author interviewed several witnesses who had been either victims of the Honduran
army's secret war from 1980 to 1984 against political dissenters or death squad
interrogators and torturers working for the army. The rôle of the US Central
Intelligence Agency in police and army training is also explored.

Politics

Central American region

382 Central America: democracy, development and change.
Edited by John M. Kirk, George W. Schuyler. New York: Praeger,
1988. 205p. bibliog.

Contributions of scholars and activists at a 1987 conference are grouped under the
categories of democracy, development and change. On pages 47-59 in the democracy
section, Judith A. Weiss addresses Honduran national identity, repression and popular
response. She surveys US economic and military hegemony and discusses popular
labour and *campesino* movements of resistance within Honduras. The work is indexed.

383 The Central America fact book.
Tom Barry, Deb Preusch. New York: Grove, 1986. 357p. maps.
bibliog.

By the authors of *Dollars and dictators* (q.v.), this guide to the politics and economics
of Central America in the 1980s offers a considerable amount of documentation
supporting the authors' thesis that US dollars continue to manipulate events in the
region. It is their contention that US government and corporations still wield control
over industry, agriculture, finance, heads of state and the military. The roles played by
the Agency for International Development, Peace Corps, US Information Agency and
others is fully explored. The section on Honduras (pages 251-68) is useful for
descriptions of contemporary political parties, *campesino* political activities, and the
activities of transnational US companies operating in the country. An essential
reference work for understanding Reagan-era policies in Central America.

384 **Central America, land of lords and lizards.**
Thorsten Valentine Kalijarvi. Princeton, New Jersey: Van Nostrand,
1962. 128p. bibliog.
The political, economic and social conditions of the five Central American nations are
described. This work is notable now for its assertion of communism creeping into each
country; it estimates that 500 members belong to the Communist Party of Honduras
and are infiltrating labour organizations and the university. Twelve tables provide
statistical data primarily on trade and economic conditions.

385 **Central America: opposing viewpoints.**
Edited by Carol Wekesser, Janelle Rohr, Karin Swisher. San Diego,
California: Greenhaven, 1990. 264p. bibliog.
'This series uses magazines, journals, books, newspapers, as well as statement and
position papers from a wide range of individuals and organizations' to present pro and
con arguments on important, controversial issues. This volume includes the opinions of
US government officials such as Elliott Abrams and James Baker III, scholars Thomas
P. Anderson, Noam Chomsky, Octavio Paz and Carlos Fuentes, and other noted
figures. It is an excellent and provocative resource of information about contemporary
US–Central American relations. One can use the index to locate references to
Honduras.

386 **Central America: the real stakes: understanding Central America**
before it's too late.
Lester D. Langley. New York: Crown, 1985. 280p. maps.
bibliog.
A professor of Latin American and diplomatic history, Langley contends that the US
government has misinterpreted the political ills of Central America as a reflection of an
East–West struggle instead of as a region struggling to establish nationhood. In a clear
and concise manner he looks at the root causes of the region's ills, important historical
events, ideologies, and how the US has aggravated the situation. The chapter 'Down in
Tegoose' tells us about contemporary Tegucigalpa, from driving habits to dress
preferences. 'Welcome to the Free Republic of Olancho' describes a successful low-
tech irrigation system and explores agrarian problems. Also highlighted is the
Salvadoran–Honduran 'Soccer War'. This would serve well as a readable, almost
chatty, introduction to this region of seemingly constant turmoil.

387 **Centroamérica en crisis.** (Central America in crisis.)
Centro de Estudios Internacionales. Mexico City: El Colegio de
México, 1980. 226p. bibliog. (Colección Centro de Estudios
Internacionales, no. 21).
A collection of articles by Central American activists and scholars concerning the
political, economic and social crises of the region in the context of international
politics. In 'Honduras, situación actual y perspectivas políticas' (Honduras, today's
situation and political perspectives) – pages 81-91 – Gustavo Adolfo Aguilar writes
about the political and economic situation from the 1950s to the 1980s and calls for the
vanguard of the rural and urban proletariat to unify for the economic, political and
social liberation of the country.

388 **Communism in Central America and the Caribbean.**
Edited by Robert Wesson. Stanford, California: Hoover Institution
Press, 1982. 177p. bibliog.

A useful collection of essays by journalists and college professors on the question of communism in Central America, the Caribbean and Guyana. The essays, written specifically for this volume, focus on contemporary politics and trace the rôle of communist political parties and leftist groups in each country. Chapter six, by Neale J. Pearson, is devoted to Costa Rica, Honduras and Panamá and includes a summary of the Honduran Communist Party activities. Each chapter ends with bibliographical notes and the text is followed by an index.

389 **Elecciones en Centroamérica.** (Elections in Central America.)
Daniel Tzur. *Estudios Centroamericanos* (El Salvador), vol. 37,
no. 402 (1982), p. 259-70.

Based on contemporary Central American publications, Tzur shows that in four relatively recent elections in Central America, both presidential and legislative, there is evidence that the United States applied a great deal of pressure to benefit its so-called vital interests. While discussing the elections in Honduras, Costa Rica, Guatemala and El Salvador, he contends that the elections have become an essential facet of US policy in Central America as it attempts to 'legitimize' the strength of the armed forces in each country.

390 **Elections and democracy in Central America.**
Edited by John A. Booth, Mitchell A. Seligson. Chapel Hill, North
Carolina: University of North Carolina Press, 1989. 214p.

The implications of recent elections for democratization in Central America are examined by panellists at the 1986 Latin American Studies Association congress. John Booth frames the analysis by broadly defining democracy as political participation and asking the scholars to assess the range, depth, and breadth of participation, the elections' freedom and fairness and their contribution to a democratic political culture. His brief assessment of Honduras is found on pages 29-31. A case-study of the 1981 Honduran presidential election is offered by Mark Rosenberg on pages 40-59. His focus is the questionable consolidation of democracy during the four-year term of Suazo Córdova in 1982-86.

391 **Honduras and Central America: at a historic juncture.**
Rigoberto Padilla Rush. *International Affairs* (Moscow), (Jan. 1988),
p. 33-42.

Provides details from a leftist perspective about the changing US policies towards Honduras during the Reagan administration and the deepening social and economic crisis and predicts that the situation may result in a social explosion.

392 **Inside Central America: the essential facts past and present on El
Salvador, Nicaragua, Honduras, Guatemala, and Costa Rica.**
Philip Berryman. New York: Pantheon, 1985. 166p.

From 1976 to 1980 Berryman was the Central American representative for the American Friends Service Committee. Prior to that he was a pastoral worker in Panamá for 10 years. In *Inside Central America*, Berryman combines his first-hand experience with political events of the region to provide a comprehensive left-of-centre analysis of US–Central American relations during Reagan's first administration, 1980-84. He contends that developments in Central America have been under-reported, misinterpreted or ignored by US media and leaders, and strives to present the perspective of the poor and unrepresented people of Central America. He supports moving from a 'Cold War' stance to further negotiations as a better approach towards peace in the region. A chronology of Central American negotiations from 1980 to 1984, a glossary, and an index are useful additions to the text.

393 **Politics in Central America: Guatemala, El Salvador, Honduras, and Nicaragua.**
Thomas P. Anderson. New York: Praeger; Stanford, California: Hoover Institution Press, 1982. 221p. bibliog. (Politics in Latin America). Revised edition, New York: Praeger, 1988. 256p. bibliog.

Valuable additions to the relatively small body of English-language literature about contemporary Central American politics. Anderson's clearly written overviews of the social and political issues of the region are followed by analyses in which he assesses the political prospects for each of the four countries. In the section on Honduras of the revised edition much attention is given to US involvement and manipulation of national politics and support of the Contras' activities there. 'Designed to be short on theory and long on political facts' these books serve as good road-maps to the political history of Central America and the numerous, persistent conflicts of the region. Although a pioneer in Central American research, it is unfortunate that most of his resources seem to be North American, and he pays scant attention to documents generated in Central America or by Central Americans. Contains an index but lacks a good map of the region.

394 **Revolutionary movements in Central America: a comparative analysis.**
Jeffery R. Goodwin. Conference paper of the American Sociological Association, 1987. (Available from University Microfilms International).

A comparative analysis of revolutionary movements in the four 'core' countries of Central America: Nicaragua, El Salvador, Guatemala, and Honduras. It is argued that differences in the political fortunes of revolutionary movements in Central America – designated as 'protostate' organizations – are best explained in terms of the specific nature of local states and of the revolutionary movements themselves.

395 **Los sistemas de partidos políticos en Centro América y las perspectivas de los procesos de democratización: II seminario, Guatemala, junio 1986.** (Political party systems in Central America and the outlook for the processes of democratization: II seminar, Guatemala, June 1986.) Guatemala: Asociación de Investigación y Estudios Sociales, [1986?]. 150p.

Papers presented at a 1986 seminar on political parties examine the conditions of political participation and representation, both regionally and within each Central American nation. On pages 75-91, Ernesto Paz, a Honduran solicitor and sociologist, addresses the current situation and future prospects in Honduras. He provides a brief overview of the origin and development of Honduran parties, the traditional National and Liberal parties, and more recent organizations developed after the Cuban

Revolution, such as PINU (Innovation and Union Party), the Christian Democrats and revolutionary parties. He also comments on the characteristics of the Honduran political and electoral process. The author concludes that Honduras has a limited and precarious democracy, with the armed forces and US embassy playing major political rôles.

Honduran characteristics

396 **Centro América: los protagonistas hablan.** (Central America: the actors speak.)
Angel Vivas Díaz, Alexis Ortíz. Caracas: Editorial Cabildo, 1986. 722p. map.

Interviews with four prominent Hondurans are published on pages 500-45. President José Azcona Hoyo, academician Carlos Roberto Reyna, Carlos Montoya of the Liberal Party and Victor Meza, director of the Honduran Documentation Centre (CEDOH) respond to political questions posed by Venezuelan journalists.

397 **La corrupción en Honduras, 1982-1985.** (Corruption in Honduras, 1982-85.)
Coordinated by Roberto Zacapa. Tegucigalpa: Centro de Documentación de Honduras, 1985. 26p. bibliog. (Série Cronologías, no. 3).

Investigative journalists of Honduras have compiled a thorough listing of incidences of corruption, incompetence, and unethical behaviour during the Suazo Córdova presidential administration. The chronologically ordered incidents corroborate CEDOH's suspicions that corruption is pervasive at all levels of society: in the military, the government, business, even in mass organizations. The conclusion is that unbridled growth of corruption is disintegrating Honduran moral and ethical foundations.

398 **Cuatro ensayos sobre la realidad política de Honduras.** (Four essays on the Honduran political reality.)
Gautama Fonseca Zúñiga. Tegucigalpa: Universidad Nacional Autónoma de Honduras, Editorial Universitaria, 1982. 134p.

These essays, previously published in the daily *Tiempo*, examine the constitutional history of Honduras, looking mainly at the powers and duties of the legislative branch of government. Political representation and participation, constitutional order and *coups d'état* are also considered. Legislative and constitutional history are particularly scrutinized for the years 1936, 1942, and 1957.

399 **Democracia y elecciones municipales: un ensayo de teoria político constitucional.** (Democracy and municipal elections: an essay on politico-constitutional theory.)
Efraín Moncada Silva. Tegucigalpa: Editorial Universitaria, 1988. 43p. (Colección Cuadernos Jurídicos, no. 2).
The author, a professor of the Honduran Institute of Juridical Research, examines legal and social issues relating to the municipal elections due to be held in November 1987 but illegally cancelled by the National Tribunal of Elections.

400 **El día que rugío la tierra.** (The day the earth roared.)
Nestór Enrique Alvarado. Tegucigalpa: [n.p.], [1969?]. 97p.
A strong condemnation of the election fraud, intimidation and violence that occurred during the 1968 local election campaigns. Citing newspaper reports and official correspondence, the author traces the acts to Nationalist Party members who supported President López Arellano. Contains numerous illustrations of politicians, and acts of violence perpetrated.

401 **Elections and beyond.**
Nacla: Report on the Americas, vol. 15 (Nov.–Dec. 1981), p. 30-6.
Main topics of this article are the political enthusiasm, economic disaster and social milieu in Honduras preceding the 1981 election in which the Liberal Party candidate, Suazo Córdova, emerged as the victor. Although the military government of General Paz García only reluctantly acquiesced to the notion of elections, most observers concluded that the voting was honest.

402 **El golpe de estado de 1904.** (The 1904 *coup d'état*.)
Víctor Cáceres Lara. Tegucigalpa: Universidad Nacional Autónoma de Honduras, Editorial Universitaria, 1985. 134p.
This compilation of articles, first published by the noted historian in the daily newspaper *El Heraldo*, details the political participants and sequence of events leading up to a *coup d'état* on 8 February 1904, when nine legislators were arrested, the legislative assembly dissolved, and Manuel Bonilla seized power. The account provides insight into the historic animosity between political parties and actors plaguing Honduras which has allowed military authority to dominate civilian political rule. It contains several illustrations.

403 **Honduran elections and democracy, withered by Washington: a report on past and present elections in Honduras, and an evaluation of the last five years of constitutional rule.**
Leyda Barbieri. Washington, DC: Washington Office on Latin America, 1986. 36p.
As the descriptive title notes, this is an evaluation of the elections for president conducted in 1981 and 1985 with scrutiny of the real power in the country: the armed forces, who had the support of the US military and executive department. The report notes that 'misplaced power and authority are the overriding problems for democracy in Honduras'. The US and the military had weakened both the civilian presidents and the political parties as they were unable to exercise any independence. Yet the desire of the Honduran people for genuine democratic participation was evident from their

Politics. Honduran characteristics

enthusiasm at election time, even though few felt that any substantive socio-economic changes or true democracy would be forthcoming. The report concludes with brief biographies of the 1985 presidential candidates and a statistical breakdown of available election results.

404 **Honduras at the crossroads.**
Mario Posas. *Latin American Perspectives*, vol. 7, no. 2-3 (1980), p. 45-56.

Posas presents a sociological analysis of the Honduran national elections to be held in April 1980. He suggests that neither a conservative military *coup* nor a revolutionary confrontation as in El Salvador will occur and predicted that a moderate reformist victory could be expected.

405 **Honduras: caudillo politics and military rulers.**
James A. Morris. Boulder, Colorado: Westview, 1984. 156p. bibliog. (Westview Profiles. Nations of Contemporary Latin America).

A central thesis for Morris is that the military régimes in contemporary Honduras have their roots in the *caudillismo*, political 'bossism', of bygone times. He deftly demonstrates this by relating the political history of Honduras from 1876 to 1956 with the era of military rule, 1972-82. His perspective is that of cultural relativism and he uses the concept of the 'cycle of political frustration' to analyse patterns of developmental experience. Also discussed are elections, the various political sectors, and the economy *vis-à-vis* the national development policy, and regional and international relations.

406 **Honduras elecciones 85: más allá de la fiesta cívica.** (Honduras elections 85: beyond the civic celebration.)
Aníbal Delgado Fiallos. Tegucigalpa: Editorial Guaymuras, 1986. 181p. bibliog.

The noted academic economist recounts and analyses in detail the 1985 presidential election won by José Azcona Hoyo of the Liberal Party. First, the establishment and development of political parties are traced, with particular attention given to their connections with the US. The US financial support for recent elections is justified through the US desire to contrast 'free and fair' elections in Honduras with those of its neighbour Nicaragua which the US government dismissed as being non-democratic. Appended tables contain a statistical breakdown of the 1985 voting which provides solid insight into the political participation and orientation of various communities as well as of the nation as a whole.

407 **Honduras: historias no contadas.** (Honduras: untold stories.)
Tegucigalpa: Centro de Documentación de Honduras (CEDOH), 1985. 218p.

A selection of essays by unnamed authors on a variety of socio-economic issues, primarily concerning political activities by the peasantry and urban working class whose voices, according to the compliers usually go unheard or unheeded in Honduras. Additional topics treated are: labour strikes, pesticide use and abuse, the Church, and Salvadoran refugees.

408 **Honduras ocupada.** (Occupied Honduras.)
Hamburg, Germany: D. Hermes, 1986. (*El Parcial*, 18 April 1986,
vol. 6, no. 18).
A compilation of photocopied news items about Honduras from both national and international Spanish-language newspapers published between 1983 and 1986. The majority are from *El Día* in Mexico City. Arrangement is by topic: political leaders, the armed forces, human rights violations, US domination, refugees, external debt, unemployment, hunger, and popular resistance.

409 **Honduras, un estado nacional?** (Honduras, a nation-state?)
Juan Arancibia Córdova. Tegucigalpa: Editorial Guaymuras, 1985.
2nd ed. 132p. bibliog.
A cogent essay examining the development (or actually lack thereof) of Honduras as a nation-state. Refers to the difficulties the dominant class has had in constructing a centralized state, due mostly to the neocolonial economic enclave imposed by US banana enterprises. The author argues that only a powerful popular movement can create a national democratic state.

410 **The iron triangle: the Honduran connection.**
Philip E. Wheaton. Washington, DC: EPICA, 1981. 25p. bibliog.
Wheaton contends that 'the Iron Triangle refers to El Salvador, Guatemala, and Honduras and to the coordinated activities of their respective military and paramilitary forces. The goal of this strategy is to suffocate the popular revolutionary movement in El Salvador through a combined operation of extermination. . . . It was the brain child of US imperialism, concocted in Washington upon critical reflection of the loss of Nicaragua. . . '. Specific mention is made of the El Salvadoran refugee situation in Honduras, the Sumpul massacre, the Movimiento Anti-Comunista Hondureño (Honduran Anti-Communist Movement, MACHO, a right-wing death squad) and repression against the Catholic Church. Wheaton, the director of EPICA (Ecumenical Program for Interamerican Communication and Action), bases his strongly critical essay against US involvement in Central America and its manipulation of the Honduran government in this plan on a variety of interviews and testimonials extracted from Central American newspapers, speeches and the mysterious and poorly cited *Materiales de reflección*.

411 **Observance of the Honduran national elections: report of a congressional study mission, November 28-30, 1981 submitted to the Committee on Foreign Affairs, US House of Representatives.**
United States Congress, House Committee on Foreign Affairs.
Washington, DC: US Government Printing Office, 1982. 15p.
Consists of reports by two Congressmen who participated in an observation mission of the 1981 elections held in Honduras in which Suazo Córdova won. The report is valuable for its overview of polling stations, political leadership and electoral results. The authors conclude that the election was conducted in a fair manner with wide popular support and without significant irregularities, fraud or subversion.

412 **Política y sociedad en Honduras: comentarios.** (Politics and society in
Honduras: commentaries)
Víctor Meza. Tegucigalpa: Editorial Guaymuras, 1981. 399p.
This volume brings together editorials, essays and commentaries previously published
by the noted social scientist in the daily newspapers *El Día* and *Tiempo* from 1975 to
1981. Meza broadly addresses social, political, economic, and cultural conditions and
concerns of Honduras during the period which comes just after a military takeover and
before the regional and national upheaval of the 1980s.

413 **Politics and the military in Honduras.**
Thomas P. Anderson. *Current History*, vol. 87, no. 533 (Dec. 1988),
p. 425-31.
Anderson, a history professor specializing in Latin America, discusses recent squabbles
between the major political parties, Liberal and National, the economy, human rights,
the military, drugs and corruption and US–Honduran relations. He concludes that the
US military should reduce its high profile in Honduras in the face of growing anti-
American sentiments.

414 **Significado histórico del gobierno del Dr Ramón Villeda Morales.**
(Historical significance of the government of Dr Ramón Villeda
Morales.)
Stefania Natalini de Castro (et al.). Tegucigalpa: Editorial
Universitaria, 1985. 220p. bibliog. (Colección Realidad Nacional,
no. 10).
Originally presented as a collective graduate thesis project, the work assesses the
government of Villeda Morales, a Liberal Party member elected president in 1957 who
held office until 1963.

415 **Suazo Córdova, a mitad de la jornada.** (Suazo Córdova: at the halfway
point of his term.)
Roberto Suazo Córdova. Tegucigalpa: Ministerio de la Presidencia,
1984. 254p.
A collection of 35 speeches given in the first two years of Suazo Córdova's presidency.
As with most political speeches, fluff abounds, but there is some substance in several
speeches about the Honduran environment and deforestation. During these years
(1983-84), he inaugurated, among other ceremonies, the second phase of the Olancho
Forest Development Programme and the National Literacy Plan.

416 **Tiburcio Carías: anatomía de una época, 1923-1948.** (Tiburcio
Carías: anatomy of an epoch, 1923-48.)
Mario Argueta. Tegucigalpa: Editorial Guaymuras, 1989.
390p. bibliog.
This is an exhaustive biography of one of the most important figures on the Honduran
political scene in the twentieth century. He held the office of president for sixteen
years and was intimately linked to the highest governing levels from 1923 through to
the early 1960s. The Latin American political characteristics of *personalismo* and
continuismo were embodied in the Carías dictatorship, which did afford a prolonged

period of political stability, albeit at the cost of freedom of expression, human rights, democracy and nation-building. Argueta, Director of the Honduran Collection at UNAH, conducted his research at the National Archives in Washington, DC, using primary sources of the US Department of State, including official diplomatic correspondence and instructions to US functionaries, in addition to using materials on political and labour organizations from the Honduran Collection at UNAH.

Political parties

417 **Azcona Hoyo, José Simón.**
Current Biography, vol. 49 (1988), p. 27-30.
Succinctly traces the political career of the centre-right president of Honduras elected on 24 November 1985. Contains excerpts from his inaugural address.

418 **Historia del Partido Nacional de Honduras.** (History of the National
Party of Honduras.)
Rafael Bardales B. Tegucigalpa: Servicopiax Editores, 1980. 158p.
Traces the roots of the Honduran National Party back to 1898, highlights election activity and results from 1902 to 1971, and presents the Party's platform for resolving the nation's ills as of 1980.

419 **Informe de balance de la actividad del Partido Comunista de Honduras:**
III congreso PCH, mayo de 1977. (Report on the activities of the
Honduran Communist Party: III Congress PCH, May 1977.)
Partido Comunista de Honduras. [Tegucigalpa?]: [n.p.], [1977 or
1978]. 75p.
Covers the national and international activities of the Honduran Communist Party in its struggle to cast off the 'stranglehold' of North American imperialists and the national bourgeoisie. Contains the resolutions of the Third Congress and salutations from representatives of the other countries attending.

420 **El maoismo en Honduras.** (Maoism in Honduras.)
Asdrubal Ramírez. Tegucigalpa: Ediciones Compol, 1974. 140p.
bibliog.
More a polemic against the 'ultra-leftism' of international adherents to Mao Tse-Tung's political philosophy, this does provide some insight into the split in the Communist Party of Honduras between supporters of the Soviet Union and of the People's Republic of China.

Politics. Political parties

421 **Orígenes, desarrollo y posibilidades de la socialdemocracia en Honduras.**
(Origins, development and possibilities of social democracy in
Honduras.)
Ernesto Paz Aguilar, Miguel Pineda. Tegucigalpa: Friedrich Ebert
Stiftung, 1986. 52p.

These two essays explore the possibilities of social democratic political ideology being
developed and influential in both Honduras and Latin America. Miguel Pineda
examines social democracy in Central America and Latin America, contrasting and
comparing it with that practised in Europe. Paz Aguilar traces the origin and
development of Honduran parties espousing this political line, from the Partido
Socialista Revolucionario (Revolutionary Socialist Party) begun in 1931 through to the
M-LIDER of 1983. Obstacles to these parties' growth have been conservative union
leaders, the low level of general political culture, and *personalismo* among other
factors. The authors express confidence that social democracy will eventually flourish
in Honduras. Noteworthy are the appended platforms of three parties: PSR (1931),
Partido Democrático Revolucionario Hondureño (Honduran Revolutionary Democratic Party) (1948), and Izquierda Democrática (Democratic Left) (1966).

422 **Partidos políticos y elecciones en Honduras, 1980.** (Political parties and
elections in Honduras, 1980.)
Arturo Fernández. Tegucigalpa: Editorial Guaymuras, 1981. 106p.
bibliog.

Results of elections held on 20 April 1980 are presented and analysed. The relative
strengths of the Liberal and National parties are compared, giving data on where their
main constituencies reside. The results show the Liberals winning 51 per cent and the
Nationals 44 per cent. An appended chart shows results of the 29 November 1981
elections, with nearly 54 per cent for the Liberals and 42 per cent for the National
Party.

423 **Party politics and elections in Latin America.**
Ronald H. McDonald, J. Mark Ruhl. Boulder, Colorado: Westview,
1989. 386p. bibliog.

Pages 111-22 deal specifically with Honduras and focus on the evolution and context of
Honduran party politics, contemporary political parties, elections, and voting statistics.
Also projects long-term trends in the political arena and includes a glossary of political
terms and an index.

424 **Plan de gobierno: opciones estratégicas para el desarrollo nacional.**
(Government plan: strategic options for national development.)
Tegucigalpa: Partido Innovación y Unidad Social Democrática, 1989.
79p.

Platform of the Innovation and Social Democratic Unity Party. Presents the party's
perspective of national problems, issues, and programme for the future (1990-94).

425 **Programa del Partido Comunista de Honduras. III Congreso, 1977.**
(Programme of the Honduran Communist Party, III Congress, 1977.)
[Tegucigalpa?]: Partido Comunista de Honduras, [1977 or 1978]. 27p.
A brief pamphlet describing the objectives of the Communist Party in general and
those of the Party in Honduras in particular.

426 **The radical right: a world directory.**
Ciar'an 'O Maol'ain. Harlow, England: Longman, 1987. (Distributed
in the US and Canada by ABC-Clio).
Describes the leadership, orientation, history and policies of radical right-wing political
groups, including those of Central America. Arrangement is in alphabetical order by
country. For Honduras, the Association for Progress, the White Hand and two defunct
groups – CAUSA and Honduran Anticommunist Movement – are included.

427 **Reorganización liberal: nuevas bases para el Partido.** (Liberal
reorganization: new footings for the Party.)
Max Velásquez Díaz. Tegucigalpa: [n.p.], 1972. 140p.
This treatise for Liberal Party reorganization and action was written one month before
the 1972 military *coup d'état* which ended a one-year interlude of civilian
administration. Colonel Oswaldo López Arellano again assumed power just as he had
done in a 1963 takeover, when a Liberal held the presidency. The disorganization of
the Party is addressed thoroughly here as the author presents a new declaration of
principles and structure, as well as a platform for action, in the hope that the venerable
Liberal Party will again be the major force in Honduran politics and government.

Military, Armed Forces and Defence

428 **Bananas, bases, and patriarchy: some feminist questions about the militarization of Central America.**
Cynthia Enloe. *Radical America*, vol. 19, no. 4 (1985), p. 7-23.
Enloe examines gender-blind interpretations and theories of political organization, imperialism and militarization that do not include the issues of domestic work, prostitution, machoism, single motherhood or wife-beating, and finds them lacking. These issues, in addition to attitudes and policies affecting masculinity and femininity, are just as important as social class and race in an analysis of US business or military operations in Central American or Caribbean countries.

429 **Breakdown in Honduras: U.S. policy in trouble.**
Leyda Barbieri, George Black. *Nacla: Report on the Americas*, vol. 18 (July–Aug. 1984), p. 9-12.
Discusses the internal coup which resulted in the transition of military command from General Gustavo Alvarez Martínez to General Walter López. Contends that the US ambassador, John Negroponte, and President Suazo Córdova were unaware of the impending coup but later issued statements implying that Suazo Córdova had engineered the change.

430 **Centroamérica: la militarización en cifras.** (Central America: the figures on militarization.)
Lilia Bermúdez T. *Revista Mexicana de Sociología*, vol. 46, no. 3 (1984), p. 27-48. bibliog.
The seemingly bottomless well of military resources available in Central America and the rôle of the US in the militarization process are considered. The author focuses on covert and overt United States participation in the military efforts of Costa Rica, Guatemala, Belize, Honduras, El Salvador, and Nicaragua. She also proposes that the distortion of the figures by the governments involved presents a barrier to an accurate account of the nature of the militarization.

Military, Armed Forces and Defence

431 **En el cielo escribieron historia.** (They wrote history in the sky.)
Orlando Henríquez. Tegucigalpa: Tipografía Nacional, 1972. 159p.
bibliog.
Describes the use of the Honduran Air Force during the El Salvador–Honduras
conflict of 1969.

432 **Female GIs in the field.**
Charles C. Moskos. *Society*, vol. 22, no. 6 (1985), p. 28-33.
Examines the situation of women in US army units in Honduras during 1984. The
author discusses how their gender affects their daily routine, personal privacy – such as
showers and sleeping arrangements – and in their effectiveness in their work. He also
notes differences in the attitudes of enlisted women and female officers.

433 **Honduran scorecard: military and democrats in Central America.**
Mark B. Rosenberg. *Caribbean Review*, vol. 12, no. 1 (1983),
p. 12-15.
Rosenberg analyses the importance of Honduras in regional and international politics
from 1960 to 1982. He pays particular attention to the forceful and dominant role of
the military in Honduran politics.

434 **Honduras.**
John Keegan. In: *World Armies*. New York: Facts on File, 1979,
p. 289-94.
After the embarrassing defeat by El Salvador in 1969, the Honduran armed forces
were increased by threefold. Keegan gives us a perceptive glimpse of the rise in
numbers of personnel and material of the Honduran armed forces after the event. He
discusses the command and constitutional status of the forces, recent operations,
organization, recruitment and training, ranks, and development up to 1977.

435 **Honduras: de república bananera a enclave militar, 1980-1984.**
(Honduras: from banana republic to military enclave, 1980-84.)
Gregorio Selser. *Revista Mexicana de Sociología*, vol. 46, no. 3
(1984), p. 241-69.
Selser provides an outline of the political events that have led to the recent
militarization of Honduras. The main subjects treated are: the installation of the
National Constituent Assembly in July 1980; the assumption of the presidency of the
Assembly by General Paz García; popular protests against tax increases proposed by
the new legislature; the Mexico City press conference of August 1982 in which
Leonides Torres Arias denounced the actions of Gustavo Alvarez Martínez, then the
Commander-in-Chief of the Armed Forces of Honduras; and the deposing of General
Alvarez Martínez and its consequences.

117

Military, Armed Forces and Defence

436 **Honduras: fuerzas armadas, dependencia o desarrollo.** (Honduras: armed forces, dependency or development.)
Rafael Leiva Vivas. Tegucigalpa: Editorial Nuevo Continente, 1973. 163p.

A historico-sociological essay probing the dynamics between the banana enclave, military forces, foreign investment, politics and the Church, and the effect their interplay has had in recent Honduran history.

437 **Honduras hoy: sociedad y crisis política.** (Honduras today: society and the political crisis.)
Margarita Oseguera de Ochoa. Tegucigalpa: CEDOH/CRIES, 1987. 221p. bibliog.

This is a valuable interpretation of the principal political and economic events plaguing Honduras since the 1980s. Written by a social science professor of the Honduran National Autonomous University, the work covers the role of the military in national politics, Honduras as a strategic location for US-backed counter-insurgency, the effects of the US presence in Honduras, and social responses to these problems. It contains may useful charts.

438 **Honduras: república alquilada.** (Honduras: republic for rent.)
Gregorio Selser. Coyoacán, México: Mex-Sur Editorial, 1983. 366p. bibliog.

Selser, an educator and journalist, suggests that Honduras has leased or rented itself to the US only because it could not sell itself outright to the dominant country. Although it has the formal appearance of being a sovereign republic, he contends that since the beginning of the 20th century it has become the quintessential dependent banana republic. This is because of its export economy, civil politicians and military régimes that acceded an inordinate amount of power to the fruit companies, such as Cuyamel and United, against the wishes of the working classes. He further states that, in addition to this humiliating status, it has become an American military enclave replacing the one formerly in Somoza's Nicaragua, and that it is used to counteract the revolutionaries and insurgents. Of particular note are his references on pages 220-7 to Israeli arms involvement in Latin America. Heavy use of the US *Congressional Record* and the Mexican newspaper *El Día* is evident as he documents his contentions.

439 **Honduras (República de Honduras).**
Adrian J. English. In: *Armed forces of Latin America: their histories, development, present strength and military potential.* London: Jane's, 1984, p. 280-93.

Thumbnail sketches of the Honduran Army, Navy and Air Force cover the history, politico-strategic position, general framework of each service, weaponry (outmoded as it is), foreign influences (mainly US with a modicum of French doctrine), and there is a brief analysis of the prospects for all the military services in the country. The few photographs included are useful for identifying uniforms and weapons currently in use.

440 **Militarismo y reformismo en Honduras.** (Militarism and reformism in
Honduras.)
Leticia Salomón. Tegucigalpa: Editorial Guaymuras, 1982. 246p.
bibliog.
While the 1980s presidential elections have allowed for civilian heads of state, the
Honduran military continues to remain the dominant power and political participant.
The author examines the historical evolution of military power and its class alignment.
Struggles of *campesinos* and labourers for land reforms and justice are shown to be
major causes for military *coups d'état* in the 1960s and 1970s. Proclamations of military
takeovers in 1956, 1963 and 1972 are appended, as are 19 very informative charts
showing armed forces organization, funding, and monetary and training assistance
from the US government.

441 **The military: willing to deal.**
Victor Meza. *Nacla: Report on the Americas*, vol. 22, no. 1 (1988),
p. 14-21.
As part of a special report on Honduras titled 'Honduras: the war comes home', Meza
writes about the US influence on the Honduran military and the unique 'parliamentary'
Army which adapts and deals with the Reagan administration, the Contras and even
with the Sandinistas.

442 **Nicaragua and Honduras: toward garrison states.**
Mark B. Rosenberg. *Current History*, vol. 83, no. 490 (1984),
p. 59-62, 87.
Rosenberg expresses concern over the increasing militarization of Central America.
Both Nicaragua and Honduras, among Latin America's poorest countries, experienced
marked deterioration in economic conditions from 1982 to 1983. He contends that
hostility between the two countries is on the upswing, largely due to US policies in
Central America. While the three countries have each proposed peace initiatives with
the goal of reducing hostilities and promoting regional stability, they have all prepared
for war while talking about peace.

443 **The Pentagon Republic of Honduras: launching pad for the
counterrevolution.**
Fred Setterberg. *Mother Jones*, vol. 12, no. 1 (1987), p. 21.
Setting the stage for a hypothetical US invasion of Nicaragua from a Honduran base,
Setterberg describes the infiltration and militarization of Honduras by overt and covert
US forces and funding sources. The article is illustrated by photographs.

444 **RPV deployment in Honduras teaches operational lessons.**
Michael A. Dornheim. *Aviation Week and Space Technology*, vol.
129, no. 2 (1988), p. 43-6.
The US military deployed remotely piloted vehicles (RPVs) in Honduras from 1984 to
1986 and experienced a series of problems in their use: inappropriate evaluation
standards, inadequate written procedures and personnel training, sporadic and limited
funding, the necessity to fly at high altitudes, turbulent climatic elements, lack of a
logistics chain, and difficulties with video imagery.

445 **Sabotage: a strategic tool for guerrilla forces.**
Harvey J. McGeorge, II, Cristine C. Ketcham. *World Affairs*, vol.
146, no. 3 (1983-84), p. 249-56.

Citing examples in Honduras and El Salvador from 1978 to 1983, the authors single out
sabotage as an important element in guerrilla warfare.

446 **The sale of F-5E/F aircraft to Honduras: hearing and markup before the
Committee on Foreign Affairs and its subcommittees on Arms Control,
International Security, and Science and on Western Hemisphere Affairs,
House of Representatives, One Hundredth Congress, first session. . .
May 19 and June 4, 1987.**
United States Congress, House Committee on Foreign Affairs.
Washington, DC: US Government Printing Office, 1987. 111p. map.

Convened to assess the foreign policy and national security implications of the
proposed sale to the Honduran government of 12 F-5E aircraft, spare parts, munitions,
support, equipment and training for US$ 75 million. A lengthy debate about the pros
and cons was followed by arguments in favour of the sale which were presented by the
then Assistant Secretary for Inter-American Affairs, Elliott Abrams, by Professor
Richard Millett, and by John Galvin, Commander-in-Chief, US Southern Command.
The only argument against the sale was proffered by Lt. Col. Edward King, a military
expert on Latin America. Contains much about the military prowess of the Central
American republics and who has what type of aircraft. Statistical tables and charts
follow the text. The sale was prohibited at that time by Joint Resolution 277.

447 **Total force policy: the changing of the guard.**
Joe Stuteville. *American Legion Magazine*, vol. 125, no. 3 (1988),
p. 18-20.

The US Army maintains 28 full combat divisions, ten of which belong to the National
Guard. This illustrated article describes these guard units which are regularly deployed
to Honduras for the overt purpose of road construction.

Foreign Relations

General

448 **Archivo de la Embajada de México en Honduras, 1908-1976: guía documental.** (Archives of the Mexican Embassy in Honduras, 1908-76: guide to documents.)
Archivo Histórico Diplomático Mexicano Genaro Estrada, coordinated by Edgar Andrade Jasso. Mexico: Secretaría de Relaciones Exteriores, 1988. 207p. (Guías para la Historia Diplomática de México, no. 5).
A catalogue of documents contained in the Archives of the Mexican Embassy in Honduras, arranged in chronological order as the documents were received and conserved. This valuable guide unlocks the contents not only of official bilateral relations, but also of Honduran relations with various states in the region and with the United States. A useful source for the study of border troubles, labour and immigration problems, population and educational concerns, domestic and foreign debt, drug trafficking, the regional political situation, and other topics. Excellent access is afforded through the subject, name and geographical indexes. Without question, this is a most useful guide for researchers needing primary sources.

449 **Between war and peace in Central America: choices for Canada.**
Edited by Lisa North and CAPA. Toronto, Canada: Between the Lines, 1990.
The organization Canada–Caribbean–Central America Policy Alternatives (CAPA) examines the roots of the Central American crisis and provides details of Canada's economic relations and developmental assistance to the Central American nations. The roles of non-governmental organizations as well as Canadian governmental agencies are considered for Honduras specifically on pages 105-7; a graph on page 111 depicts Canada's direct aid to Honduras from 1981 to 1989. Solutions for aiding Salvadoran

and Nicaraguan refugees in Honduras are considered on pages 131-48. Recommendations are offered for Canadian policy-makers on assistance, refugee relief, peacekeeping rôles and diplomatic initiatives.

450 **Central America and the Middle East: the internationalization of the crisis.**
Edited by Damián J. Fernández. Miami, Florida: Florida International University, 1990. 239p. bibliog.

The geopolitical dimension of the Central American crisis is examined from a new perspective, the spiderweb theory of conflict. In eight essays, the traditional models of conflict are rejected: the East–West bipolar approach and the North–South perspective are considered to miss the national aspects of conflict and underestimate the connections between revolutionaries and world powers. The spiderweb model recognizes more participants, more dimensions, a higher degree of internationalization, prolonged duration, and more elusive conflict resolution. The essayists apply the theory by examining the roles played in Central America by Israel, the Palestine Liberation Organization (PLO), Libya and Iran. Honduras is mentioned as being a recipient of Israeli arms and technical assistance and Ariel Sharon's 1982 visit which followed the visit of General Gustavo Alvarez Martínez to Israel is recounted. Besides broadening the theoretical perspective of the conflict, this work is valuable for its examination of Jewish life in Central America. It is indexed.

451 **Diplomacia y deuda externa: el caso de Honduras, 1897-1912.**
(Diplomacy and foreign debt: the case of Honduras, 1897-1912.)
Rodrigo Quesada Monge. *Anuario de Estudios Centroamericanos* (Costa Rica), vol. 10 (1984), p. 69-80. bibliog.

Using Foreign Office documents in the Public Record Office, Council of Foreign Bondholders reports, and other secondary sources, the author discusses the foreign debt crises of Honduras between 1867 and 1879. During this time Honduras had contracted debts with London bondholders that totalled £5.4m. The London bondholders' efforts to collect the debts and the activities of J. P. Morgan with the U.S. State Department to assume the London interests in Honduras are highlighted. The author concludes that it is evident that the United States played a major rôle and England a secondary rôle in the events of the day and that Honduras was a bystander to the events that concerned its economic and political status.

452 **Diplomacia política y desarrollo nacional de Honduras.** (Political diplomacy and national development of Honduras.)
Héctor Roberto Herrera Cáceres. Tegucigalpa: Universidad Nacional Autónoma de Honduras, Editorial Universitaria, 1983. 200p.

Discusses how to maintain an effective relationship between university education and professional work as a Honduran representative abroad, whether as a diplomat or entrepreneur. The author served as the Honduran ambassador to Belgium, Luxembourg and the Netherlands from 1977 to 1983 and as UNAH professor of international law and foreign relations. Here he has gathered some of his previous lectures and speeches together with new material on the philosophy of diplomatic service *vis-à-vis* foreign relations.

453 **Honduras: en busca del encuentro, 1978-1987.** (Honduras: in search of a common ground, 1978-87.)
Coordinated by Juan Arancibia Córdova, Adolfo Aguilar Zinser, Rodrigo Jauberth Rojas. Mexico: Centro de Investigación y Docencia Económicas, 1987. 156p. bibliog.
A collection of essays dealing with Mexican–Honduran relations. The work grew from a 1985 seminar sponsored by the Centre for Economics Study and Teaching. The first section traces the economic situation of Honduras from 1979 to the mid-1980s. Section two deals with Mexican–Honduran economic and cultural relations and the opinions of the Honduran public and business sectors with regard to Mexico. In conclusion, the author contends that Mexico has fallen short in its support of Honduras, at least in the political and economic arenas, and suggests several solutions to strengthen Mexican–Honduran ties. Provides an insightful contrast between the relatively weak ties of Honduras to Mexico in comparison to the dominating role of the US in Honduran affairs. The text is followed by several statistical tables and bilateral documents.

454 **Incidente de "La Masica" entre Honduras y la Gran Bretaña: reclamación por la muerte de un súbdito inglés y por lesiones a otros dos.** (The Masica incident between Honduras and Great Britain: claim for the death of a British subject and the injuries of two others.)
Ministerio de Relaciones Exteriores. Tegucigalpa: Tipografía Nacional, 1913. 164p.
Includes all the documents relating to a claim submitted by Great Britain for the killing of a British subject and the wounding of two others by Honduran soldiers at Masica. It sheds light on the stressed relationship between the countries at the time.

455 **Northern shadows: Canadians and Central America.**
Peter McFarlane. Toronto, Canada: Between the Lines, 1989. 245p. bibliog.
Canadian economic and political relations with Central America are chronicled. Canadian influence in Honduras results largely from Catholic missionaries who have numbered over 120 in the field. Recently, economic aid to Honduras has approached nearly five million dollars in 1983-84. The Canadian government has usually followed the US standard policy, but a large network of social activists continues to push Canada to stand for peace, justice and independence in Central America.

456 **Tigre Island and Central America. Message from the President of the United States, transmitting documents in answer to a resolution of the House respecting Tigre Island, &c., &c. ...**
United States Department of State. Washington, DC: US Government Printing Office, 1850. 328p. maps. (31st Congress, 1st session. House Ex. doc. 75).
Contains the texts of 48 documents submitted by President Fillmore to the US House of Representatives upon their request for information concerning the occupation by the British government of Tigre Island in the Gulf of Fonseca. The documents, written between 1847 and 1850, include diplomatic correspondence between John Clayton,

Foreign Relations. With other Central American states

E. G. Squier, George Bancroft, James Buchanan, and others instrumental in establishing and consolidating the US presence in Central America.

457 **Tratados internacionales de Honduras.** (International treaties of Honduras.)
Rafael Leiva Vivas. Tegucigalpa: Universidad Nacional Autónoma de Honduras, 1970. 84p.

A listing, with brief descriptions, of several dozen Honduran international treaties.

458 **Yearbook of the United Nations.**
United Nations Office of Public Information. New York: United Nations, 1947- . annual.

An annual publication which offers succinct descriptions of UN-related projects in member countries. Through use of the index one can check for references to Honduran activities and documents. Most projects fall under the realms of social or health conditions and development assistance.

With other Central American states

459 **Análisis del conflicto entre Honduras y El Salvador.** (Analysis of the conflict between Honduras and El Salvador.)
Marco Virgilio Carías, Rolando Valerio Hernández, Gustavo Adolfo Aguilar B. Tegucigalpa: Universidad Nacional Autonóma de Honduras, Facultad de Ciencias Económicas, 1969. 118p. bibliog.

Published nine months after the Salvadoran invasion of Honduras, this volume presents the fresh opinions and research of several Honduran economists as to why the ill-fated war occurred. Using statistics and historical documents (dating back to the 1800s) the authors attempt to demonstrate that the root of the problem had been the aggressive, anti-Central American and pro-US imperialism direction that the Salvadoran military and oligarchy had followed when the Hondurans resisted continuing to be the release valve for the burgeoning Salvadoran population. Class struggles in both countries, the CIA, US imperialism, the trend in El Salvador to change from an agrarian to a mixed economy, and problems with the Central American Common Market (CACM) are also considered as contributory factors to the war. The study also shows how CACM statistics could be misinterpreted to lead one to believe that Honduras was more economically unstable than it actually was and might have led El Salvador to believe that the country could be easily conquered. Appendix no. 5 consists of a chronological table of hostilities between the two countries from 1967 to 1969.

460 **La batalla de Washington.** (The battle of Washington.)
Jorge Fidel Durón. Tegucigalpa: Imprenta Calderón, 1969. 2nd ed.
30p.

The former Honduran Minister of Foreign Relations presents a condensed version of the events leading to the resolutions of the Organization of American States (OAS) concerning the conflict between El Salvador and Honduras in 1969, the so-called Soccer War. The resolutions condemmed El Salvador's invasion and required its immediate withdrawal from invaded Honduran territory.

461 **Conexión en Tegucigalpa: el somocismo en Honduras.** (Connection in
Tegucigalpa: Somozism in Honduras.)
Roberto Bardini. Puebla, México: Universidad Autónoma de Puebla,
[1982]. 91p.

An Argentine journalist exposes the connection between the Nicaraguan counter-revolutionaries living in Honduras and officials of the Honduran government and military by focusing on an aeroplane accident that occurred in 1981. The Honduran Air Force plane was carrying a high-level Honduran military official and a Nicaraguan pro-Somoza counter-revolutionary, Steadman Fagot Muller.

462 **El conflicto Honduras–El Salvador y el orden jurídico internacional,**
1969. (The Honduras–El Salvador conflict and the international judicial
order, 1969.)
James Rowles. Ciudad Universitaria Rodrigo Facio, Costa Rica:
EDUCA, 1980. 303p. bibliog.

An American professor of international law examines, almost hour by hour, the causes and consequences of the 1969 conflict, with particular attention given to the rôle of international bodies: the Organization of American States, Inter-American Commission on Human Rights and the United States. At the time of publication, ten years after the event, diplomatic relations were still suspended between the two nations.

463 **La Contra en Honduras.** (The Contras in Honduras.)
Tegucigalpa: Centro de Documentación de Honduras (CEDOH), 1987.
35p.

An illustrated, chronological exposé of the presence of anti-Sandinista para-military forces ensconced on Honduran territory along the border with Nicaragua, from their initial actions in 1981 as ragtag counter-revolutionaries to their peak of strength and number in 1987. CEDOH investigates the Contras' supply, training and funding by the US and their protection by the Honduran military and government, even though the Contras were displacing Honduran farmers on their own land and contributing to internal concern about their growing presence and demands upon limited resources. By 1987 it was recognized that Honduras might face a critical dilemma if thousands of armed men continued to live on Honduran soil. This report includes positions taken by unions, and by student, popular, and several business and professional organizations in Honduras denouncing the Contra presence.

464 **El diferendo hondureño–salvadoreño: su evolución y perspectivas.**
(The Honduran–Salvadoran differences: evolution and perspectives.)
H. Roberto Herrera Cáceres. Tegucigalpa: Universidad Nacional
Autónoma de Honduras, Facultad de Ciencias Jurídicas y Sociales,
1976. 215p. bibliog. (Colección Investigaciones Jurídicas).
The rupture caused by the 1969 conflict between Honduras and El Salvador was still
unresolved after seven years, with economic as well as diplomatic consequences to
both nations. In an attempt to sort out the differences, the noted law professor
examines each nation's attitudes toward negotiating a settlement and offers a strategy
for Honduras to follow. He also examines the yet-to-be reconciled issue of sovereignty
in the Gulf of Fonseca. A bibliography and ten legal documents pertaining to the
resolution of the diplomatic stalemate are appended.

465 **Documentos y doctrinas relacionados con el problema de fronteras:
El Salvador, Honduras.** (Documents related to the border problem:
El Salvador, Honduras.)
San Salvador: Editorial Delgado, 1985. 409p. maps. bibliog.
An important and useful source for the study of border, territorial and sovereignty
issues between El Salvador and Honduras. Gathers together and reproduces, in
thematic order, all of the relevant major documents necessary to understand the
complex situation: legal dispositions, International Court of Justice decisions,
constitutions, historical documents and opinion papers by experts. The documents date
from 1563 to 1983. The work includes several detailed maps.

466 **Guatemala–Honduras boundary arbitration. Brief on behalf of
Guatemala on the question concerning the competency of the
International Central American tribunal to take cognizance of the
boundary question between Guatemala and Honduras.**
Washington, DC: [Government of] Guatemala, 1931. 133p.
A submission to the multinational tribunal of the US, Costa Rica and Chile concerning
the treaty of 16 July 1930 between Guatemala and Honduras. Signed by Carlos
Salazar, agent for Guatemala and Charles Cheney Hyde, Adrián Recinos, Manuel
Echeverría y Vidaurre, counsel for Guatemala.

467 **Guatemala–Honduras boundary arbitration; reply of Guatemala to the
counter-case of Honduras submitted to the Arbitral tribunal composed
of: the Hon. Charles Evans Hughes, chief justice of the United States of
America; Hon. Luís Castro Ureña, from Costa Rica; Hon. Emilio Bello
Codesido, from Chile. Under treaty of July 16, 1930.**
Washington, DC: Judd & Detweiler, 1932. 183p. maps.
A submission by Carlos Salazar, agent for Guatemala, this was also published in
Spanish with the title, *Arbitraje de límites entre Guatemala y Honduras.* In addition,
it contains a report relating to the construction of the hypsometric map of Guatemala
drawn under the supervision of the engineering staff of the Guatemala boundary
commission, by order of the government of the republic. It is useful for the
examination of boundary problems between the two countries.

468 **Guatemala–Honduras boundary arbitration; the case of Guatemala submitted to the Arbitral tribunal composed of: the Hon. Charles Evans Hughes, chief justice of the United States of America; Hon. Luís Castro Ureña, from Costa Rica; Hon. Emilio Bello Codesido, from Chile. Under treaty of July 16, 1930. [And Annexes]**
Washington, DC: [Government of Guatemala], 1932. 2 vols. maps.
Yet another submission stating the case of Guatemala in the boundary dispute between the two countries. This is signed by Carlos Salazar, the agent for Guatemala, and others and dated February 1932. Published also in Spanish with the title, *Arbitraje de límites entre Guatemala y Honduras; alegato presentado por Guatemala.* . . .

469 **Honduras–Guatemala boundary arbitration; counter-case of Honduras in answer to the case of Guatemala.**
Washington, DC: [Government of Honduras], 1932. 591p. maps.
Presents the Honduran perspective of the boundary dispute and contains maps intended to serve for both the Spanish and English version of the counter-case above. The three major disagreements concerned the Montagua river as a boundary, the Gulf of Fonseca–Ulúa boundary line and the Merendón mountains as a boundary. We find here presentations of the Honduran counsel including interpretations of historical documents and English-language versions of documents dating from 1525 to 1913. Both titles and explanatory text are in Spanish and English. The Spanish text is entitled, *Arbitraje de límites entre Honduras y Guatemala; réplica.* . . . The work also includes, on pages 588-91, an 'Index of publications cited by the representation of Honduras which are at the disposal of the Honorable Special boundary tribunal'.

470 **The Honduras–Nicaragua boundary dispute, 1957-1963: the peaceful settlement of an international conflict.**
Wayne Earl Johnson. PhD dissertation, University of Denver, Colorado, 1964. 186p. bibliog.
The first submission to the International Court of Justice (ICJ) regarding a boundary dispute was that between Honduras and Nicaragua in 1957. The territory at issue was that of the wedge-shaped strip of land known as the Mosquito Coast. After brief incidences of violence, a peaceful resolution was achieved through the efforts of many persons, the ICJ, and the Organization of American States.

471 **Honduras y El Salvador ante la Corte Internacional de Justicia.**
(Honduras and El Salvador before the International Court of Justice.)
H. Roberto Herrera Cáceres. Tegucigalpa: Centro de Documentación de Honduras, 1987. 87p.
The continuing contention between Honduras and El Salvador over their national boundaries and sovereignty over islands in the Gulf of Fonseca receives substantial attention from this noted expert in international law. Three essays written between 1977 and 1987 are included. He analyses the 1980 peace treaty (also reproduced) which re-establishes formal relations disrupted by the 1969 conflict. The 1987 essay addresses the resolution of borders submitted to the International Court of Justice and the text of that agreement is also given in full.

Foreign Relations. With other Central American states

472 **Land's end.**
Nacla: Report on the Americas, vol. 15 (Nov.–Dec. 1981), p. 12-25.
An editorial article about the social ills and interrelationships of the Central American republics, with particular emphasis on Honduras. Specific topics covered include the Soccer War, López Arrellano's plan for national unity and its failure, multinationals and their role in local politics, the 'Bananagate' scandal (when Eli Black, United Brands chairman tossed his briefcase through a skyscraper window and followed it 44 floors down to the street, thus prompting the Securities and Exchange Commission to investigate a US$ 1.25 million bribe to a Honduran official), and the Horcones massacre.

473 **Letter addressed by Doctor Marco A. Soto to President General Justo Rufino Barrios and answer to it.**
Marco Aurelio Soto, Justo Rufino Barrios. New York: Las Novedades, 1883. 48p.
This exchange of letters in Spanish and English between the presidents of Guatemala and Honduras during 1883 offers an example of the polemicism and political turbulence of the isthmus during that era. It reflects their mutual recriminations and accusations, with each claiming the other is about to seek to intervene in his country. The letters are accompanied by a series of newspaper articles that constitute part of the violent verbiage that characterized their relations.

474 **Opinion and award: Tribunal especial de límites entre Guatemala y Honduras.** (Special boundary tribunal between Guatemala and Honduras.)
Special Boundary Tribunal (Guatemala–Honduras boundary arbitration). Washington, DC: [n.p.], 1933. 98p. 2 maps.
Traces the history of boundary arbitration between the two countries and settles the boundary question as based on the 1930 treaty between the two countries. English and Spanish versions are on opposite pages. It was signed on 23 January 1933 by Charles Evans Hughes, president of the tribunal, and by Luís Castro Ureña and Emilio Belio Codesido, arbitrators.

475 **The war of the dispossessed: Honduras and El Salvador, 1969.**
Thomas P. Anderson. Lincoln, Nebraska: University of Nebraska Press, 1981. 203p. maps. bibliog.
In setting forth his analysis of the underlying reasons for the four-day conflict known as the Soccer War, Anderson provides a penetrating social and political history of both nations, showing how many factors contributed to the outbreak. The strength of this work lies in his assessment of the two militaries and his detailed reconstruction of the military tactics employed. The 100-hour conflict exacted a toll of 2,000 fatalities with hundreds of thousands of persons dispossessed, regional unification deferred, and instability continuing through to the present day. The book includes a detailed index.

With USA

476 **The case of the invisible aid.**
Philip L. Shepherd. *Nacla: Report on the Americas*, vol. 22, no. 1 (1988), p. 31-40.

Analyses US involvement in Honduran political and military matters from 1981 to 1988, and cites US intervention: [from] 'broadest national fiscal and monetary policies down to the smallest grassroots development projects, the Agency for International Development has been calling the shots'.

477 **El caso de las Islas Santanilla.** (The case of the Santanilla Islands.)
Carlos A. Ferro. Tegucigalpa: Oficina de Relaciones Públicas, Presidencia de Honduras, 1972. 2nd ed. 160p.

The preface to this edition proudly announces the final resolution of the question of sovereignty over the Swan Islands, long disputed between Honduras and the United States. When this work first appeared in 1969, the US still denied Honduran sovereignty, so the author, Argentine ambassador to Honduras, compared the Swan Islands question to that of jurisdiction over the Falklands. His argument successfully swayed the US Department of State, as is made clear in the appended documents. A treaty recognizing Honduran sovereignty was signed in 1971, with official ceremonies conducted in 1972.

478 **El caso Matta: radiografía de la violencia.** (The Matta case: an examination of the violence.)
Leticia Salomón. *Boletín Bimestral de Análisis*, vol. 2 (April 1988), p. 52-69.

On 7 April 1988, violent anti-American demonstrations took place after the arrest and seizure of an alleged drug trafficker, Juan Ramón Matta Ballesteros. This analysis of the tumultuous event cites deep-rooted resentment of the US policies in Central America and Honduras as causes of the demonstrations.

479 **Confronting revolution: security through diplomacy in Central America.**
Edited by Morris J. Blachman, William M. Leogrande, Kenneth Sharpe. New York: Pantheon, 1986. 438p.

Fifteen articles by respected specialists, written expressly for this volume, analyse the reasons for the failure of US policies in Central America and the lack of viable policy alternatives for the region and for each country within it. With regard to Honduras, the US-sponsored militarization of that country and how it has engendered an opposition that could result in even more problems for the country is solidly documented and argued.

480 **Diplomacia de las cañoneras: Honduras, 1924.** (Gunboat diplomacy: Honduras, 1924.)
Gregorio Selser. *Cuadernos Americanos*, vol. 42, no. 5 (1983), p. 118-27.

In this study of North American 'gunboat diplomacy', Selser explores the use of US military ships and marines and United Fruit's freight boats, dubbed the 'banana fleet' as a strong-arm force in Honduran politics of the 1920s.

481 **Enclave y sociedad en Honduras.** (Enclave and society in Honduras.)
Antonio Murga Frassinetti. Tegucigalpa: Universidad Nacional Autónoma de Honduras, 1978. 248p. bibliog.

The author proposes that the economic history of Honduras is that of the interrelationship of the expansionist dynamics of North American companies interested in linking Honduran exports with the capitalist world market. He seeks to explain the process of 'foreignization' or 'de-nationalization' of the local economic system, with particular attention to the mining and plantation sectors. Finally, he analyses the rôles of the local oligarchy and immigrants in capital expansion and suggests that the oligarchy became totally subordinate to foreign interests that dominated the country's economy. The time-frame covered is from the late 1800s to the 1930s. The text is accompanied by statistical charts and several useful appendices, including political documents, the incorporation of the Tela Railroad Company, and article reprints concerning major economic issues of the period.

482 **Forging peace: the challenge of Central America.**
Richard R. Fagen. New York: Blackwell, 1987. 161p. bibliog.

Fagen, a Latin Americanist at Stanford University and previously director of the liberal organization Policy Alternatives for the Caribbean and Central America, sets forth the notion that 'US policy initiatives towards Central America founded on humane and democratic principles can successfully serve the US national security requirements while promoting prosperity and fairness within the region'. 'Peace through democracy' and 'security through development' are argued to be better ways to achieve positive goals than through militarization. Pages 98-110 deal specifically with Honduras, but use of the detailed index will uncover more information throughout the text. The book is indexed.

483 **La hegemonia de los Estados Unidos en Honduras, 1907-1932.** (United States hegemony in Honduras, 1907-32.)
Marvin Barahona. Tegucigalpa: Centro de Documentación de Honduras, 1989. 264p. bibliog.

Barahona analyses the three decades of Honduran–US relations in which the two countries formulated an unbalanced relationship of hegemony and dependency. His well-documented study, based on research at a number of European, North and Central American archives, evaluates the evolution and effects, in the Honduran context, of the encounter between the industrialized, capitalist culture of the North with the agrarian culture of Honduras. The effects of the Great Depression and the beginnings of labour organization for economic justice are chronicled. The study concludes with the 1932 election of Carías. It contains several charts and graphs.

484 **Honduras: an oasis of peace?**
James A. Morris. *Caribbean Review*, vol. 10, no. 1 (1981), p. 38-41.
Examines the recent attention the United States has given Honduras and asserts that it
is the result of a desire to regain political influence in Central America and to diminish
leftward changes. Morris considers that there is an attempt to return Honduras to
constitutional rule by elections and progressive government.

485 **Honduras and U.S. policy: an emerging dilemma. Hearing before the
Subcommittee on Inter-American Affairs of the Committee on Foreign
Affairs, House of Representatives, Ninety-seventh Congress, second
session, September 21, 1982.**
United States Congress House Committee on Foreign Affairs,
Subcommittee on Inter-American Affairs. Washington, DC: US
Government Printing Office, 1982. 108p. bibliog.
A hearing concerning the US policy toward Honduras as of 1982. Significant
participants in the hearing were Stephen Bosworth, Deputy Assistant Secretary of
State for Inter-American Affairs; Professor Richard Millett; Lt. Col. John Buchanan,
USMC (Retired), Center for Development Policy. The discussions covered several
'terrorist' incidents, increased US military assistance, Nicaraguan activity in Honduras,
and the fragile civilian–military relationship. Interspersed among the testimonies are
reprints of articles on the US involvement in Honduras and the political situation as of
1982.

486 **Honduras: el sometimiento incondicional a la estrategia regional de los
EE.UU: una documentación de prensa.** (Honduras: unconditional
submission to the regional strategy of the US: documentation from the
press.)
Hamburg, Germany: El Parcial, 1983. 126p. map. (*El Parcial*, 9).
An illustrated compilation of new articles from various sources, many from *El Día* in
Mexico; most are in Spanish, but some are in English and German. As the work's
subtitle indicates, these articles show the overwhelming influence of US military and
political policy and its effects on the economic and social spheres of Honduras, as well
as its dominance over the Honduran government and armed forces.

487 **Honduras: guerra y anti-nacionalidad.** (Honduras: war and anti-
nationality.)
Ventura Ramos Alvarado. Tegucigalpa: Editorial Guaymuras, 1987.
205p.
A well-known Honduran journalist explores the thesis that the US application of the
doctrine of 'national security' has resulted in the complete loss of Honduran self-
determination. He urges Hondurans to reject cultural imperialism of any sort, and
politicians to renovate their political thinking in order to make the transition to an
authentic democracy' based on popular sovereignty. The lack of a national identity in
military personnel and civilians in powerful positions, and low-intensity warfare
(viewed as high-intensity by many Central Americans), are also treated as factors
contributing to political and social unrest.

488 **Honduras, portaviones terrestre de los EE.UU.** (Honduras, aeroplane
landing strips for the US.)
Hamburg, Germany: D. Hermes, 1988. 137p. (*El Parcial*, 26 Dec.
1988, vol. 9, no. 26).
A compilation of photocopied articles from various newspapers, written in 1986-88,
primarily in Spanish but with a few in English or German. Topics concern political
persecution, drug trafficking, US military assistance, and Honduran economic,
diplomatic, social and political conditions of the period.

489 **Honduras: seis meses de gobierno de 1983.** (Honduras: six months of
government in 1983.)
Ernesto I. Castellanos. *Estudios Centroamericanos: ECA*, vol. 38
(Sept. 1983), p. 759-68.
Looks specifically at the military plans of the Reagan administration in the first six
months of 1983 in the context of the years since 1980 when it was decided that
Honduras might serve as a useful chess-piece in the war against the Sandinistas.
Discusses human rights violations of the early 1980s, political opposition and
ideological struggles, and the activities of several specific groups such as CAUSA and
the Asociación para el Progreso de Honduras (Association for Honduran Progress).

490 **Los inicios de la diplomacia del dólar: Honduras, 1911-1912.**
(The incipiency of dollar diplomacy: Honduras, 1911-12.)
Gregorio Selser. *Cuadernos Americanos*, vol. 42, no. 6 (1983),
p. 127-43.
Before the North American fruit companies became economic empires in Central
America there were local statesmen and politicians who, 'contaminated by the fever of
progress', wanted to develop their countries modelled on European and North
American examples. The first major economic fiasco occurred in the 1860s and 1870s
with British loans to build an inter-oceanic railway. In 1909, the US stepped in to
assume control over that debt and subsequently a series of treaties and pacts were
made giving the US a significant upper hand in future economic, commercial and
political matters. Selser, a leading historian, offers details of the Knox–Paredes treaty,
the 'Hornet' and 'Tacoma' gunboat incidents, and United Fruit machinations.

491 **Police aid and political will: U.S. policy in El Salvador and Honduras,
1962-1987.**
Washington, DC: Washington Office on Latin America, 1987. c.80p.
Co-authored by Washington Office on Latin America (a watchdog coalition of religious
and academic groups concerned about Latin American economic, political and social
conditions) staff members Jim Lobe and Anne Manuel, and based on materials
gathered in 1987, this document summarizes the chequered history of US police
training in El Salvador and Honduras from 1962 to 1987. There is a long history of
efforts by the US government to assist foreign police forces, but it was not until 1962
and the creation of the Office of Public Safety (OPS) that police assistance became a
national priority of the Kennedy administration. OPS aid was distributed among three
categories: equipment, US advisers providing in-country training for police management and operations, and training for mid- to senior-level police officers in the US. In
spite of remarkable growth, the Office was dissolved by Congress in 1974, due to many

perceived failures, bureaucratic rivalries and, most importantly, the perception by Congress and the public that it was aiding police forces that were guilty of grave violations of human rights. The authors also discuss Section 660 of the Foreign Assistance Act, Reagan administration philosophy, the McCollum Amendment, the question of political will in and between the US, Honduras and El Salvador, and the recent history of police training in the two Central American countries.

492 The soft war: the uses and abuses of U.S. economic aid in Central America.
Tom Barry, Deb Preusch.   New York: Grove, 1988. 304p. bibliog.

The authors describe US economic aid to Central America as 'intervention with a smile', but their thorough investigation of the underside of US humanitarian and economic assistance supports their conclusion that the region's majority population would be better off without the assistance, as it is fuelling the economic and political crisis. The strategies of the US Agency for International Development are critically examined in the first part of the book. The second part examines the political uses of US economic assistance and also the activities of the American Institute for Free Labor Development. While Nicaragua, El Salvador and Guatemala receive more specific attention, Honduras is mentioned throughout the text. This work is essential to understanding the escalating dimensions of US economic intervention in Honduras and the region in the 1980s. It is indexed.

493 The tragic course and consequences of U.S. policy in Honduras.
Philip L. Shepherd.   *World Policy Journal*, vol. 2, no. 1 (1984), p. 109-54.

Shepherd blasts President Ronald Reagan, accusing him of having used the Honduran government to further counter-revolution in Nicaragua and counter-insurgency in El Salvador, all the while leaving the Honduran people to their own devices to withstand successive arbitrary and undemocratic régimes.

494 Two approaches to an understanding of U.S.–Honduran relations.
Mark Rosenberg, Philip L. Shepherd.   Miami, Florida: Latin American and Caribbean Center, Florida International University, 1983. 51p. (Occasional Papers Series. Dialogues, no. 14).

Scholars with abundant experience in Honduras analyse the effect of US foreign policy which has resulted in a steady increase in the level of involvement on the part of Honduras in the Central American conflict. They note that the internal conditions within Honduras have been completely disregarded, setting back Honduran political independence and socio-economic development. The goals and objectives of the US towards Honduras have been failures, they suggest, because the wrong aims have been pursued. The presentation by Rosenberg is 'The current situation in Honduras and US policy'; that of Philip L. Shepherd is entitled 'United States foreign policy and Honduras: how and why it has failed'.

495   U.S. ends and means in Central America: a debate.
Ernest Van den Haag, Tom J. Farer.   New York: Plenum, 1988. 241p.
bibliog.

A renowned conservative, Ernest Van den Haag, and a Tory liberal, Tom J.
Farer, engage in frank debate over the US rôle in Central America. In a lively tone they
struggle with issues such as US interests in Central America, the Contras, US and
international law, and alternatives to the US policies of the 1980s. The text is followed
by a brief bibliography and a serviceable, but limited, index.

496   U.S. involvement in Central America: three views from Honduras.
David Ronfeldt, Konrad Kellen, Richard Millett.   Santa Monica,
California: RAND, 1989. 71p.

A RAND think-tank report prepared for a project studying the local effects of US
involvement in Central America. The study identifies key themes in the philosophy of
the Honduran élite, based on interviews conducted in 1985 and 1986 with Victor Meza,
Gustavo Alvarez Martínez and César A. Batres. Despite ideologies ranging from left
to right, those interviewed showed surprising consistency, all emphasizing the
importance of nationalism and sharing concern over the rôle of the US, a country
which was perceived as an unreliable ally and whose inconsistency could endanger
disruptive anti-American sentiments.

497   U.S. policy in Central America: the endless debate.
Darío Moreno.   Miami, Florida: Florida International University
Press, 1990. 186p. bibliog.

A clearly written analysis of the formulation of US foreign policy in Central America,
showing that its failure stems, in large part, from the Vietnam War. Divergent
strategies towards the Third World are exemplified by the Carter administration's
liberal internationalism where social and economic underdevelopment are considered
to be the root causes of conflict; the Reagan administration's cold warriors viewed the
crisis as an East–West confrontation. The author explores the conflicts between these
theories for formulating US policy and their strategic implementation. Very little is
written specifically about the tactical use of Honduras as the US staging ground, but
one example shows arm-twisting by US diplomats to keep President Azcona Hoyo
from complying with the Esquipulas or Arias Peace Plan. The work ends with a brief
analysis of Bush's Central American policy which aimed at undermining the
Sandinistas, something which it appears to have done with success. The work includes
an index.

498   U.S. policy in Honduras and Nicaragua: hearing before the Subcom-
mittee on Western Hemisphere Affairs of the Committee on Foreign
Affairs, House of Representatives, Ninety-eighth Congress, first session,
March 15, 1983.
United States Congress House Committee on Foreign Affairs,
Subcommittee on Western Hemisphere Affairs.   Washington, DC: US
Government Printing Office, 1983. 123p.

This hearing was convened to review the administration's assistance request and
policies toward Honduras and Nicaragua. The opinions of several US and Central
American academics are presented, including Richard Millett, Mark Rosenberg, John

Booth and others. Useful for the study of US–Honduran–Nicaraguan relations in the early 1980s. An interesting appendix includes a letter referring to the use of Puerto Rican National Guardsmen in Pentagon-sponsored military exercises.

499 **U.S. relations with Honduras – 1985: hearing before the Subcommittee. . .Ninety-ninth Congress, first session, February 6, 1985.**
US Congress House Committee on Foreign Affairs, Subcommittee on Western Hemisphere Affairs.   Washington, DC: US Government Printing Office, 1985. 75p.
Consists of lengthy statements by Mark Rosenberg, Richard Millett and Max Singer about the political situation of Honduras from 1981 to 1985 and about US involvement. It includes charts of exiled generals under Suazo Córdova, and statements concerning 'disappeared' persons and other human rights violations.

500 **War and peace in Central America.**
Frank McNeil.   New York: Scribner's, 1988. 310p. bibliog.
McNeil, a career State Department official, served as ambassador to Costa Rica from 1980 to 1983 when he was recalled as a result of his advocacy of a diplomatic track to US–Central American foreign policy to supplement Reagan's well-developed military track. His insider's perspective of US (read Reagan-era) policy foibles and follies vis-à-vis Central America lend credence to this interesting analysis of Central American politics from the late 1970s to the late 1980s. The main strength of the book lies in the detailed, telling intricacies of international policy-making, priority setting and diplomacy. This unusual and close perspective makes it a valuable contribution in spite of its brevity and cursory treatment of history and politics.

501 **Wilson doctrine: how the speech of President Wilson at Mobile, Alabama, has been interpreted by the Latin-American countries.**
Policarpo Bonilla.   New York: [n.p.], 1914. 42p.
A response to Woodrow Wilson's address of October 1913 in which he publicly stated his intention to oppose foreign (i.e., European) intervention in the hemisphere in the name of democracy. In this statement the president of Honduras summarizes Latin American reaction and speaks for the region, noting that Latins fear Yankee intervention more than they do the European efforts, both because of proximity and because of Wilson's policies.

135

Constitution, Laws and Judicial System

502 **Análisis comparativo de las constituciones políticas de Honduras.**
(Comparative analysis of the political constitutions of Honduras.)
Edited by Ramiro Colindres Ortega. Tegucigalpa: Corporación
Editora Nacional, 1988. 4th ed., corrected and enlarged. 139p. bibliog.

The complete text of the 1982 constitution is printed in full, and there are brief
summaries of the several constitutions preceding 1982. Honduras was a member of the
short-lived Central American Republic whose constitution was promulgated in 1823;
the first constitution by Honduras as an independent nation was in 1839; other
constitutions were passed in 1865, 1873, 1880, 1894, 1906, 1908, 1924, 1936, 1957, and
1965. The author notes that the 1982 constitution, while advanced in its concepts, is
implemented only partially in reality, as many of its articles represent only the good
intentions of the legislators. An autonomous electoral tribunal is introduced in this
document to separate political partisanship from influencing national elections.

503 **Boletín del Congreso Nacional.** (Bulletin of the National Congress.)
Tegucigalpa: Congreso Nacional, [1982?]- .

Presents transcriptions of the plenary meetings. There are numerous errors in volume
designation and many issues were published out of chronological order. Some
supplements are called *Boletín Especial* and earlier volumes were issued under the title
Boletín Legislativo del Congreso Nacional (c.1958). It is published on an irregular
basis.

504 **Breve historia constitucional de Honduras.** (A short constitutional
history of Honduras.)
José Francisco Martínez.   Tegucigalpa: Asembleas Constituyentes,
Congresos Ordinarios y Extraordinarios, Consejos de Estado, Consejos
de Ministros, 1979. 239p. bibliog.
A journalist and professor makes objective comments about historical and political
imperatives that resulted in the various constitutions under which Hondurans have
lived from 1825 to 1965. In this three-part work he presents a brief legislative history,
and the principal characteristics of the Honduran constitution and the national
assemblies. There are several plates of illustrations depicting national symbols such as
buildings, the national emblem, tree and flower.

505 **Competencia territorial del poder judicial hondureño.** (Territorial
obligations of Honduran judicial power.)
Armando Urtecho López.   Tegucigalpa: Universitaria, 1988. 42p.
(Colección Cuadernos Jurídicos, no. 3).
Describes the territorial limitations and obligations of all Honduran judicial circuits.

506 **Derecho mercantil.** (Commercial law.)
Laureano F. Gutiérrez Falla.   Buenos Aires: Editorial Astrea, 1985- .
bibliog.
In this first volume we find a heavily footnoted review of commercial law in Honduras
as of 1985. Based on a study of the *Código de Comercio* (Code of Commerce) of
Honduras promulgated in 1950, the author makes comparisons with the mercantile
codes of other countries such as Italy and Belgium. He also analyses statutes
concerning the start-up of a business, mergers and acquisition, stocks, contracts, debts
and liquidation. This work would be of immense value to anyone desirous of
establishing a business in the country. The contents of volume 1 concerned business.
Subsequent volumes seem not yet to be available.

507 **La estadística en Honduras.** (Statistics in Honduras.)
Tegucigalpa: Ministerio de Economía, Dirección General de Estadística
y Censos, 1977. 110p.
A compilation of laws, regulations, and decrees concerning the accumulation and
publication of statistics, specifically by the General Office of Statistics and Censuses.

508 **Estatuto jurídico de la Bahía de Fonseca y régimen de sus zonas
adyacentes.** (Juridical statute of the Bay of Fonseca and regulation of its
adjacent zones.)
Roberto Herrera Cáceres H.   Tegucigalpa: Universitaria, 1989. 288p.
5 folding maps. bibliog.
The Gulf (or Bay) of Fonseca is of fundamental economic and strategic interest for the
three surrounding nations: El Salvador, Honduras and Nicaragua. Although the three
nations are in agreement regarding their exclusive sovereignty over the waters *vis-à-vis*
the international community, each country maintains divergent opinions about their
legal rights and jurisdictions within the boundaries of the water body. Herrera Cáceres,
professor of international law at UNAH, explores the most important issues at stake,
including geographical, historical and juridical questions.

Constitution, Laws and Judicial System

509 **Export–import laws and decrees of Honduras and implementing regulations, 1976-1988.**
Tegucigalpa: Ministry of Commerce, 1988. 101 leaves.

Eighteen laws, agreements, decrees, exemptions and implementing regulations concerning export and import processing and regulation are compiled and published here in English. Four items date from the latter 1970s; the remainder are dated from 1984 through to August 1988, that is, issued during the presidency of José Azcona Hoyo. Decree no. 356 issued on 6 December 1972 established several free-trade zones; the Puerto Cortés Free Zone was decreed on 19 July 1976. The last agreement included concerns over the procedure of migratory facilities to foreign investors and merchants.

510 **Expropriation in Central America and Panama: processes and procedures.**
Robert C. Casad.   Buffalo, New York: W. S. Hein, 1975. 188p. bibliog.

The process of expropriation of private property and the procedures to accomplish this are examined for each Central American country and Panamá. Honduras is treated on pages 43-59. Its basic constitutional provisions as promulgated in 1965 and relating to private property and expropriation are first set forth, the state's power of expropriation and the purposes for which it is permitted are examined, and the expropriation procedures are outlined. The expropriation laws treat foreigners and Hondurans alike. Modifications to these processes and procedures may have occurred since publication of this work.

511 **La Gaceta, diario oficial de la República de Honduras.** (The Gazette, Official Record of the Republic of Honduras.)
Tegucigalpa: Government of Honduras, 1876- .

A daily publication of laws, decrees, ministerial orders and decisions, and legal notices published by the government. It also includes international agreements. The title and agency names vary and it lacks an index.

512 **Historia constitutional e institucional de Honduras, y derecho interno y derecho internacional.** (Constitutional and institutional history of Honduras and domestic law and international law.)
Ramón E. Cruz.   Tegucigalpa: [n.p.], 1976. 3rd enlarged ed. 133p. bibliog.

A compilation of nine articles written between 1957 and 1970 by Cruz and others about the constitutional history of Honduras (with comparisons of the 1965 and 1967 constitutions), international relations and relations with Nicaragua. An earlier edition was published in Tegucigalpa by Imprenta López in 1964[?].

513 **Historia del poder judicial de Honduras.** (History of the judicial power
of Honduras.)
Carlos Arita Palomo. Tegucigalpa: Universidad Nacional Autónoma
de Honduras, Editorial Universitaria, 1982. 44p.

A brief history of the Supreme Court of Justice from 1821 to 1982 written by a former
presiding justice of the Suazo administration. It is especially useful for the
identification of individuals who served on the bench during each presidential
administration.

514 **Honduras.**
Thomas H. Reynolds, Arturo A. Flores. In: *Foreign law:
current sources of codes and legislation in jurisdictions of the
world (Vol. 1, Western hemisphere).* Littleton, Colorado: Fred
B. Rothman, 1989. 16p.

A brief summary of Honduran laws and where to locate them. The bibliography is in
alphabetical order by subject and includes both Spanish-language sources and English
when the original has been translated. It appears that the laws relating to air, banking,
business, citizenship, copyright, commercial code, civil procedure, insurance, labour,
mining, natural and marine resources, oil, property, social security and trademarks are
available in English translations in a variety of sources. One may consult this volume to
discover where.

515 **Honduras law digest.**
In: *Martindale-Hubbell Law Digest. Canadian and International Law
Digest.* Summit, New Jersey: Martindale-Hubbell, 1991.

Contains twelve pages of summarized and translated information about nearly all
aspects of Honduran law from absentees to wills. Citations are given for specific codes
and sections.

516 **Honduras y la problemática del derecho internacional público del mar.**
(Honduras and the problem of international maritime law.)
H. Roberto Herrera Cáceres. Tegucigalpa: UNAH, 1975. 264p.
bibliog. (Colección Investigaciones Jurídicas).

A high-level government official and solicitor, the author sets forth the Honduran
position on its maritime sovereignty as presented at the third United Nations
Conference on the Law of the Sea in 1974. Appendices (p. 209-61) contain documents
as they were presented at the conference.

517 **The independence of the supreme courts in Latin America: a review of
the literature.**
Joel G. Verner. *Journal of Latin American Studies* (Great Britain),
vol. 16, no. 2 (1984), p. 463-506. bibliog.

The author notes that scholars have paid scant attention to the assessment of the
independence of supreme courts in Latin America. Generally speaking, the scholarly
consensus is that there exists a wide variety of reasons why the courts are politically
dependent and dominated by their political environments. There are, however,
noticeable variations among the countries and over time. He classifies the courts of

Constitution, Laws and Judicial System

countries in six groups along an independent–dependent continuum: independent-activist, attenuated-activist, stable-reactive, reactive-compliant, minimalist (Peru, Ecuador, Bolivia, Panamá, El Salvador, Guatemala, and Honduras), and personalist.

518 **La justicia penal en Honduras.** (Criminal justice in Honduras.)
Luís Salas, José María Rico.   San José, Costa Rica: Editorial
Universidad Centroamericana, 1989. 192p.

Discusses the underpinnings of the Honduran criminal justice system from a theoretical and methodological perspective and within its social, historical and political context.

519 **Labor law and practice in Honduras.**
Anna Stina Ericson.   Washington, DC: US Department of Labor,
Bureau of Labor Statistics, 1961. 37p. map. bibliog. (BLS report, no.
189).

Intended to provide background material for US businessmen and other Americans employing local workers in Honduras in the 1960s. Provides very detailed information concerning the conditions of employment, hours, pay, holidays, record and reports, employee services, compensations, and the like. Students of contemporary labour history will find the statistical tables and charts dating from the late 1950s useful.

520 **Legislación de aguas en América Central, Caribe y México: El Salvador,
Haiti, Honduras, Jamaica, México, Nicaragua, Panamá, República
Dominicana.** (Maritime legislation in Central America, the Caribbean
and Mexico: El Salvador, Haiti, Honduras, Jamaica, Mexico,
Nicaragua, Panama, Dominican Republic.)
Prepared by Magno Tulio Sandoval.   Rome: Organización de las
Naciones Unidas para la Agricultura y la Alimentación (FAO),
1975- . bibliog. (Estudios Legislativos, no. 8).

A compilation of laws, decrees, agreements and regulations concerning water rights for the named countries. It includes bibliographical references to specific treaties and laws.

521 **Legislación indigenista de Honduras.** (Indian legislation in Honduras.)
Ernesto Alvarado García.   México: Instituto Indigenista
Interamericano, 1958. 97p. (Ediciones Especiales del Instituto
Indigenista Interamericano, no. 35).

A compilation of laws and decrees dating from 1829 to 1953 concerning the treatment of Indians and the disposition of their lands. There have been very few juridical dispositions on behalf of the Indian population because, in theory at least, they are to be considered brothers and equals in the eyes of the law without regard to race and cultural background. Yet, the author laments, there are many cases where they have been woefully exploited and taken advantage of by the better-educated Ladinos.

522 **Leyes municipales iberoamericanas.** (Iberoamerican municipal laws.)
Manuel Ortuño. Madrid: Unión de Ciudades Capitales
Iberoamericanas, 1989. 4 vols. bibliog. (Colección de Estudios
Municipales).
Pages 297-361 of volume four contains the full text of the Honduran constitution and
the laws relating to municipal and political conduct.

523 **La mujer ante la legislación hondureña.** (Women in Honduran
legislation.)
Francisco J. Blanco. Tegucigalpa: Talleres Tipo-Litográficos Aristón,
1955. 203p.
A compilation of dispositions relating to women. Extracted from the laws, codes and
regulations of the country, the dispositions concern family and marriage, public health,
education, prostitution, labour, civil rights, and other topics.

524 **Recopilación de las constituciones de Honduras, 1825-1965.**
(A compilation of Honduran constitutions, 1825-1965.)
Tegucigalpa: La Universidad, 1977. 619p. (Publicación del Instituto de
Investigación Jurídica, no. 7).
In three parts, the volume reproduces 20 distinct versions of Honduran constitutions,
approved or not, complete with sections and articles. In part one, the two constitutions
were in effect while the Spanish were in control (1808-12); part two presents the
Federal Constitutions of 1824, 1835, 1898 and 1921; part three presents other
constitutions in effect or proposed from 1825 to 1965. A very useful volume for
studying the constitutional history of Honduras.

525 **A statement of the laws of Honduras in matters affecting business.**
Dante Gabriel Ramírez, Roberto Ramírez. Washington, DC:
General Secretariat, Organization of American States, 1981. 4th ed.,
revised and enlarged. 292p.
Written expressly for businessmen, attorneys and others interested in legislation
concerning business affairs. Each volume of the series emphasizes the commercial,
industrial, labour law and related matters of a given member nation. Transportation,
natural resources, family, economic controls and health are other topics treated in this
volume on Honduras. Each section mentions general principles and the specific articles
of regulation in the constitution and appropriate codes of law. Use of this document is
severely hampered by the lack of a table of contents or an index. This volume
supersedes the earlier three editions published by the Inter-American Development
Commission (1st ed., 1947) and the Legal Division, Pan American Union (2nd and 3rd
eds, 1965).

Administration and Local Government

526 **Honduras: an area study in government.**
William Sylvane Stokes. Madison, Wisconsin: University of
Wisconsin Press, 1950. 351p.

According to Stokes, the Honduran political system has endured monarchy, empire, federation, representative-republic, military dictatorship, semi-parliamentary rule and elected presidents as forms of government for its people. In his work the author sets out to explore the various forms of Honduran government by a thorough investigation of archival materials, and public and private Honduran libraries. He also conducts interviews with politicians, and representatives of high society and the common people, and gives us observations of politics and government in action. He adeptly traces the political evolution from discovery to the late 1940s, discusses the various constitutions, analyses the organizations and procedures of colonial and modern courts and describes the 'spoils system' electoral system. There is a translated copy of the 1936 constitution on pages [301]–28.

527 **Honduras: monumentos históricos y arqueológicos.** (Honduras:
historical and archaeological monuments.)
Daniél Fernando Rubín de la Borbolla, Pedro Rivas. México:
[Pan American Institute of Geography and History], 1953. 98p. map.
(Monumentos Históricos y Arqueológicos de América, 8).

A presentation of the legislation enacted to preserve and protect the Honduran national patrimony from 1845 through to 1952. Many of the decrees specifically concern administration of the archaeological treasures located at the Copán site. Forty photographs of stelae and temples at Copán are included. Colonial religious architecture and artefacts of Comayagua are illustrated by another 21 photographs.

528 **Honduras y su división político-territorial.** (Honduras and its political divisions.)
J. Alfonso Berganza D. Tegucigalpa: [n.p.], 1982. 20p.
A brief history of the administrative and political divisions of Honduras. Several maps show the changes in the divisions.

529 **Housing policies in Central America: political and economic constraints.**
James A. Goodrich. *Habitat International*, vol. 6, no. 4 (1982), p. 461-70.
By means of a comparative analysis of housing policies in Honduras, El Salvador and Costa Rica the author discusses parallels in governmental performance and policy content, political and economic restraints that limit options for housing choices, problems of institutional change, and housing policy subsystems.

530 **Los municipios de Honduras.** (The municipalities of Honduras.)
Carmen Fiallos. Tegucigalpa: Editorial Universitaria, 1989. 347p. tables. (Colección Realidad Nacional, no. 24).
Provides descriptions of the 18 departments and 289 municipalities of Honduras. Each entry includes historical, geographical, population, legal and social information. The entries are arranged in alphabetical order by department, and then municipality.

531 **Plan de desarrollo metropolitano del Distrito Central: EDOM 1975-2000.** (Central District metropolitan development plan: EDOM 1975-2000.)
Dirección General de Urbanismo. Comayaguela: SECOPT, 1976. 100p. maps.
The plan consists of a brief history of urban development in Tegucigalpa, charts showing the growth of the city, and commercial, residential and industrial area plans for various sectors of the city. The work includes useful maps of the zones under consideration. The plan is also known as EDOM (Esquema Director de Ordenamiento Metropolitano) 1975-2000.

Statistics

532 **Anuario estadístico.** (Statistical yearbook.)
Tegucigalpa: Dirección General de Estadística y Censos, 1952- .
A comprehensive compilation of demographic, economic, social and cultural data for the national level and for departments. This description is based on the 1982 edition. Earlier volumes were issued under the agency's earlier name *Dirección general de censos y estadísticas*. Volumes are also available as part of Chadwyck-Healey's *Latin American and Caribbean official statistical series on microfiche* (Cambridge: Chadwyck-Healey, 1979-).

533 **Boletín estadístico mensual.** (Monthly Statistical Bulletin.)
Tegucigalpa: Banco Central de Honduras, Departamento de Estudios Económicos, 1972- .
Provides statistical tables on money and banking, public finance, external commerce and national accounts. Also summarizes new economic, financial and fiscal legislation. This title continues the *Boletín estadístico* published by the same body.

534 **Consumer markets in Central America, 1984 edition.**
London: Euromonitor, 1984.
Pages 83-108 are concerned with Honduras. The purpose of these business reports is to assist in the assessment of the potential of developing regions as consumer markets. Drawing upon statistical information from a variety of sources, including the OAS, national statistics, IMF, UN and others, there is a country-by-country survey of major consumer markets, giving imports and sales in categories such as foodstuffs, pharmaceuticals, household goods and electrical appliances.

535   **Cuentas nacionales de Honduras, 1975-1984.** (National Budget for
       Honduras, 1975-84.)
       Tegucigalpa: Banco Central de Honduras, [1985?]. 69p.

A wealth of statistical data is presented on the national income and gross national
product (GNP) of Honduras for a ten-year period. It chiefly consists of tables clearly
depicting a breakdown of financial data. Following the United Nations' stipulated
methodology, the participants in the national transactions are grouped by three
sectors: business, individuals and non-profit institutions, and the government.

536   **Estadísticas del producto e ingreso nacional, 1925-1952, según un
       sistema de contabilidad económica.** (Statistics for national production
       and income, 1925-52, according to a system of economic accounting.)
       Manuel Tosco. Tegucigalpa: [n.p.], 1954. 109p.

A treasure trove of time-series statistical information about and analyses of Honduran
gross national product and income from 1925 to 1952.

537   **Honduras en cifras.** (Honduras in figures.)
       Tegucigalpa: Banco Central de Honduras, Departmento de Estudios
       Económicos, 1963- .

A brief summary of data in all sectors of Honduran life: economics, society, commerce
and industry, education, electricity and water, national product and consumption,
balance of payments, tourism and cooperatives. The description is based on the
1984-86 edition, published in 1987. It includes tables and graphs. The bibliographer
has verified the existence of compilations for the years 1963-64, 1971-73, 1975, and
1982-88.

538   **Statistical yearbook.**
       United Nations Department of Economic and Social Affairs, Statistical
       Office. New York: United Nations, 1948- . annual.

Published in English and French, this annual compendium offers a tremendous amount
of statistical data on a wide variety of topics including manpower, agricultural and
industrial production, population, manufacturing, mining, infrastructure, energy,
housing, health, education, science and technology. Some charts include time-series
data from the previous decade.

539   **Statistical yearbook for Latin America and the Caribbean, 1989.**
       United Nations Economic Commission for Latin America and the
       Caribbean. Santiago de Chile: United Nations, 1990. c.800p.

An annual publication that represents a compilation of hundreds of statistical tables
concerning Latin America and the Caribbean and covering a wide range of socio-
economic data. Tables include data on social development and welfare, economic
growth, domestic prices, capital formation and financing, trade balance, debt,
population, national accounts, production, social conditions, and other topics.

Economics

540 **An analysis of credit use in the Honduran agrarian reform sector.**
Randy Steven Stringer. PhD dissertation, University of Wisconsin,
Madison, 1984. 285p. (DAI 45/02A, p. 586).

Land reform is a relatively recent phenomenon in Honduras. More than 90 per cent of
the redistribution has taken place since 1972 and virtually all has occurred since 1962.
Most of the land has come from the public sector, and this has created two problems.
First, the Honduran government has not had the time to establish an effective
institutional infrastructure to administer the reform. Second, most reform beneficiaries
are settled on low-quality land. The focus of this study is on providing credit to
reformed-sector *campesinos*. Its main themes are the obstacles which block the
efficient use of production credit in the reformed sector. An important conclusion is
that while credit may be a necessary condition for improving the economic
performance of the reform groups, it is not a sufficient one under the present 'rules of
the game'. [Based on the author's abstract].

541 **Bananos y política: Samuel Zemurray y la Cuyamel Fruit Company en
Honduras.** (Banana plantations and politics: Samuel Zemurray and the
Cuyamel Fruit Company in Honduras.)
Mario Argueta. Tegucigalpa: Universidad Nacional Autónoma de
Honduras, Editorial Universitaria, 1989. 153p. maps. bibliog.

One of the main reasons Honduras has been stereotyped as a 'banana republic' comes
from the plantations established along the north coast by three banana companies:
Standard Fruit, United Fruit and Cuyamel Fruit. The establishment and operations of
the latter company and its founder are scrutinized in this work which offers an
economic and political history of Honduras at the beginning of this century and shows
the web of intrigue and manipulation which allowed the fruit companies to operate this
banana enclave. Articles about this company published at an earlier date are reprinted
in the appendix.

542 **Central America: the future of economic integration.**
Edited by George Irvin, Stuart Holland. Boulder, Colorado; San
Francisco; London: Westview 1989. 206p. bibliog.

In this collection of essays written by university professors and Central American
specialists, various aspects of the reconstruction of the region's industrial and trading
system from the 1960s onwards are addressed. The rôle of the European Community is
given special attention as is the crisis of the Central American Common Market. The
contributors suggest that the European Community could play a unique rôle in
engendering the economic integration of the five countries while promoting more
effective and efficient models for growth. The work contains graphs and tables to
illustrate salient points by contributors.

543 **Central American cauldron.**
Richard Millett. *Current History*, vol. 82, no. 481 (Feb. 1983),
p. 69-73, 81-2.

A renowned authority on Central America, Millett discusses some of the economic and
political problems of Central America in the early 1980s.

544 **Central American Recovery and Development Task Force report to the
International Commmission for Central American Recovery and
Development.**
Edited by William Ascher, Ann Hubbard. Durham, North Carolina:
Duke University Press, 1989. 462p. bibliog.

These fifteen essays first critically assess the prospects for regional development by
synthesizing knowledge of Central America's domestic and economic problems, and
then go on to offer specific creative recommendations for policy-makers. Honduran
examples abound throughout the essays, but regional development is the main focus.
Some chapters discuss topics little covered elsewhere; notable essays are those on
environmental conservation, ecotourism, health care, and opportunities for women.
Central American debt and the prospects for regional economic integration are
addressed and illustrated. The work is also valuable for its appraisals of US
development initiatives such as the Alliance for Progress, the Caribbean Basin
Initiative (CBI), and the Kissinger Commission report. Relationships among trade,
aid, and reforms are clarified through these analyses.

545 **Centroamérica en el siglo XVIII: un intento de explicación económica y
social.** (Central America in the eighteenth century: an attempt at an
economic and social explanation.)
Juan Carlos Solorzano Fonseca. *Estudios Sociales Centroamericanos*
(Costa Rica), vol. 11, no. 32 (1982), p. 11-22. bibliog.

Using documents from the Archives of the Indies in Seville, the author attempts to
analyse economic and social transformations, exploitation, social organization, and the
political life of Central America from the late seventeenth century through to the
eighteenth century, and then to relate these to the tensions of early nineteenth-century
Central America. As Spanish descendants began to establish large cattle ranches and
Indians lost control of agricultural production many changes occurred in Honduras,
Nicaragua, and El Salvador. This and other social transformations had their roots in
the Indian uprisings of the nineteenth century and the confrontations between

Economics

Guatemala and the other Central American provinces over economic and political problems during the 1820s and 1830s.

546 **Coffee and its economic role in selected Latin American countries.**
Neil B. Ridler. *Desarrollo Rural en las Américas*, vol. 12, no. 2 (1980), p. 157-63. bibliog.
Considers the costs and benefits of the coffee boom as they affected Costa Rica, Honduras, Guatemala, Nicaragua, El Salvador and Colombia. Ridler cites the unprecedented fiscal, monetary and political problems generated after 1975 which resulted from over-dependency on the international coffee market.

547 **La construcción del sector público y del Estado nacional de Honduras, 1876-1979.** (The making of the public sector and national state of Honduras, 1876-1979.)
Mario Posas, Rafael del Cid. Ciudad Universitaria Rodrigo Facio, Costa Rica: Editorial Universitaria Centroamericana, 1981. 254p. bibliog.
The authors explore the expansion and functional differentiation of the Honduran state apparatuses as seen through signs of international and domestic capital investment and a class struggle. After an in-depth historical analysis of Honduran politics and economics from 1876 to 1979, the authors, both sociologists, conclude that with the régime of Juan Manuel Gálvez (1949-54), institutional modernization got its major impetus and continued uninterrupted for 30 years in response to pressures from 'imperialist' international organizations.

548 **Country profile: Guatemala, El Salvador, Honduras.**
London: Economic Intelligence Unit. 1986- . annual.
An annual summary of economic data for the countries named. Serves as a companion publication to *Country report: Guatemala, El Salvador, Honduras*. Prior to 1986 it was called the *Quarterly Economic Review of Guatemala, El Salvador, Honduras*.

549 **Country report: Guatemala, El Salvador, Honduras.**
London: Economic Intelligence Unit. 1986- . quarterly.
The 'analysis of economic and political trends every quarter' regularly monitors political, economic and business conditions on a quarterly basis. It tracks quarterly economic indicators and highlights important events that have an effect on economic trends in each country. Useful for regular comparative and time-series statistics, it uses a worldwide network of specialists and sources of data. A companion publication to the annual *Country profile: Guatemala, El Salvador, Honduras* (q.v.). It was formerly titled *Quarterly Economic Review of Guatemala, El Salvador, Honduras*.

550 **La crisis económica en Honduras, 1981-1984.** (The economic crisis in
Honduras, 1981-84.)
Introduction by Antonio Murga Frassinetti, analysis and evaluations by
the United Nations Economic Commission for Latin America (ECLA).
Tegucigalpa: Centro de Documentación de Honduras (CEDOH):
Postgrado Centroamericano de Economía, 1985. 158p. bibliog.

This first joint effort between the Honduran Documentation Centre and the Central
American Postgraduate School of Economics and Planning Development offers a
collection of essays concerning the serious economic crisis facing Honduras since 1980.
The first chapter of the work is a careful review of the major factors of the crisis from
1981 to 1984, written by Antonio Murga Frassinetti while he was a visiting professor at
UNAH. After a relatively accelerated and sustained economic period from 1955 to
1978 Murga cites factors such as the political crises of the Central American region,
fiscal deficits, (im)balance of payments, high loan rates and the vulnerability of an
economy based on exported products as a few of the reasons for the Honduran
economic crisis after 1980. Subsequent chapters are year-by-year analyses of economics
statistics compiled by the United Nations Economic Commission for Latin America
and Honduran agencies. Included are many tables representing all aspects of the
nation's economic status, e.g., GNP, expenditures, exports, and principal economic
indicators.

551 **Crisis y reactivación económica.** (Crisis and economic reactivation.)
Miguel Calix Suazo. [Tegucigalpa?]: [n.p.], 1987. 230p.

As a professor in the Faculty of Economic Sciences, UNAH, and former director of
the Department of Economic Studies at the Central Bank, Calix Suazo is highly
qualified to examine and suggest strategies for improving the economic plight of
Honduras. In this work, he presents a dozen lucid essays concerning various aspects of
inflation; monetary policy and the energy crisis; public and private banking within a
Central American context. His chapter on the energy problems facing the nation and
his recommendations is a particularly interesting one.

552 **De estructura económica y banca central: la experiencia de Honduras.**
(Concerning economic structure and central banking: the experience of
Honduras.)
Carlos F. Hidalgo. Madrid: [n.p.], 1963. 133p. bibliog.

The interplay between the Central Bank and the structure of the national economy is
the main focus of this doctoral study. National income, the history of the Central
Bank, taxation, all aspects of agricultural production for export and domestic
consumption are a few of the major issues discussed. The book includes several tables.

553 **The determinants of international reserves in the small open economy:
the case of Honduras.**
Paul Burkett, Javier Ramirez, Mark Wohar. *Journal of
Macroeconomics*, vol. 9, no. 3 (1987), p. 439-50. bibliog.

The authors examine the international-reserve changes occurring in Honduras from
1960 to 1983 when the currency exchange rate was fixed at two lempira to the US
dollar. Their conclusions indicate that changes in Central Bank credit were a reaction
to changes in the income terms of trade.

Economics

554 **Development and destruction: interrelated ecological, socioeconomic, and nutritional change in southern Honduras.**
Susan C. Stonich. PhD dissertation, University of Kentucky, 1986. 409p. (DAI 47/03A, p. 0963).
This study examines the multi-level and interrelated effects of economic development on the ecological, socio-economic, and nutritional systems of southern Honduras. Viewing development in evolutionary perspective, this research traces the uneven history of attempts to develop the region economically from the time of the Spanish Conquest to the 1890s and the resultant integration of the region into the world economic system. The research concludes that development has exacerbated inequalities in access to land, making most households increasingly dependent on wage labour, migration, and transfer payments from family members living outside the co-residential unit. Simultaneously, the emphasis on export agriculture has not provided adequate employment opportunities. The result has been widespread resource scarcity (land as well as wage labour/cash alternatives) and nutritional inadequacy for large segments of the population. [From the author's abstract].

555 **Dollars and dictators: a guide to Central America.**
Tom Barry, Beth Wood, Deb Preusch. New York: Grove, 1983. 282p.
The Preface claims that 'with detailed documentation, *Dollars and dictators*, offers a clear definition of imperialism. It is a meticulous accounting of the complex political–economic cultural component of US society that dominates Central American life'. In Part one the authors demonstrate how free-market policies further the pattern of concentrated wealth, power and foreign control over domestic development agendas. Several chapters highlight agriculture, industry, finance, the military, and foreign aid. Part two consists of case-studies. That of Honduras appears on pages 163-79 and is very useful for its list of US companies and subsidiaries operating in Honduras as of 1983. Appendices include a chronology from 1900 to 1982 of US involvement in the region, and comparative statistics for businesses in Central America.

556 **Economics of sorghum and soil erosion control technologies for small hillside farmers in southern Honduras.**
Miguel Angel López Pereira. PhD dissertation, Purdue University, 1990. 249p. (DAI 51/09A, p. 3163).
The author's abstract explains that 'the two technologies analyzed are stone walls and ditches combined with permanent legume trees for erosion control of the the hillside lands, and the new sorghum cultivars, Sureno and Catracho, combined with chemical fertilizer and insecticide. The objectives of this study were to estimate the potential impact of these technologies, as well as key resource constraints and government agricultural policies, on the income and productivity of small farmers in the region.'

557 **The economies of Central America.**
John Weeks. New York: Holmes and Meier, 1985. 209p. bibliog.
Provides a general overview of the political economy of Central America. Data on Honduras are included in sections on gross national product, balance of payments, agricultural production, manufacturing, foreign trade, and foreign debt. The author

notes the major problem confronting Honduras in the 1980s was the balance of payments. He projects that a restructuring of Central American economies will be enforced by negative growth, declining living standards, and economic disintegration. The text is followed by an index.

558 **Estudio económico de la aldea de Flores.** (Economic study of the town of Flores.)
Tegucigalpa: Instituto de Investigaciones Económicas y Sociales, Universidad Nacional Autónoma de Honduras, 1964. 76p. bibliog.

The socio-economic study of the community of Flores in Comayagua Department was conducted for the purpose of formulating an agricultural development plan. It discusses land tenancy, urban markets, communication, transportation, demographics, agricultural techniques, cattle raising and other factors affecting production. The many statistical tables provide an in-depth examination of a typical Honduran village in the 1950s to 1960s period.

559 **Growth and crisis in the Central American economies, 1950-1980.**
Hector Pérez Brignoli. *Journal of Latin American Studies* (Great Britain), vol. 15, no. 2 (1983), p. 365-98. bibliog.

The author traces the economic conditions of Central America that gave rise to the current political crisis in the region. He proposes that the change from the prosperity of the 1950s to the crisis of 1978-79 was accompanied by increasing economic inequality, and that that created conditions which fostered social conflict and political mobilization.

560 **Honduras: a problem in economic development.**
Vincent Checchi. Westport, Connecticut: Greenwood, 1977. 172p. maps. bibliog. (Reprint of the 1959 ed. published by Twentieth Century Fund, New York).

Provides an overview of the economic development of Honduras at mid-century, with an assessment of the country's growth potential. Checchi examines the infrastructure, extractive and manufacturing industries, labour force, tourism, and financial situation. He summarizes the negative and positive factors for economic growth and recommends a programme for development which remains a challenge for Honduras: improve education, promote foreign investment and tourism, control inflation, conserve natural resources, build roads, and promote Central American economic integration.

561 **Honduras: crisis económica y proceso de democratización política.** (Honduras: economic crisis and the process of political democratization.)
Tegucigalpa: Centro de Documentación de Honduras, 1990. 105p. bibliog.

Three chapters, written by prominent academics of the Honduran College of Economists, delve into the process of democratization, the economic crisis of the 1980s, and the College's recommendations for the 1990s.

562 **Impuesto sobre la renta y lo contencioso administrativo.** (Income tax
and administrative disputes.)
Enrique Flores. San José, Costa Rica: Editorial Universitaria
Centroamericana, 1973. 542p. bibliog.

An in-depth examination of Honduran income tax law with particular reference to
national and international (double taxation) concerns. This work is of interest mainly
to students of tax law.

563 **Informe económico.** (Economic Report.)
Tegucigalpa: Banco Central de Honduras, Departamento de Estudios
Económicos, 1983- . annual.

An annual review of the Honduran and world economies. It is accompanied by a
lengthy statistical appendix.

564 **Los límites de la acción estatal bajo situaciones reformistas: los casos de
Honduras (1972-1975) y Panamá (1968-1980).** (The limits of state
action in reformist situations: the cases of Honduras, 1972-75, and
Panama, 1968-80.)
Rafael del Cid. *Estudios Sociales Centroamericanos*, vol. 13, no. 38
(1984), p. 13-39. bibliog.

Based on the public documents of Panamá and Honduras. The author compares and
contrasts reforms in Panamá and Honduras which he considers to have contributed to
the expansion and diversification of the public sector. As public-sector investment rose
rapidly and foreign debt increased, the large public external debt became unwieldy for
weak economies and made them dependent upon external fluctuations. Payments on
the foreign debt resulted in disaster for the local economy and contributed to moving
these societies into a downward spiral of underdevelopment and economic chaos.

565 **The Morgan–Honduras Loan, 1908-1911.**
Juan E. Paredes. New Orleans: The author, 1911-12. 3 vols.

An account of the Honduran debt situation, denouncing the government of President
Miguel Dávila and the arrangement with Morgan, which was adopted owing to a
conflict of claims that arose when British bondholders demanded custody of the railway
because of non-payment of outstanding loans, and the government signed agreements
granting custody to the British while giving an American control of the same line,
resulting in an Anglo-American clash. At the suggestion of Washington, a new loan
was worked out with Morgan and Co., involving a financial receivership, which the
author denounces as a violation of the nation's sovereignty. The volumes consist of
collections of the pertinent correspondence, agreements, and other documents, with
some narration.

566 **Nineteenth-century Honduras: a regional approach to the economic history of Central America, 1839-1914.**
José Guevara Escudero. PhD dissertation, New York University, 1983. 510 leaves. maps. bibliog. (Available from University Microfilms International).

A thorough investigation of the Honduran socio-economic structure after gaining independence and becoming a sovereign nation through World War I. The author provides substantial geographical data, noting the social and spatial distribution of the population and the towns, and investigates land distribution and usage. He analyses the economies of three distinctive geographical areas and their interaction with the national and regional economies. He notes that the rugged topography hindered large-scale economic development, so the economy was largely pastoral and subsistence farming. The economy did maintain diverse exports and trading partners until the Liberal Party reforms which advanced the mining and banana sectors and re-oriented the national economy towards the US market. The author's use of primary sources such as censuses, foreign trade reports, customs invoices, and ship registers provides a wealth of economic data which he has compiled into numerous tables. For its contribution to understanding political economy, social structure, and demography, this is an essential work for an otherwise little-studied period in Honduran economic history.

567 **Peasant economy and agrarian reform in the north-central highlands of Honduras.**
Phillip Ray Herr. PhD dissertation, Columbia University, 1988. 380p. (DAI 49/10A, p. 3070).

Agrarian reform has been frequently mentioned as one of the primary reasons Honduras has not been influenced by the strong pressures for social change that have been felt in neighbouring Central American nations. This study, based on fieldwork undertaken in 1981 and 1984-85, analyses the dynamics of the reform process in Honduras and the conditions that give rise to peasant mobilization and resistance. The findings indicate that the general deterioration of rural living conditions, caused by the expansion of commercial agriculture and the increased concentration of land, has resulted in insecure tenure arrangements for peasant households. Dependence on off-farm labour has increased in the wake of these changes, leaving many households in a precarious economic situation. Consequently, peasants have forged alliances with unions and local development brokers in order to obtain land, and have occupied parcels of land near their communities. [Author's abstract].

568 **The political economy of Central America since 1920.**
Victor Bulmer-Thomas. Cambridge; New York: Cambridge University Press, 1987. 416p. map. bibliog.

This is an excellent scholarly examination of economic development in Central America from the consolidation of the export-oriented model in the 1920s through to the mid-1980s. The nature and rôle of economic factors in the present regional crisis is also explored. Textual information is supported quantitatively by numerous charts and tables and by a statistical appendix containing 15 tables with yearly data from 1920 to 1984 for each country, including Honduras. Political and economic references to Honduras are ample throughout this essential study.

Economics

569 **Políticas de ajuste en Centroamérica.** (Adjustment policies in Central America.)
Victor Bulmer-Thomas, Ennio Rodríguez Céspedes, Eduardo Valladares. San José, Costa Rica: Facultad Latinoamericana de Ciencias Sociales, 1987. 119p. bibliog. (Cuadernos de Ciencias Sociales, no. 2).

A paper presented at a 1986 seminar on the Central American economic crisis and focusing on the crisis and politics of stabilization and adjustment in Honduras is included as one of three reports. The other two examine Costa Rica and the entire region. The distinguishing features of the Honduran model of behaviour is set forth by Valladares who demonstrates that prices are much more stabilized in Honduras than elsewhere, with less real deterioration of wages. He considers the major destabilizing element to be the enormous and growing deficit in the balance of payments.

570 **The politics of economic stabilization: IMF standby programs in Latin America, 1954-1984.**
Karen L. Remmer. *Comparative Politics*, vol. 19, no. 1 (1986), p. 1-24.

The politics of economic stabilization in several Latin American countries, including Honduras, is evaluated with regard to the implementation of International Monetary Fund (IMF) programmes from 1954 to 1984. The question of authoritarianism as a necessary condition for achieving economic stability, and the IMF standby arrangements under democratic and authoritarian régimes, are scrutinized.

571 **Privatization in developing countries: ideal and reality.**
Lim Gil-Chin, Richard J. Moore. *International Journal of Public Administration*, vol. 12, no. 1 (1989), p. 137-61. bibliog.

The authors examine the issue of privatization, using Honduras as a case-study. 'Direct administration' and 'contracting out' are compared for three construction-related activities: urban upgrading for housing projects, rural roads, and primary schools. The conclusions indicate that the usual expectations of contracting out were not met due to institutional barriers and the lack of market competition.

572 **A revolving fund to provide the capital for self-help: rural women's small production units in Honduras.**
Stephen Jarrett. *Assignment Children*, vol. 51-52 (1980), p. 141-53.

In an effort to improve its rural development programme for children's services, a revolving credit fund was created by the Honduran government for organized groups of women interested in starting small production projects. A fruit and vegetable bottling cooperative in La Antigua and a children's clothing production unit in Colomoncagua were two successful projects from which all funds were fully recuperated, thus ensuring funding for other self-help projects.

573 **The short-run relationship between inflation and output changes in developing countries: the case of Latin America (El Salvador, Guatemala, Honduras).**
Farhad Saboori.   PhD dissertation, Indiana University, 1985. 189p.
(DAI 46/09A, p. 2759).

The relationship between output growth, inflation and monetary growth is analysed for the three small open economies of El Salvador, Guatemala, and Honduras, for the period 1960-82. One of the issues discussed is the response of real output changes to the unanticipated rate of inflation. While most studies in industrial countries have shown a positive response of real output to unanticipated price changes, the opposite results emerge in developing countries, particularly those with high and variable inflation rates. [Author's abstract].

574 **The structural roots of crisis: economic growth and decline in Honduras, 1950-1984.**
Hugo Rolando Noé Pino.   PhD dissertation, University of Texas, Austin, 1988. 257p. (DAI 49/11A, p. 3458).

Honduras experienced rapid economic growth during the period between 1950 and 1979. During the first half of the 1980s, however, a severe economic crisis hit the country. This study adopts a radical structuralist approach and determines that the reasons for crisis were not only the contraction of the world economy at the beginning of the 1980s, but also the structural characteristics of the pattern of economic growth in Honduras between 1950 and 1979. These characteristics are caused by the existence of dualism and dependency in the economy. [Author's abstract].

575 **Studies in the economics of Central America.**
Victor Bulmer-Thomas.   New York: St. Martin's, 1988. 246p. bibliog.

This book brings together several excellent essays written by the British scholar between 1983 and 1987, on the general theme of Central American economics. The first part embraces long-term studies looking at the transformation of the economy from 1920 and identifies the strengths and weaknesses of an agricultural export-driven model. Part two concerns the issues surrounding the rise and fall of the Central American Common Market. Lastly, in the section entitled 'Central America in Crisis', the author investigates the economic decline from 1979 to 1987 and the balance of payments. Each article is followed by a section of bibliographical notes which reveal research based upon Honduran government and international agency documents. The work contains statistical tables and an index.

576 **Taxes and tax harmonization in Central America.**
Virginia G. Watkin.   Cambridge, Massachusetts: Law School of Harvard University, 1967. 519p. maps. bibliog.

Now quite dated, this work provides substantial data on taxation in Honduras in the mid-1960s. The tax laws enacted prior to 31 March 1966 are compiled on pages 306-72. Customs duties, sales, transactions and miscellaneous taxes, property taxes, income tax, inheritance and gift taxes are all thoroughly examined.

Investment, Finance, Banking and Currency

577 **Agricultural lending costs in Honduras.**
C. E. Cuevas, D. H. Graham. In: *Undermining rural development with cheap credit*, edited by D. W. Adams, D. H. Graham, J. D. von Pischke, p. 96-103. Boulder, Colorado: Westview, 1984.
An overview of problems related to borrowing money for large and small agricultural projects in Honduras.

578 **Aspectos monetarios de la economía de Honduras.** (Monetary policies of the Honduran economy.)
Edmundo Valladares. Tegucigalpa: Banco Central de Honduras, Departamento de Estudios Económicos, 1970. 158p. bibliog.
In his introduction to the analysis of the Honduran monetary policy the author studies the policies and practices as they were in the late 1960s. Initial chapters deal with the supply and demand for capital along with theoretical instruments for evaluating the monetary policies of the recent past. Subsequently the author, an official in the Economic Studies Department of the Central Bank, presents a simplified model of the Honduran economy with the proposed monetary policy in a national context. He concludes with a chapter on short-term monetary planning. Throughout the text he offers theoretical suggestions for improving the economic policies of Honduras. Since this study is full of statistical charts and economic equations it would be very useful to anyone studying the economic history of Honduras.

579 **Business Latin America.**
New York: Business International Corporation, 1966- . weekly.
An excellent weekly business report on events and trends in Latin America, with frequent coverage of Central America and occasional articles on Honduras.

580 **Catálogo de monedas y medallas de proclama de Centro América y Panamá.** (Catalogue of coins and commemorative medallions of Central America and Panama).
Felipe Siliézar Ramos. Guatemala: Eros, [1977?]. (Distributed in the US by Almanzar's Coins of the World, San Antonio, Texas).
A photographic guide to the coins of Central America dating from 1733 to 1976 and including those minted in or for Honduras.

581 **Central American monetary union.**
John P. Young. Washington, DC: Agency for International Development, 1965. 180p.
A seasoned economist in Central American affairs lays out a plan for uniform currency as part of a Central American economic integration programme. His report makes comparisons with the European Economic Community and offers a great deal of information on the regional economics of Central America.

582 **The copper coinages of the Republic of Honduras, 1878-1920.**
Tom DeLorey. *Numismatist*, vol. 102, no. 9 (1989), p. 1416-24, 1479-84.
A numismatist specializing in Honduran coinage, DeLorey candidly chronicles the tumultuous history of the many copper issues by Honduras from the late nineteenth and early twentieth centuries. Minting coins in Honduras has been challenging at best since the Tegucigalpa Mint opened in 1823 under the short-lived rule of Augustín Iturbide. Over the years, the Mint opened and closed as political circumstances changed, with final closure occurring in 1920. Since 1931, Honduran coins have been struck in the US Mint. The difficulties in obtaining minting equipment – dies, punches, metals and engravings – in addition to the political upheavals, has resulted in many unique issues of questionable quality. His analyses of alterations-by-exigency to punches and dies are quite amusing.

583 **El escándalo del ferrocarril: ensayo histórico.** (The railroad scandal: historical essay.)
Alfredo León Gómez. Tegucigalpa: [n.p.], 1978. 198p. bibliog.
A detailed analysis of the unfortunate events that unfolded as a result of loans made to Honduras by European bankers in the nineteenth century for the purpose of building an inter-oceanic railroad. The author minutely describes the tragic and dramatic financial fiasco that undermined the international credit of the country for many decades.

584 **External shocks and fiscal deficits in a monetary model of international reserve determination: Honduras, 1960-83.**
Mark Wohar, Paul Burkett. *Applied Economics* (UK), vol. 21, no. 7 (1989), p. 921-9. bibliog.
The authors tested a simultaneous equation model of reserve determination which dealt with the effects of external interest rates, income terms of trade, real income and the domestic credit of the Central Bank during the period from 1960 to 1983.

Investment, Finance, Banking and Currency

585 **Historia de la moneda de Honduras.** (History of Honduran coins.)
Arturo Castillo Flores. Tegucigalpa: Banco Central de Honduras,
1974. 233p., 31 leaves of plates. bibliog.
An authoritative history of the coin in Honduras. Unfortunately the table of contents is
difficult to find, coming as it does after the main text. The work includes chapters on
the coin in pre-Columbian times, colonial times, during the periods of Independence
and Federation, after Federation, the official lempira coin and the Central Bank of
Honduras as the sole coin minter. The text is followed by a photographic section
depicting hundreds of coins.

586 **Historia financiera de Honduras. Informes de las misiones Arthur N.
Young, 1920-21, Bernstein, 1943, y del Fondo Monetario Internacional,
1949.** (Financial history of Honduras. Reports from the Arthur N.
Young, 1920-21, Bernstein, 1943, and International Monetary Fund,
1949 missions.)
Tegucigalpa: Banco Central de Honduras, 1921-50. 3 vols in one. map.
Contains three separate studies by foreign financial consultants about the Honduran
economic situation from 1920 to 1949, and provides many statistical tables on national
income and expenditures.

587 **Honduras investment guide.**
Tegucigalpa: Investment Promotion Office, General Directorate of
Foreign Trade, 1986. 33p.
This illustrated guide to investment opportunities in Honduras for the entrepreneur
provides background country information in addition to details about potential
commercial projects in private enterprise. The legal aspects of doing business in
Honduras are lightly touched upon.

588 **Intermediation costs and scale economies of banking under financial
regulations in Honduras.**
Carlos E. Cuevas. PhD dissertation, Ohio State University, 1984.
291p. (DAI 45/06A, p. 1826).
Transaction costs borne by financial intermediaries and borrowers are the focus of this
study. The effects of financial regulations on intermediaries' costs and borrowers' costs
are analysed. Particular attention is given to interest-rate regulations and selective
credit policies. Translogarithmic cost functions are the basis for measuring and
analysing the costs of the National Agricultural Development Bank of Honduras, the
largest private commercial bank in the country. [Based on the author's abstract].

589 **Memoria anual.** (Annual Report.)
Tegucigalpa: Banco Central de Honduras, Departamento de Estudios
Económicos, 1951- . annual.
Devoted primarily to an account of the Bank's activities during the year, the report
also contains a review of the economy paralleling that in the *Informe económico*
published by the Bank (q.v.). The title varies slightly. Over the years, the Bank has
also published a number of other series such as *Revista trimestral*, and *Boletín*.

590   **A monetary history of Honduras, 1950-1968.**
      Frank Falero, Jr.   Lexington, Kentucky: Office of Business
      Development and Government Services, College of Business and
      Economics, University of Kentucky, 1972. 115p. bibliog.
Centres on the history of the development of Honduras in terms of its monetary policy
from 1950 to 1972. Special consideration is given to the creation, organization, goals
and policies of the Central Bank which, in turn, greatly affected the monetary policies
pursued by the bank. Finally, a spectral and cross-spectral analysis of the bank's
policies is made in order to detect lead and lag relationships that might have affected
overall economic development. The author has used and reproduced a number of
equations and statistical tables to illustrate his points.

591   **The right to a periodic dividend in Honduras.**
      Laureano F. Gutiérrez Falla.   *Arizona Journal of International and
      Comparative Law*, vol. 1987, p. 73-100.
The right of company stockholders to receive periodic dividends is not expressly
established in Honduran law, but when analysed together, several sections in the *Civil
Code* and basic precepts in commercial law lead one to conclude that such a right does
exist. A professor of law at UNAH bases this study and his conclusions on a thorough
analysis of the pertinent codes and sections in Honduran law and draws analogies with
the laws of other countries.

Trade, Commerce, Industry and Mining

592 **Central America: regional integration and national political development.**
Royce Q. Shaw. Boulder, Colorado: Westview, 1978. 242p. bibliog.
Difficulties encountered by the Central American Common Market are surveyed and analysed. The effects of the internal Honduran political situation which contributed to the 1969 Soccer War with El Salvador, and attempts at reconstruction after the war and through to 1978, are considered on pages 129-79.

593 **Comercio exterior de Honduras.** (Honduran foreign trade.)
Tegucigalpa: Ministerio de Economía, Dirección General de Estadística y Censos, 1978- . quarterly.
Summarizes data and statistics relating to the import and export commerce of Honduras. Formerly entitled *Comercio exterior de Honduras: Exportación* and *Comercio exterior de Honduras: Importación*.

594 **El Salvador and economic integration in Central America: an econometric study.**
Gabriel Siri. Lexington, Massachusetts: Lexington Books, 1984. 204p. bibliog. (Wharton Econometric Studies Series).
Although focused upon El Salvador, this study of necessity includes data on Honduran trade with El Salvador and other countries in the region. The author has developed a macroeconomic model of El Salvador which forms the basis of his study, but he also developed mini-models of the Central American economies, including Honduras. Of particular note is a section analysing the effects of the 1969 war between Honduras and El Salvador (pages 190-6). The work is indexed.

595 **Empresas del sector social de la economía.** (Businesses of the social sector of the economy.)
Sigfrido Burgos Flores.   Honduras: Lithopress Industrial, 1986. 237p. bibliog.
Discusses cooperation and cooperative endeavours between the business and social sectors of the economy.

596 **La explotación bananera en Honduras: capítulos del deshonor nacional.** (The banana trade of Honduras: chapters of national dishonour.)
Enrique Flores Valeriano.   Tegucigalpa: Departmento Editorial de la UNAH, 1979. 229p.
An indictment of the dependency of Honduran economics and politics on the multinational banana monopolies of the Northern coast. Examines the 1975 scandal of United Fruit's US$ 1.25 million payment in bribes to Honduran officials and the continued influence of the Tela Railroad Company and Standard Brands. The appendix includes a dozen documents detailing concessions and contracts with the banana companies.

597 **Export agriculture and the crisis in Central America.**
Robert G. Williams.   Chapel Hill, North Carolina: University of North Carolina Press, 1986. 257p. bibliog.
The US policy of encouraging export expansion and diversification and other measures for the promotion of private-sector growth as a means to promote social stability in Central America is challenged in this excellent examination of the cotton and cattle trades which are considered the most successful examples of this policy. Reasons for each boom, its beneficiaries and its effects on the average person are explored, and the relationship between the export-oriented policy and the political crisis is examined. This work provides statistics on cotton and beef production and export for Honduras and, more importantly, recounts incidents of the effects of this policy in Honduras, such as little-known peasant repressions and three massacres in Olancho which took place in 1975. This is a most valuable socio-economic study which provides a substantial challenge to the US economic cure for Central American instability.

598 **Facts relating to the Rosario Mine.**
New York and Honduras Rosario Mining Company.   New York: N. F. Seeback, 1882. 20p.
Extracts from reports regarding the Company's silver mine, seeking to promote investment.

599 **Foreign direct investment of expatriate entrepreneurs: the case of Honduras.**
David Robert Befus   PhD dissertation, University of Miami, 1986. 162p. (DAI 47/11A, p. 4132).
The purpose of the study was to identify the investment activity of expatriate entrepreneurs and profile their personal characteristics. The expatriate entrepreneurs' investment activity is compared to that of multinational companies, and their personal

characteristics are compared to other entrepreneurial populations. The economic development impact of expatriate investors is explored. [From the author's abstract].

600 **La formación del estado y el orígen minero-mercantil de la burguesia hondureña.** (The formation of the state and the mining-mercantile origins of the Honduran bourgeoisie.)
Guillermo Molina Chocano. *Estudios Sociales Centroamericanos* (Costa Rica), vol. 9, no. 25 (1980), p. 55-89.

During the administrations of Marco Aurelio Soto and Ramón Rosa, the liberal reform movement fostered the revitalization of mining as the main component of capitalist expansion in Honduras from 1875 to 1930. A small, native bourgeoisie developed, thanks to European and North American capital and technology, and redirected state resources to benefit the mining industry. The success in mining resulted in a growing demand for domestic and foreign consumer products which encouraged the bourgeoisie into commercial endeavours.

601 **A geographic analysis of the beef cattle industry in Honduras.**
Ralph H. Alderman. PhD dissertation, Michigan State University, 1973. 198p. bibliog. (Available from University Microfilms International).

Research on specific industries in Honduras is rare. This thoughtful analysis of the cattle industry whose primary purposes are beef production and exportation focuses on the geographical distribution of the industry and provides insights into management, labour, and social implications.

602 **Honduras: an export market profile.**
H. C. Bolling. Washington, DC: US Department of Agriculture, 1984. 196p. (Foreign Agricultural Economic Report).

Describes Honduras as a modest but steady consumer of US agricultural goods that may purchase as much as $75 million of US farm products by 1990. That would be an increase of only $51 million since 1980, a year in which the United States exported more than $41 billion of agricultural commodities worldwide. It is suggested that Honduras increased farm imports throughout the seventies because of population growth instead of an expanding economy. One of the poorest countries in Central America, it is predicted that Honduras will probably continue to experience a sluggish economic growth and greater external debt in the eighties. The report includes several statistical tables.

603 **Honduras rotaria.**
Tegucigalpa: Rotary Club of Tegucigalpa, 1943- . irregular.

The official organ of the Rotary Club of Tegucigalpa offers news about local business and businessmen.

604 **Honduras: the new El Dorado.**
New Orleans: J. G. Hauser, 1909. 24p.

A brief and glowing description of the nation's resources and development, stressing its prospects and the high returns to investors. The focus is on gold-mining prospects, but copper is also discussed.

605 In quest of El Dorado: precious metal mining and the modernization of Honduras, 1880-1900.
Kenneth V. Finney. New York: Garland, 1987. 454p. bibliog. (South American and Latin American Economic History Series).
An excellent in-depth socio-economic study of the development of gold and silver mining in late 19th-century Honduras.

606 The international directory of importers: South/Central America.
Healdsburg, California: Distributed by Blytmann International, 1983- . biennial.
A biennial source listing the 42 major importing firms in Honduras. Arranged in alphabetical order by country, it provides, again in alphabetical order, the name, addresses, telephone number, current major imports and number of employees. Following the alphabetical list is a classified section by product type.

607 International investment of expatriate entrepreneurs: the case of Honduras.
David R. Befus (et al.). *Journal of Small Business Management (JSBM)*, vol. 26, no. 3 (1988), p. 40-7.
A fascinating investigation of expatriate entrepreneurs in Honduras which revealed a thriving international business sector in the developing country. Based on a survey conducted in 1985, the study gathered information concerning the motivation for investment, types of companies started, market orientation, and individual profiles of the entrepreneurs.

608 International narcotics control strategy report.
Washington, DC: US Department of State, Bureau of International Narcotics Matters, 1991. 397p.
Pages 151-4 describe activities in Honduras to counteract the drug trade. Because of its poorly policed coastline, it continues to serve as a trans-shipment location for cocaine. A large radar system is being installed to permit better tracking and a National Drug Council was established in 1990. Small amounts of cannabis are cultivated in scattered, small plots. Local abuse of drugs is limited but will presumably increase. An admittedly unreliable statistical table of seizures and arrests follows the text.

609 Labour in the colonial mining of Honduras.
Linda Newson. *Americas (Academy of American Franciscan History)*, vol. 39, no. 2 (1982), p. 185-203. bibliog.
Different types of labour were used simultaneously in the gold and silver mines of colonial Honduras, but their importance changed from century to century. The use of black slaves was more prevalent in the early 'golden age' of gold mining. During the 17th century when profitability was minimal, Indian labour drafts predominated, and free labour became increasingly important in the 18th century. Newson's research is based on documents in the Archivo General de Indias.

Trade, Commerce, Industry and Mining

610 **Luchas del movimiento obrero hondureño.** (Struggles of the Honduran labour movement.)
Mario Posas. San José, Costa Rica: Editorial Universitaria Centroamericana, 1981. 274p. maps. bibliog. (Colección Seis).

The organization and struggles of the North Coast workers in the banana enclave are vividly recounted, with an in-depth history of the 1954 strike which resulted in the legalization of the workers' organizations. Statistical data on the United Fruit Company and banana industry ranges from 1945 to 1956. The appendix includes documents by the organizers of the unions directed toward the Tela Railroad Company.

611 **Production and politics in Central America's convulsions.**
Samuel Stone. *Journal of Latin American Studies* (Great Britain), vol. 15, no. 2 (1983), p. 453-69.

Stone examines production and political factors in five Central American countries from the 1960s to the early 1980s. He reasons that differences in the availability of land for export crops, labour and capital have an affect on the methods and customs applied to cultivate the main export products. The differences have a direct effect on the evolution of governments: in the northern countries (Guatemala, El Salvador, Honduras), the ruling families have served an economic function, whereas in Nicaragua and Costa Rica it has become political.

612 **Silver mining in Colonial Honduras.**
Linda A. Newson. *Revista de Historia de América*, no. 97 (Jan.–June 1984), p. 45-76. maps. bibliog.

A serious historical study of silver mining in colonial Honduras, based on primary source documents, in which the economic factors, labour and social ramifications of the industry are considered. The article includes several tables and charts.

613 **Training for development of small industries: an analysis of four approaches applied in Honduras.**
Julio Daniél Ramírez de Arellano. PhD dissertation, University of Massachusetts, Amherst, 1985. 384p. (DAI 46/03A, p. 0590).

This study explores variables that seem to affect the results in four different cases of training in programmes for the development of small industries in Honduras. Prior to the presentation and analysis of each case, data about small industries in Honduras are provided, and the programmes where the cases were implemented are also described. Recommendations made at the end of the study deal with topics such as the previous experience field personnel should have, the practical orientation of training, and the use of the entrepreneurs' innovations and experiences as an input for training. [Author's abstract].

Forestry

614   The cattle are eating the forest.
Billie R. DeWalt.   *Bulletin of the Atomic Scientists*, vol. 39, no. 1
(1983), p. 18-23.
A critical look at the changes in land use from the production of basic food grains by
peasants to livestock production for export by wealthier individuals. It challenges the
notion that food shortages in developing countries are due to overpopulation and
asserts that cattle grazing results in deforestation, a decline in the production of grain
crops, and increases competition between poor farmers and cattle for limited
resources. The author asserts that the primary beneficiaries of this trend are North
American pets and their owners who are the ultimate consumers of Central American
beef.

**615   Conservation and indigenous human land use in the Río Platano
watershed, Northeast Honduras.**
Edited by Jeffrey W. Foehlich, Karl H. Schwerein.   Albuquerque,
New Mexico: University of New Mexico, Latin American Institute,
1983. 94p. maps. bibliog. (Research Paper Series. University of New
Mexico, Latin American Institute, no. 12).
A comprehensive survey of the Río Platano Biosphere Reserve, which enjoys a
measure of official protection since it falls within the limits of a national archaeological
park. This final report of a 1981 University of New Mexico survey includes much
background information on man's past and present utilization of the region;
mammalian and floral documentation; and concludes with recommendations for the
future of this endangered ecosystem. Some of the recommendations are: the relocation
of some cultivated fields from upstream closer to the inhabited areas; restrictions on
hunting and fishing should be instituted; transportation and travel difficulties should
not be ameliorated (although they do recommend limited tourism and scientific
expeditions); and a quota system to prevent overfishing.

616 **Diagnóstico socio-económico sobre el consumo y producción de leña en Honduras.** (Socio-economic analysis of wood consumption and production in Honduras.)
Jeffrey Ronald Jones, Alfonso Pérez G. Turrialba, Costa Rica: Centro Agronómico Tropical de Investigación y Enseñanza CATIE, Departmento de Recursos Naturales Renovables, 1982. 80p. bibliog. (Applied Anthropology Documentation Project, no. 913).

With the objective of identifying critical and potentially critical areas of deforestation, the Proyecto Leña y Fuentes Alternas de Energia surveyed over 425 farmers and 75 owners of fuelwood-consuming industries and fuelwood merchants. The fuelwood market in Honduras is highly developed, with over 30 per cent of farm families purchasing all or part of their fuelwood. Large cities such as Tegucigalpa, San Pedro Sula and Choluteca pose the greatest problems since local fuelwood sources are seriously depleted. The analysis of the survey has produced many statistical tables, but no recommendations to remedy the situation. An English summary is provided.

617 **Honduras: women make a start in agroforestry.**
M. Wiff. *Unasylva*, vol. 36, no. 4 (1984), p. 21-6.

A brief report on Honduran women working on agroforestry development projects.

618 **A program for fostering the economic growth and development of the Republic of Honduras through investments in forestry.**
Seymour I. Somberg. PhD dissertation, Duke University, 1962. 251p. bibliog.

As he explains in his abstract, the author attempts to demonstrate the possible effects of the development of the forestry subsector of an underdeveloped economy upon the total economy of a nation possessing abundant natural forest resources.

619 **Survey of pine forests: Honduras. Final report.**
Rome: United Nations Development Programme, Food and Agricultural Organization of the United Nations, 1968. 80p. maps.

The report, prepared for the Government of Honduras by the Food and Agriculture Organization (FAO), describes the remaining pine forests and indicates types of pines and their geographical distributions.

Agriculture, Land Tenure and Agrarian Reform

620 **Agrarian structure and political stability in Honduras.**
   J. Mark Ruhl. *Journal of Inter-American Studies and World Affairs*,
   vol. 26, no. 1 (1984), p. 33-68. bibliog.
Ruhl contends that in spite of its poverty, Honduras seems to be more politically stable
than El Salvador. Compared to El Salvador, Honduras has had fewer of the small
marginal farms and instead maintains more medium-sized land holdings resulting in a
lower proportion of landless and extremely poor peasants, and an active land reform
programme. Thus, Honduran *campesinos* have had an interest in the existing system
and some independence. The article is based on documents from the Honduran
government, the Inter-American Development Bank and other agencies.

621 **Agricultural credit in Honduras.**
   Economic Commission for Latin America.   New York: United
   Nations, 1950. 38p.
A study of the credit situation in 1950, with recommendations for the improvement of
financing available to agriculture.

622 **Bananas: from Manolo to Margie.**
   George Ancona.   New York: Clarion, 1982. 48p.
Follows the route of a banana from Manolo in Honduras, where it is grown, to Margie
in North America, where it is eventually consumed. The ample illustrations and
photographs provide a glimpse of rural Honduran life on a 'finca', a large farm or
plantation.

Agriculture, Land Tenure and Agrarian Reform

623 **Bibliografía agrícola de Honduras, 1977-1979.** (Agricultural bibliography of Honduras, 1977-79.)
Tegucigalpa: Centro de Documentación e Información Agrícola, Secretaría de Recursos Naturales, 1980. 105p.
A major bibliography of Honduran sources for agriculture and land tenure. There is also an earlier version published by the same centre: *Bibliografía agrícola nacional: suplemento*, 1972-1977 (1978. 51p.).

624 **Compilación de los estudios básicos del diagnóstico del sector agrícola.** (Compilation of the basic studies relating to the analysis of the agricultural sector.)
Tegucigalpa: Ministerio de Recursos Naturales, Consejo Superior de Planificación Económica y Agencia para el Desarrollo Internacional, 1978. 562p.
A major compilation of a wide variety of studies conducted by many agencies pertaining to the agricultural sector.

625 **Declaración del Partido Comunista de Honduras sobre la Ley de Reforma Agraria.** (Declaration of the Honduran Communist Party on the Agrarian Reform Law.)
Partido Comunista de Honduras. Tegucigalpa: Comisión Política del Comité Central del Partido Comunista de Honduras, 1975. 15p.
The pros and cons, as interpreted by the Honduran Communist Party of the Agrarian Reform Law passed on 30 December 1974. Aspects viewed as pros include the limit of 'territorial' property, the creation of *empresas asociativas de campesinos* (rural workers' cooperatives), restrictions of the semi-feudalistic forms of agricultural production, and the revision of concession and rental contracts. Negative aspects include limits on the *empresas asociativas*, problems with lands left fallow, and conservation of the capitalist *latifundios* [estates].

626 **Diversity, distribution and use of edible and ornamental plants in home gardens in Honduras.**
Lynn Ellen Doxon. PhD dissertation, Kansas State University, 1988. 209p. (DAI 49/07B, p. 2443).
Seventy-five Honduran gardens were analysed in five geoclimatic locations. The types and uses of plants found are catalogued, and qualitative descriptions given of 30€ species found growing in the gardens. Sixty-four per cent of these species were ornamentals, 25 per cent were food plants, 10 per cent were medicinal, and the rest were used for household, seasoning or other uses. This research established that the complexities of Honduran garden systems make a stable and reliable food production system. [Based on the author's abstract].

627 **El café en Honduras.** (Coffee in Honduras.)
Eduardo Baumeister. *Revista Centroamericana de Economía*, vol. 11,
no. 4 (1990), p. 33-78.
In this article, Baumeister thoroughly analyses the Honduran coffee industry from the
early 1970s to 1989. He focuses on the government support of this important
agricultural sector, marketing conditions, the processes of production, and commercialization and exportation. The article contains numerous graphs and tables and a
lengthy bibliography.

628 **Estrategia de desarrollo y reforma agraria: la opción hondureña.**
(Strategy for development and agrarian reform: the Honduran
option.)
Clodomir Santos de Morais. Tegucigalpa: Programa de
Capacitación Campesina para la Reforma Agraria, 1975. 129p.
(Serie didactica, no. 7).
Contains four essays on economic development through agrarian reform, including an
address by President López Arellano on the national plan for development.

629 **Estructura agraria en áreas del Valle de Sula.** (Agricultural structure in
areas of Sula Valley.)
Enrique Astorga Lira. Tegucigalpa: Talleres Gráficas del INA, 1975.
2nd ed. 85p.
Looks at cooperative agricultural efforts in the Sula Valley area.

630 **Evaluación de los asentamientos y cooperativas campesinas en
Honduras.** (Evaluation of rural settlements and cooperatives.)
Enrique Astorga Lira. [Tegucigalpa?]: [Instituto Nacional Agrario],
1975. 2nd ed. 84p.
Based on information provided by the National Census of Settlements and
Cooperatives of the National Agrarian Institute, the author assesses the changes in
land tenure and crop production after the 1972 agrarian reforms. Positive results listed
include: previously abandoned lands used for production; 12,000 families saw higher
earnings; a rise in employment; fewer social tensions in the rural zone; and a more
positive image for the government. Limitations or obstacles included: still not enough
land for all farmers; lack of financing; and weak coordination on the part of
responsible government agencies.

Agriculture, Land Tenure and Agrarian Reform

631 **La evolución de la pobreza rural en Honduras.** (The evolution of rural poverty in Honduras.)
   Guillermo Molina Chocano, Ricardo Reina.   Santiago, Chile: Organización Internacional del Trabajo, Programa Mundial del Empleo, Programa Regional del Empleo para América Latina y el Caribe, 1983. 93p. bibliog.

In four chapters, the authors present a study of the socio-economic characteristics of small-farm workers from the availability of land, crops planted and harvested, ability to produce enough for marketing to other work opportunities, and income generation. The process of agrarian reform and its impact on the agricultural sector and evolution of rural poverty in the framework of overall Honduran economic development are also covered.

632 **The Honduran Agrarian Reform under Suazo Córdova, 1982-1985. An assessment.**
   J. Mark Ruhl.   *Inter-American Economic Affairs*, vol. 39, no. 2 (Fall 1985), p. 63-80. bibliog.

Evaluates the effects of agrarian reform during the administration of Suazo Córdova.

633 **Honduras and the Perry Land Grant: a new field for the farmer, stockman, lumberman and laborer.**
   Chicago: American–Honduras Company, 1888. 55p.

An account of the land grant on the south Caribbean coast of Honduras, which the Honduran government sold to the Company, authorizing settlement and immigration. Most of the volume, which is designed to encourage immigration, is a collection of glowing comments on the unlimited agricultural potential of the region and the crops that could be grown there. The grant clearly lies in the region of the disputed border with Nicaragua.

634 **Honduras: los límites del reformismo castrense, 1972-1979.**
   (Honduras: the limits of Castroist reform, 1972-79.)
   Mario Posas, Rafael del Cid.   *Revista Mexicana de Sociología*, vol. 42, no. 2 (1980), p. 607-48.

In 1972, President Osvaldo López Arellano initiated a programme of land reform. However, most of the land redistributed was state-owned and his reform left large *latifundios* [estates] as they were. His proposals for woodland resources were also unsuccessful and eventually he was overthrown and replaced by Alberto Melgar Castro. Although Melgar Castro's government emphasized economic growth, his administration was equally unsuccessful in tackling land-reform problems and was plagued by drug scandals, graft and bribery. Melgar Castro was forced to resign by the armed forces and a three-man junta was formed to replace him.

635   Los índios de Honduras y la situación de sus recursos naturales.
       (Honduran Indians and their natural resources.)
       L. Fernando Cruz Sandoval.   *América Indígena* (Mexico), vol. 44,
       no. 3 (1984), p. 423-46. bibliog.
The author provides estimates of the Indian population in tabular form and analyses
Honduran legislation concerning its natural resources. He asserts that a significant
number of Indians have no legal rights to the land they have always occupied and that
many titled Indian lands have been illegally taken over by non-Indians. From the early
twentieth century to the 1970s most of the national resources were controlled or owned
by the state and no action had been taken by the national agrarian officials.

636   **Key policy issues for the reconstruction and development of Honduran
       agriculture through agrarian reform.**
       Kenneth H. Parsons.   Madison, Wisconsin: Land Tenure Center,
       University of Wisconsin-Madison, 1978. 22p.
In this supplement to an earlier report *Agrarian reform in Southern Honduras* (Land
Tenure Center, Paper no. 67, March 1976), Parsons states the key policy issues
necessary for reconstruction and development in the agrarian sector as he looks at
processes of agricultural development and increasing employment in agriculture. He
also considers various kinds of farming systems that might be beneficial: individual,
cooperative, communal, and mixed.

637   **Land titling in Honduras: the baseline survey as a means of targeting
       development asssistance.**
       Edgar G. Nesman, Mitchell A. Seligson, Earl Jones.   Rural
       Sociological Society Conference proceedings, 1985. (Available from
       University Microfilms International).
In 1983 the National Agrarian Institute of Honduras initiated a titling assistance
project for peasant farmers who had settled on national lands. Over 700 farmers were
interviewed in 1983 in order to determine the situation at the start of the titling
project. The same farmers were to be interviewed after five years. The results of the
interview indicated that the titling beneficiaries were stable, lived in poverty, lacked
formal education, had little credit experience, yet were interested in receiving technical
advice and had a positive attitude towards land titling.

638   **Man, crops and pests in Central America.**
       George Ordish.   London: Pergamon; New York: Macmillan, 1964.
       119p. (Biology in Action Series, vol. 3).
Insects and fungi that attack the primary agricultural crops of Central America are
described, and methods for natural and artificial control given. The work includes
several illustrations of pests.

Agriculture, Land Tenure and Agrarian Reform

639 **El modelo hondureño de desarrollo agrario.** (The Honduran model of agrarian development.)
Clodomir Morais (et al.). Tegucigalpa: Programa de Capacitación Campesina para la Reforma Agraria, 1975. 141p. bibliog.

Three essays examining the state of agricultural economic development and the possibilities of obtaining increased development through agrarian reform. Several statistical tables are presented.

640 **Modernity and public policies in the context of the peasant sector: Honduras as a case study.**
Carlos O'Brien Fonck. Ithaca, NY: Cornell University, 1972. 148p. bibliog. (Cornell University, Latin American Studies Program. Dissertation series, no. 32).

An astute investigation by an experienced agricultural economist into the agricultural public policies and lack of modernization in the peasant sector of Honduras. Although the public policies of the 1960s to 1970s aimed at expanding farm output, the technocrats, bureaucracy and power structure then in place impeded any improvement in the agricultural output by peasant farmers in the rural zones in favour of the larger farm operators with substantial capital, power and influence. The author discusses many aspects of the economy from 1950 to 1970 and includes many tables and charts of statistics related to farm sizes, family income, farm production, corn, bean and livestock sales and regression analysis. Basing his work on a variety of Honduran governmental papers, United Nations documents and English-language journal articles, he concludes that without genuine peasant pressure groups such as labour unions and associations there would be little change in the distribution of wealth in the Honduras of the future.

641 **Public policy, peasants, and rural development in Honduras.**
Charles D. Brockett. *Journal of Latin American Studies*, vol. 19, no. 1 (1987), p. 69-86.

In this article, Brockett sets out to evaluate the intent, impact and adequacy of US and Honduran public policies related to rural development in Honduras since the 1950s. The author discusses the successes and failures of the US Agency for International Development programmes in the area of agricultural development and the recent history of agrarian reform in Honduras. He concludes that recent trends have not resulted in massive land redistribution in the early 1980s and that many of the country's economic problems are due to the promotion of commercial export agriculture since 1950.

642 **Roots of rebellion: land and hunger in Central America.**
Tom Barry. Boston: South End Press, 1987. 220p. bibliog.

Who owns the land and how it is used is the focus of this investigation of the underlying causes of regional political and economic conflict. The author contends that the greater importance given to export-oriented agriculture rather than to local food needs has benefited a small national élite and the transnational corporations. National food security needs to be the guiding policy for the resolution of the land and hunger crises. Peasant movements for agrarian reform in Honduras are covered on pages 144 to 149; data on land use, malnutrition, exports, and other related topics are sprinkled throughout the text. The book contains illustrations.

643   A study of sorghum diseases in Honduras, their importance under
      different cropping systems, and strategies for their control.
      George Clayton Wall.   PhD dissertation, Texas A&M University,
      1986. 120p. (DAI 47/07B, p. 2710).

Twenty-one sorghum diseases were identified in different sorghum-growing regions of
Honduras, of which eight were studied with regard to their effect on sorghum yield.
Sources of resistance to sorghum downy mildew, gray leaf spot, oval leaf spot, ladder
spot, acremonium wilt, and zonate leaf spot were identified by screening various
international and local nurseries at several locations between 1983 and 1985. [Author's
abstract].

Transportation and Communication

644 **Honduras.**
Frederic M. Halsey. In: *Railway expansion in Latin America: descriptive and narrative history of the railroad systems of Argentina, Peru, Venezuela, Brazil, Chile, Bolivia and all other countries of South and Central America.* New York: Moody Magazine and Book Co., 1916, p. 134-41.
It sounded like a capital idea, but like so many good ideas, the Honduran Interoceanic Railway, conceived by E. G. Squier, fell victim to international political problems and entrepreneurial jealousies. Subsequent efforts by the Honduran government resulted in a few miles of track laid at exorbitant cost and, consequently, high foreign debts. Halsey provides a succinct and coherent overview of the financial arrangements made from 1850 to 1914. Railway routes laid in that period totalled no more than 300 miles, consisted of at least two different gauges, and were operated primarily for the exportation of agricultural produce.

645 **Honduras and the Interoceanic Railway: report on the line and its prospects, being the result of recent personal visits.**
William Alexander Brooks. London: Pottle & Son, 1874. 24p.
A report on the prospects and plans for the railway, written by an enthusiastic supporter of the scheme.

646 **Honduras Interoceanic Railway Company, Limited: prospectus, preliminary report.**
Ephraim George Squier. New York: Tubbs, 1854. 2nd ed., 63p.; London: Charles Whittingham, 1857. 100p. maps.
A detailed survey of the proposed railway and its route, with discussion of the engineering aspects and terrain, stressing its feasibility and prospects. The author was a promoter of the project, and this work was one of his major efforts to secure investment for its completion.

647 **Honduras: its present difficulties and future prospects.**
London: Spottiswoode, 1872. 25p.

A brief tract by a bondholder arguing in favour of pursuing the Honduras Interoceanic
Railway with all possible speed. He contends that political disturbances in that nation
are normal and minor and that the railway would be highly profitable when completed,
and hence that bondholders should be patient and support further investment to rush
the project to completion, ignoring temporary setbacks. The anonymous author
contends that construction of a canal elsewhere in the isthmus is unlikely and would
not in any case have much effect on the profitability of the railway.

648 **Honduras rural roads: old directions and new.**
John Maxwell Hamilton.   Washington, DC: Agency for International
Development, 1981. 60p. 2 maps. (Project Impact Evaluation, no. 17).

A survey of the road system in Honduras and recommendations for new ones.

649 **The Pan American Highway system: a compilation of official data on the
present status of the Pan American Highway system in the Latin
American Republics.**
Washington, DC: Travel Division, Pan American Union, 1969. 79p.
maps. bibliog.

This interesting book provides a brief account of the evolution of the highway, then
describes the route country by country. The 151 paved miles in Honduras are described
on pages 28-9. It is noted that the most interesting parts of the country are not along
this route, and a detour is suggested to Tegucigalpa.

650 **Railways of Central America and the West Indies.**
Rodney W. Long.   Washington, DC: Department of Commerce,
Bureau of Foreign and Domestic Commerce, 1925. (Trade Promotion
Series, no. 5).

This works 'presents very detailed information with respect to all railways in this
territory, covering such phases as the development of the line, the mileage, operating
officials, methods of purchases, finances, traffic statistics, characteristics of the right-of-
way, number of employees, motive power, rolling stock, repair shops and equipment.'
[Letter of submission, p. xvi]. The report, which is the most detailed this bibliographer
has seen concerning the early development of Central American railways, was
prepared through the cooperation of many manufacturers of railway equipment and
railway companies. The section for Honduras appears on pages 54-79 and includes a
historical survey, the full text for the Agrícola de Sula (a subsidiary of Cuyamel Fruit
Company) concession of May 1920, maps, photographs and many diagrams of railway
equipment in use at the time. A must for research on the history of rail transportation
in the region.

651 **Report of Capt. Robert Fitz-Roy, Royal Navy, to the Earl of
Clarendon, on the proposed Honduras Interoceanic Railway.**
Robert Fitz-Roy.   London: Chiswick Press, 1856. 15p.

A brief statement of the case for the feasibility and profitability of the Honduras
railway, rating it superior to other projects and locations.

Transportation and Communication

652 **Report to the directors of the Honduras Interoceanic Railway Company.**
Ephraim George Squier. London: [n.p.], 1858. 102p. maps.
An official report designed to encourage investment in this project, paralleling the author's earlier efforts, and with the usual rich description and emphasis on the feasibility of its construction.

653 **Visionaries and swindlers: the development of the railways of Honduras.**
Delmer G. Ross. Mobile, Alabama: Institute for Research in Latin America, 1975. 134p. maps.
Traces the rise and fall of several railway schemes in Honduras and the many frustrations experienced by the nation as it attempted to promote development by remedying its lack of railways. The principal problem was lack of financing. Neither North Americans or Europeans were prepared to invest in an inter-oceanic railway due to evidence of shady dealings and unfavourable loan terms. Ultimately, lines to the banana plantations became the only lines in the country and all were located on the northern coast. The work is based on published sources and some United Fruit Company documents, and is indexed.

Labour and Trade Unions

654 **AIFLD in Central America: agents as organizers.**
Tom Barry, Deb Preusch.   Albuquerque, New Mexico: Inter-
Hemispheric Education Resource Center, 1990. 76p. bibliog.

A highly informative report documenting the extensive operations of the American
Federation of Labor-Committee for Industrial Organization (AFL-CIO) in Central
America through the American Institute for Free Labor Development (AIFLD),
established in 1959 after the Cuban revolution. The origins, history, financial
operations, training and development programmes of the AIFLD are covered in detail.
Activities in each Central American country are examined and it is noted that
Honduras has been a favoured base of operations where AIFLD works primarily
through the Confederation of Honduran Workers (CTH). The author opines that 30
years of involvement have not contributed to improved conditions for workers and
peasants and that it has indeed prevented the emergence of a radical worker–peasant
alliance by using anti-communism to pit labour groups against each other. There is a
contingent within the US trade unions attempting to change the AFL-CIO's traditional
support of US intervention in foreign labour unions and a list of these groups is
appended to the text along with a 'who's who' of AIFLD and other union
organizations.

655 **Bananas, labor, and politics in Honduras, 1954-1963.**
Robert MacCameron.   Syracuse, NY: Maxwell School of Citizenship
and Public Affairs, Syracuse University, 1983. 166p. maps. bibliog.
(Foreign and Comparative Studies. Latin American Series, no. 5).

In 1954 the employees of the United Fruit Company went on strike for better wages
and working conditions. This act soon grew into a bitter, nationwide general strike.
MacCameron examines the historical background to the protest, describes the strike
process and the interplay between labour organization, labour legislation and politics.
Sources for his research came from the National Archives of Honduras, the National
Library of Honduras and various US government documents, including State
Department correspondence. There are several tables and maps to accompany the
text.

Labour and Trade Unions

656 **Breve historia de las organizaciones sindicales de Honduras.** (Brief history of Honduran labour organizations.)
Mario Posas. [Tegucigalpa?]: Friedrich Ebert Stiftung, [1987 or 1988]. 87p. bibliog.

This is a succinct overview of the many labour organizations of Honduras, both past and present, for wage workers and the peasantry. The first organization created was a mutual aid society for artisans in 1884. This type of association was at its most important in the 1920s with 25 groups enrolling 6,000 members. These societies then founded the Federación Obrera Hondureña in 1921, the first labour confederation. A more militant confederation was founded in 1929 on the North Coast, the Federación Sindical Hondureña. This and other organizations influenced by Marxist proponents continued to expand their base of operations among the important banana plantation workers. Their efforts led to the 1954 strike during which workers passionately challenged their inequitable economic and social conditions and won the right to organize legally. This victory led to new organizations – some of them aligned with particular political parties – formed with outside sources of funding, such as those affiliated with the AFL-CIO's AIFLD (see item no. 654) whose underlying purpose was to thwart Cuban revolutionary influence on the union's leadership. Several recently established organizations are described. Overall, this brief history provides an excellent summary that would be useful to anyone studying the development of labour organizations in Central America or Honduras.

657 **Central America and the Dominican Republic: trade union training for women workers – some encouraging years.**
Petra Ulshoefer. *Labour Education*, no. 61 (1985), p. 18-19.

This article is a description of a project set up to assist national trade union centres with their goals towards the organizing and training of women workers. It provides an overview of the establishment of women's committees as support structures for trade union confederations. The effects of the programme and the responses of women trade unionists are evaluated.

658 **La crisis económica de Honduras y la situación de los trabajadores.**
(The economic crisis of Honduras and the workers' situation.)
Mauricio Montes. Tegucigalpa: Ediciones SITRAUNAH, 1982. 151p. bibliog.

In the early 1980s, during a difficult economic period and after the Sandinista victory in Nicaragua, numerous economic studies were carried out in Honduras, many with the purpose of showing how capitalism had woefully failed, and concluding that the only correct, new path to prosperity was that of socialism. This is one such work. While looking at the agricultural situation in Honduras, problems with industrialization, large landholdings, foreign capital and the deficit, the author traces Honduran economic history from the early 1970s to the early 1980s.

659 **Diagnóstico de los recursos humanos en Honduras, 1960-1972: introducción al estudio del potencial humano.** (An analysis of human resources in Honduras, 1960-72: introduction to the study of the human potential.)
Tegucigalpa: Grupo de Recursos Humanos, Secretaría Técnica del Consejo Superior de Planificación Económica, 1973. 229p.

An analysis of the labour supply in Honduras for the period indicated, with recommendations for future occupational training.

660 **Foreign labor trends: Honduras.**
United States Bureau of International Labor Affairs. Washington, DC: US Department of Labor, 1989. 8p. (Foreign Labor Trends, FLT 89-62).

An annual review of labour laws and conditions based on sources from the Honduran government. The latest issue available to this compiler was 1989 and it covered, very briefly, all aspects of labour from unions to international labour relations.

661 **Historia del movimiento obrero en América Latina. Vol. 2: Guatemala, Honduras, El Salvador, Nicaragua, Costa Rica, Panamá.** (History of the labour movement in Latin America. Vol. 2: Guatemala, Honduras, El Salvador, Nicaragua, Costa Rica, Panama.)
Edited by Pablo González Casanova. Mexico City: Siglo Veintiuno, 1985. 319p.

An excellent study of the history of the labour movement in Latin America, focusing on the 20th century and with contributions by numerous scholars.

662 **Historia del movimiento obrero hondureño.** (History of the Honduran labour movement.)
Víctor Meza. Tegucigalpa: Editorial Guaymuras, 1980. 170p. bibliog.

An impressive history of the working-class movement and its contributions to the socio-political development of Honduras from the late 1800s through to the 1970s. The accomplishments and failures of the various trade unions are recounted and analysed. Special attention is accorded to the grand banana strike in 1954 which the author declares to have been the most important confrontation between labour and capital in Honduran history.

663 **Historia laboral de Honduras: de la conquista al siglo XIX.** (Labour history of Honduras: from the Conquest to the 19th century.)
Mario Argueta. Tegucigalpa: Secretaría de Cultura y Turismo, Dirección General de Cultura, Departamento de Publicaciones, 1985. 204p. bibliog.

An accomplished historian and bibliographer examines Honduran economic and political history from the mid-1500s to the end of the 19th century. Emphasizing the perspective of the under-represented majority, he focuses on the experiences of the blacks, native peoples and poor labourers in the *repartimientos* [assessment of taxes], *encomiendas* [patronage], *haciendas* [estates], and mining enterprises. The work received the Premio de ensayo Rafael Heliodoro Valle in 1983. Use of the work is somewhat hindered by the lack of an index.

664   **The Honduran trade union movement, 1920-1982.**
Richard Swedberg.   Cambridge, Massachusetts: Central America Information Office, 1983. 44p. bibliog.

Swedberg's study traces the growth and development of labour unions in Honduras and the struggle by wage workers for economic and political justice. Descriptions of early organizing efforts in the North Coast banana plantations and the repression they faced is particularly valuable for understanding the conditions which led to the historic 1954 banana strike and the subsequent codification of labour laws and legalization of unions. Labour's progress has been thwarted through repression by the state, banana company policies, US interference and manipulation through the American Institute for Free Labor Development, and, more recently, through the US militarization of Honduras. Labour activists, always harassed, have increasingly been subjected to human rights violations, and the author concludes that labour's demands for economic and political justice have largely remained unmet.

665   **Honduras, el empleo en el plan nacional de desarrollo, 1979-1983.**
(Honduras, employment in the National Development Plan, 1979-83.) Regional Employment Program for Latin America and the Caribbean, prepared by Hector Szretter (et al.).   Santiago, Chile: PREALC, 1980. 116p. bibliog. (Documento de Trabajo / PREALC, 181).

The objective of this study is to evaluate the effects of the National Development Plan for 1979-83 on labour supply in the rural, industrial and basic services sectors of economic activity. Unfortunately, due to the apparent unavailability of information about the transportation, communication and financial sectors, there is no analysis of the labour supply in those fields. The study includes many statistical tables with data from the early 1970s and estimates up to 1983.

666   **Impacto social de las conquistas laborales hondureñas.** (Social impact of Honduran labour victories.)
Ernesto Alvarado Reina.   San Pedro Sula, Honduras: E. Alvarado Reina, 1984. 105p.

The author, a solicitor and notary, explains the basic facts pertaining to Honduran labour laws with the aim of improving worker–manager/owner relations. Commentaries range from the concepts of 'seventh day' and 'thirteenth month' pay, minimum wage, and collective contracts, to unemployment and the corruption of public administrators.

667   **Informal and formal market participation of rural Honduran women.**
Sharon M. Danes, Mary Winter, Michael B. Whiteford.   East Lansing, Michigan: Michigan State University, 1985. 34p. (Working paper, no. 82). bibliog.

This paper 'examines factors that affect women's participation in the market sector. The data were collected in Moroceli, Honduras, in 1981. Participation in the market sector was divided into three categories: not working outside the home, participation in the informal market sector, and participation in the formal market sector. The analysis included cross-tabulation and regression.' [Author's abstract].

668 **Momentos estelares de la participación de la CTH en la vida política nacional.** (Highlights of CTH participation in national political life.)
Mario Posas. Tegucigalpa: Friedrich Ebert Stiftung, 1987. 99p. bibliog.

A history of the powerful Confederation of Honduran Workers (CTH), founded in 1964 and with a current membership of over 200,000. Key events and individual accomplishments are examined as well as combined efforts undertaken with other labour organizations for the advancement of the economic and social welfare of the working class and peasantry. The effect of the CTH on political behaviour is shown through the 1985 confrontation which changed the electoral process inside political organizations. Although briefly mentioned, the CTH's strong affiliation with the American Institute For Free Labor Development is glossed over. Other works need to be consulted to gain a complete picture of CTH's history and political involvement.

669 **El movimiento campesino hondureño: un panorama general, siglo XX.** (The Honduran peasant movement: a general panorama, 20th century)
Mario Posas. In: *Historia política de los campesinos latinoamericanos* (Political history of the Latin American peasantry), coordinated by Pablo González Casanova. Mexico: Siglo Veintiuno Editores, 1984-85, vol. 2, p 28-76. bibliog.

Traces the history of the Honduran rural labour movement from the late 1880s to the early 1980s, with emphasis on that of the *campesinos* [peasants] who did not work strictly for wages from large foreign companies. After analysing the rise and demise, the successes and failures of many rural organizations, the author concludes that the rural, rugged individualist is giving way to a unified peasantry with a sense of class solidarity and the ability to mobilize for interests beneficial to its constituents. Although peasant movements have served to debilitate somewhat the power base of some large, traditional landowners and to modernize the rural sector, the strong conservative reaction from urban social forces has conspired, according to the author, to inhibit the rural classes from reaping total agrarian reform.

670 **Multinationals square off against Central American workers.**
Anne M. Street. *Business and Society Review*, no. 52 (Winter 1985), p. 45-9.

NCC Industries, a multinational garment corporation, has closed down many unionized factories in the past few years. One of them, Hondbra, threw more than 200 Honduran women out of work. Shortly after the factory closed, the Trade Union Federation of Workers of Northern Honduras (FESITRANH) convinced the Honduran government that is should assist in training the workers to sew garments other than the brassières they had formerly produced. The major tasks now facing the company include market development and having enough work for all of the workers.

671 **Problems and promises: vocational development for disabled youth in Honduras.**
Daniel N. Kucij. (Paper presented at the 65th Annual Convention of the Council for Exceptional Children, Chicago, 20-24 April 1987). 1985. 62p.

The author investigates issues in vocational development for handicapped youth in Honduras with the objective of identifying promising employment opportunities where minimal investments of technical aid would have maximum benefits. Interviews were conducted with the parents of handicapped youths, employers and technical assistant agencies. The document concludes with suggestions for a public awareness campaign, professional training, encouragement of integrated school services and employment-generating activities.

672 **The role of the private sector as a provider of industrial training: the case of the Honduran furniture industry.**
Mary Catherine Ott. PhD dissertation, University of California, Davis, 1984. 215p. (DAI 46/02A, p. 0492).

Vocational training programmes in Latin America have emphasized publicly funded solutions to skilled labour shortages. Nevertheless, the private sector remains the dominant source of skilled industrial manpower in many developing countries. This research documents and analyses the contribution firms make to human capital accumulation in a developing country. The case-study is carpentry training in the Honduran furniture industry.

673 **El sector laboral hondureño durante la reforma liberal.** (The Honduran labour sector during the Liberal reforms.)
Mario R. Argueta. Tegucigalpa: Universidad Nacional Autónoma de Honduras, Editorial Universitaria, 1981. 30p. bibliog.

Analysis of the development of the labour sector during the Liberal reform period starting with Marco Aurelio Soto's rise to power in 1876 and ending at the turn of the century. Argueta focuses on the agricultural, mining, infrastructural and artisan sectors of the labour force.

674 **Summary of the labor situation in Honduras.**
Washington, DC: US Bureau of Labor Statistics, 1959. 25p. bibliog.

Prepared for the International Cooperation Administration, Office of Labor Affairs, this overview of the Honduran labour force, labour legislation and trade union movement from 1950 to 1959 was intended to serve as background material for future technical cooperation. The work outlines the provisions of the labour code in effect at the time and provides a significant amount of wage and labour data. Appendices list the trade unions in both Tegucigalpa and the North Coast Federation.

675 **El surgimiento de la clase obrera hondureña.** (The rise of the Honduran working class.)
Mario Posas Amador. *Anuario de Estudios Centroamericanos*, vol. 9 (1983), p. 17-35. bibliog.

Posas documents the problems of mining, banana and urban workers from 1900 to 1920. Wages were low, working conditions unhealthy and hazardous, housing was substandard, and there was a high rate of alcoholism. He contrasts these conditions of the majority with the more favourable situation of the United Fruit Company workers. He also cites the importation of black Caribbean workers as a contribution to further depression of wages, an increase in racial tensions, and exploitation of the working class.

676 **Survey on priority needs for qualified human resources in four Central American and Caribbean countries: Costa Rica, Dominican Republic, Honduras, Republic of Panama.**
Carried out jointly by the Istituto italo-latino americano (IILA) and the Intergovernmental Committee for Migration (ICM). [n.p.]: [n.p.], 1983. 351p. bibliog.

Compiled at the request of the presidents of the four countries, this report addresses the paucity of specialized human resources available locally yet critically needed for the implementation of social and economic development plans. The objectives of the survey were to determine specific priority needs within the national planning of the four countries, and to gather and process available information for a report to be submitted to the governments which might contribute to the financing of the recruitment and placement of highly qualified personnel. The survey focused on public and semi-public institutions and identified the need for over 600 experts in the sectors considered. For Honduras these sectors included agriculture, forestry, industry, mining, energy, public works and infrastructure, research and technology, administration, education, and social infrastructure.

677 **Tendencias ideológicas actuales en el movimiento obrero hondureño.** (Present ideological tendencies in the Honduran labour movement.)
Mario Posas. *Anuario de Estudios Centroamericanos* (Costa Rica), vol. 6 (1980), p. 25-54. bibliog.

Basing his work on labour minority reports, union publications, newpapers, and secondary sources, Posas provides a history of trade unionism in Honduras dating back to the World War I era. Trade unions for the most part were government-controlled and tied to US entrepreneurial interests. As they grew stronger, more aggressive and independent after World War II, the government perceived them to be subversive and subjected them to increasingly severe repression, a policy that continued through to 1979.

Environment and Ecology

678 **The dynamics of social processes and environmental destruction: a Central American case study.**
Susan C. Stonich. *Population and Development Review*, vol. 15 (June 1989), p. 269-96. bibliog.
This article is based on a conference paper and on Stonich's doctoral dissertation written in 1986. She presents evidence that there is a link between agricultural development, the land tenure system, steady demographic changes, the accumulation of capital and the deterioration and destruction of the environment in Southern Honduras. A map, tables, and charts support her contentions.

679 **Hacia una Centroamérica verde: seis casos de conservación integrada.**
(Towards a green Central America: six cases of integrated conservation.)
Stanley Heckandon Moreno (et al.). San José, Costa Rica: Editorial DEI, 1990. 142p. maps. (Colección Ecología–teología).
The ecology of Central America and the need for conservation of its natural resources are examined. A chapter on Honduras (pages 53-68) by Rigoberto Romero and Francisco Martínez investigates water resources for Tegucigalpa whose population continues to increase even though insufficient water supply has been a perpetual challenge. The essay provides data and a map on Tigra National Park outside Tegucigalpa.

680 **Honduras, perfil ambiental del país: un estudio de campo.** (Honduras, an environmental profile of the country: a field study.)
Paul Campanella. McLean, Virginia: JRB Associates, 1982. 201p. bibliog.
Assesses the environmental situation and government policies regarding the conservation and protection of natural resources in Honduras. It includes several photographs.

681 **Natural resources and economic development in Central America: a regional environmental profile.**
H. Jeffrey Leonard. New Brunswick, New Jersey: Transaction Books, 1987. 279p. bibliog.

A very useful source for the study of natural resource use, abuse and exploitation in Central America. Leonard analyses the socio-economic trends of the region and the impact of these trends on the landscape. With specific regard to Honduras, problems stemming from deforestation, illegal wildlife trade, land degradation, use of pesticides, timber production and water usage are among the topics discussed. This scholarly work is well documented and supported by numerous, detailed tables, time-series charts and lists, and includes an index.

682 **La situación ambiental en Centroamérica y el Caribe.** (The environmental situation in Central America and the Caribbean.)
Edited by Ingemar Hedstrom. San José, Costa Rica: Departamento Ecuménico de Investigaciones, 1989. 318p. bibliog. (Colección Ecología–teología).

The ecology of Central America and the environmental policies of its governments are examined in this collection of essays. A chapter on Honduras by Juan Almendares (pages 61-101) considers the ecological effects of the North American military occupation, noting yellow rain, deforestation, and sexually transmitted diseases as having the most deleterious long-term effects on the human ecology and environment of Honduras.

Education

683 **Adult education program of Acción Cultural Popular Hondureña.**
Robert Anthony White. St. Louis, Missouri: St. Louis University,
1972. c.200p. bibliog.
Presents a study of the radio schools conducted by the Movement for Popular
Development from 1950 to 1972. White describes the surge of *campesino* protests for
greater rural development, the three major prongs of the educational programme
(literacy, agriculture, and health), and the promotion of effective political organization
in rural zones.

684 **An agricultural curriculum for the common cycle of general culture of
rural Honduras.**
Anamaria Gómez Rodas de Varela. PhD dissertation, Oregon State
University, 1988. 189p. (DAI 49/10A, p. 3008).
The study attempted to identify the skills needed in agriculture for rural youth in
Honduras and to develop an appropriate agricultural education curriculum at the
Common Cycle of General Culture (lower middle-school level) of the current
educational system. Recommendations were developed for implementation of the new
curriculum as an integral component of the Common Cycle, a teacher preparation
programme, an agricultural youth organization, and programme institutionalization.
[Author's abstract].

685 **Alfabetización y mujeres: la experiencia del proyecto IHDER-ANACH.**
(Literacy and women: the IHDER-ANACH experiment.)
Edited and coordinated by Jan Ooijens (et al.). Tegucigalpa:
Editorial Guaymuras; The Hague: Centre for the Study of Education in
Developing Countries 1990. 169p. maps. bibliog.
A detailed report of a literacy campaign aimed at Honduran peasant women that was
conducted in Cortés department. The socio-economic conditions of the country women
are well documented, and the reasons for undertaking the literacy project are set forth,

as well as the methodology for accomplishing its aims and objectives. One of the more interesting conclusions of the project was that the effectiveness of the literacy classes was greatly improved when they were conducted for women only.

686 **Education in Central America.**
George R. Waggoner, Barbara Ashton Waggoner. Lawrence, Kansas: University Press of Kansas, 1971. 180p. bibliog.

Although somewhat dated, the information contained in the chapter on Honduras still provides a valuable historical overview. Pages 71-87 contain brief sections on background, legal and constitutional bases, administration of the system, pre-primary, primary, secondary, and higher education. Five statistical tables show the numbers and distribution of students and graduates, budgets, and per capita student expenditures.

687 **Education in Central America and the Caribbean.**
Edited by Colin Brock, Donald Clarkson. London; New York: Routledge, 1989. 322p. bibliog.

Case-studies of educational conditions in Caribbean countries are provided for six nations. The politics of adult education in Central America is the focus of one chapter by Gonzalo Retamal. On pages 189-95 he looks at specific projects in Honduras such as the project of Radio Suyapa.

688 **Education in Honduras.**
Maury Weldon Thompson, Marjorie C. Johnston. Washington, DC: Government Printing Office, 1955. 33p. maps. bibliog. (Department of Health, Education and Welfare Bulletin 1955, no. 7).

One of a series on basic education in the American republics initiated in 1943 by the US Office of Education. The study is divided into two parts: background country information, and information on the Honduran educational system as it was in the early 1950s. Several tables are included which give sample programmes of study from elementary through to university-level courses and vocational programmes. Worthy of special note is the timeline on page 9 of the national educational system.

689 **Education in Honduras: a case study of an underdeveloped Latin American republic.**
Fernando Hidalgo. Lynchburg, Virginia: Lynchburg College, 1969. 160p. bibliog. (MEd thesis). 160p. bibliog.

The objective of Hidalgo's study is to provide a picture of the Honduran educational system of the 1960s, its background and future direction. He includes the curricula (preschool to college level) used in the most important schools of the time, a description of the structure and administration of the system and mentions legislation of importance to education. He attributes many of the ills of the school system and the resultant low level of literacy to the overwhelming and negative influence of the Jesuits who, in his opinion, were more interested in an educated upper class than peasantry. But he also blames the lack of professional teacher-training, the absence of relevant (i.e., vocational) curricula and difficult economic conditions. It appears to be very thorough coverage for the period concerned.

Education

690 **Historia de la universidad.** (History of the university.)
Jose Reina Valenzuela. Tegucigalpa: Universidad Nacional
Autónoma de Honduras, 1976. 252p. bibliog.

The author provides details on the evolution of higher education in Honduras, firmly placing the triumphs and travails into conjunction with the political climate of the times. Particularly important is the inclusion of the full texts of laws and decrees establishing and regulating higher educational institutions. The 1975 inaugural message of University Rector Jorge Arturo Reina, in which he sets forth the goals and objectives of the University, is also included.

691 **Honduras.**
George Kurian. In: *World education encyclopedia*, vol. 3, edited by
George Thomas Kurian. New York; Oxford: Facts on File, 1988,
p. 1510-13.

Brief mention is made of education in the colonial period, followed by an overview of the pre-primary, primary, secondary and higher educational systems in place today. The author also devotes a paragraph each to administration, finance, non-formal education, and the teaching profession.

692 **Honduras.**
D. Vega. In: *The encyclopedia of comparative education and national
systems of education,* edited by T. Neville Postlewaite. Oxford:
Pergamon, 1988, p. 329-32. Also in: *The international encyclopedia of
education*, vol. 4, editors-in-chief, Forsten Husen and T. Neville
Postlewaite. New York; Oxford: Pergamon, 1985, p. 2300-3.

After a brief socio-economic description of Honduras, the author focuses on the aims, structure, administration and finance of the Honduran educational system from primary to university level. Also mentioned are aspects of teacher supply, curriculum, examinations, promotions and the major problems. Reference is made to statistics from the late 1960s to the early 1980s.

693 **Honduras, Republic of**
In: *The international encyclopedia of higher education*, vol. 5, editor-in-
chief, Asa S. Knowles. San Francisco, California: Jossey-Bass, 1977,
p. 2047-52. bibliog.

Summarizes the history of the education system of Honduras from the colonial days and the 'Society of Enterprising Thought and Good Taste' (a literary society) to the late 1970s. It is more detailed than the other entries in this section. The legal basis of the educational system, admission requirements, programmes and degrees offered, and student financial aid and access to education are some of the topics discussed that were not found in other sources.

694 **Innovation and Entrepreneurship Development Center: Honduras.**
Leony Yu-Way, Martín Zuniga. *Journal of Small Business Management (JSBM)*, vol. 25, no. 4 (1987), p. 70-3.

In response to an alarming 41 per cent unemployment rate, the Entrepreneurship Development Center was established to promote economic growth and employment. Through the training of business students, improvement of the performance of existing small businesses, identification of new markets and the provision of assistance to would-be entrepreneurs it is hoped that the employment situation will see an upswing.

695 **Lucha por la paz y la cultura.** (Struggle for peace and culture.)
Juan Almendarez. San José, Costa Rica: Editorial Universitaria Centroamericana, 1982. 297p. bibliog.

A collection of articles and public addresses by the rector of the UNAH, focusing on the themes of maintaining the autonomy of the university and keeping it free from government interference in Central America, and on the mission of the university to promote peace in the region. The chapter on science and technology discusses the medical needs of the country. Many of Almendarez' activities and ideas did not suit some members of the military, political or business sectors, nor all the faculty of UNAH and he was replaced by a more conservative rector. He has since become an active human rights monitor and international peace advocate.

696 **A participatory methodology for literacy and health education: the IPREFA integrated project in Choloma, Honduras.**
Luís María Aller Atucha, Catherine D. Crone. *Assignment Children*, vol. 51-52 (1980), p. 141-61.

From July 1978 to June 1980, the Ministries of Public Health and Social Assistance and the Honduras Family Planning Association conducted an integrated rural project that focused on literacy circles. The central thesis of the project in Choloma was a literacy programme based on the perceived needs of the populace. The 1980 evaluation cited satisfactory operation with high impact in several areas and success in many of the stated objectives.

697 **Pensamiento universitario centroamericano.** (University thought in Central America.)
Carlos Tunnerman B. Ciudad Universitaria Rodrigo Facio, Costa Rica: Editorial Universitaria Centroamericana, 1980. 521p. bibliog.

A collective tribute to Central American universities on the occasion of the tricentenary of the founding of the University of San Carlos in Guatemala. Some thirty essays address specific institutions of higher education, but the main topics are autonomy, objectives, reforms, research, and operations which are applicable to all Central American universities. One document specifically concerning Honduras is presented on pages 123-34. Prepared by the organizing committee for the First Meeting of the University Community (Primer Encuentro de la Comunidad Universitaria) held in 1974 at the National Autonomous University of Honduras (UNAH), the paper concerns the role of the University in the present era. UNAH's mission is presented as contributing to the social transformation of Honduras from a dependent and underdeveloped country.

Education

698 **Perspectiva de la enseñanza de la medicina en Honduras.** (Outlook on medical education in Honduras.)
Ramón Alcerro Castro. Tegucigalpa: Universidad Nacional Autónoma de Honduras, Editorial Universitaria, 1982. 214p. bibliog.
An assessment and evaluation of medical school training in Honduras, specifically at the UNAH. Contains a substantial bibliography on pages 128-33.

699 **Plan de desarrollo universitario, 1967-1970.** (University development plan, 1967-70.)
Alberto Mendoza Morales. Tegucigalpa: Universidad Nacional Autónoma de Honduras, [1966?]. 118p. bibliog.
Sets forth the goals and objectives of the National Autonomous University of Honduras (UNAH) for the years 1967 to 1970. Although these plans rarely come to complete fruition in such financially impoverished countries, they serve well to identify the situation of the institution and provide the framework under which the institution operates at a given time. This plan outlines the characteristics of the University: legal status, student and teaching bodies, administration, libraries, physical plant, budget, and future goals. The work contains maps, illustrations, statistical tables and graphs.

700 **Principios de la reforma universitaria: consideraciones sobre los deberes de la universidad y primeras recomendaciones sobre la manera de cumplirlos.** (Principles of university reform: considerations on the obligations of the university and recommendations on how to accomplish them.)
Rudolph P. Atcon. Tegucigalpa: Universidad Nacional Autónoma de Honduras, 1960. 39p.
Sets forth the mission of the ideal Latin American university, the difficulties of realizing goals, and a possible new structure for the Universidad Nacional Autónoma de Honduras.

701 **La universidad como factor de transformación social.** (The university as a factor in social transformation.)
Manuel Antonio Santos. Honduras: Centro Universitario de Estudios Generales, Universidad Nacional Autónoma de Honduras, 1977. 54p.
This work is most valuable for its discussion of autonomy, but it also contains useful information about the status of teaching, research and outreach of the National University in the early 1970s.

702 **Universities in the business of repression: the**
academic–military–industrial complex and Central America.
Jonathan Feldman. Boston, Massachusetts: South End Press, 1989.
371p. bibliog.
This investigation focuses on the links between US educational institutions and the US
military and transnational corporations that conduct research and development
projects for military purposes. An extensive appendix lists those transnational
corporations connected to Central American intervention, noting (when known) their
sales and activities in Honduras.

Science and Technology

703 **Central America and the Caribbean, development assistance abroad.**
New York: Technical Assistance Information Clearing House,
American Council of Voluntary Agencies for Foreign Service, 1983- .
Published by an 'information center specializing in the socio-economic development
programs abroad of US voluntary agencies, church missions, foundations, an[d] other
nonprofit organizations', this is a compilation of timely information about American
technical and development assistance, with specific reference to resources and concerns
of the private non-profit sector. Pages 164-85 deal with Honduras. Each entry contains
the name of the agency, contact person and address, programme description,
personnel, programme initiation, cooperating organizations, and expenditures for fiscal
year 1982. Before the entries for each country, there is a statement referring to the
total number of participating organizations and a total amount of programme
expenditure in dollars. This publication continues various individual country reports
published since 1966.

704 **Experiencia en la transferencia de información científica y técnica a
través del Centro de Información Industrial del Banco Central de
Honduras: CIIBANTRAL.** (The experience of scientific and technical
information transfer through the Centre for Industrial Information of
the Central Bank of Honduras: CIIBANTRAL).
José Ricardo Freije M.   In: *The transfer of scholarly, scientific and
technical information between North and South America.*   Metuchen,
New Jersey: Scarecrow, 1986. 701p.
A brief description of the services of the Centre and its use of automation.

705 **Promoting democracy: microfilming the Honduran voter registry was more than the ordinary project.**
Ramiro Valderama. *Inform* (Silver Springs, Maryland), vol. 3, no. 6 (1989). p. 36-43.

An example of north–south technology transfer. In 1988 the US Agency for International Development proposed to assist the Honduran National Electoral Tribunal and the National Registry of Persons in the processing of vital information about the Honduran citizenry and the creation of a useful voter registry. The primary objectives of the project were to: preserve historical and statistical information dating from 1880 by transcribing and inputting it into a central database; review and compare transcribed information to ensure that only one file existed for each individual; and to produce other useful statistical reports and research based on the data in the central file. Each stage of the project is described and the information would be useful to anybody in charge of a project in which computers are introduced to non-computer users. In the section 'Lessons' a number of excellent points to keep in mind are listed whenever an attempt is made to transfer technology or conduct a multinational project.

Literature

706 **Antología del cuento hondureño.** (Anthology of Honduran short
stories.)
Jorge Luís Oviedo.   Tegucigalpa: Unidos, 1988. 167p.
Twenty short stories by fifteen practitioners of the craft are presented after an
introductory historical essay by the compiler, himself an accomplished author.
Included are two authors from the 1920s Renovation group and several from the
Generation of 1950, but with the majority flourishing today. Very brief bio-
bibliographies are followed by the stories of: Arturo Martínez Galindo, Marcos Carías
Reyes, Víctor Cáceres Lara, Alejandro Castro, Pompeyo del Valle, Julio Escoto,
Jorge Luís Oviedo, and others.

707 **Los barcos.** (The boats.)
Roberto Quesada.   Tegucigalpa: Baktun, 1988. 216p.
La Ceiba is the setting for this strong story about the back-breaking work of pineapple
harvesting. The title of the novel is derived from the boats that periodically come to
collect the Standard Fruit Company produce, but also serve as a reminder of US
domination of Honduras. Carnival, dances and amorous plots have their place in the
novel, but the workers' struggle for fair treatment is the overriding theme.

708 **Breve reseña del cuento hondureño.** (Brief review of the modern
Honduran short story.)
Manuel Salinas Paguada.   *Cuadernos Hispanoamericanos: revista
mensual de cultura hispánica* (Spain), vol. 124, no. 371 (1981),
p. 385-96. Also published in: *Cahiers du monde hispanique et luso-
brésilien*, vol. 36 (1981), p. 63-74.
Presented at the international colloquium on the Hispanic American short story, Paris,
May 1980, this paper reviews, decade by decade, the development of modern short
stories in Honduras from the 1920s to the present and shows how they reflected the
political, economic, and social events of the era. In the 1920s, creolism, *costumbrismo*

[traditionalism], regionalism and cosmopolitanism were the main trends. Later, the '35 generation' reflected a more conservative perspective, while the more liberal political situation of the 1950s expanded literary horizons. From the 1960s and 1970s the following authors are examined: Eduardo Bahr, Julio Escoto, Oscar Acosta, Marcos Carías Zapata, Roberto Castillo, Edilberto Borjas, and José Porfirio Barahona.

709 **Cinco poetas hondureños.** (Five Honduran poets.)
Selected by Hernán Antonio Bermúdez. Tegucigalpa: Editorial Guaymuras, 1981. 102p.
Selections of the contemporary poetry of Alexis Ramírez, Rigoberto Paredes, José Luis Quesada, Ricardo Maldonado, and Horacio Castellanos Moya.

710 **Clementina Suárez.**
A. Guillén Zelaya. Tegucigalpa: López, 1982. 177p., [105]p. of plates.
In this tribute to the first lady of Honduran arts and letters, Guillén Zelaya has organized nearly sixty anecdotal essays by her contemporaries extolling her literary and cultural accomplishments. The poet, born in Olancho, early expressed her independence and artistic inclinations, living or travelling in Mexico and other Latin American countries before returning to live in Tegucigalpa's Barrio La Hoya where her home today doubles as an art gallery. Her legion of admirers include most of Latin America's foremost 20th-century artists, who have found her to be a challenging and enticing portrait subject for their art. This volume includes over one hundred colour and black-and-white reproductions of over 90 artists' representations of Clementina Suárez. Her vibrancy, mystery and enchantment are depicted in a variety of media from her youth through to her older age. As one essayist notes, it is possible to know Clementina through these artists and to know the artists through Clementina.

711 **Clementina Suárez: su lugar en la galería de mujeres extraordinarias.**
(Clementina Suárez: her place in the gallery of extrordinary women.)
Janet N. Gold. Tegucigalpa: [Talleres Gráficas del Editorial Guaymuras], 1990. 30p.
Gold, a doctoral student, interviews Suárez and traces the life of this most prolific and famous poetess of Honduras. She also makes comparisons with other great women of the arts, specifically Isadora Duncan and Gertrude Stein.

712 **Diccionario de escritores hondureños.** (Dictionary of Honduran authors.)
Mario R. Argueta. Tegucigalpa: Centro Técnico Tipolitográfico Nacional, 1986. 110p.
Compiled by the director of the Honduran Collection at the Honduran National Autonomous University, this slim volume is arranged in alphabetical order by author surname and provides birth and death dates, the place of birth, bibliographical entries, and critical commentaries on the importance of each writer's works.

Literature

713 **Enriqueta and I.**
Argentina Díaz Lozano, translated from the Spanish by Harriet de
Onís. New York: Farrar & Rinehart, 1944. 217p. map.

Daughter of an itinerant and peripatetic elementary school teacher, Díaz Lozano recounts her rather unusual, bittersweet childhood and early adolescence as she and her mother travelled from post to post in western and northern Honduras from 1914 to 1924. Although the writer focuses mainly on the relationship between mother and daughter, she reveals much about life and its hardships in rural Honduras, San Pedro Sula and Tegucigalpa in the early decades of this century. Her compassion, affection and respect for her compatriots is pervasive and when comparing her reminiscences with those of Harry Franck (see item no. 89) one wonders if they were in the same country at roughly the same time. The story ends as its subject turns fifteen and is sent off to boarding-school in Tampa, Florida. The author has won a number of literary prizes in Cuba, the US and Honduras and this volume was the non-fiction prize winner in the second Latin American literary prize competition. The autobiography with its scattered sketches is quite readable and a very pleasant way to pass an afternoon.

714 **Exaltación de Honduras: antología.** (Exaltation of Honduras: anthology.)
Selected by Oscar Acosta, Pompeyo del Valle. Tegucigalpa:
Universidad Nacional Autónoma de Honduras, 1971. 333p. bibliog.

Over 100 poems about Honduras by 37 Honduran poets. The anthology is divided into thematic sections, such as bestiary, Morazán, women, town, vegetation, lakes and rivers, family, and others. Following the poems are bio-bibliographical sketches of varying lengths about each contributor: the earliest was José Trinidad Reyes born in 1799; the latest, Oscar Acosta, was born in 1933.

715 **Hablan cinco teatristas hondureños.** (Five Honduran dramatists speak.)
Claire Pailler. *Cahiers du monde hispanique et luso-brésilien*, vol.
40 (1983), p. 83-5.

Written in Spanish or French, Pailler reports on some of the resolutions of the first Honduran National Congress of Theatre held in July 1982. At the forefront is the resolution to create and foster theatre by the people for the people while supporting workshops, seminars, forums and theatrical companies.

716 **Honduras literaria; colección de escritos en prosa y verso, precedidos de apuntes biográficos.** (Literary Honduras; a selection of authors in prose and verse, preceded by biographical notes.)
Rómulo Ernesto Durón y Gamero. Tegucigalpa: Ministerio de
Educación Pública, 1957-58. 2 vols in 7. (Colección Juan Ramón
Molina, no. 3-9).

A selection of poetry and prose written by respected Hondurans. The compiler has prefaced each selected author with a brief biographical sketch. The numbering of this set is rather tricky. The volumes containing poetry are designated as numbers 3-5 of the *Colección* and given volume numbers of 1-3. The first of these volumes contains poems by José Trinidad Reyes, Juan Ramón Reyes and Guadalupe Gallardo, among others. The second volume (no. 4 of the *Colección*) includes Josefa Carrasco, Ramón Reyes, Rómulo E. Durón, Carlos Gutiérrez, Miguel Fortín, and others. Volume 3 (no.

5 of the *Colección*) presents the works of José Domínguez, Froylán Turcios, and Valentin Durón, with others. The prose volumes, numbers 6 and 7 of the *Colección*, contain a potpourri of memoirs, speeches and commentaries concerning a variety of issues by the likes of Dionisio Herrera, Cecilio del Valle, Francisco Morazán, Juan Lindo, and other prominent persons of bygone days. Numbers 8 and 9 were not available to this compiler.

717 **Imagenes: ensayos.** (Images: essays.)
Raúl Gilberto Trochez. Tegucigalpa: [n.p.], 1973. 281p.
A collection of short essays about Honduran and Latin American poets and authors by the poet and then director of the National Library. It includes an essay on the origin of the National Library and National Archives.

718 **Juan Ramón Molina, 1875-1908.**
Ramon L. Acevedo. In: *Latin American writers*. New York: Scribner, 1989, vol. 2, p. 539-42.
Although his life was short, Molina is considered the national poet of Honduras and one of the foremost writers of Spanish America's *modernismo* movement. A poet, journalist and short-story writer, he also served as the editor of several newspapers in Guatemala and Honduras and was designated sub-secretary of the Department of Economic Development and Public Works. The bio-bibliographical article concludes with a selected bibliography of biographical and critical studies.

719 **Literatura hondureña contemporanea: ensayos.** (Contemporary Honduran literature: essays.)
Helen Umaña. Tegucigalpa: Editorial Guaymuras, 1986. 286p.
A compilation of previously published newspaper and journal articles on contemporary Honduran literary figures of the 20th century, written by a professor of literature at the National Autonomous University of Honduras who also served as the editor of the literary journal, *Tragaluz*. Fifteen male writers and poets (the most notable being Roberto Sosa) and one poetess (Clementina Súarez) are profiled. There are photographs and brief bio-bibliographical sketches of each subject. Some writers profiled have published merely one work, whereas others, such as Roberto Sosa, have been quite prolific. Unfortunately, the original source of publication and date is lacking.

720 **Literatura hondureña: selección de estudios críticos sobre su proceso formativo.** (Honduran literature: a selection of critical studies about its formative process.)
Rigoberto Paredes. Tegucigalpa: Unidos, 1987. 300p. bibliog.
A selection of studies concerning the formative process of Honduran literary expression. Its broad focus encompasses various periods, their representative genres, and works and authors who have made outstanding contributions. Included are general studies, theatre, poetry, narrative, and essay.

Literature

721 **Memorias.** (Memoirs.)
Froylán Turcios. Tegucigalpa: Universidad Nacional Autónoma de
Honduras, Editorial Universitaria, 1980. 419p. bibliog. (Colección
Letras Hondureñas, no. 5).
The autobiography of a leading Honduran intellectual who edited a number of Central
American literary journals and served in several high-level government posts.

722 **Muerte más aplaudida.** (Death highly praised.)
Jorge Luís Oveido. Tegucigalpa: Unidos, 1989. 65p.
Sixteen modern, ironic short, sometimes very short, stories that reveal many facets of
life in Honduras.

723 **Narradoras hondureñas.** (Honduran women narrators.)
Helen Umaña. Tegucigalpa: Editorial Guaymuras, 1990. 166p. bibliog.
The noted Honduran literary critic analyses the narrative work of three Honduran
women: Lucila Gamero de Medina (1873-1964), Paca Navas de Miralda (1900-69),
and Argentina Díaz Lozano (1914-). Brief biographical data is provided for each
author and the novels of each are summarized and critiqued. An overview of the
present situation of female writers is also provided.

724 **Olancho y su poesia.** (Olancho and her poetry.)
Heriberto Rodríguez Barahona. Tegucigalpa: Imprenta Calderón,
1972. 120p.
An anthology of over 120 poems by 24 poets (eight of them women) born in the
department of Olancho. Among those included are: Juan Ramón Reyes, Froylán
Turcios, Alfonso Guillén Zelaya, Miguel Angel Osorio, Clementina Suárez, Victoria
Bertrand, Ada María Navas, Juanita Zelaya, Adilia Cardona, Mélida Fiallos, Hostilio
Lobo, and Aura Enoé Clix.

725 **Poesía contemporánea: 11 poetas hondureños.** (Contemporary poetry:
11 Honduran poets.)
Tegucigalpa: Consejo Metropolitana del Distrito Central, 1978. 11 vols.
Each volume contains examples of the poetry of one contemporary poet: Clementina
Suárez, Jorge Federico Travieso, Jaime Fontana, Antonio José Rivas, Pompeyo del
Valle, Roberto Sosa, Oscar Acosta, José Adan Castelar, Edilberto Cardona Bulnes,
Rigoberto Paredes, and José Luís Quesada.

726 **The portrait and the mirror: a biography of Honduran poet Clementina
Suárez.**
Janet N. Gold. PhD dissertation, University of Massachusetts, 1990.
421p. (DAI vol. 51/11A, p. 3763).
The author's abstract tells us that 'This is the first full-length biography of this
matriarch of Honduran letters. It differs from other portraits of Ms. Suárez in its
length, its point of view and its narrative strategy. Told from the perspective of an
outsider observing and interacting with another culture, it begins with a brief history of
the Suárez-Zelaya family, followed by a retelling of Ms. Suárez' life that is broadly
chronological but that weaves together her past, present and future with a reading of

her work that foregrounds her use of poetry as a workshop in the construction of herself.'

727 **Rafael Heliodoro Valle, 1891-1959.**
Georgett M. Dorn. In: *Latin American writers*. New York: Scribner, 1989, vol. 2, p. 721-4.

'A man for all seasons', Valle proved to be a versatile intellect, a dedicated journalist, a historian with encyclopaedic knowledge who worked endlessly to expand the cultural horizon of his fellow North and Latin Americans. His bio-bibliography is followed by an impressive selected bibliography of first editions, historical works, bibliographies compiled by Valle and biographical and critical studies.

Language

728 **The Bay Islands English of Honduras**
Elissa Warantz.   In: *Central American English*, edited by John
Holm.   Heidelberg, Germany: Gross, 1983, p. 71-94. bibliog.
Most of the Bay Island's 10,000 inhabitants speak English as their mother tongue and
Spanish as their second language. In Chapter 3 of this volume, Warantz provides a
brief sociolinguistic history of the Bay Islands, ethnolinguistic groups and transcriptions
of recorded conversations exemplifying the unique speech patterns found on Utila
Island.

729 **Colonial languages of the *Gobierno* of Guatemala: a review of the
primary sources.**
Lawrence H. Feldman.   *Journal of Mayan Linguistics*, vol. 5, no. 2
(1986), p. 1-15. bibliog.
Presents new data about dozens of native languages spoken during the colonial period
in the *Gobierno* of Guatemala (which included Honduras) from two hitherto unknown
manuscripts: *Memoria de los padres y sacerdotes que están ocupados en beneficios en
este Obispado de Guatemala* (1607) (Memoirs of the priests working for the benefit of
the Bishopric of Guatemala) by Juan Ramírez; and *Memoria de los curatos, pueblos,
curas, doctrineros, coadjutores, y feligreses y idiomas de que se compone el Obispado
de Guatemala* (1739) (Memoirs of the parishes, towns, priests, coadjutors, and
parishioners and languages that constitute the Bishopric of Guatemala) by Gayoso.
Based on original manuscripts, Feldman provides information about what colonial
inhabitants of the region claimed were the native languages of given communities.

730 The development of the Paya sound-system.
Dennis Graham Holt. PhD dissertation, University of California, Los
Angeles, 1985. 310p. (DAI 47/06A, p. 2144).

This study deals with the Paya language of northeastern Honduras, the northernmost
member of the Chibchan family of languages, which includes most of the languages of
southern Central America and a number of languages of northwestern South America.
Until the present study, Paya had been a little-known language whose genetic affinities
had been a matter of conjecture. The study consists of three main sections: an analysis
and discussion of the synchronic phonology of Paya, constituting the first rigorous look
at Paya phonology in the light of the linguistic theories that have developed since the
work of Conzemius (1928); a comparative analysis involving Paya and five other
languages of the Chibchan family; and a determination and discussion of the historical
sound-laws that must have operated during the development of Paya from Proto-
Chibchan. [Author's abstract].

731 El español hablado en Honduras. (The spoken Spanish of Honduras.)
Compiled by Atanasio Herranz. Tegucigalpa: Editorial Guaymuras,
1990. 299p. bibliog.

An anthology of articles about the provincialisms and variations of Spanish as spoken
in Honduras compiled by a Spanish romance philologist. The language is analysed in
three linguistic planes: phonetic, morpho-syntactic and lexico-semantic. Included are
articles by Lipski, van Wijk and Membreno. Following the main text, there are two
excellent lengthy annotated bibliographies on Honduran linguistics and Spanish in
Latin America.

732 Favorite idioms and expressions used in Honduras.
Compiled by Thomas Harold Walz. Tegucigalpa: [n.p.], [1964?].
147p. bibliog.

Although a bit dated, this compendium of expressions should still prove useful to the
interested visitor to Honduras. Written for anyone who may be staying for an extended
period, the book includes lists of idioms and expressions with English translations,
taboo Spanish words (with non-taboo English translations), hand and body gestures
with diagrams, and an explanation of the *Voseo* as used in Honduras. The volume is
based on a year (1963) of word collecting in all regions of Honduras.

733 Fonética y fonología del español de Honduras. (Phonetics and
phonology of Honduran Spanish.)
John M. Lipski. Tegucigalpa: Editorial Guaymuras, 1987. 144p.
bibliog.

Lipski investigates the variations in the Spanish language as spoken in different regions
of Honduras. The phonetics and phonology of provincialisms and dialects are analysed.
The final 'n' and the reduction of the 's' are treated in separate chapters as particularly
notable Honduran variations of the Spanish language.

734 **Hondureñismos.** (Hondurenisms.)
Alberto Membreno. Tegucigalpa: Editorial Guaymuras, 1982. 3d ed.
232p.

This reprint of the third edition of a dictionary originally published in 1912 (Mexico: Tipografía Muller Hermanos) consists of approximately 3,000 words and phrases used in Honduras at the turn of the century. Compiled by an ex-president of the country, definitions vary from single works to lengthy explanations with exemplary sentences, rhymes or excerpts from texts. The etymology of a word is generally not given. Vulgar words, 20th-century terms, and vocabulary for flora and fauna are omitted, but many indigenous words are included. It seems to be the only major lexicographical study of the country.

735 **Instability and reduction of /s/ in the Spanish of Honduras.**
John M. Lipski. *Revista Canadiense de Estudios Hispánicos*, vol. 11, no. 1 (1986), p. 27-47. maps. bibliog.

A linguistic survey focusing on the peculiarities of the /s/ in Honduran speech. Lipski, an authority on the Spanish of Latin America, discusses the varying usage of the phoneme /s/, its instability in the language, aspiration of the /s/ in certain cases and other details of the Honduran dialect. Lastly, the author offers a geographical survey that demonstrates great regional variations in the tiny country.

736 **Léxico del delincuente hondureño: diccionario y análisis linguístico.**
(A lexicon of Honduran delinquent slang: dictionary and linguistic analysis.)
Elba María Nieto S. Tegucigalpa: Editorial Universitaria, 1986. 216p. bibliog. (Colección Letras Hondureñas, no. 25).

An investigation of the specialized language developed by juvenile delinquents as a means of identification, communication and differentiation. The work begins with a general characterization of slang in its social context, followed by a listing of terms and phrases by category. Each term has a phonological transcription, etymology, grammatical function, a definition, an example of use, and synonyms. The seven categories of words are: money, arms, drugs, authorities, family, the body, and miscellaneous. The book will be useful to linguists as well as lawyers, social workers and others concerned with delinquent Honduran youths.

The Arts

737 **Alfarería lenca contemporánea de Honduras.** (Contemporary Lenca
    pottery of Honduras.)
    Alessandra Castegnaro de Foletti. [Tegucigalpa?]: Editorial
    Guaymuras, 1989. 373p. bibliog.
The author presents the richness, utility and beauty of contemporary Lenca pottery
through profuse illustrations and a well-researched text. This female-dominated
'cottage' industry of the Lenca is analysed by region, production methods and
commercialization. The book contains many charts, tables, maps, and drawings.

738 **La Campa y su cultura popular tradicional la producción de la
    cerámica.** (La Campa and its traditional ceramics production.)
    Mario Ardón Mejía. *América Indígena*, vol. 44, no. 3 (1984),
    p. 573-88. maps. bibliog.
The inhabitants of La Campa, situated in the department of Lempira, have a long
history of pottery production for commercial purposes. Here the author presents the
techniques for production, the designs, and the history of this local artisan industry. He
includes black-and-white photographs and tables outlining production problems.

739 **Canciones de Honduras = Songs of Honduras.**
    Compiled by the Oficina del Folklore Nacional de la Secretaria de
    Educación Pública de Honduras and transcribed by the Sección de
    Música de la Unión Panamericana. Washington, DC: Unión
    Panamericana, 1975.
'This collection of Honduran songs was assembled and recorded on tape by the
National Folklore Office of Honduras. The recordings were then transcribed in the
form seen in this publication.' Two sharply contrasted musical styles are included, one
which is well represented in urban towns, the other more likely to be heard in rural
communities and sung by descendants of Africans. Most of the music on the tape was
recorded by the Los Catrachos trio.

The Arts

740 **Conservación de las pinturas de Pablo Zelaya Sierra.** (Conservation of the paintings of Pablo Zelaya Sierra.)
José Rolando Caballero C.   *Mesoamérica* (Guatemala), vol. 9 (June 1985), p. 178-81.

Offers a biographical sketch of the Honduran artist, Pablo Zelaya Sierra, born in Ojojona in 1896, and describes the techniques used to restore his paintings housed in the Honduran Institute of Anthropology and History. Four examples of his work are reproduced as photographs.

741 **La danza folklórica hondureña.** (Honduran folk dance.)
Rafael Manzanares A.   Tegucigalpa: Partido Nacional de Honduras, 1972. 32p.

In this pamphlet, Manzanares presents choreographical notes for seventeen Honduran folk dances, and commentary on several others. Honduran folk dance benefits from an admixture of *criollo*, indigenous and African influences with regional differences and emphases. He also discusses typical costumes and provides rough sketches of nine of these.

742 **Datos históricos sobre la plástica hondureña.** (Historical facts about Honduran plastic arts.)
Raúl Fiallos Salgado.   Tegucigalpa: [n.p.], 1989. 129p.

A professor who is well known among the artists and cultured people of Honduras writes about the history of painting in Honduras. Biographical sketches of the best-known artists, commentary on church artwork, and various exhibitions are described. The work includes black-and-white photographs of artists and an art school.

743 **De Guatemala a Nicaragua: diario del viaje de un estudiante de arte.** (From Guatemala to Nicaragua: travel diary of an art student.)
Manuel González Galván.   Mexico City: Universidad Nacional Autónoma de Mexico, 1968.

This very interesting travel diary kept by a Mexican art student as he journeyed through Central America in 1958 contains (on pages 86-107) his impressions of Honduran colonial architecture. He describes, in great detail, the façade and the interior of the beautiful cathedral at Comayagua, including the paintings and other artwork, the church of La Merced in Comayagua, Los Dolores in Tegucigalpa, and the principal cathedral located on the main plaza in the capital city. Sixteen photographic plates clearly reveal the architectural details.

744 **Historia de la música de Honduras y sus símbolos nacionales.** (History of music in Honduras and her national symbols.)
H. Cargalv.   Tegucigalpa: Lithopress Industrial, 1983. 90p. bibliog.

Provides history, criticism and biographical information about the world of music in Central America. Cargalv includes several music scores and portraits in addition to synopses of the history of the national hymns of El Salvador, Guatemala, Nicaragua and Costa Rica.

745 **Homenaje a Isidro España.** (In honour of Isidro España.)
   Helen Umaña. *Tragaluz*, vol. 2, no. 14 (1986), p. 4-10.
Born in La Ceiba in 1945, Isidro España has dedicated his life to bringing theatre into the lives of his Honduran compatriots. An accomplished writer, actor and director, he has concentrated on developing worker and student theatre companies, as well as the National Theatre Company. Umaña offers an overview of his career, excerpts from an interview with him, and the comments of several intellectuals and actors who have known him.

746 **Imagen cívica de Honduras: compilación de documentos cívicos e
   históricos.** (The civic image of Honduras: a compilation of civic and
   historical documents.)
   Javier Barahona Duarte. Tegucigalpa: [n.p.], 1985. 152p. map.
A handy reference book for the national symbols and anthems of Honduras. Here you will find the words and some music (and even how to conduct the music) to hymns of Honduras, Morazán, to the pine tree (the national tree), to mother, Lempira, Columbus, and several other songs dear to the hearts of the citizenry. The compiler also supplies the words to the national anthems of other Central American nations, a description of the flag and the national emblem, and lists all the presidents and heads of state from 1821 to 1982.

747 **La mujer hondureña bajo el cielo del arte, la ciencia y su influencia
   social.** (Honduran women in the realms of art, science and her social
   influence.)
   Raúl Arturo Papoaga. Tegucigalpa: [n.p.], 1985. 128p.
A curious little tome in which the author, a poet of sorts, pays homage to the women of his country. He provides brief biographies of notable and not so notable women in the areas of letters, art and music, and gives listings of accomplished women in scientific fields. The work is hampered by the lack of birth or death dates and a name index. The biographies are not presented in any discernibly logical order, being in neither alphabetical nor chronological arrangement. A valiant first attempt at making a biographical reference tool about Honduran women, but one hopes that a more logically arranged tool with greater detail will appear in the future.

748 **La pintura en Honduras.** (Painting in Honduras.)
   Luís Marinas Otero. Tegucigalpa: Secretaría de Cultura, Turismo e
   Información, 1977. 30p.
The text by a former Spanish diplomat to Honduras covers the succinct history of the plastic arts as practised in Honduras from the 18th to the 20th century. The works and lives of Pablo Zelaya Sierra, Confucio Montes de Oca, Max Euceda, Carlos Zúñiga Figueroa, Roberto M. Sánchez, Mario Castillo, Dante Lazzaroni Andino, Miguel Angel Ruíz, Ricardo Aguilar, Moises Becerra, and José Antonio Velásquez are briefly described. This short work contains black-and-white illustrations of the painters and examples of their art.

749 **Towards a cultural policy for Honduras.**
Alba Alonso de Quesada.   Paris: Unesco, 1978. 73p. bibliog. (Studies
and Documents on Cultural Policies).

One of a series of country studies done by Unesco members with a view to comparing
the principles and methods of cultural policy, evaluation of cultural needs,
administrative structures, personnel training, legislation, budgeting, and the like.
Prepared by the Secretariat of State for Culture, Tourism and Information in
Tegucigalpa, the illustrated study is divided into two parts: the development of
Honduran culture, and the present efforts to devise a new cultural policy. It is
especially useful for its description of the government agencies and civic organizations
concerned with cultural development.

Libraries and Archives

750 **Análisis del uso del *Indice Agrícola de América Latina y del Caribe* en Honduras.** (Analysis of the use of the *Latin American and Caribbean Agricultural Index* in Honduras.)
Emily López de Alvarado, Martha Moradel Díaz. *Revista AIBDA*, vol. 4, no. 1 (1983), p. 1-10.

Reports on the results of a survey conducted at Honduran regional and local agricultural centres regarding the use of the agricultural index by agronomists, specialists and librarians. Questionnaire responses indicated minimal awareness of the existence of the index and the authors conclude that the State Agriculture Information and Documentation Centre should increase its promotional activities.

751 **Boletín de la Biblioteca y Archivo Nacional.** (Bulletin of the National Library and Archives.)
Tegucigalpa: Biblioteca Nacional, 1939- . irregular.

An irregularly published journal focusing on archival and library research and news.

752 **Development and function of the National System of School Libraries in Honduras and a proposal concerning the education of school librarians.**
Edited and translated by Sigrun Klara Hannesdottír. In: *Education of school librarians, some alternatives.* München, Germany: K. G. Saur, 1982, p. 43-58. (IFLA Publication, 22).

This collection of papers presented at the Seminar for the Education of School Librarians for Central America contains one submitted by the Technical Services for the Support of Educational Programmes of the Secretary of Public Education which reports on the progress made in the school library system from 1968 to 1977. With some assistance from Unesco, services were developed in 17 of the 18 departments with a total of 115 new libraries established (a modest 2.24 per cent of all primary schools in the country) and 22,000 books distributed. Many other accomplishments are cited. Cogent proposals and objectives are set forth to further the education of school librarians at the Francisco Morazán Teacher Training College or the National Library.

753 **Primary school library system in Honduras.**
A. Ballon.   *Unesco Bulletin of Libraries*, vol. 23, no. 6 (1969),
p. 293-9.

Describes the status of public, primary school libraries, most of which are in the Tegucigalpa area.

754 **Republic of Honduras, Libraries in**
Jorge Fidel Durón.   In: *The encyclopedia of library and information science*, vol. 25.   New York: M. Dekker, 1978- , p. 239-41.

The article tells of the development of publicly accessible libraries and librarianship which has been slow in Honduras. The first public library dates back to 1880 and 100 years later there are still only about 200 libraries – with fewer than 500,000 volumes. This article takes a cursory glance at the development of public libraries and cites the Directory and Inventory prepared by the Honduran Association of Librarians and Archivists as a major source of information.

Books, Publishing, Journalism and Mass Media

755 **The coming of age of development communication.**
Judy Brace. *Media in Education and Development*, vol. 17, no. 2 (1984), p. 78-82.

Brace offers a survey of key projects in development communication since the formation of the Information Centre on Instructional Technology in 1972. She includes Nicaragua's Radio Mathematics for the primary grades, Guatemala's Basic Village Education Project, and mass media as a means to disseminate health information in Honduras and The Gambia.

756 **Historia de la cultura hondureña.** (History of Honduran culture.)
Rafael Heliodoro Valle. Tegucigalpa: Editorial Universitaria, Universidad Nacional Autónoma de Honduras, 1981. 235p. bibliog.

Five essays by the noted Honduran intellectual who died in 1959 are compiled to present a history of Honduran journalism, book publishing, folklore, intellectual life, and accomplishments. A brief essay provides information on the first book published in Honduras and subsequent rare and important books. The longest essay is a bibliographical study of journalism in Honduras from 1829 to 1953, noting names of publications, directors, and editors.

757 **Honduras.**
John Spicer Nichols. In: *World press encyclopedia*. New York: Facts on File, 1982, p. 437-66.

Provides background information, general characteristics, the economic framework, press laws, and censorship of the press for all countries of the world. It includes newspapers and their circulations, radio and television.

758 **La imprenta en Honduras, 1828-1975.** (The printing industry in
Honduras, 1828-1975.)
Miguel Angel García.   Tegucigalpa: Universidad Nacional Autonóma
de Honduras, Editorial Universitaria, 1988. 301p. (Colección Letras
Hondureñas, no. 35).

This history of the printing industry in Honduras is focused primarily on publishing in
the nineteenth century after the first enterprise was established in Tegucigalpa in 1828.
The author discusses both private and government presses, with special attention given
to the official *La Gaceta*. Over 300 publishers are mentioned chronologically by year of
establishment, from 1828 to 1975. An extensive appendix lists the laws and regulations
concerning the press issued from 1832 to 1901.

759 **Políticas nacionales del libro.** (National book policies.)
Centro Regional para el Fomento del Libro en América Latina y el
Caribe. Bogota: CERLAL, 1980-[83?]. 4 vols.

Prepared for presentation at the International Book Fair (London, 1982), the four-
volume set outlines the national policies concerning the production of books in Latin
America and the Caribbean. Pages 33-6 of volume 3 concern Honduras and cover,
very briefly, the development of public and private publication houses and seven
national literary prizes.

760 **Presencia en el tiempo de una asociación intelectual.** (The coming of age
of an intellectual association.)
Juan Ramón Ardón.   Tegucigalpa: Editorial Universitaria,
Universidad Nacional Autónoma de Honduras, 1984. 280p. (Colección
Letras Hondureñas, no. 20).

An illustrated history of the Honduran Press Association and journalism.

761 **Retazo de la historia cultural de San Pedro Sula: diccionario
periodístico, diccionario de autores, cronología de la imprenta.**
(Fragments of the cultural history of San Pedro Sula: dictionary of
journalists, dictionary of authors, chronology of the press.)
Rubén Antúñez Castillo.   San Pedro Sula, Honduras: Imprenta
Antúñez, 1966. 227p.

A detailed history of journalism, printing and writing in San Pedro Sula.

Professional Publications

762 **Economia política.** (Political economics.)
Tegucigalpa: Instituto de Investigaciones Económicas y Sociales, Universidad Nacional Autónoma de Honduras, 1963- . irregular.

Publishes articles by national specialists concerning problems of development and economic integration, industrial policy, and demography in Latin America. It usually contains statistics, graphs, tables or maps.

763 **Estudios antropológicos e históricos.** (Anthropological and historical studies.)
Tegucigalpa: Instituto Hondureño de Antropología e Historia, 1978- . biennial.

A series dedicated to the promotion of anthropological studies on Honduran subjects.

764 **Estudios centroamericanos.** (Central American studies.)
San Salvador: Universidad Centroamericano José Simeón Cañas, 1945- . bi-monthly.

A leading academic, scholarly journal from Central America, it often contains articles about Honduras by Honduran specialists.

765 **Estudios sociales centroamericanos.** (Central American social studies.)
San José, Costa Rica: Consejo Superior Universitario de Centroamérica, 1971- . quarterly.

A key academic journal publishing articles on a variety of social issues written by both Central American and non-Central American specialists. It frequently has articles on Honduras.

Professional Publications

766   **Foro hondureño: revista mensual de ciencias jurídicas y sociales.**
(Honduran forum: monthly journal of juridical and social sciences.)
Tegucigalpa: Sociedad de Abogados, 1930- . monthly.
Dedicated to the study of law and social sciences, especially for Central and South America. It occasionally publishes critical book reviews.

767   **Revista.** (Journal.)
Tegucigalpa: Sociedad de Geografía e Historia de Honduras, 1904-59.
irregular.
Although it has now ceased publication, it is a valuable source of research on the history and geography of Honduras.

768   **Yaxkin.**
Tegucigalpa: Instituto Hondureño de Antropología e Historia, 1975- .
A scholarly journal dedicated to publishing original research and translated articles focusing on Honduran antiquities, anthropology and history. Many articles are enhanced by photographs, maps, tables, diagrams or charts.

Encyclopaedias and Directories

769 **La enciclopedia histórica de Honduras.** (Historical encyclopaedia of
Honduras.)
Tegucigalpa: Graficentro Editores, 1989. 11 vols published of a
projected 12.

A rather poor example of an encyclopaedia, but better than nothing at all. Numerous
but poor-quality illustrations, an inadequate index (a scant eleven pages), oversized
typography and a glossary that omits the most basic of administrative terms are a few
of its detractions. A valiant attempt at producing a useful reference tool for a country
lacking such items, but one hopes that a future work will contain all of the pertinent
facts accurately and index them thoroughly.

770 **Index to Spanish American collective biography.**
Sara de Mundo Lo.   Boston: G. K. Hall, 1981-85. 4 vols.

It is often very difficult to track down biographical information about important (or
less important) Latin American figures. This reference set is an invaluable aid in
providing access to information about thousands of such persons. In the set as a whole,
the compiler has indexed approximately 4,000 works of collective biography containing
information on over 100,000 biographees with 220,000 entries. The third volume of the
set covers the Central American and Caribbean countries. After a general section, the
work is arranged by country in alphabetical order. Each country is subdivided by
discipline, also in alphabetical order. There are author, short-title and biographee
indexes.

Encyclopaedias and Directories

771 **Private organizations with U.S. connections, Honduras: directory and analysis.**
Albuquerque, New Mexico: Inter-Hemispheric Education Resource Center, 1988. 77p. bibliog.

A directory containing analyses of over 500 non-governmental organizations and churches operating in Honduras and with financial or other connections to US private organizations, churches or to the US government. The listing is in alphabetical order by English name or Spanish acronym, with full cross-referencing in the index. Addresses and telephone numbers are given for each non-governmental organization (NGO). Operational size, whether it is a recipient of US government funds, and whether food aid is a programme component are given for each NGO, then specific focus and projects undertaken are analysed. This work reveals the pervasiveness of NGOs whose presence in all areas of Honduras has tripled since 1980.

772 **South America, Central America, and the Caribbean, 1991.**
London: Europa, 1990. 3rd. ed. 683p. maps. bibliog.

Very up-to-date information on Honduras appears on pages 353-68 in the third edition of this spin-off of the *Europa yearbook*. A brief historical overview was written by Helen Schooley and an overview of Honduran economic conditions by Paul Hackett with revisions by Phillip Weare. Government officials are named, political organizations identified, and diplomatic representation noted. Newspapers, periodicals, publishing houses, and radio and television stations are listed. Statistical information for banking, insurance, trade, industry, mining and other sectors is given for 1984-86.

Bibliographies

773 **Anuario bibliográfico hondureño.** (Honduran annual bibliography.) Tegucigalpa: Editorial del Ministerio de Educación Pública. 1961- .
An attempt to document all publications concerning Honduras. This bibliographer was able to verify the existence of this unannotated bibliography for the years 1961-63 and 1980-82.

774 **Bibliografía hondureña.** (Honduran bibliography.) Miguel Angel García. Tegucigalpa: Banco Central de Honduras, 1971-72. 2 vols.
García attempts to document all publications (books, pamphlets and speeches) published in or about Honduras that are housed in local libraries or archives or mentioned in the *Tentative bibliography of the belles-lettres of the republics of Central America* (Henry Grattan Doyle. Cambridge, Massachusetts: Harvard University Press, 1935) and *A guide to the official publications of the other American republics* (see item no. 780). It is organized by year of publication, then alphabetically by author or title. For many items, a location is given. Volume one covers the years 1620-1930; volume two, 1931-60. At the end of volume two there is a handy author index for both volumes.

775 **A bibliography of Latin American bibliographies.** Arthur E. Gropp (et al.). Metuchen, New Jersey: Scarecrow Press, 1968- .
A listing of bibliographies, both in book format or journal articles, in all disciplines emanating from or about Latin America. The latest subsequent editions have been compiled by Lon Loroña and tend to appear in five-year cumulations.

Bibliographies

776   **A bibliography of United States–Latin American relations since 1810.**
Compiled and edited by David F. Trask, Michael C. Meyer, Roger R.
Trask.   Lincoln, Nebraska: University of Nebraska Press, 1968. 441p.

A massive, unannotated, selected bibliography of eleven thousand published
references on 19th- and early 20th-century foreign relations between the Americas.
The title is a little misleading since it does encompass sources relevant for the study of
history, economics and general politics for the countries concerned. *The supplement to
a bibliography of United States–Latin American relations since 1810*, by Michael Meyer
contains an additional 3,500 briefly annotated items.

777   **Central America in the nineteenth and twentieth centuries: an annotated
bibliography.**
Kenneth J. Grieb.   Boston: G. K. Hall, 1988. 573p. (Reference
Publications in Latin American Studies).

A meticulously compiled research tool with detailed annotations representing many
disciplines, including economics, history, literature, political science, and sociology.
The general Central American chapter is followed by chapters for each country. The
library locations for each entry are a useful addition for researchers.

778   **The Central American agrarian economy: a bibliography.**
Compiled by the staff of the Land Tenure Center Library.   Madison,
Wisconsin: Land Tenure Center Library, 1975-78. 2 vols. (Training &
Methods Series, nos 26, 27).

An unannotated bibliography of books, government documents and journal reprints in
files of the Land Tenure Center. Most materials date from early 1960 to the mid-1970s.
Pages 46-66 of Part two concern Honduras and cover agriculture, economic affairs,
land tenure, reform and use, politics and government, social affairs, and statistics. A
good source for ephemeral materials. Part one covers Belize, Costa Rica, and El
Salvador, while Part two covers Guatemala, Honduras, Nicaragua, and Panamá.

779   **Guía para el investigador de la historia colonial hondureña: hacia una
periodización de la historia colonial hondureña: un ensayo temático
bibliográfico.** (Researchers' guide for Honduran colonial history:
periodization of Honduran colonial history: a bibliographical, thematic
essay.)
Mario Argueta.   Tegucigalpa: Universidad Nacional Autónoma de
Honduras, Editorial Universitaria, 1985. 43p. bibliog.

A noted historian and archivist, Argueta offers a periodization of Honduran history
based on his interpretations of significant historical research. He reviews what he
considers to be major historical analyses of Honduran history in the format of a
bibliographical essay then proceeds to expand upon his conclusions and periodization.
He notes that it could be done by economic, social, demographic, ecological or
politico-administrative criteria, by trends or by a combination thereof. For each factor
above he notes the important national events that could be used in determining the
start and finish of specific periods, i.e., pestilence, mining, illness, or Spanish–Indian
contact.

780 **A guide to the official publications of the other American Republics. Vol. 13, Honduras.**
Henry V. Besso. Washington, DC: Library of Congress, 1947. 31p.
Reprinted by Johnson Reprint Corporation, 1964.

The guide lists serials, series and monographs issued by the Honduran government from 1821 to 1946 and now housed in the Library of Congress. The arrangement is by government branch, followed by other agencies and an index. In the reprinted edition, Honduras appears in Volume 2.

781 **Handbook of Latin American studies.**
Cambridge, Massachusetts: Harvard University Press, 1935-51; Gainesville, Florida: University of Florida Press, 1952-78; Austin: University of Texas Press, 1979- . annual.

An outstanding resource for the study of 20th-century Latin American bibliography and a primary tool for the area in the social sciences and humanities. Since 1965, alternate volumes deal with the social sciences or humanities. Each volume is organized by discipline, then country, with essays and annotated entries contributed by leading scholars. The author and subject indexes allow for easy access to numerous entries about Honduras in English or Spanish.

782 **Hispanic American periodicals index.**
Los Angeles, California: Center for Latin American Studies, University of California, Los Angeles, 1978- .

An annual index to over 200 periodicals published in or about Latin America. Articles are arranged in author and subject-specific order and may be in Spanish, English, French, German, Portuguese, or Italian. Each volume contains numerous references to Honduras, but lacks annotations. The journals are indexed exhaustively with the exception of minor notices. Some volumes contain book reviews, others do not. A valuable complement to the *Handbook of Latin American studies* (q.v.).

783 **Honduras bibliography and research guide.**
Colin Danby, Richard Swedberg. Cambridge, Massachusetts: Central America Information Office, 1984. 333p.

According to the authors' preface, this is the first time a serious effort to organize Honduran bibliographical sources has been undertaken outside Honduras. In addition to the numerous, unannotated bibliographical citations in English, Spanish and French, which are arranged in nine subject categories, it contains very good lists of periodicals and organizations concerned with Honduras. Advice as to where to obtain materials – research library collections in the US, US and Honduran archives, and book dealers – is given, but it is pointed out that much of what is included in the bibliography may be difficult to obtain. The commentaries at the beginning of each section provide valuable guidance for researchers. Government publications are listed under Honduras and the responsible agency in the author index. An extremely useful resource for anyone doing research about Honduras even though it does lack a subject-specific index and annotations.

Bibliographies

784 **Indice de la bibliografía hondureña.** (Index to Honduran bibliography.)
Fidel Jorge Durón. Tegucigalpa: Imprenta Calderón, 1946. 211p.
Comprises 3,000 briefly annotated citations about Honduras or written by Honduran authors from 1821 to 1946. It is arranged alphabetically by author or title and includes pamphlets, books, laws, doctoral theses, and periodical titles. It is a continuation, revision and more precise version of Durón's *Repertorio bibliográfico hondureño* (q.v.) which he compiled for the first Honduran book exhibition.

785 **Investigación y tendencias recientes de la historiografía hondureña: un ensayo bibliográfico.** (Research and recent tendencies in Honduran historiography: a bibliographical essay.)
Mario Argueta. Tegucigalpa: Editorial Universitaria, 1981. 28p. bibliog.
A bibliographical essay on the historiography of Honduras from the colonial period to the present. Argueta, a noted historian, indicates where lacunae exist and makes suggestions about foreign archives where further research on specific periods could be conducted. He also notes fertile fields for further study such as cultural evolution, agricultural development, urbanization and social stratification. Most sources cited are in either English or Spanish with French and German sources totally excluded. Although it lacks an index, this essay would serve well as a starting point for the incipient historian.

786 **Latin America in the nineteenth century: a selected bibliography of books of travel and description published in English.**
Edited by Curtis A. Wilgus. Metuchen, New Jersey: Scarecrow Press, 1973. 184p.
An annotated bibliography of 19th-century travellers' accounts by a wide variety of officials and adventurers. Dozens of entries include references to Central America and Honduras.

787 **Repertorio bibliográfico hondureño.** (An index to Honduran bibliography.)
Jorge Fidel Durón. Tegucigalpa: Imprenta Calderón, 1943. 68p.
Contains, in addition to the Honduran bibliography, lists of the books collected by the National Library for its first Exposición y Feria del Libro Hondureño (Honduran Exhibition and Book Fair), including material contributed by Guatemala, Chile and the United States.

788 **Tendencias e investigaciones recientes de la sociología hondureña: un ensayo bibliográfico.** (Trends and recent research in Honduran sociology: a bibliographical essay.)
Mario Argueta. Tegucigalpa: Editorial Universitaria, 1986. 60p. bibliog.
This bibliographical essay examines the development of sociological research and the study and teaching of sociology in Honduras through brief descriptions of books and articles grouped together broadly by topic. Political sociology and socio-economic works are included in this essay, which intentionally omits works published prior to

1954. The work provides a valuable overview of sociological investigation undertaken primarily by Hondurans (although a few foreign works are cited) and it offers suggestions for future research. Access is somewhat hindered by the lack of an index.

Indexes

There follow three separate indexes: authors (personal and corporate); titles; and subjects. Title entries are italicized and refer either to the main titles, or to other works cited in the annotations. The numbers refer to bibliographical entries, not to pages.

Index of Authors

A

Abrams, E. M. 161, 173, 385
Acevedo R. L. 718
Acker, A. 14, 330
Acosta, O. 714
Acosta Bonilla, B. 311
Adams, D. W. 577
Adams, R. N. 310
Aguilar, G. A. 387, 459
Aguilar Zinser, A. 453
Aguirre, J. M. 72
Agurcía Fasquelle, R. 160
Alcero Castro, R. 698
Alderman, R. H. 601
Aller Atucha, L. M. 696
Almendares, J. 682
Almendarez, J. 695
Alonso de Quesada, A. 749
Alvarado, E. 320
Alvarado, N. E. 400
Alvarado García, E. 521
Alvarado Reina, E. 666
American–Honduras Company 27
Ancona, G. 622
Anderson, T. P. 337, 385, 393, 413, 475
Andrade Jasso, E. 448
Andrews, E. W. 86
Antúñez Castillo, R. 761
Aplicano Mendieta, P. 142
Aquiles Euraque, D. 205
Arancibia Córdova, J. 409, 453
Arbingast, S. A. 39
Archivo Histórica

Diplomático Mexicano 448
Ardón, J. R. 760
Ardón Mejía, M. 738
Arellano, J. E. 304
Argueta, M. 186, 192, 231, 234-5, 238, 416, 541, 663, 673, 712, 779, 785, 788
Arita Palomo, C. 513
Ascher, W. 544
Ashmore, W. 138
Astorga Lira, E. 629-30
Atcon, R. P. 700

B

Bailey, P. E. 348
Baily, J. 66, 221
Baker, J. 385
Ballon, A. 753
Balow, T. 3
Bancroft, G. 456
Bancroft, H. H. 185
Barahona, M. 483
Barahona Duarte, J. 746
Barbieri, L. 403, 429
Bardales B., R. 182, 418
Bardini, R. 461
Barrios, J. R. 473
Barry, T. 6, 383, 492, 555, 642, 654
Baumeister, E. 627
Becerra, L. 159, 189, 369
Befus, D. R. 599, 607
Behm, H. 358
Bell, C. N. 87

Benítez Manaut, R. 339
Benjamin, M. 319-20
Bennett, F. P. 108
Benyo, J. C. 123
Berganza D., J. A. 528
Bermúdez, H. A. 709
Bermúdez T., L. 430
Berryman, P. 392
Bertrand Anduray, M. L. de 316
Besso, H. V. 780
Bianchi, C. C. 257
Blachman, M. J. 479
Black, G. 429
Blanco, F. J. 523
Blanco, G. 298
Blumenschein, M. 297
Boddy, P. H. 340
Bolling, H. C. 602
Bonilla, M. 44
Bonilla, P. 501
Booth, E. M. 345
Booth, J. A. 390, 498
Bossert, T. J. 346
Boundary Tribunal 474
Boyer, J. C. 329
Brace, J. 755
Brock, C. 687
Brockett, C. D. 324, 641
Brooks, W. A. 645
Brown, E. L. 366
Brown, J. S. H. 86
Buchanan, J. 456
Buckley, T. 92
Bulmer-Thomas, V. 568-9, 575
Burgos Flores, S. 595
Burkett, P. 553, 584
Bustillo dc Young, L. 51

C

Caballero C., J. R. 740
Cáceres Lara, V. 190, 229, 402, 706
Calix Suazo, M. 541
Camarda, R. 273
Campanella, P. 680
Canterero, R. 334
CAPA (Canada–Caribbean–Central America Policy Alternatives) 449
Carcamo Tercera, H. 196
Cardenal, R. 295
Cargalv, H. 744
Carías, C. M. 294
Carías, M. V. 459
Carney, J. G. 306
Carpenter, A. 3
Carr, A. F. 23
Casad, R. C. 510
Castegnaro de Foletti, A. 737
Castellanos, E. I. 489
Casteñada, H. de 1
Casteñada S., G. A. 201
Castillo Flores, A. 585
Catherwood, F. 84
Centro de Estudios Internacionales 387
Centro Regional para el Fomento del Libro 759
Cevallos, F. P. 290
Chamberlain, R. S. 213
Chamorro Zelaya, P. J. 230
Chapman, A. M. 136, 266-7, 269
Charles, C. 71
Chater, J. 54
Checchi, V. 560
Chirinos, L. 335
Chomsky, N. 385
Clark, C. M. 129
Clarkson, D. 687
Clayton, J. 456
Cohen, M. 256
Colindres Ortega, R. 187, 502
Comisión de Límites 41
Committee on Population and Demography 247
Comparato, F. E. 78
Conzemius, E. 263, 730
Cornelius, R. M. 349
Crone, C. D. 696
Crowley, T. M. 279
Cruz, G. A. 95, 119
Cruz, R. E. 512
Cruz Reyes, V. C. 353
Cruz Sandoval, L. F. 635
Cuevas, C. E. 577, 588
Culbert, T. P. 147
Custudio López, R. 376

D

Danby, C. 783
Danes, S. M. 313, 667
Daniel, J. B. 26
Dasher, T. 360
Davidson, W. V. 28, 219, 264
Davies, M. H. 328
Davis, I. L. 108
Dawson, F. G. 129, 223
de Mundo Lo, S. 770
de Onís, H. 713
del Cid, J. R. 249, 547, 564, 634
del Valle, P. 225, 287, 706, 714
Delgado Fiallos, A. 406
DeLorey, T. 582
Deutsch, H. B. 232
DeWalt, B. R. 614
Diagram Group 40
Díaz Chávez, F. 240
Díaz Lozano, A. 713
Dilling, Y. 277
DiLorenzo, K. 255
Dixon, B. 148
Domschke, E. 248
Dorn, G. M. 727
Dornheim, M. A. 444
Doxon, L. E. 626
Drake, J. C. 129
Drucker, L. 371
Dunkerley, J. 183
Durham, W. H. 252
Durón, J. F. 460, 754, 784, 787
Durón, R. E. 220
Durón y Gamero, R. E. 716

E

Eckelberry, D. R. 111
Edwards, M. 9
Eldridge, J. 271, 278
English, A. J. 439
Enloe, C. 428
Eppler, D. B. 36
Epstein, J. F. 139
Ericson, A. S. 519
Erwin, T. L. 109
Espino, F. 340
Evans, H. E. 118

F

Fagen, R. R. 482
Falero, F. 590
Farer, T. J. 495
Fash, B. W. 172
Fash, W. L. 160, 171-2
Feldman, J. 702
Feldman, L. H. 729
Ferguson, W. M. 141
Fernández, A. 422
Fernández, A. G. 210
Fernández, D. J. 450
Ferro, C. A. 477
Fiallos, C. 530
Fiallos Salgado, R. 742
Figueroa, M. 351
Finney, K. V. 206, 605
Fitz-Roy, R. 651
Fleishman, J. 363
Flores A. A. 514
Flores, E. 562
Flores Valeriano, E. 596
Floyd, T. S. 197
Foehlich, J. W. 615
Fonck, C. O. 640
Fonseca Zúñiga, G. 398
Foote, D. 341, 354
Fox, R. W. 250
Franck, H. A. 89, 713
Frantzuis, A. von 78
Frehsee, R. 52
Freije M., J. R. 704
Freter, A. 147, 154
Fuentes, C. 385
Funes de Torres, L. 376

G

Galindo, J. 166
Galvão de Andrade Coelho, R. 258

Gannon, R. 37
García, M. A. 758, 774
García de Palacio, D. 78
Gardner, D. 103
Garrett, K. 157
Gates, W. 166
Gayoso 729
Gerrard, A. H. 133
Gerstle, A. I. 169
Ghoshal, A. 279
Gil-Chin, L. 571
Gillenkirk, J. 312
Godfrey, H. F. 58
Goff, F. 35
Gold, J. N. 711, 726
Gómez, A. L. 583
Gómez Rodas de Varela,
  A. 684
González C., D. 286
González Casanova, P.
  661, 669
González Galván, M. 743
Goodman, F. D. 94
Goodrich, J. A. 529
Goodwin, J. R. 394
Gordon, G. B. 149, 153,
  164, 166
Goyer, D. 248
Graham, D. H. 577
Granados Garay, R. 51
Greenbaum, I. F. 113
Greenfield, D. W. 104
Grieb, K. J. 777
Griffith, W. J. 181
Gropp, A. E. 775
Guardiola, G. 211
Gudeman, S. 325
Guest, I. 275
Guevara Escudero, J. 566
Guillén Zelaya, A. 710
Gutiérrez Falla, L. F. 506,
  591
Guzmán, J. 315
Gwynne, J. A. 110

H

Hackett, P. 772
Hafernik, J. E. 115
Haight, J. 60
Halsey, F. M. 644
Hamilton, J. M. 648

Hancock, R. 83
Hannesdottír, S. K. 752
Hargreaves, B. 101
Hargreaves, D. 101
Harris, W. D. 333
Healey, P. 127
Hedstrom, I. 682
Heliodoro Valle, R. 188,
  215, 225, 231, 756
Helms, M. W. 270
Henderson, J. S. 125
Henríquez, O. 431
Henry, O. 65
Hernández, R. V. 459
Hernández Chévez, E. 34
Herr, P. R. 567
Herranz, A. 731
Herrera Cáceres, H. R.
  452, 464, 471, 508, 516
Hezlep, W. L. 39
Hidalgo, C. F. 552
Hidalgo, F. 689
Hill, G. W. 309
Hill, K. 247
Hohmann, H. 151
Holland, S. 542
Holm, J. 728
Holt, D. G. 730
Houlson, J. H. 64
Houwald, G. von 291
Hubbard, A. 544
Huguet, J. W. 250
Hunter, C. B. 135
Hurlbert, S. H. 93
Husen, F. 692
Huston, R. G. 75

I

Intergovernmental
  Committee for
  Migration (ICM) 676
Irvin, G. 542
Istituto italo-latino
  americano (IILA) 676
IUCN Conservation
  Monitoring Centre 33

J

Jahn, E. A. 56
Janowitz, B. 350, 364, 368

Jarrett, S. 572
Jauberth Rojas, R. 453
Johannessen, C. L. 22, 32
Johnson, R. K. 104
Johnson, W. E. 470
Johnston, M. C. 688
Jones, E. 637
Jones, J. K. 113
Jones, J. R. 616
Jones, R. E. 359
Joyce, R. A. 130
Juarros, D. 221

K

Kalijarvi, T. V. 384
Karnes, T. L. 177
Keegan, J. 434
Keenagh, P. 79
Kellen, K. 496
Kelly, J. 131
Kendall, C. 325, 341, 354
Kerns, V. 259
Ketcham, C. C. 445
Kinley, D. 243
Kirk, J. M. 382
Knowles, A. S. 693
Koch, S. D. 96
Kramer, F. 326
Kucij, D. N. 671
Kurian, G. T. 691

L

La Val, R. K. 116-17
Land Tenure Center
  Library 778
Lange, F. W. 127
Langlais, L. 53
Langley, L. D. 386
Lanza Sandoval, F. 51
Lapper, R. 244
Lara Pinto, G. 261
Lascaris Comneno, C. 180
Leiva Vivas, R. 222, 227,
  236, 436, 457
LeMoyne, J. 381
Lentz, D. L. 97
Leogrande, W. M. 479
Leonard, H. J. 681
Lester, M. 77

Levy, C. K. 107
Leyland, J. 63
Lipski, J. M. 731, 733, 735
Lobe, J. 491
Loftin, M. T. 309
Loker, W. M. 121
Lombard, T. R. 15
Lombardi, C. L. 50
Lombardi, J. V. 50
Long, R. W. 650
Longyear, J. M. 156
López de Alvarado, E. 750
López Pereira, M. A. 556
Loroña, L. 775
Loveland, C. A. 259
Loveland, F. O. 259
Lunardi, F. 202, 212
Luque, C. 204, 245

M

McBirney, A. R. 38
MacCameron, R. 655
McConahay, M. J. 343
McDonald, M. 331
McDonald, R. H. 423
McFarlane, P. 455
McGeorge, H. J. 445
McLellan, D. L. 352
MacLeod, M. J. 184
McNeil, F. 500
Mallory, J. K. 167
Mangurian, D. 335
Manuel, A. 271, 370, 373, 491
Manzaneras A., R. 293, 741
Maol'ain, C. O. 426
Marinas Otero, L. 4, 217, 748
Marineros, L. 112
Martínez, F. 679
Martínez, J. F. 504
Martínez, M. F. 198, 216
Martínez, S. 288-9
Martínez Castillo, M. F. 200
Martínez Gallegos, F. 112
Martorell, R. 341, 344, 354
Marx, W. G. 299
Mata Gamarra, J. I. 345, 356
Maudslay, A. P. 94, 133, 141, 166, 168

May, J. M. 352
Mejía, M. 191, 225, 285
Meléndez Chaverrí, C. 233
Melick, E. M. 305
Mell, C. D. 100
Membreno, A. 731, 734
Membreno, J. B. Y. 30
Méndez, J. E. 377
Mendoza Morales, A. 699
Messenger, L. C. 134
Meyer, H. K. 193
Meyer, J. R. 120
Meyer, M. C. 776
Meza, V. 231, 412, 441, 662
Millett, R. 496, 498-9, 543
Mock, N. B. 355
Molina Chocano, G. 600, 631
Moncada Silva, E. 399
Monroe, B. L. 105
Monteiro, P. V. M. 42
Montes, M. 658
Montúfar, L. 228
Moore, R. J. 571
Moradel Díaz, M. 750
Morais, C. 639
Morales, J. 231
Morales y Sánchez, A. 132
Moreno, D. 497
Moreno, S. H. 679
Morlan, A. E. 73
Morley, S. G. 166
Morris, F. B. 20
Morris, J. A. 405, 484
Mortensen, D. V. 327
Moskos, C. C. 432
Mundigo, A. 362
Muñóz, J. 168
Munro, D. G. 86, 243
Murga Frassinetti, A. 481, 550
Myers, H. M. 29
Myers, P. V. N. 29

N

Nadolny, E. S. 338
Natalini de Castro, S. 414
Natera, G. 347
Naylor, R. A. 207
Nelson, A. 378
Nesman, E. G. 637

New York and Honduras
    Mining Company 598
New York Navigation and
    Colonization
    Company 31
Newson, L. 214, 262, 609,
    612
Nichols, J. S. 757
Nieto S., E. M. 736
Norsworthy, K. 6
North, L. 449
Novak, J. A. 349

O

O'Gara, C. 344
Oficina del Folklore
    Nacional 739
Ooijens, J. 685
Oquelí, R. 224-5, 308
Ordish, G. 638
Orentlicher, D. 275
Ortega, P. 292
Ortíz, A. 396
Ortuño, M. 522
Oseguera de Ochoa, M. 437
Ott, M. C. 672
Oviedo, J. L. 706, 722
Oyuela, L. de 317

P

Padilla H., A. L. 314
Padilla Rush, R. 391
Pailler, C. 715
Painter, J. 244
Paredes, D. 282
Paredes, J. E. 565
Paredes, R. 720
Parsons, K. H. 636
Partido Comunista de
    Honduras 419, 625
Paxman, J. 88
Paz, E. 395
Paz, O. 385
Paz Aguilar, E. 421
Pearson, N. J. 388
Peckenham, N. 195
Pérez, A. 616
Pérez Brignoli, H. 174, 559

224

Pérez Estrada, A. 203
Pérez Estrada, T. 203
Perry, E. W. 24
Pineda, M. 421
Pineda Portillo, N. 5
Pino, H. R. N. 574
Pischke, J. D. von 577
Pochet Coronado, R. M.
  303
Pope, K. 125, 145
Popoaga, R. A. 747
Porpora, D. V. 374
Porter, W. S. 65
Posas, M. 404, 547, 610,
  634, 656, 668-9, 675,
  677
Postlewaite, T. N. 692
Preusch, D. 383, 492, 555,
  654
Primante, D. A. 358
Proyecto Centroamericano
  de Estudios Socio-
  Religiosos
  (PROCADES) 296

Q

Quesada, R. 707
Quesada Monge, R. 451
Quiñónez, E. 192

R

Ramírez, A. 420
Ramírez, D. G. 525
Ramírez, J. 525, 553, 729
Ramírez, R. 525
Ramírez de Arellano, J. D.
  613
Ramos Alvarado, V. 487
Record, S. J. 100
Regional Employment
  Program for Latin
  America and the
  Caribbean 665
Reina, J. A. 690
Reina, R. 631
Reina Valenzuela, J. 199,
  218, 231, 234, 690
Remmer, K. L. 570

Rener, F. 291
Retamal, G. 687
Reynolds, T. H. 514
Rice, D. S. 147
Richmond, D. 67
Richter, E. 253
Rico, J. M. 518
Ridgely, R. S. 110
Ridler, N. B. 546
Rivas, P. 527
Robicsek, F. 158
Robinson, E. J. 137
Rodgers, I. 277
Rodríguez, M. 175
Rodríguez, N. P. 283
Rodríguez Barahona, H.
  724
Rodríguez Céspedes, E.
  569
Rohr, J. 385
Rojas, M. 182
Romero, R. 679
Ronfeldt, D. 496
Rosa, M. A. 209
Rosa, R. 231
Rosenberg, M. B. 194,
  390, 433, 442, 494,
  498-9
Ross, D. G. 653
Rowles, J. 462
Royce, J. Q. 141
Rubín de la Borbolla, D. F.
  527
Rudolph, J. D. 7
Ruhl, A. B. 68
Ruhl, J. M. 423, 620, 632

S

Saavedra, D. 307
Sabloff, J. A. 143
Saboori, F. 573
Sagástume F., A. S. 241
Salas, L. 518
Salinas Paguada, M. 708
Salomón, L. 12, 440, 478
Salvin, O. 94
Sanders, W. T. 162
Sandoval, M. T. 520
Santos, M. A. 701
Santos de Morais, C. 628
Scherzer, K. 90

Schmidt, A. 276
Schooley, H. 242, 772
Schortman, E. 138
Schuyler, G. W. 382
Schwerein, K. H. 615
Sección de Música de la
  Unión Panamericana
  739
Seligson, M. A. 390, 637
Selser, G. 435, 438, 480, 490
Setterberg, F. 443
Sharpe, K. 479
Shaw, M. 284
Shaw, R. Q. 592
Sheets, P. 144
Shepherd, P. L. 194, 476,
  493-4
Sherman, W. L. 178
Siliézar Ramos, F. 580
Singer, M. 499
Siri, G. 594
Skutch, A. F. 103, 111
Smith, Sir Grafton Elliot
  133
Snarr, D. N. 366-7
Solien González, N. L. 260
Solorzano Fonseca, J. C.
  545
Soltera, M. 77
Somberg, S. I. 618
Soto, M. A. 473
Spinden, H. J. 166, 168
Spink, M. L. 170
Squier, E. G. 8, 78, 81, 85,
  231, 456, 646, 652
Stephens, J. L. 74, 84, 166,
  168
Stokes, W. S. 526
Stone, D. Z. 126-8, 146,
  188, 310
Stone, S. Z. 322, 611
Stoner, K. L. 50
Stonich, S. C. 554, 678
Street, Anne M. 670
Strcct, Annie 195
Stringer, R. S. 540
Strome, D. R. 271
Stromsvik, G. 152, 163, 168
Stuart, D. 157
Stuart, G. E. 157
Stuteville, J. 447
Suazo Córdova, R. 415
Sutherland, C. H. N. 99
Swedberg, R. 664, 783

225

Swett, C. 91
Swisher, K. 385
Szretter, H. 665

T

Teggart, F. J. 43
Thompson, M. W. 688
Thompson, W. 82
Tojeira, J. M. 300
Torres, J. F. 323
Torres Adrián, M. J. 321
Tosco, M. 536
Trask, D. F. 776
Trask, R. R. 776
Trinidad Reyes, J. 714
Trochez, R. G. 717
Tunnermann B., C. 697
Turcios, F. 239, 721
Turcios Ramírez, S. 209
Tzur, D. 389

U

Ugalde, A. 361
Ulshoefer, P. 657
Umaña, H. 719, 723, 745
UN Dept of Economic and
    Social Affairs 246, 538
UN Economic Commission
    for Latin America
    [and the Caribbean]
    (ECLA) 539, 545, 621
UN Environment
    Programme 33
UN Office of Public
    Information 458
Urban, P. 138, 150
Ureña Morales, G. 200
Urtecho López, A. 505
US Board on Geographic
    Names 49
US Bureau of International
    Labor Affairs 660

US Congress, House
    Committee on Foreign
    Affairs 411, 446, 485,
    498
US Dept of State 456

V

Valderama, R. 705
Valdez, R. 117
Valladares, Edmundo 578
Valladares, Eduardo 569
Vallejo H., H. R. 237
Valverde, J. 298
Van den Haag, E. 495
Van Ost, J. R. 60
Van Wijk, 731
Vaux, P. D. 106
Vega, D. 692
Velásquez Díaz, M. 427
Veliz, V. 122
Verner, J. G. 517
Villalobos-Figueroa, A. 93
Vivas Díaz, A. 396
Vogrin, A. 151
Von Hagen, V. W. 76, 84,
    268

W

Waggoner, B. A. 686
Waggoner, G. R. 686
Wagner, Mandy 114
Wagner, Moritz 90
Waldéz, W. 336
Wall, G. C. 643
Walz, T. H. 732
Warantz, E. 728
Watkin, V. G. 576
Wauchope, R. 265
Weare, P. 772
Webster, D. 147, 165
Weddle, K. 11

Weeks, J. 557
Weiss, J. A. 382
Wekesser, C. 385
Wells, S. M. 33
Wells, W. V. 69, 231
Wesson, R. 388
West, R. C. 25
Wheaton, P. E. 410
White, R. A. 683
Whiteford, M. B. 313, 667
Wiff, M. 617
Wilde, M. 274
Wilensky, J. M. 60
Williams, H. 38
Williams, R. G. 597
Wilgus, C. A. 786
Wilson, L. D. 120
Winn, W. B. 301
Winter, M. 313, 667
Winter, N. O. 70
Witten, S. M. 379
Wohar, M. 553, 584
Wolffsohn, A. 98
Wonderley, A. 125, 140
Wood, B. 555
Wood, S. L. 102
Woodward, R. L. 176,
    181, 226
Wortman, M. L. 179

Y

Yankelevich, P. 231
Yde, J. 124
Young, J. P. 581
Young, T. 80
Yu-Way, L. 694

Z

Zacapa, R. 397
Zelaya Bonilla, J. E. 345
Zelaya Carranza, S. 208
Zúñiga, M. 694

Index of Titles

A

*According to our ancestors:
Folk texts from
Guatemala and
Honduras* 284
*Acontecimientos
sobresalientes de la
Iglesia de Honduras,
1900-1962: Primeros
pasos para la
elaboración de una
historia de la Iglesia
hondureña* 295
*Acute respiratory infection
control program pilot
study in Honduras* 340
*Adult education community
projects and planned
parenthood* 328
*Adult education program
of Acción Cultural
Popular Hondureña*
683
*Adventures in the far
interior of South
Africa* 63
*Agrarian reform in
Southern Honduras*
636
*Agricultural credit in
Honduras* 621
*Agricultural curriculum for
the common cycle of
general culture of rural
Honduras* 684
*Agricultural ecology and
prehistoric settlement
in the El Cajón region
of Honduras* 121
*AIFLD in Central
America: agents as
organizers* 654
*Alfabetización y mujeres: la
experiencia del
proyecto INDEX-
ANACH* 685
*Alfarería lenca
contemporánea de
Honduras* 737

*Análisis arqueológico de la
cerámica de Piedra
Blanca* 122
*Análisis comparativo de las
constituciones políticas
de Honduras* 502
*Análisis del conflicto entre
Honduras y el
Salvador* 459
*Analysis of credit use in the
Honduran agrarian
reform sector* 540
*Anglo-Spanish struggle for
Mosquitia* 197
*Antología del cuento
hondureño* 706
*Anuario bibliográfico
hondureño* 773
Anuario estadística 532
*Apuntamientos para una
historia colonial de
Tegucigalpa y su
alcaldía mayor* 198
*Aquatic biota of Mexico,
Central America and
the West Indies* 93
*Arbitraje de límites entre
Guatemala y
Honduras* 467-9
*Archaeological
investigation of intra-
community social
organizations at La
Ceiba, Comayagua,
Honduras* 123
*Archaeological
reconnaissance of
northwestern
Honduras: a report of
the work of the Tulane
University–Danish
National Museum
Expedition, 1935* 124
*Archaeology in
northwestern
Honduras: interim
report of the Proyecto
Arqueológico Sula* 125
*Archaeology of central and
southern Honduras*
126
*Archaeology of lower
Central America* 127
*Archaeology of the north
coast of Honduras* 128
*Archaeology on the
Mosquito Coast: a
reconnaissance of the
pre-Columbian and
historic settlement
along the Río Tinto*
129
*Die Architektur von Copán
(Honduras):
Vermessung,
Plandarstellung,
Untersuchung der
baulichen Elemente
und des raumlichen
Konzepts* 151
*Archivo de la Embajada de
México en Honduras,
1908-1976: guía
documental* 448
*Area handbook for
Honduras* 7
*Areas silvestres de
Honduras* 95
*Armed forces of Latin
America: their
histories, development,
present strength and
military potential* 439
*Aspectos monetarios de la
economía de
Honduras* 578
*Assessment of the public
health sector in
Honduras (1975-1985)*
342
*Atlas of Central America
and the Caribbean* 40

B

*Ball courts at Copán: with
notes on courts at La*

Unión, Quirigua, San
Pedro Pinula, and
Asunción Mita 152
Bananas: from Manolo to
Margie 622
Bananas, gold and silver;
oro y plata 307
Bananas, labor and politics
in Honduras, 1954-
1963 655
Bananos y política: Samuel
Zemurray y la
Cuyamel Fruit
Company en
Honduras 541
Los barcos 707
Bark and ambrosia beetles
of North and Central
America (Coleoptera,
Scolytidae): a
taxonomic monograph
102
La batalla de Washington
460
Beautiful Honduras:
experiences in a small
town on the Caribbean
1
Between war and peace in
Central America:
choices for Canada
449
Bibliografía agrícola de
Honduras, 1977-1979
623
Bibliografía agrícola
nacional: suplemento,
1972-1977 623
Bibliografía hondureño 774
Bibliografía sociopolítica
de Honduras 308
Bibliography of Latin
American
bibliographies 775
Bibliography of United
States–Latin American
relations since 1810
776
Biologia centrali-
americana, zoology,
botany and
archaeology 94
Birds of tropical America
103

Blackwood's Magazine 78
Blennioid fishes of Belize
and Honduras . . .
their systematics,
ecology, and
distribution 104
Blue blaze: danger and
delight in strange
islands of Honduras 64
Boletín de la Biblioteca y
Archivo Nacional 751
Boletín de la Defensa
Nacional 239
Boletín del Congreso
Nacional 503
Boletín estadístico mensual
533, 589
Breve historia
constitucional de
Honduras 504
Breve historia de las
organizaciones
sindicales de Honduras
656
Brief history of Central
America 174
Business Latin America
579

C

Cabbages and kings 65
Cádiz experiment in
Central America, 1808
to 1826 175
El café en Honduras 627
Cahiers du monde
hispanique et luso-
brésilien 708
Cambridge History of
Latin America 226
Canciones de Honduras =
Songs of Honduras
739
Carías: el caudillo de
Zambrano, 1933-1948
241
Carías, el último caudillo
frutero 240
Carta dirijida al Rey de
España 78
Cartografía de la América
Central: publicaciones

de la Comisión de
Límites 41
El caso de las Islas
Santanilla 477
Catálogo de monedas y
medallas de proclama
de Centro América y
Panamá 580
Catalogue of Latin
American flat maps,
1926-1964 42
Catalogue of Admiralty
charts and other
hydrographic
publications, 1983 59
Catalogue of maps of
Hispanic America 43
Caverns of Copán,
Honduras. Report on
explorations by the
Museum, 1896-97 153
Central America, a nation
divided 176
Central America and the
Caribbean,
development assistance
abroad 703
Central America and the
Middle East: the
internationalization of
the crisis 450
Central America:
democracy,
development and
change 382
Central America:
describing each of the
states . . . their natural
features, products,
popular, and
remarkable capacity
for colonization 66
Central America fact book
383
Central America:
Guatemala, Honduras,
Belize . . . Panama 53
Central America: how to
get there and back in
one piece with a
minimum of hassle 67
Central America in the
nineteenth and
twentieth centuries: an

annotated bibliography 777

Central America, land of lords and lizards 384

Central America: opposing viewpoints 385

Central America: regional integration and national political development 592

Central America report 16

Central America: the future of economic integration 542

Central America: the real stakes: understanding Central America before it's too late 386

Central American agrarian economy: a bibliography 778

Central American English 728

Central American monetary union 581

Central American Recovery and Development Task Force report to the International Committee for Central American Recovery and Development 544

Central Americans: adventures and impressions between Mexico and Panama 68

Centro América: los protagonistas hablan 396

Centroamérica en crisis 387

Cerro Palenque, Valle del Ulúa, Honduras: terminal classic interaction on the southern Mesoamerican periphery 130

Characteristics of rural life and the agrarian reform in Honduras 309

Children of the volcano 330

Cinco poetas hondureños 709

Classic Maya collapse at Copán, Honduras: a regional settlement perspective 154

Clementina Suárez 710

Clementina Suárez: su lugar en la galería de mujeres extraordinarias 711

Comayagua antañona, 1537-1821 199

Comercio exterior de Honduras 593

Comizahual: leyendas, tradiciones y relatos de Honduras 285

Communism in Central America and the Caribbean 388

Compendio de la historia de la ciudad de Guatemala 221

Competencia territorial del poder judicial hondureño 505

Compilación de los estudios básicos del diagnóstico del sector agrícola 624

Complete visitor's guide to Mesoamerican ruins 131

Conexión en Tegucigalpa: el somocismo en Honduras 461

Conflict in Central America 242

El conflicto Honduras–El Salvador y el orden jurídico internacional, 1969 462

Confronting revolution: security through diplomacy in Central America 479

Conquest and colonization of Honduras, 1502-1550 213

Conservation and indigenous human land use in the Río Platano watershed, Northeast Honduras 615

La construcción del sector

público y del Estado nacional de Honduras, 1876-1979 547

Consumer markets in Central America, 1984 edition 534

La Contra en Honduras 463

Copán ayer y hoy: guía breve 155

Copán ceramics: a study of southeastern Maya pottery 156

Copán, home of the Mayan gods 158

Copán: tierra de hombres y dioses 159

Copantl, jardín maya 'La Concordia' 132

Coral reefs of the world 33

La corrupción en Honduras, 1982-1985 397

Cost of conquest: Indian decline in Honduras under Spanish rule 214

Country profile: Guatemala, El Salvador, Honduras 548-9

Country report: Guatemala, El Salvador, Honduras 548-9

La crisis económica de Honduras y la situación de los trabajadores 658

La crisis económica en Honduras, 1981-1984 550

Crisis y reactivación económica 551

Cristóbal de Olid, conquistador de México y Honduras 215

Cruising guide to the Bay Islands 60

Cuadernos Hispanoamericanos: revista mensual de cultura hispánica 708

Cuando las tarántulas atacan 369

4 [cuatro] aproximaciones a Ramón Rosa 225

Cuatro ensayos sobre la realidad política de Honduras 398

Cuentas nacionales de Honduras, 1975-1984 535

Cultural surveys of Panama – Nicargua – Guatemala – El Salvador – Honduras 310

Curiosidades y bellezas de Honduras 34

D

Danlí en el recuerdo 286

La danza folklórica hondureño 741

Datos históricos sobre la plástica hondureña 742

De estructura económica y banca central: la experiencia de Honduras 552

De Guatemala a Nicaragua: diario del viaje de un estudiante de arte 743

Declaración del Partido Comunista de Honduras sobre la Ley de Reforma Agraria 625

Democracia y elecciones municipales: un ensayo de teoria político constitucional 399

Demographic Yearbook 246

Derecho mercantil 506

Los derechos humanos en Honduras 376

Description of the ruins of Copán 166

Development and destruction: interrelated ecological, socioeconomic, and nutritional change in southern Honduras 554

Development of the Paya sound-system 730

El Día 412, 438

El día que rugío la tierra 400

Diagnóstico do los recursos humanos en Honduras, 1960-1972: introducción al estudio del potencial humano 659

Diagnóstico socio-económico sobre el consumo y producción de leña en Honduras 616

Diccionario de escritores hondureños 712

Diccionario histórico–biográfico hondureño 186

Diccionario histórico-geográfico de las publicaciones de Honduras 44

El diferendo hondureño–salvadoreño: su evolución y perspectivas 464

Diplomacia política y desarrollo nacional de Honduras 452

Dirección general de censos y estadísticas 532

Directorio geográfico de las congregaciones protestantes de Honduras por departamentos, municipios y áreas urbanas 296

Distribution of several branches of Mayance linguistic stock 166

Distributional survey of the birds of Honduras 105

Diversity, distribution and use of edible and ornamental plants in home gardens in Honduras 626

Documentos, historia de Honduras 216

Documentos y doctrinas relacionados con el problema de fronteras: El Salvador, Honduras 465

Dollars and dictators: a guide to Central America 383, 555

El dominio insular de Honduras, estudio histórico-geográfico 201

Don't be afraid, Gringo: a Honduran woman speaks from the heart: the story of Elvia Alvarado 320

E

Ecology of malnutrition in Mexico and Central America: Mexico, Guatemala, British Honduras, Honduras, . . . Panama 352

Ecology of the freshwater fishes of central Honduras: neotropical, reservoirs, food partitioning, reproduction 106

Economia política 762

Economics of sorghum and soil erosion control technologies for small hillside farmers in southern Honduras 556

Economies of Central America 557

Education in Central America 686

Education in Central America and the Caribbean 687

Education in Honduras 688

Education in Honduras: a case study of an underdeveloped Latin American republic 689

Education of school
    librarians 752
El Salvador and economic
    integration in Central
    America: an
    econometric study 594
Elections and democracy in
    Central America 390
Elephants and ethnologists
    133
Empresas del sector social
    de la economía 595
En el cielo escribieron
    historia 431
La enciclopedia histórica de
    Honduras 769
Enciclopedia histórica de
    Honduras: obra
    fundamental de
    información y consulta
    e imprescindible
    auxiliar pedagógico
    para maestros 187
Enclave y sociedad en
    Honduras 481
Encyclopedia of
    comparative education
    and national systems
    of education 692
Encyclopedia of library
    and information
    science 754
Les enfants de la mort:
    univers mythique des
    indiens Tolupán
    (Jicaque) 266
Enriqueta and I 713
Eragrostis
    pectinacea–pilosa
    complex in North and
    Central America
    (Gramineae:
    Eragrostoideae) 96
Escama de oro y otra de
    plata: figuras y
    ficciones de la
    tradición oral
    hondureña 287
El escándalo del
    ferrocarril: ensayo
    histórico 583
El español hablado en
    Honduras 731
La estadística en Honduras
    507

Estadístico del producto e
    ingreso nacional, 1925-
    1952, según un sistema
    de contabilidad
    económica 536
Estampas de Honduras 188
Estatuto jurídico de la
    Bahía de Fonseca y
    régimen de sus zonas
    adyacentes 508
Estrategia de desarrollo y
    reforma agraria: la
    opción hondureña 628
Estructura agraria en áreas
    del Valle de Sula 629
Estudio económico de la
    aldea de Flores 558
Estudio sobre la
    participación de la
    mujer en el desarrollo
    económico y social de
    Honduras 311
Estudios antropológicos e
    históricos 763
Estudios centroamericanos
    764
Estudios sociales
    centroamericanos 765
Ethnographical survey of
    the Miskito and Sumu
    Indians of Honduras
    and Nicaragua 263
Europa yearbook 772
Evaluación de los
    asentamientos y
    cooperativas
    campesinas en
    Honduras 630
La evolución de la pobreza
    rural en Honduras 631
Evolución histórica de
    Honduras 189
Exaltación de Honduras:
    antología 714
Excavaciones en el área
    urbana Copán 162
Excavations at
    Guarabuqui, El
    Cajón, Honduras:
    frontiers, culture areas,
    and the southern
    Mesoamerican
    periphery 134
Exploraciones y aventuras
    en Honduras, 1857 69

Explorations and
    adventures in
    Honduras, comprising
    sketches of travel . . .
    and a review of the
    history and general
    resources of Central
    America 69
Explotación bananera en
    Honduras: capítulos
    del deshonor nacional
    596
Export agriculture and the
    crisis in Central
    America 597
Export–import laws and
    decrees of Honduras
    and implementing
    regulations, 1976-1988
    509
Expropriation in Central
    America and Panama:
    processes and
    procedures 510

F

Facts relating to the
    Rosario Mine 598
Failure of union: Central
    America, 1824–1975
    177
Familia, trabajo y
    reproducción social:
    campesinos en
    Honduras 321
Favorite idioms and
    expressions used in
    Honduras 732
Fechas de la historia de
    Honduras 190
Fertility and mortality
    changes in Honduras,
    1950–1974 247
Field guide to dangerous
    animals of North
    America, including
    Central America 107
Field guide to the birds of
    Mexico and Central
    America 108
Five republics of Central
    America, their political

231

and economic
development and their
relations with the
United States 243
Fodor's Central America 54
El folklore en la tierra de
los pinos 288
El folklore en los tiempos
coloniales 289
Folklore hondureño;
tradiciones, leyendas,
relatos y cuentos
populares de la ciudad
de Comayagua 290
Fonética y fonología del
español de Honduras
733
Forced native labor in
sixteenth-century
Central America 178
Forced to move 273
Foreign direct investment of
expatriate
entrepreneurs: the case
of Honduras 599
Foreign labor trends:
Honduras 660
Foreign law: current
sources of codes and
legislation 514
Forging peace: the
challenge of Central
America 482
Foro hondureño: revista
mensual de ciencias
jurídicas y sociales 766
Francisco Morazán 228
Francisco Morazán y sus
relaciones con Francia
227
La fundación de la ciudad
de Gracias a Dios y de
las primeras villas y
ciudades de Honduras
en los documentos y
erradas narraciones de
los historiadores 202

G

La Gaceta, diario oficial de
la República de
Honduras 511

Gazetteer of Honduras:
names approved by the
US Board of
Geographic Names 45
Geographic analysis of the
beef cattle industry in
Honduras 601
Geography of the savannas
of interior Honduras
22
Gobernantes de Honduras
en el siglo 19 229
El golpe de estado de 1904
402
Government and society in
Central America,
1680-1840 179
Ground-beetles of Central
America (Carabidae)
109
Guatemala and her people
of today; . . . to which
are added chapters on
British Honduras and
the republic of
Honduras, with
reference to the other
countries of Central
America 70
Guatemala–Honduras
boundary arbitration.
Brief on behalf of
Guatemala on the
question concerning
the competency of the
International Central
American tribunal 466
Guatemala–Honduras
boundary arbitration;
the case of Guatemala
submitted by the
Arbitral tribunal . . .
Under treaty of July
16, 1930 468
Guatemala–Honduras
boundary arbitration;
reply of Guatemala to
the counter-case of
Honduras submitted to
the Arbitral tribunal
. . . Under treaty of
July 16, 1930 467
Gubida illness and religious
ritual among the

Garífuna of Santa Fé,
Honduras: an
ethnopsychiatric
analysis 257
Guía de las ruinas de
Copán 163
Guía de los parques
nacionales, refugios de
vida silvestre, reservas
biológicas y
monumentos naturales
de Honduras 95
Guía para el investigador
de la historia colonial
hondureña: hacia una
periodización de la
historia colonial
hondureña: en ensayo
temático bibliográfico
779
Guía para investigadores de
Honduras 46
Guide to ancient Maya
ruins 135
Guide to the birds of
Panama: with Costa
Rica, Nicaragua, and
Honduras 110
Guide to the official
publications of the
other American
republics 774, 780

H

Hacia una Centroamérica
verde: seis casos de
conservación integrada
679
Handbook of Latin
American Studies 781-
2
Handbook of Middle
American Indians 265
Handbook of national
population censuses:
Latin America and the
Caribbean, North
America and Oceania
248
La hegemonia de los
Estados Unidos en

Honduras, 1907-1932
483
El Heraldo 402
Heritage of the
conquistadors: ruling
classes in Central
America from the
Conquest to the
Sandinistas 322
Hieroglyphic stairway,
ruins of Copán: report
on explorations by the
Museum 164
High jungles and low 23
Highlights: a confidential
report, Central
America and Panama
17
Los hijos de la muerte: el
universo mítico de los
Tolupán-Jicaques,
Honduras 266
Los hijos del copal y la
candela 267
Hispanic American
Periodicals Index 782
Historia constitucional e
institucional de
Honduras, y derecho
interno y derecho
international 512
Historia de Honduras 191-2
Historia de la cultura
hondureño 756
Historia de la Federación
de la América Central,
1823-1849 230
Historia de la moneda de
Honduras 585
Historia de la música de
Honduras y sus
símbolos nacionales
744
Historia de la universidad
690
Historia de las ideas en
Centroamérica 180
Historia del movimiento
obrero en América
Latina. Vol. 2:
Guatemala, Honduras
. . . Panamá 661
Historia del movimiento
obrero hondureño 662

Historia del Partido
Nacional de Honduras
418
Historia del poder judicial
de Honduras 513
Historia financiera de
Honduras. Informes
de las misiones Arthur
N. Young, 1920-21,
Bernstein, 1943, y del
Fondo Monetario
Internacional, 1949
586
Historia laboral de
Honduras: de la
conquista al siglo XIX
663
Historia política de los
campesinos
latinoamericanos 669
Historical analysis of the
tropical forest tribes of
the southern border of
Mesoamerica 136
Historical dictionary of
Honduras 193
Historical geography of the
Bay Islands,
Honduras: Anglo-
Hispanic conflict in the
western Caribbean 28
History of Central America
185
Home in Honduras: the
Blumenscheins pioneer
in La Suiza 297
Homenaje a la ciudad de
Gracias a Dios en el
CD aniversario de su
fundación, 1536-1936
203
Honduran elections and
democracy, withered
by Washington: a
report on past and
present elections in
Honduras, and an
evaluation of the last
five years of
constitutional rule 403
Honduran trade union
movements 664
Honduran women: the
marginalized majority
332

Honduras 2-5, 24, 47, 217,
231
Honduras: a country guide
6
Honduras: a country study
6-7
Honduras: a crisis on the
border 275
Honduras: a problem in
economic development
560
Honduras: an area study in
government 526
Honduras: an export
market profile 602
Honduras and the
Interoceanic Railway:
report on the line and
its prospects, being the
result of recent
personal visits 645
Honduras and the Perry
Land Grant: a new
field for the farmer,
stockman, lumberman
and laborer 633
Honduras and U.S. policy:
an emerging dilemma
485
Honduras bibliography and
research guide 783
Honduras: caudillo politics
and military rulers 405
Honduras: civilian
authority–military
power: human rights
violations in the 1980s
372
Honduras confronts its
future: contending
perspectives on critical
issues 194
Honduras: crisis económica
y proceso de
democratización 561
Honduras: descriptive,
historical and statistical
8
Honduras, el empleo en el
plan nacional de
desarrollo, 1979-1983
665
Honduras: el sometimiento
incondicional a la

233

estratega regional de
los EE. UU. 486
Honduras elecciones 85:
más allá de la fiesta
cívica 406
Honduras: en busca del
encuentro, 1978-1987
453
Honduras en cifras 537
Honduras: fuerzas
armadas, dependencia
o desarrollo 436
Honduras: general
descriptive data 10
Honduras: guerra y anti-
nacionalidad 487
Honduras hoy: sociedad y
crisis política 437
Honduras: Iglesia y cambio
social 298
Honduras in pictures 11
Honduras: índice anotado
de los trabajos
aerofotográficos y los
mapas topográficos y
de recursos naturales
48
Honduras Interoceanic
Railway Company,
Limited: prospectus,
preliminary report 646
Honduras investment guide
587
Honduras: its present
difficulties and future
prospects 647
Honduras literaria:
colección de escritos en
prosa y verso,
precedidos de apuntes
biográficos 716
Honduras: monumentos
históricos y
arqueológicos 527
Honduras: official standard
names approved by the
US Board on
Geographic Names 49
Honduras on the brink: a
report on human rights
based on a mission of
inquiry 373
Honduras: panorama y
perspectivas 12

Honduras, perfil ambiental
del país: un estudio de
campo 680
Honduras: portrait of a
captive nation 195
Honduras: post report 13
Honduras: república
alquilada 438
Honduras rotaria 603
Honduras rural roads: old
directions and new 648
Honduras: state for sale
244
Honduras: the land of great
depths 71
Honduras: the making of a
banana republic 14
Honduras: the new El
Dorado 604
Honduras: the reply of
Colonel José M.
Aguirre to some unjust
strictures published
against that republic by
the New York Times
72
Honduras This Week: your
Central American
weekly review 18
Honduras, un estado
nacional? 409
Honduras Update 19
Honduras: without the will
373
Honduras y El Salvador
ante la Corte
Internacional de
Justicia 471
Honduras y la
problemática del
derecho internacional
público del mar 516
JHonduras y su división
político-territorial 528
Honduras–Guatemala
boundary arbitration;
counter-case of
Honduras in answer to
the case of Guatemala
469
Honduras–Nicaragua
boundary dispute,
1957-1963: the
peaceful settlement of

an international
conflict 470
Hondureñismos 734
Hondureños en la
independencia de
Centroamérica 218
Hoosier in Honduras 73
House of the Bacabs,
Copán, Honduras 165
Housing in Honduras; La
vivienda en Honduras
333
How holocausts happen:
the United States in
Central America 374
Human rights in Central
America: a report on
El Salvador,
Guatemala, Honduras
and Nicaragua 373,
375
Human rights in Honduras
after General Alvarez
378
Human rights in Honduras:
Central America's
sideshow 373
Human rights in Honduras,
1984 376
Human rights in Honduras:
signs of "the Argentine
method" 377

I

Imagen cívica de
Honduras:
compilación de
documentos cívicos e
históricos 746
Imagenes: ensayos 717
Impacto social de las
conquistas laborales
hondureñas 666
La imprenta en Honduras,
1828-1975 758
Impuesto sobre la renta y lo
contencioso
administrativo 562
In quest of El Dorado:
precious metal mining
and the modernization

of Honduras,
1880-1900 605
In search of refuge 277
Incidente de "La Masica"
entre Honduras y la
Gran Bretaña:
reclamación por la
muerte de un súbdito
inglés y por lesiones a
otros dos 454
Incidents of travel in
Central America,
Chiapas and Yucatán
74, 84
Income levels, income
distribution, and levels
of living in rural
Honduras: a summary
and evaluation of
quantitative and
qualitative data 323
Incredible yanqui: the
career of Lee
Christmas 232
Index to Spanish American
collective biography
770
Indice de la bibliografía
hondureño 784
Informal and formal
market participation of
rural Honduran
women 667
Informe de balance de la
actividad del Partido
Comunista de
Honduras: III
congreso PCH, mayo
de 1977 419
Informe económico 563,
589
Inscriptions at Copán 166
Inside Central America: the
essential facts past and
present on El
Salvador, Nicaragua,
Honduras, Guatemala,
and Costa Rica 392
Interaction on the southeast
Mesoamerican
frontier: prehistoric
and historic Honduras
and El Salvador 137
Intermediation costs and

scale economies of
banking under
financial regulations in
Honduras 588
International directory of
importers: South/
Central America 606
International encyclopedia
of education 692
International encyclopedia
of higher education
693
International narcotics
control strategy report
608
Investigación y tendencias
recientes de la
historiografía
hondureña: un ensayo
bibliográfico 785
Iron triangle: the
Honduran connection
410
Los irresponsables: ensayo
sobre la niñéz
abandonada en
Honduras 334

J

Jicaque (Torrupán) Indians
of Honduras 268
José Cecilio del Valle:
sabio centroamericano
233
Journey in Honduras and
jottings by the way 75
Jungle in the clouds: a
naturalist's
explorations in the
Republic of Honduras
76
La justicia penal en
Honduras 518

K

Key policy issues for the
reconstruction and
development of
Honduran agriculture

through agrarian
reform 636

L

Labor law and practice in
Honduras 519
Lady's ride across Spanish
Honduras 77
Land, power, and poverty:
agrarian
transformations and
political conflict in
Central America 324
Land titling in Honduras:
the baseline survey as a
means of targeting
development assistance
637
Late ceramic horizons in
north-eastern
Honduras 139
Late classic Maya
economic
specialization:
evidence from the
Copán obsidian
assemblage 167
Latin America in the
nineteenth century: a
selected bibliography
of books of travel and
description published
in English 786
Latin American and
Caribbean official
statistical series on
microfiche 532
Latin American history: a
teaching atlas 50
Latin American writers
718, 727
Legislación de aguas en
América Central,
Caribe y México 520
Legislación indigenista de
Honduras 521
Los lencas de Honduras en
el siglo XVI 269
Letter addressed by Doctor
Marco A. Soto to
President General

Justo Rufino Barrios and answer to it 473
Letter to King of Spain: being a description of the ancient provinces . . . an account of the languages, customs and religion . . . and a description of the ruins of Copán 78
Léxico del delicuente hondureño: diccionario y análisis lingüístico 736
Leyes municipales iberoamericanas 522
Life and nature under the tropics: or, Sketches of travels among the Andes, and on the Orinoco, Río Negro, and Amazon 29
Life histories of Central American birds 111
Literatura hondureña contemporanea: ensayos 719
Literatura hondureña: selección de estudios críticos sobre su proceso formativo 720
Lito the shoeshine boy 335
Lucha por la paz y la cultura 695
Luchas del movimiento obrero hondureño 610

M

El machismo en Honduras 314
Mamíferos silvestres de Honduras 112
Man, crops and pests in Central America 638
El maoismo en Honduras 420
Marco Aurelio Soto: reforma liberal de 1876 234
Market incorporation and out-migration of the peasants of Western Honduras 326
Martindale-Hubbell Law Digest 515
Marvels of Copán: a handy illustrated guide 168
Maya ruins in Central America in color: Tikal, Copán and Quirigua 141
Maya–Lenca ethnic relations in late classic period Copán, Honduras 169
Mayangna yulnina kulna balna = Tradiciones orales de los índios Sumus 291
Los mayas en Honduras: visión de un mundo extinguido 142
Memoria anual [Banco Central de Honduras] 589
Memoria de los curatos, pueblos, curas, doctrineros, coadjutores, y feligreses y idiomas de que se compone el Obispado de Guatemala 729
Memoria de los padres y sacerdotes que están ocupados en beneficios en este Obispado de Guatemala 729
Memoria del Congreso sobre el Mundo Centroamericano de su Tiempo: V Centenario de Gonzalo Fernández de Oviedo 200
Memorias [Froylán Turcios] 721
Memorias de un sampedrano 204
Memories of a Central American: El Salvador, Honduras, Nicaragua (Contras), et cetera 315
Merchants and industrialists in northern Honduras: the making of a national bourgeoisie in peripheral capitalism, 1870-1971 205
Merchants, miners and monetary structures: the revival of the Honduran import trade, 1880-1900 206
Mesoamérica 20
Metates as socioeconomic indicators during the Classic Period at Copán, Honduras 170
Middle America: its lands and its peoples 25
1954 en nuestra historia 238
1862 224
Militarismo y reformismo en Honduras 440
El modelo hondureño de desarrollo agrario 639
Modernity and public policies in the context of the peasant sector: Honduras as a case study 640
Momentos estelares de la participación de la CTH en la vida política nacional 668
Monetary history of Honduras, 1950-1968 590
Monografía de la mujer hondureña 316
Monografía del Departamento de Copán 30
Morazán, defensor de la unión de Centroamérica 182
Morgan–Honduras Loan, 1908-1911 565
Mortalidad en la niñéz en Centroamérica, Panamá y Belice: 1970-1985 357
Mortalidad en los primeros años de vida en países de la América Latina, Honduras, 1969-1970 358

Mosquito Coast: an
account of a journey
through the jungles of
Honduras 79
Motoring in Central
America and Panama:
a compilation of
information on the
Pan American
Highway 55
Movimientos populares en
la historia hondureño
del siglo XIX; período
nacional 235
Muerte más aplaudida 722
La mujer ante la legislación
hondureña 523
La mujer hondureña bajo
el cielo del arte, la
ciencia y su influencia
social 747
Mündliche Überlieferungen
der Sumu-Indianer 291
Los municipios de
Honduras 530

N

Narradoras hondureñas 723
Narrative of a residence on
the Mosquito Shore:
with an account of
Truxillo, . . . Bonacca
and Roatan, and a
vocabulary of the
Mosquitian language
80
National Geographic 9
Natural resources and
economic development
in Central America: a
regional environmental
profile 681
Negros caribes de
Honduras 258
New archaeology and the
ancient Maya 143
New El Dorado: a short
sketch of Honduras,
C.A., its people,
climate, natural
resources, and vast
mineral wealth 26

New Honduras: its
situation, resources,
opportunities, and
prospects
New York Times 72
Nineteenth-century
Honduras: a regional
approach to the
economic history of
Central America,
1839-1914 566
Nociones de taxonomía
vegetal 99
Northern shadows:
Canadians and Central
America 455
Notas sobre la evolución
histórica de la mujer en
Honduras 317
Notes on Central America:
particularly the states
of Honduras and San
Salvador: their
geography, . . .
resources,
productions, etc., and
the proposed
Honduras
International Railway
81, 85
Noteworthy records of bats
from El Salvador,
Honduras, and
Nicaragua 113
Nutritional status of
preschool children in
Honduras where
sorghum is consumed
359

O

Observance of the
Honduran national
elections: report of a
congressional study
mission, November
28-30, 1981 submitted
to the Committee on
Foreign Affairs, US
House of
Representatives 411

Olancho: an account of the
resources of the State
of Honduras in
Central America,
especially of the
Department of
Olancho 31
Olancho y su poesía 724
Opinion and award:
Tribunal especial de
límites entre
Guatemala y
Honduras 474
Orígenes, desarrollo y
posibilidades de la
socialdemocracia en
Honduras 421

P

Pacific coasts of Central
America and United
States pilot 61
El Padre Subirana y las
tierras concedidas a los
índios hondureños en
el siglo XIX 219
Palaeoecology of the Ulúa
Valley, Honduras: an
archaeological
perspective 145
Pan American highway
guide: a
comprehensive travel
guide to Mexico,
Central America [and]
South America, . . .
1968-1969 56
Pan American Highway
system: a compilation
of official data on the
present status . . . in
the Latin American
Republics 649
Panorama histórico de la
Iglesia en Honduras
300
Partidos políticos y
elecciones en
Honduras, 1980 422
Party politics and elections
in Latin America 423

Pátrios lares: leyendas, tradiciones, consejas 292

Peasant economy and agrarian reform in the north-central highlands of Honduras 567

Penny ante imperialism: the Mosquito Shore and the Bay of Honduras, 1600-1914 207

Pensamiento universitario centroamericano 697

Perceptions of selected goals in village development for Honduras by three levels in the development chain 327

Perspectiva de la enseñanza de la medicina en Honduras 698

Phenetics and ecology of hybridization in buckeye butterflies (Lepidoptera: Nymphalidae) 115

Los pinares de Honduras 98

La pintura en Honduras 748

Pioneer Protestant missionaries in Honduras 301

Plan de desarrollo metropolitano del Distrito Central: EDOM 1975-2000 531

Plan de desarrollo universitario, 1967-1970 699

Plan de gobierno: opciones estratégicas para el desarrollo nacional 424

Plantas comunes de Honduras 99

Poesia contemporánea: 11 poetas hondureños 725

Police aid and political will: U.S. policy in El Salvador and Honduras, 1962-1987 491

Política y sociedad en Honduras: comentarios 412

Political economy of Central America since 1920 568

Políticas de ajuste en Centroamérica 569

Políticas nacionales del libro 759

Politics in Central America: Guatemala, El Salvador, Honduras, and Nicaragua 393

Populating a green desert: population policy and development: their effect on population redistribution, Honduras, 1876-1980 249

Population and urban trends in Central America and Panama 250

Por las sendas del folklore 293

Portrait and the mirror: a biography of Honduran poet Clementina Suárez 726

Power in the isthmus: a political history of modern Central America 183

Pre-Columbian man finds Central America: the archaeological bridge 146

Precolumbian population history in the Maya lowlands 147

Presencia de Máximo Gómez en Honduras 236

Presencia en el tiempo de una asociación intelectual 760

Primer Encuentro Nacional sobre Desarrollo Urbano: cuarto centenario de Tegucigalpa 251

Principios de la reforma universitaria: consideraciones sobre los deberes de la universidad y primeras recomendaciones sobre la manera de cumplirlos 700

Private organizations with U.S. connections, Honduras: directory and analysis 771

Problems and promises: vocational development for disabled youth in Honduras 671

Proceedings of the XXXVIIIth International Congress of Americanists 270

Program for fostering the economic growth and development of the Republic of Honduras through investments in forestry 618

Programa del Partido Comunista de Honduras. III Congresso, 1977 425

La provincia de Tegucigalpa bajo el gobierno de Mallol, 1817-1821: estudio histórico 220

Q

Quarterly Economic Review of Guatemala, El Salvador, Honduras 548

R

Radical right: a world directory 426

Railway expansion in Latin America: descriptive and narrative history of the railroad systems of . . . South and Central America 644

Railways of Central America and the West Indies 650

Rainbow countries of Central America 82

Rainbow republics, Central America 83

Ramón Rosa y el positivismo en Honduras 237

Recopilación de las constituciones de Honduras 524

Reflexión sobre la formación de la conciencia política: de la diocesis de Santa Rosa de Copán: para las comunidades cristianas 302

Los refugiados en Honduras, 1980-1986 280

Los refugiados salvadorenos en Honduras 281

Reorganización liberal: nuevas bases para el partido 427

Relación verdadera de la reducción de los índios infieles de la provincia de la Tagusigalpa, llamados Xicaques 304

Relationships, residence and the individual: a rural Panamanian community 325

Repertorio bibliográfico hondureño 784, 787

Report of Capt. Robert Fitz-Roy, Royal Navy, to the Earl of Clarendon, on the proposed Honduras Interoceanic Railway 651

Report to the directors of the Honduras Interoceanic Railway Company 652

Research guide to Honduras 51

Researches in the Uloa Valley, Honduras. Report on explorations by the Museum, 1896-97 149

Resumen del plan nacional de desarrollo, 1974-1978 318

Retazo de la historia cultural de San Pedro Sula: diccionario periodístico, diccionario de autores, cronología de la imprenta 761

Revision of the Mexican and Central American spider wasps of the subfamily Pompilinae (Hymenoptera, Pompilidae) 118

Revista [Sociedad de Geografía e Historia] 767

Revista trimestral [Banco Central] 589

Las revoluciones en Honduras 245

Revolutionary movements in Central America: a comparative analysis 394

Role of the private sector as a provider of industrial training: the case of the Honduran furniture industry 672

Roots of rebellion: land and hunger in Central America 642

S

Sailing directions enroute for the west coasts of Mexico and Central America 62

Sale of F-5E/F aircraft to Honduras: hearing and markup before the

[US] Committee on Foreign Affairs . . . 1987 446

Savannas of interior Honduras 32

Scarcity and survival in Central America: ecological origins of the Soccer War 252

Search for the Maya: the story of Stephens and Catherwood 84

El sector laboral hondureño durante la reforma liberal 673

Seed sowing in Honduras 305

Serpientes venenosas de Honduras 119

Sex roles and social change in native lower Central America societies 259

Short-run relationship between inflation and output changes in developing countries: the case of Latin America (El Salvador, Guatemala, Honduras) 573

Significado histórico del gobierno del Dr. Ramón Villeda Morales 414

Los símbolos nacionales de Honduras 196

Los sistemas de partidos políticos en Centro América y las perspectivas de los procesos de democratización 395

La situación ambiental en Centroamérica y el Caribe 682

Situation of human rights in Honduras, 1989 380

Snakes of Honduras 120

Social support among the urban poor of Honduras: a multivariate model of individual and environmental influences on support 363

Soft war: uses and abuses of U.S. economic aid in Central America 492

Sojourners of the Caribbean: ethnogenesis and ethnohistory of the Garífuna 260

South America, Central America, and the Caribbean, 1991 772

South American handbook 54, 57

Spanish Central America: a socioeconomic history, 1520-1720 184

Spanish Honduras: its rivers, lagoons, savannas . . . transportation and natives 27

Statement of the laws of Honduras in matters affecting business 525

States of Central America 8, 85

Statistical and commercial history of the Kingdom of Guatemala, . . . from original records in the archives, actual observations and other authentic sources 221

Statistical yearbook 538

Structural roots of crisis: economic growth and decline in Honduras, 1950-1984 574

Student in Central America, 1914-1916 86

Studies in Spanish-American population history 262

Studies in the economics of Central America 575

Study of sorghum diseases in Honduras, their importance under different cropping systems, and strategies for their control 643

Suazo Córdova, a mitad de la jornada 415

Summary of the labor situation in Honduras 674

Sumus in Nicaragua and Honduras: an endangered people 271

Supplement to a bibliography of United States–Latin American relations since 1810 776

Survey of pine forests: Honduras. Final report 619

Survey on priority needs for qualified human resources in four Central American and Caribbean countries: Costa Rica, Dominican Republic, Honduras, Republic of Panama 676

Systems of labor organization in Late Classic Copán, Honduras: the energetics of construction 173

Systems of settlement in the precolombian Naco Valley, northwestern Honduras 150

T

Tangweera: life and adventures among gentle savages 87

Taxes and tax harmonization in Central America 576

Tegucigalpa de mis recuerdos; La Galería de los indispensables; Gobernantes de Honduras desde 1824 hasta 1978 209

Tegucigalpa, Hospital General, 1880–souvenir–1927 365

Tegucigalpa This Week 18

Tendencias e investigaciones recientes de la sociología hondureño: un ensayo bibliográfico 788

Tentative bibliography of the belles-lettres of the republics of Central America 774

Through the volcanoes: a Central American journey 88

Tiburcio Carías: anatomía de una época, 1923-1948 416

Tiempo 398, 412

Tigre Island an Central America. Message from the President of the United States, transmitting documents in answer to a resolution of the House 456

To be a revolutionary: an autobiography 306

Towards a cultural policy for Honduras 749

Tradición oral indígena de Yamaranguila 294

Tradiciones tegucigalpenses 211

Tráfico de esclavos negros a Honduras 222

Tragaluz 719

Training for development of small industries: an analysis of four approaches applied in Honduras 613

Tramping through Mexico, Guatemala and Honduras: being the random notes of an incurable vagabond 89

Transfer of scholarly, scientific and technical information between North and South America 704

Tratados internacionales de Honduras 457

Travels in the free states of Central America: Nicaragua, Honduras, and San Salvador 90

Trip to British Honduras, and to San Pedro, Republic of Honduras 91

Tropical trees found in the Caribbean, South America, Central America, Mexico 101

Two approaches to an understanding of U.S.–Honduran relations 494

U

Undermining rural development with cheap credit 577

La universidad como factor de transformación social 701

Universities in the business of repression: the academic–military–industrial complex and Central America 702

Update Latin America 21

US Congressional Record 438

U.S. ends and means in Central America: a debate 495

U.S. involvement in Central America: three views from Honduras 496

U.S. policy in Central America: the endless debate 497

U.S. policy in Honduras and Nicaragua 498

U.S. relations with Honduras – 1985 499

V

El Valle de Comayagua, documentos para la historia 212

Violent neighbors: El Salvador, Central America and the United States 92

Visionaries and swindlers: the development of the railways of Honduras 653

Vital registration systems in five developing countries: Honduras, Mexixo, Philippines, Thailand, and Jamaica 254

Volcanic history of Honduras 38

W

Wanderungen durch die mittel-amerikanischen Freistaaten 90

War and peace in Central America 500

War of the disposessed: Honduras and El Salvador, 1969 475

Wilson doctrine: how the speech at Mobile, Alabama, has been interpreted by the Latin-American countries 501

With the Miskitos in Honduras 272

Works of Hubert Howe Bancroft: History of Central America 185

World education encyclopedia 691

World press encyclopedia 757

Y

Yaxkin 68

Yearbook of the United Nations 458

Your Central America guide 58

Index of Subjects

A

Abduction 369, 499
Abrams, Elliott 446
Accommodation 52, 54, 57
Acosta, Oscar 708, 714,
  725
Administration 39, 327,
  526-31, 676
  Spanish 213, 216-17, 220
Adoption 325, 336, 343
Adult education 328, 683,
  687
Advanced Seminar on
  Lower Central
  American
  Archaeology (1980)
  127
Adventurism 14, 209
Aerial maps 48
AFL-CIO 654, 656
Africans in Honduras 222,
  663, 675
  influence on folk dance
  741
Agalta valley 208
Agrarian problems 386
  see also Land reform;
  Land tenure
Agrarian reform see Land
  reform
Agrarian Reform Act
  (1972) 319
  Law (1974) 625
Agrícola de Sula 650
Agricultural credit 577,
  588, 621, 637
Agricultural curriculum
  684
Agricultural development
  558, 636, 639, 678, 785
  see also Economic
  development; Export
  economies
Agricultural ecology 121
Agricultural experts 676
Agricultural exports 552,
  554, 643
  see also Export
  economies

Agricultural pests 638
Agricultural production
  557
Agricultural resources 9
Agricultural techniques
  558
Agriculture 15, 22, 24, 42,
  82, 307, 324, 327, 383,
  538, 555, 620-43, 673,
  683
  Mayan 143
  see also products by
  name
Agriculture Information
  and Documentation
  Centre 750
Agroforestry 617
Aguilar, Ricardo 748
AID see [US] Agency for
  International
  Development
AIFLD see American
  Institute for Free
  Labor Development
Alcohol 347
Alcoholism 675
Alliance for Progress 333,
  544
Altar Q 155
Altars 155
  see also by name
Alvarado, Elvia 320
Alvarado, Jorge de 200
Alvarez Martínez, Gustavo
  375-8, 429, 435, 450,
  496
Amapala 77, 89, 206
American Anthropological
  Association
  Conference (1985) 137
American Convention on
  Human Rights 371
American Friends Service
  Committee 392
American Institute for
  Free Labor
  Development
  (AIFLD) 492, 654,
  656, 664, 668

American Museum of
  Natural History 135,
  139
American–Honduras
  Company 27
Americas Watch
  Committee 373, 377
Anarchy 231
Anglo-Spanish rivalry 197
Animals 23
  see also Fauna
Anteater 76
Anthony's Key Resort 52
Anthropology 763, 768
  see also Ethnic groups;
  and peoples by name
Anti-American sentiments
  413, 478, 496
Antillean people 310
Aquatic fauna 93
Aquatic flora 93
Arce, Manuel José 182
Archaeology 28, 30, 42,
  64, 74, 84, 94, 121-50,
  265, 527, 768
Architecture 137, 290, 743
  Tegucigalpa 210
  see also Copán
Archives 198, 216, 264,
  290, 483, 526, 750-4,
  783, 785
  French 227
  see also by name
Archives of the Indies,
  Seville 213, 262, 545,
  609
Archives of the Mexican
  Embassy 448
Argentina 377
Arias Peace Plan 497
Armed forces 12, 242, 376,
  389, 395, 403, 408,
  428-47
  see also Military, the;
  US military presence
Art and artists 290, 740,
  742, 748
Artefacts see Archaeology
Arts 737-49
  see also by genre

Arthropods 107
Artisans 673
  see also Pottery
Asia 133
Assassination see Death
  squads
Association for
  [Honduran] Progress
  426, 489
Asunción Mita 152
Atlántida 34, 128
Atlases see Maps, atlases
  and gazetteers
Audiencia of Guatamala
  78, 262
Autobiographies
  Díaz Lozano, Argentina
  713
  Turcios, Froylán 721
Automation 704
Azcona Hoyo, José Simón
  380, 394, 406, 417,
  497, 509

B

Bahr, Eduardo 708
Balance of payments 537,
  550, 557, 569, 575
Ball courts 130, 152
Banana companies see
  Multinational banana
  companies
Banana empires 14, 409,
  436, 541
Banana workers' strike
  (1954) 238, 610, 655-6,
  662, 664
'Bananagate' scandal 472
Bananas 174, 307, 566,
  610, 622
Bancroft Library,
  University of
  California 185
Banking 514, 551, 772
Barahona, José Porfirio
  708
Barba amarilla 76
Barbadians 255
Barbareta 60
Basic Valley Education

Project, Guatemala
  755
Batres, César A. 496
Bats 113, 116-17
Battles 50
Bay Islands 28, 32-3, 52,
  79, 85, 114, 139, 201,
  258, 310, 728
Becerra, Moises 748
Beef 326, 329
Beetles 102, 109
Belgium 452, 506
Belio Codesido, Emilio
  474
Belize 54, 73, 104, 130-1,
  255, 259, 430, 778
  see also British
  Honduras
Bertrand, Victoria 724
Bibliographies 773-88
  agriculture 623, 778
  economics 776-8
  fauna 105
  foreign relations 776
  geography 28
  government 778, 780,
  783
  historiography 785
  history 178, 181, 184,
  207, 776-7, 779
  Land Tenure Center 778
  law 514
  literature 777
  native peoples 261, 265
  periodicals 782-3
  politics 776-8
  sociology 322, 777, 781,
  788
  travel 786
Biographies 186, 231, 770
  Azcona Hoyo, José 417
  Carías, Tiburcio 241, 416
  Christmas, Lee 232
  Molina, Juan Ramón
  718
  Suárez, Clementina 710,
  726
  Valle, José del 233
  Valle, Rafael Heliodoro
  727
  Zelaya Sierra, Pablo 740
  see also Literature
Birds 63, 103, 105, 108,
  110-11

Birth statistics 246, 250
Bishop, A. E. 301
Bishops 199
Black, Eli 472
Black River region 29,
  223
  see also Río Tinto
Blumenschein, John 297
Boca ceramics 130
Bolivia 355, 517
Bonilla, Manuel 402
Border troubles 448, 465,
  474
  see also Boundaries
Borjas, Edilberto 708
Bosworth, Stephen 485
Botany see Flora
Boundaries 41, 50
  arbitration 466-70
  see also Border troubles
Bourbon legacy 175
Bourbon reforms 179
Bourgeoisie 189, 205,
  419
Breast-feeding 344, 350,
  355
Bribery 472, 596, 634
Britain
  relations with Honduras
  451, 454
British Central American
  Land Company 80
British Honduras 91
British influence 28, 87
British involvement 207
British Museum 64
British Office for Overseas
  Development 98
Buccaneering 28
Buchanan, John 485
Bugs see Insects
Bush administration 497
Business developments 18,
  453, 579, 603, 694
  see also Labour laws
Butterflies 115

C

Cabañas, Trinidad 191
Cabo Honduras 263
Cáceres, Alonso de 200

Cáceres Lara, Víctor 706
Cádiz experiment 175
Calderón, Francisco 304
Cambodian art 133
Campesino political
activity 382-3, 440,
640, 642, 669, 683
Campesinos 306, 309,
320-1, 329, 540, 620
Canada 279
relations with Honduras
449, 455
Canada–Caribbean–
Central America
Policy Alternatives
(CAPA) 449
Cannabis 608
CAPA *see*
Canada–Caribbean–
Central America
Policy Alternatives
Capital investment 547,
578, 611
Capitalism 189, 205, 329,
481, 658, 678
Captaincy-General in
Middle America 221
Cardona, Adilia 724
Cardona Bulnes, Edilberto
725
Carías Andino, Tiburcio
240-1, 416, 483
Carías régime 307
Carías Reyes, Marcos 706
Carías Zapata, Marcos 708
Caribbean Basin Initiative
(CBI) 544
Caribbean coast 1, 23, 65,
130, 207, 235, 633
Caribbean islands 40
Carnegie Institution 162
Carrasco, Josefa 716
Carrera, Rafael 182, 189
Carter administration 497
Cartography *see* Maps,
atlases and gazetteers
Cassel, J. G. 301
Castelar, José Adan 725
Castellanos Moya, H.
709
Castillo, Mario 748
Castillo, Roberto 708
Castro, Alejandro 706
Castro Ureña, Luís 474

Catacamas 32
Cathedrals 212
Comayagua 743
Tegucigalpa 743
Catherwood, Frederick 84
Catholic Church 185, 195,
199, 213, 217, 290,
407, 410, 436
and state 234, 242, 303
Catholic faith 267
Cattle 545, 558, 597, 601,
614
Caudillismo 405
CAUSA 426, 489
Caves 34, 153
Cayos Cochinos 60
CBI *see* Caribbean Basin
Initiative
CEDOH *see* Honduran
Documentation
Centre
CELADE 357
-Canada 358
Censorship 373, 757
Census data 247-8, 264,
358, 566
Central America *see*
countries by name
Central American
Common Market 253,
459, 542, 575, 592
Central American crisis 12,
174, 391, 449-50, 494,
559, 569
Central American
Postgraduate School
of Economics and
Planning
Development 550
Central American
Republic 502
Central American union
182
Central Bank 552-3, 584-5,
589-90
Central Intelligence
Agency (CIA) 459
Centre for Economics
Study and Teaching
453
Centre for Industrial
Information 704
Centronycteris maximiliani
113

Ceramic fragments 122,
126, 139
Ceramics *see* Pottery
Cerro Palenque 130
Chamber of Commerce
and Industry,
Tegucigalpa 18
Chartering 60
Cheney Hyde, Charles 466
Chibchan languages 730
Chiefdoms 214
Children 330, 335
abandoned 334
mortality 357
Chile 446, 787
China 420
Chinese art 133
Cholera 353
Choloma 696
Choluteca 32, 56, 188, 233,
378, 616
Chorotega Malalaca 188
Chorotega people 142
Chortí people 142
Christian Democrats 303,
395
Christian Socialism 306
Christmas, Lee 89, 232
Church organizations 771
CIA *see* US Central
Intelligence Agency
Cities 5, 54, 202
Civil registration 254
Civil rights 316, 523
Civil war 14
Class conflict 303
see also Campesinos;
Popular rebellion;
Social classes
Class struggle 459, 547
see also Campesinos;
Peasants; Popular
rebellion; Social
classes
Climate 15, 40, 42, 62, 69,
81, 99, 105
Clinics 342
Clothing 71
Coats of arms 40
Cocaine 608
Coffee 174, 627
boom 546
Coins 580, 582, 585
Cold War 497

Colombia 349
coffee boom 546
Colomoncagua 572
Colón 128
Colonial heritage 174, 179
Colonialism 178, 187
Colonization 31, 187, 214,
262
Columbus, Christopher 3,
190, 746
Comayagua 32, 86, 126,
128, 175, 179, 188,
199-200, 218, 234, 323,
527, 558
archives 198, 216
churches 743
legends 290
prostitution 331
valley 137, 148, 212, 261
Comayaguela 209
Commerce 213, 217, 221
Commercial law 506, 514,
525, 591
Commercial opportunities
18
see also Investment
Committee for the Defense
of Human Rights 376
Committee of Relatives of
Missing Detainees 376
Common Cycle of General
Culture 684
Communications 6, 42,
558, 644-53, 665
Communism 312, 384, 388
Communist Party of
Honduras 384, 388,
419-20, 425, 625
Concession of land 208,
219, 625
Confederation 175, 177
constitutions (1824,
1835) 182
Confederation of
Honduran Workers
(CTH) 654, 668
Conquistadors 212, 214,
269, 322
see also Spanish
Conquest: and by
name
Conservation 33, 527, 544,
560, 679
policy 680

Constitutional history 398,
502-25
Constitutions 465, 526
(1823) 502
19th-century 502, 504,
524
20th-century 502, 504,
522, 524
(1936) 526
(1982) 502
Consumer markets 534
Contadora Act 339
Continuismo 416
Contra–Sandinista conflict
271, 331
Contraband trade 223
Contraception 348
and fertility 349-50
Contraceptive Prevalence
Surveys 349
Contras 69, 278, 369, 393,
441, 463, 495
Convent 212
Conzemius, Edward 730
Cooperatives 572, 625,
629, 636
Copán 9, 53, 58, 76, 78, ·
83-4, 187, 265, 301
archaeology 30, 74, 94,
135, 143, 146, 151-73,
527
demography 147
Copán Regional Museum
131
Copán valley 137, 153-4
Copán–Chamelecón valley
124
Copper 604
see also Coins
Copyright 514
Coral reefs 33, 52, 60
Cornell University 125, 150
Corruption 397, 413, 666
Cortés 128, 205, 685
Cortes de Cádiz 218
Cortés, Hernán 142, 215
letters 202
Cosmopolitanism 708
Costa Rica 466, 500, 611,
778
birds 110-11
coffee boom 546
economic crisis 569
ethnic groups 255, 263

health 346, 349
history 174, 177, 183
housing policy 529
military 430
national symbols 744
politics 388-9
Costumbrismo 708
Costumbrista literary style
211
Cotton 329, 597
Council of Foreign
Bondholders 451
Counter-insurgency 437,
461, 493
Counter-revolutionaries
see Counter-
insurgency
Countryside 1, 76, 681
see also Lakes; and other
physical features by
name
Coups d'état 398, 402, 440
(1972) 427
Crabs 34
Credit 540, 553
see also Agricultural
credit; International
credit
Creole 708
Criollo influence 741
Criminal justice 518
CTH see Confederation of
Honduran Workers
Cuba 236, 713
Cuban revolution 395, 654,
656
Cultivated plants 22
Cultural characteristics 7,
87
Cultural policy 749
Culture 2, 88, 186-7, 193,
233, 785
see also Ethnic groups;
Statistics; and peoples
by name
Cuna people 259
Currency 69, 553, 581
Current events 16-21
Cuscatlán 78
Customs and excise 566,
576
Customs and traditions
71-2, 126, 185, 209, 211
see also Ethnic groups;
and peoples by name

Cuyamel Fruit Company 438, 650
  see also Zemurray, Samuel

D

Daily life 1, 3, 9, 321
  Mayan 142-3
  native people 263
Dances 288-9, 293, 707, 741
Danlí 32, 286
Dávila, Miguel 565
Death squads 371, 373, 380-1, 410
  see also Murder
Debt 448, 451, 490, 539, 544, 550, 565
  see also External debt
Defence 428-47
Deforestation 415, 614, 616, 681-2
Democracy 194, 382, 390, 395, 403, 561
Democratic Left 421
Demography *see* Population
Dengue fever 351
Dependency theory 240, 574
Detention 372-3, 380
Developing countries 573
  see also by name
Development assistance 458, 544, 703
Development plans
  (1974-78) 318
  (1979-83) 665
Development policy 382, 405, 640-1
Diarrhoeal diseases 341, 354
Díaz Lozano, Argentina 713, 723
Dictatorship 416
Diplomatic correspondence 416, 456
Diplomatic developments 18
Diplomatic initiatives 449

Diplomatic relations 462, 464
  see also Foreign relations; International relations
Disappearance *see* Abduction
Diseases 682
  see also Health; Public Health; *and diseases by name*
Displaced persons 331
Dividends 591
Diving 52
Documents 465
  16th-century 216
  see also Archives; Bibliographies
Domínguez, José 716
Drugs 413
  trafficking 448, 478, 488, 608, 634
Duncan, Isadora 711
Durón, Rómulo E. 716
Durón, Valentin 716

E

Earthquakes 90, 151
  (1915) 190
Ecclesiastical divisions 50, 218
Echeverría y Vidaurre, Manuel 466
ECLA *see* UN Economic Commission for Latin America
Ecology 106, 352, 554, 615, 678-82
Economic activity 39, 47, 214
  women and 311, 313
Economic conditions 27, 87, 238, 242, 384, 387, 412, 442, 453, 488, 550, 559, 574, 586, 656, 689, 772
Economic development 18, 184, 194, 205, 213, 298, 326, 542, 554, 560, 568, 599, 628, 631, 633, 639, 675, 762

Economic events 6, 191, 437, 708
Economic history 481, 566, 578, 658, 663
Economic integration 544, 554, 560, 581, 762
Economic issues 12, 20, 543, 545
Economic justice 483, 664
Economic prospects 27, 544
Economic stability 569-70
Economics 16, 74, 179, 233, 540-76, 776-8
Economy 5, 11, 22, 27, 71, 81, 183, 195, 318, 413
  see also Statistics
Ecotourism 544, 615
Ecuador 517
Ecumenical Program for Interamerican Communication and Action (EPICA) 410
Education 10, 47, 82, 204, 233-4, 317-18, 327, 448, 523, 537-8, 560, 637, 676, 683-702
El Cajón 134, 137
El Carbón 208
El Dorado 69
El Paraíso 286, 378
El Salvador 9, 78, 81, 92, 491, 508, 517, 611, 778
  agrarian structure 620
  archaeology 131
  coffee boom 546
  economics 548-9
  fauna 113
  history 183, 238
  housing policy 529
  inflation 573
  military 430, 445
  national symbols 744
  politics 312, 389, 394
  relations with Honduras 459, 465, 470
  USA 493
  social change 545
  social structure 326, 337, 339
  trade 594
  US economic aid 492
  see also Refugees

El Salvador-Honduras
conflict (1969) 192,
252-3, 386, 431, 434,
460, 464, 472, 475,
592, 594
El Triunfo de la Cruz 215
Elections 389-90, 395,
399-401, 403-4, 411,
484
see also Political parties;
Presidential elections
Electoral system 526
Electrical appliances 534
Elites 322
Elitist rebellions 235
Encyclopaedia 769
Energy 318, 538
crisis 551
experts 676
English speakers 197
Enoé Clix, Aura 724
Entrepreneurs 207
Entrepreneurship
Development Center
694
Environment 6, 415, 544,
678-82
policy 682
Epidemics 184
Erosion 151
control 556
Escoto, Julio 706, 708
España, Isidoro 745
Espino, Fernando 304
Esquema Director de
Ordenamiento
Metropolitano 1975-
2000 (EDOM) 531
Esquipulas Peace Plan 497
Ethnic groups 12, 255-72
Ethnobotany 97
Ethnography 187
see also Ethnic groups
Ethnohistory 87, 178, 260
Ethnomedicine 256-7, 267,
310, 354
Euceda, Max 748
European [Economic]
Community 542, 581
European settlers 129
Exchange rate 553
Expatriate entrepreneurs
599, 607
Experts needed 676

Exploitation 545, 675
Explorers 50, 136, 202
Export economics 174,
252, 438, 550, 552,
567-8, 575, 611, 614,
641-2
Exports 10, 329, 481, 509,
550, 597, 627, 642
see also Import–export;
and products by name
Expropriation 510
External debt 408, 448,
557, 564, 602, 644, 658
Extrajudicial execution
373, 375, 380

F

F-5E aircraft 446
Fagot Muller, Steadman
461
Falkland Islands 477
Family planning 328, 342,
348-50, 362, 696
see also Sterilization
Family structure 325
Fauna 29, 33, 64, 69, 73,
76, 93-5, 102-20
Federación Obrera
Hondureña 656
Federación Sindical
Hondureña 656
Federation 174, 179, 191,
228, 230
disintegration 226
Federation of Honduran
Women's Associations
332
Fertility see Family
planning
Feudal aristocracy 189
Fiallos, Mélida 724
Fillmore, Millard,
President 456
Finance 383, 533, 539, 555,
560, 665
First aid 107
Fiscal law 533, 562
First Meeting of the
University Community
697
Fishes 107
blennioid 104

freshwater 106
Fishing 60
Flags 40, 196, 746
Flints 157
Flora 29, 33, 69, 73,
93-101, 615, 626
Flores 558
Folklore 284-94, 739, 756
Fontana, Jaime 725
Food 71, 534
security 642
shortage 614
Food and Agriculture
Organization (FAO)
619
Forced labour 178, 184,
269
Foreign aid 449, 455, 492,
555
Foreign Assistance Act 491
Foreign debt see External
debt
Foreign investment see
Investment
Foreign involvement 242
Foreign Office, London
451
Foreign policy 194, 446
Foreign relations 16-17, 50,
224, 448-58
bibliography 776
within Central America
459-75
with USA 476-501
Forestry 614-19, 676, 681
Fort Omoa 197, 222
Fortín, Miguel 716
France 224, 227, 439
Franciscan mission 304
Francisco Morazán
Teacher Training
College 752
Fuelwood 616
Fungi 638
Furniture industry 672

G

Gallardo, Guadalupe 716
Gálvez, Juan Manuel 547
Galvin, John 446
Gambia, The 755

Gamero de Medina, Lucila
723
Gardens 626
Garífuna people 28, 235,
255-60, 284, 310
Garment workers 670
Gazetteers see Maps,
atlases and gazetteers
Genealogy 322
General Archives of the
Government
(Guatemala) 213
General Captaincy of
Guatemala 218
General Office of Statistics
and Censuses 507
General Secretariat for
Urban Studies 46
Genocide 374
Geochemistry 35
Geography 2, 4, 22-7, 53,
64, 74, 90, 126-7, 193,
767
regional 28-32
Geology 5, 33-9, 105, 125
Geophysics 35
Geopolitics 450
Geothermal energy 37
Geothermal sites 35-6
GNP see Gross national
product
Gold 184
mines 222, 604-5, 609
Gómez, Máximo 236
Government 3, 5, 10-11,
19, 217, 239, 511, 778,
780, 783
brought to trial 370-1
see also Local
government
Governors of Copán 155
Gracias a Dios 190, 202-3,
378
Grasses 96
Graves 156
Great Depression 483
Grid references 45
Gross national product
(GNP) 535-6, 550, 557
Growth potential 560
Guanaja 60, 190
Guarabuqui 134
Guatemala 37, 517, 611,
778

archaeology 131
archives 198, 216
coffee boom 546
confrontation 545
economics 548-9
education 755
folklore 284
health 346
history 175, 179, 183
inflation 573
maps 40-1
military 430
national symbols 744
politics 339, 389, 394
relations with Honduras
466-9, 473-4
US economic aid 492
violence 337
Guatemala City 89, 200,
221
Guerrillas 6, 242, 275, 281,
330, 445
Guillén Zelaya, Alfonso
724
Gulf of Fonseca 456, 464,
469, 471, 508
Gulf of Mexico 59
'Gunboat diplomacy' 480
Gutiérrez, Carlos 716
Guyana 388

H

Habsburg rule 179
Handicapped people 671
Harvard–Smithsonian
project 150
Hasandigubida 257
Health 318, 327, 340-68,
458, 683
see also Statistics
Health education 340, 356,
755
see also Family planning;
Immunization
Health services see Public
health; Social services
Health-care training 340
Henderson, J. S. 150
Herbs 97
Herrera, Dionisio [de] 180,
229, 716

Hieroglyphics 155, 160,
164
see also Mayan
hieroglyphics
Higher education 686,
690-1, 697-8
see also University
education; and
establishments by
name
Higueras 213
Historiography 181, 785
History 2, 4, 8, 10-11, 13-15,
40, 50, 53, 69, 74,
186-96, 767-8, 776, 779
Central America 174-85
colonial (1502-1821) 187,
198-9, 213-23
local 197-212
19th century 224-37
20th century 238-45
Holocene period 145
Hondbra 670
Honduran Air Force 431,
439
Honduran Anti-
Communist
Movement (MACHO)
410, 426
Honduran Association of
Librarians and
Archivists 754
Honduran Chamber of
Tourism 18
Honduran Documentation
Centre (CEDOH)
396-7, 463, 550
Honduran Ecology
Association 112
Honduran Federation of
Campesina Women
332
Honduran Institute of
Anthropology and
History 125, 129, 162,
165, 740
Honduran National School
of Forestry Sciences
98
Honduran Navy 439
Honduran Press
Association 760
Honduran Women's Day
332

Honduran–American
    Chamber of
    Commerce 18
Honduras Family Planning
    Association 696
Horcones massacre 472
Hornet incident 490
Hospitals 342, 361, 365,
    368
Hot springs 34
Hotels *see* Accommodation
Household goods 534
Housing 71, 251, 318, 323,
    333, 367, 538, 675
    policy 529
    privatization 571
Houston, Texas 283
Hughes, Charles Evans 474
Human rights 19, 21 194,
    242, 369-81, 408, 413,
    489, 491, 499, 664, 695
Human Rights Watch 373
Humuya drainage system
    106
    river valley 121, 124
Hunger 408, 642
    see also Nutrition
Hurricane Fifi 192, 366-7
Hyde, Charles Cheney 466
Hydrography 40, 42

I

Iconography 141, 165
IMF *see* International
    Monetary Fund
Immigration 31, 633
Immigration problems 448
    see also Refugees
Immunization 345
Implements 144
Import–export 18, 593
Imports 206, 509, 602, 606
Impoverishment 174
Income distribution 323
Income tax law *see* Fiscal
    law
Independence 14, 174-5,
    179, 189, 218, 226,
    317, 455
indigenous art 133
indigenous artefacts 64

indigenous influence 741
indigenous peoples 214,
    261-72, 310, 635, 663
    legislation regarding 521
    see also by name
indigenous revolts 213, 545
indigenous social systems
    214
Indo-China 133
Industry 383, 538, 542,
    555, 665, 762, 772
    experts 676
    small 613
Inequalities 174, 554, 559,
    656
Infant health 344
Infant mortality 340, 357-8
Inflation 551, 560, 573
Information Centre on
    Instructional
    Technology 755
Infrastructure 538, 540,
    560, 673
    experts 676
Innovation and [Social
    Democractic] Union
    Party 395, 424
Inscriptions 164, 166
Insects 107, 118, 638
Intellectual trends 185
    *see also intellectuals by
    name*
Inter-American
    Commission of
    Women 316
Inter-American
    Commission on
    Human Rights 462
Inter-American Court of
    Human Rights 370-1,
    373, 379
Inter-American
    Development Bank
    250, 620
Inter-American Highway
    55
Inter-Hemispheric
    Education Resource
    Center 6
International Bureau of
    the American
    Republics 10
International Congress of
    the Book (1982) 759

International Court of
    Justice (ICJ) 465,
    470-1
Internation credit 583
    see also Railways
International labour
    relations 660
International law 495
International Monetary
    Fund (IMF) 534, 570
International relations 3,
    86, 405, 512
    see also specific countries
International treaties 457,
    471
Interoceanic Railway 81,
    85, 583, 644-7, 651-2
Interrogation 381
Intibuca 267
Investment 26-7, 436, 509,
    560, 587, 598-9, 607,
    646-7
    public-sector 564
IPGH *see* Panamerican
    Institute of Geography
    and History
Iran 450
Iriona 258
Iron working 129
Irrigation 386
Israel 450
Italy 506
Iturbide, Augustín 582

J

Jamaica 223
Jamaicans 255
Jesuits 300, 306, 689
    see also by name
Jewish life in Central
    America 450
Jicaque people 76, 97, 136,
    219, 264, 266, 268,
    284, 304, 310
Joint Resolution 277 446
Journalism 756, 760-1
Judicial circuits 505
Judicial system 502-25
Jungle
    coastal 79
    highland 76

tropical 75
Junonia 115
Jurisdictional problems 213
Justice 455, 664
see also Criminal;
Economic; Social
justice
Juticalpa 32
Juvenile delinquents 736

K

Kennedy administration 491
King, Edward 446
King of Spain 78
Kinship 325
Kissinger Commission 544
Knox–Paredes treaty 490

L

La Antigua 572
La Campa 738
La Ceiba 34, 115, 123, 745
La Concordia national park 132
La Entrada 137
La Merced church, Comayagua 743
La Paz 267
La Suiza 297
La Unión 152
La Virtud refugee camp 273, 282
Labour 80, 554, 560, 609, 611-12, 654-77
Labour laws 316, 514, 519, 660, 666, 674
affecting women 523
codified 238, 664
Labour movements 382, 440, 483, 610, 661, 669
Labour problems 448
Labour relations 660, 666
Ladino people 310, 325, 521
Lake Petén 63
Lake Yojoa 146, 265, 297
Lakes 34, 714

see also by name
Land 5, 11, 23, 611
see also Concession
Land reform 242, 298, 309, 319-20, 324, 440, 540, 567, 620-43, 670
Land tenure 252, 324, 374, 554, 558, 566-7, 620-43, 658, 678
Land Tenure Center bibliography 778
Land use 42, 47, 155, 331, 614-15, 642
Landless families 319, 324, 329, 620
Landowners 198, 324
Language 42, 269, 728-36
Latin America see countries by name
Latin American Studies Association Congress (1983) 276
(1986) 390
Law 502-25, 690, 758, 766
Lazzaroni Andino, Dante 748
Legends see Folklore
Legislative history 398, 635
Lempira 203, 267, 738, 746
Lempira rebellion (1537) 189
Lenca people 142, 169, 267, 269, 294, 304
pottery 737
León 200
Literal Party 395-6, 401, 406, 413-14, 422, 427, 566
Liberal reform 231, 234, 600, 673
Liberty unity 179
Liberation theology 302-3
Libraries 750-4
see also by name
Library of Congress 780
Libya 450
Life expectancy 323
Lifestyle 1, 71, 214, 268
Lindo, Juan 716
Literacy 328, 415, 683, 685, 689, 696
Literary prizes 759
Linguistics see Language
Literature 706-27

see also genres, novelists, poets by name
Living conditions 13, 89, 567
Lobo, Hostilio 724
Local government 526-31
López, Walter 429
López Arellano, Oswaldo 400, 427, 472, 628, 634
Los Alamos National Laboratory 35-6
Los Catrachos trio 739
Los Dolores church, Tegucigalpa 743
Luxembourg 452

M

M-LIDER 421
Maceo 236
Machismo 314, 337, 428
MACHO see Honduran Anti-Communist Movement
Mahogany trees 3
Maldonado, R. 709
Mallol, Narciso 220
Malnutrition see Nutrition
Mammals 112, 615
Manufacturing 538, 557, 560
Mao Tse-Tung 420
Maoism 420
Maps, atlases and gazetteers 39-51
Marginalized groups see Guerrillas; Refugees; Street vendors; Women
Marine parks 33
Maritime charts 59
Marriage 234
statistics 246
Martí, José 236
Martínez Galindo, Arturo 706
Masculinity see Machismo
Masica incident 454
Mass media 755, 772
Mass Media and Health Practices Project 341
Massacre at Lempa River (1981) 273

near Santa Rosa de
Copán (1980) 281
Matagalpa people 136
Matta Ballesteros, Juan
Ramón 478
Maya Lowlands 130, 145,
154
demography 147
Maya people 84, 142-3,
153, 159, 162, 165,
173, 187
collapse 154, 285
Mayan hieroglyphics 132,
141
Mayan ruins 141
see also Copán; *and
others by name*
McCollum Amendment
491
Media 6
see also Mass media
Medical education 698
Medicine 97, 695
see also Ethnomedicine
Melgar Castro, Alberto
634
Mercantile codes 506
Merendón mountains 469
Mesa Grande refugee
camp 281-2
Mesoamerica *see countries
by name*
Metates [grinding stones]
170
Mexico 25, 57, 84, 108,
131, 173, 255, 265,
314, 347
relations with Honduras
453
war with France 224
Mexico City 408, 435
Meza, Victor 396, 496
Middle America *see
countries by name*
Middle American
Research Institute 124
Migration 252, 329, 554
statistics 246, 250
Militarism 195, 440
Militarization *see* Armed
forces; Military, the;
US military presence
Military government 401,
405

see also Coups d'état;
Human rights;
Military, the
Military research and
development 702
Military, the 7, 14, 16, 42,
213, 239, 275-6, 320,
410, 428-47, 555
see also Human rights
Millett, Richard 446, 485
Mineral deposits 35
Mineral resources 9, 24,
26, 42
see also Copper; Gold;
Silver
Mining 10, 15, 42, 69, 184,
210, 538, 560, 566,
600, 605, 609, 663,
673, 772
Mining operators 198
Mining workers 675
Ministry of Culture and
Tourism 129, 749
Ministry of [Public] Health
356, 368, 696
Ministry of Social
Assistance 696
Miscegenation 262
Miskito people 87, 129,
136, 263, 270, 272,
274, 299, 378
Missionaries 87, 208, 219,
269, 297, 301, 304-6,
455
see also Moravians; *and
missionaries by name*
Mitchell-Hedges, F. A. 64
Modernismo 718
Molina, Juan Ramón 718
Monetary policy 551, 578,
598
Monetary union 581
see also Economic
integration
Monkeys 63
Monoculture 184
Montana de la Flor 310
Montejo, Francisco de 200,
213
Montes de Oca, Confucio
748
Montoya, Carlos 396
Morat 60
Moravians 87, 299

Morazán, Francisco 177,
179-80, 182, 189, 191,
227-8, 714, 716, 746
Morgan, J. P. 451, 565
Moroceli 313, 667
Mortality statistics 246,
250, 323
see also Infant mortality
Mosquitia *see* Mosquito
Coast
Mosquito Coast 79, 85,
197, 207, 223, 258,
263, 291, 470
Motor vehicles 55
Multinational banana
companies 240, 315,
438, 472, 596
see also by name
Murder 369, 374, 376
see also Death squads
Museum of the American
Indian 64
Museums 131
see also by name
Music 289, 744
Musical instruments 288,
293
Myths 266
see also Folklore

N

Naco phase 125
Naco valley 137, 150
Naco Valley Survey
Project 150
Nation-states 174, 179,
226, 409
National Agrarian Institute
630, 637
National Agricultural
Development Bank
588
National Archives of
Honduras 655, 717
National Archives,
Washington 416
National Autonomous
University of
Honduras (UNAH)
697-700
autonomy 695, 701

herbarium 99
Honduran Collection 416, 712
National Census of Settlements and Cooperatives 630
National Center for Health Statistics 254
National characteristics 231, 382, 487
National Congress 503
National Congress of Theatre 715
National Constituent Assembly (1980) 435
National development plans *see* Development plans
National Drug Council 608
National Electoral Tribunal 705
National Folklore Office 739
National Geographic Institute of Honduras 45, 51
National Guard 447
National hymns 744, 746
National income 535-6, 552, 586
National Library 655, 717, 752
National Literacy Plan 415
National Museum of Honduras, Tegucigalpa 131
National parks 95, 132, 679
National Party 395, 413, 418, 422
National product 323, 535, 537
National Registry of Persons 705
National security 7, 194, 446, 482, 487
National symbols 196, 504, 744, 746
National System of School Libraries 752
National Theatre Company 745
National Tribunal of Elections 399
Nationalism 177, 496

Nationalist Party 400
Natural resources 3, 26-7, 33-8, 48, 53, 81, 252, 514, 525, 560, 604, 635, 679, 681
policy 680
Navarro, Pedro 212
Navas, Ada María 724
Navas de Miralda, Navas 723
Nazis 374
NCC Industries 670
Negroponte, John 429
Nepal 349
Netherlands 452
New York Navigation and Colonization Company 31
Newspapers 757, 772
Nicaragua 73, 87, 144, 463, 508, 611, 778
coffee boom 546
education 755
fauna 110, 113
health 346
history 183, 197, 238
military 430, 438, 442-3
national symbols 744
politics 312, 339
refugees 9, 274
relations with Honduras 461, 470, 512
with USA 493
social change 545
US economic aid 492
see also Border troubles; Sandinistas
Non-governmental agencies 449, 771
North Americans 28
North Coast [Federation] 32, 60, 610
trade unions 656, 664, 674
Novels 707, 723
Nutrition 318, 323, 329, 352, 359, 554, 642

O

OAS *see* Organization of American States

Obsidian 144, 167
Occupational training 659
Office of Labor Affairs International Cooperation Administration 674
Office of Public Safety (OPA) 491
Olanchito 32
Olancho 69, 128, 208, 386
massacres 597
poetry 724
rebellions 235
Olancho Forest Development Programme 415
Olid, Cristóbal de 215
Omoa 63
OPA *see* Office of Public Safety
Oral rehydration therapy 341, 354
Order of Mercy 212
Organization of American States (OAS) 370, 460, 462, 470
statistics 534
Ornithology *see* Birds
Orphanages 334, 338
Osorio, Miguel Angel 724
Oviedo, Jorge Luís 706, 722

P

Pacific coast 62, 111
Pacific Ocean 59, 61
PAHO *see* Pan-American Health Organization
Pakistan 279
Palaeoecology 145
Palestine Liberation Organization (PLO) 450
Pan-American Health Organization (PAHO) 357
Pan-American Highway 56, 649
Panamá 40, 54, 61, 89, 110, 255, 388, 392, 510, 517, 564, 778

Panama Canal 255
Panamerican Institute of
  Geography and
  History (IPGH) 46
Para-military groups 6,
  410, 435, 440, 463
Paredes, Rigoberto 709,
  725
Party politics 14
Patronage 663
Paya people 28, 129, 136,
  208, 219, 730
Paya region 128
Paz García, Policarpo 401,
  435
Peabody Museum 162
Peace 332, 392, 455
  initiatives 442, 497, 695
  -keeping 449
Peace Corps 383
Pearl Lagoon 23
Peasants 189
  see also Campesinos;
  Popular rebellion
Penca people 23
Pentagon 498
People 5, 11, 23, 53, 71,
  73-4, 76, 80-2, 88, 187,
  193
  see also Maya; Miskito;
  and others by name
Perry Land Grant 633
Persecution 373, 488
Personalismo 416, 421
Peru 517
Pesticides and pest control
  407, 638, 681
Petitions 216
Pharmaceutical services
  360
Pharmaceuticals 534
Philippines 355
Philosophy 180
Photography, underwater
  52
Physicians 361
Pine forests 98, 619
Pineapples 707
Pitt, William 223
Place-names 45, 49
Plantanares 37
Playa de los Muertos 146

PLO see Palestine
  Liberation
  Organization
Poetry 203, 709, 714, 716-
  17, 720, 724-5
  see also poets by name
Police 491
Policy Alternatives for the
  Caribbean and Central
  America 482
Political activists
  persecuted 372
Political asylum 283
Political characteristics 7,
  14, 396-416
Political conditions 238,
  242, 387, 412, 488
Political economy 557, 566
Political events 6, 92, 191,
  224, 229-30, 295, 392,
  437, 708
Political intrigue 213
Political issues 12, 20, 543,
  545
Political mobilization 559
Political participation 398,
  406-7
Political parties 320, 417-
  27, 656
  see also Politics; and
  parties by name
Political system 12
  see also Democracy;
  Elections; Political
  parties
Politics 13, 15-17, 19, 69,
  74, 82, 179, 183, 185-
  6, 239, 382-427, 436,
  526, 776-8
Pompilinae 118
Popular rebellion 189, 235,
  408-9, 567
Population 39, 42, 44, 47,
  90, 246-54, 262, 448,
  558, 566, 678, 762
  (1680-1840) 179
  policy 249
  see also Statistics
Port facilities 27
  Pacific 206
Positivism 237
Pottery 126, 137, 140, 146
  Lempira 738
  Lenca 737

Mayan 132, 156
Poverty 269, 302, 306, 332,
  362-3, 392, 620, 631,
  637
Pre-Columbian
  Mesoamerica 140, 187
  see also Archaeology
Prehistory 40
  see also Archaeology
Presidential elections 440
  (1922) 245
  (1954) 238
  (1981) 403
  (1985) 403, 406
  (1990) 278
Press, the 757
Prices 569, 573
Primary schools 571, 686,
  691
  libraries 752-3
Printing industry 758, 761
Private property 510, 514
Privatization 571
Problems 3
  see also Children;
  Poverty; Refugees;
  Social issues
Professional publications
  762-8, 782-3
Prostitution 331, 428, 523
Protestant churches 296,
  301
Proyecto Arqueológica
  Copán 154-5, 160,
  162, 165
Proyecto Arqueológico
  Sula 145
Proyecto Leña y Fuentes
  Alternas de Energia
  616
Public health 342, 365,
  523, 525, 544
  see also Family planning;
  Health education;
  Immunization
Public holidays 83, 293
Public Record Office,
  London 451
Public services 234
Publishing 756, 759, 772,
  787
Puerto Barrios 258
Puerto Cortés 86
  Free Zone 509

Puerto Rico 498

Q

Quesada, José Luís 709, 725
Quetzal bird 76
Quirigua 147, 152

R

Racial tension 675
Radio 757, 772
Radio Mathematics, Nicaragua 755
Radio schools, Honduras 683
Radio Suyapa 687
Radiocarbon dating 127
Railways 27, 650, 653
  British loans 490, 565, 583
  surveying mission 75
  see also by name
Rainfall 28
Rainforest 99
Rama people 259
Ramírez, Alexis 709
Ramón Reyes, Juan 716, 724
Rancho Ires phase 125
RAND 496
Reagan administration 383, 391-2, 441, 489, 491, 497, 500
Reagan, Ronald 493
Recinos, Adrián 466
Reef structure 33
Refugees 9, 273-83, 330, 376-8, 407-8, 410, 449
  see also Statistics
Regional development 544
  see also Central American Common Market; Economic integration
Regional emblems 196
Regionalism 708
Relief agencies see Hurricane Fifi; Refugees

Religion 295-306, 337
  see also Church; Missionaries
Religious architecture 199
Religious art 199
Religious practices 216-17
  see also Ethnic groups; and peoples by name
Remotely piloted vehicles (RPVs) 444
Rent see Land tenure
Repression 195
Reptiles 63, 107
Republican experiment 179
Research 676, 751
  see also Archives; Bibliographies
Respiratory diseases 340
Restaurants 54, 57
Revolutionary Democratic Party 421
Revolutionary movements 394, 450
Revolutionary Socialist Party (PSR) 421
Reyna, Carlos Roberto 396
Right-wing political parties 426
Río Chamelecón 150
Río Guayape Valley 32
Río Montagua 469
Río Negro 29
  see also Río Tinto
Río Platano Biosphere Reserve 615
Río San Juan 263
Río Tinto 29, 80, 129
Rivalry 175, 179
Rivas, Antonio José 725
Rivers 714
  see also by name
Road system 9, 55, 82, 560, 571, 648
Roatán 33, 52
Rock formations 38
Rosa, Ramón 225, 237, 600
Rosario Mine 598
Rotary Club of Tegucigalpa 603
Ruins see Archaeology
Ruíz, Miguel Angel 748
Rural development 572, 641

see also Agrarian problems; Agricultural development; Peasant class; Villages
Rural life see Social structure
Rural politics 195
  see also Campesino political activity

S

Sabotage 445
Sailing 59-62
Salazar, Carlos 466-8
Sambo-Miskito allies 197
San Buenaventura 304
San Esteban 32
San Lorenzo 323
San Marcos de Colón 56
San Pedro Pinula 152
San Pedro Sula 9, 58, 77, 202, 204-5, 250-1, 305, 368, 616, 713, 761
San Salvador 90, 251
Sánchez, Roberto M. 748
Sanctuary Movement 374
Sandinistas 441, 463, 489, 497, 658
Santa Bárbara 128, 137-8
Savannas 22, 32, 99
Schools see Education
Science and technology 538, 695, 703-5
Scuba-diving 60
Sculpture 290
Secession 218
Secondary education 686, 691
Securities and Exchange Commission 472
Seibal 147
Self-help projects 572
Semi-feudalism 189, 625
Seminar for the Education of School Librarians 752
Settlement 26, 31-2, 44, 60, 66, 80, 184, 219, 633
  see also Archaeology; and settlements by name

255

Seville
  archives 198, 216, 545
Sex roles 259
Sexually transmitted
  diseases 682
Sharks 114
Sharon, Ariel 450
Sherds see Ceramic
  fragments
Ship registers 566
Short stories 706, 708, 722
Sierra, Terencio 229
Siguatepeque 32
Silver 3, 69, 184, 200, 210,
  598, 605, 609, 612
Slang 736
Slavery 178, 189, 222, 262,
  269
  abolition 222
Sloth 76
Smallpox 353
Snakes 76, 120
  poisonous 119
Soccer War see El
  Salvador–Honduras
  conflict
Social Christian movement
  303
Social classes 189, 240,
  428, 547
  (1680-1840) 179
Social conditions 3-4, 69,
  71, 74, 81, 90, 92, 179,
  185, 238, 307-39, 412,
  458, 488, 656
  see also Statistics
Social conflict 559
Social customs 217, 224,
  286
  see also Ethnic groups;
    and peoples by name
Social democracy 421
Social development 298,
  567, 676
Social events 6, 191, 708
Social issues 12, 328-39,
  765-6
Social justice 194, 332
Social security 238, 316,
  514
Social services 338, 340-68
  women and 311
Social structure 319-27,
  566, 785

Socialism 658
Society of Enterprising
  Thought and Good
  Taste 693
Socio-economic
  characteristics 7, 558,
  566, 631, 681, 685, 692
Socio-politics 308, 662
Sociology 322, 777, 781,
  788
Soil 3, 32, 42, 105, 121, 145
Somalia 279
Somoza Debayle,
  Anastasio 438, 461
Songs 739
Sorghum 556
  diseases 643
SOS Children's Village 315
Sosa, Roberto 719, 725
Soto, Marco Aurelio 234,
  600, 673
Sovereignty 464-5, 477,
  487, 508, 565
Soviet Union 420
Spain 218, 223
  see also under Spanish
Spaniards 28
Spanish Conquest 78, 125,
  136, 150, 187, 214, 554
Spanish dominion 184, 213
  see also History, colonial
Spanish forts 222
  see also by name
Spanish governors 199
  see also by name
Spanish Honduras 91
Spanish speakers 197, 728,
  731-3, 735
Spiritual beliefs 257-8
  see also Religion;
    Religious practices
Sports 54
Squier, E. G. 644
  see also Interoceanic
  Railway
Standard Brands 596
Standard Fruit Company
  541, 707
Standard of living 313, 557
Stanford University Food
  Research Institute 344
Statistics 8, 13, 221, 307,
  321, 507, 532-9, 772
  business 555

  cultural 532
  economic 532-4, 537-9,
  548-50, 563, 566, 568,
  578, 586, 640
  health 357, 538
  national development
  665
  population 246-7, 250-1,
  254, 532, 538-9
  refugees 280
  social 532, 537-9
Stein, Gertrude 711
Stela B, Copán 133
Stelae 155, 160, 163, 171
  see also by name
Stephens, John Lloyd 84
Sterilization 350, 364, 368
Street vendors 330
Strikes 238, 407
Stromsvik, Gustav 30
Strong, W. D. 150
Suárez, Clementina
  710-11, 719, 724-6
Suazo Córdova, Roberto
  390, 397, 401, 411,
  415, 429, 499, 513, 632
Subirana, Manuel de Jesús
  208, 219, 264
Subsistence farming 566
Suffrage 332
Sugar plantations 222
Sugar processing 129, 329
Sula valley 125, 137, 150,
  629
Sulaco drainage system 106
  river valley 121, 134, 261
Sumpul massacre 410
Sumu people 136, 263,
  271, 274, 291
Superstitions 288
Supreme Court of Justice
  513
Swamps 99
Swan Islands 33, 477

T

Tacoma incident 490
Talanga 32
Tax increases 435
Taxation 552, 576, 663
  see also Fiscal law

Teacher training 689, 692
Technical assistance 450,
    671, 703
Technical cooperation 674
Technology transfer 23,
    676, 704-5
    see also Science and
    technology
Tegucigalpa 9, 32, 58, 83,
    86, 89, 175, 179, 205,
    209-11, 218, 227, 234,
    266, 365, 368, 386, 713
    (1578-1821) 198, 340
    architecture 743
    archives 198
    battle 245
    children 335, 338, 344
    fuelwood 616
    Mint 582
    population 250-1
    poverty 363-4
    printing 758
    school libraries 753
    trade unions 674
    urbanization 531
    water supply 679
Tela 9
Tela Railroad Company
    481, 596, 610
Television 757, 772
Tenampua 126
Thailand 279, 349
Theatre 715, 720, 745
Tigra National Park 679
Tigre Island 146, 456
Tikal 147
Titling assistance project
    637
Tol people 264
Toltec people 285
Tolupán people 266
Tombs 156
Topography 40, 42, 48, 51,
    566
Torres Arias, Leonides 435
Torrupán people 268, 310
Torture 369, 372-3, 376,
    380-1
Tourism 52-8, 537, 560
    see also Ecotourism
Tourist centres 40, 57
Towns 40, 44, 54, 73, 202
    see also by name
Trade 47, 69, 82, 146, 224,

326, 384, 539, 542,
    544, 557, 594, 772
    Mayan 143
    reports 566
Trade Union Federation of
    Workers of Northern
    Honduras
    (FESITRANH) 670
Trade winds 610, 654-77
    see also Labour
    movements
Trademarks 514
Trans-Pacific contact 133
Transaction costs 588
Transfer payments 554
Transportation 27, 39-40,
    42, 54-7, 224, 318,
    525, 558, 644-53, 665
Travellers' accounts 63-92,
    786
Travesía 146
Travieso, Jorge Federico
    725
Treaties 457, 466, 471, 490,
    520
Trees 100-1
Trinidad Reyes, José 716
Tropical climate 99
Trujillo 65, 72, 190, 197,
    222-3, 258
Tuberculosis 356
Turcios, Froylán 68, 716,
    721, 724
Turrupán 76

U

Ulúa boundary line 469
Ulúa valley 124, 128, 130,
    145, 149
    polychromes 139, 146
UN Conference on the
    Law of the Sea
    (1974) 516
    see also Water rights
UN Economic Commission
    for Latin America
    (ECLA) 550
UN High Commission for
    Refugees (UNHCR)
    273, 275, 282
UN projects 458

UN statistics 534
UNAH see National
    Autonomous
    University of
    Honduras
Underdevelopment 330,
    564
Unemployment 324, 339,
    408, 666, 694
Unesco 749, 752
UNHCR see UN High
    Commission for
    Refugees
Unicef 357
United Brands 472
United Fruit Company 23,
    438, 480, 490, 541,
    596, 610, 653, 655, 675
United Nations see entries
    under UN
United Provinces of
    Central America 222
United States of America
    see entries under
    America[n], North
    Americans, US
University education 452
University of New Mexico
    615
University of San Carlos,
    Guatemala 697
Urbanization 251, 531, 785
[US] Agency for
    International
    Development (AID)
    [USAID] 254, 311,
    383, 476, 492, 641, 705
US Board on Geographic
    Names 45, 49
US Central Intelligence
    Agency 459
US Civil War 91, 224
US Department of State
    373, 380, 416, 477, 655
US farm products 602
US foreign relations 6, 86,
    282
    with Honduras 476-501
US hegemony 383-3, 389,
    393, 395, 403, 408,
    428, 441, 483, 486, 707
US House of
    Representatives 456
US military presence 88,

238, 312, 331, 413,
430, 432, 437, 443,
447, 682
US Office of Education
688
US police training 491
US presence since 1821
195, 242
see also US military
presence
US refugee policy 279
US–Canadian border 61
US–Central American
relations 385, 442
US–Honduran relations
413, 476-501
USAID see US Agency for
International
Development
Utila 60, 728

V

Vaccination 345
Valle, Cecilio del 716
Valle, José de 180, 233
Valle, Pompeyo del 706,
725
Valle, Rafael Heliodoro
727
Vegetation 22, 28, 32, 40,
42, 121, 714
Velásquez, José Antonio
748
Velásquez Rodríguez,
Manfredo 371, 373,
379
Vietnam War 497
Villages 83, 145
development 327
Villeda Morales, Ramón
414

Violence 337, 400
Visitación Padilla
Committee 332
Vocational training 671-2,
688
Volcanic history 38

W

Wages 569, 630, 655, 664,
669, 674-5
see also Labour
movements
Walker, William 190
Washington Office on
Latin America 491
Wasps 118
Water 22, 35, 40, 537
resources 679, 681
rights 520
Waterfowl 63
Wealth 323
distribution 640
Weapons 144, 439, 450
Weather 60
see also Climate
Welfare *see* Social services
West Africa 257
West Indies 25
Westinghouse Health
Systems 349
White Hand 426
Whitman, Walt 68
WHO *see* World Health
Organization
Wildlife 40
reserves 95
Wilson, Woodrow 501
Witness[es] for Peace 277,
374
Women 6, 311, 313,
316-17, 332, 714

education 685
intellectuals 747
legislation affecting 523
market participation 667
opportunities 544
Women workers 657
Working class 189, 675
see also Labour
Working-class movement
see Labour
movements
World Health
Organization (WHO)
354
World Vision 281
World War I 566, 677
World War II 677

Y

Yamaranguila 294
Yarumela 323
Yoro 32, 128
Young people 337, 736
Yucatán 200
Yure drainage system 106
Yuscarán 325

Z

Zambu people 79
Zamorano 32
Zelaya, Juanita 724
Zelaya Sierra, Pablo 740,
748
Zemurray, Samuel 14, 126,
322
see also Cuyamel Fruit
Company
Zúñiga Figueroa, Carlos
748

Map of Honduras

This map shows the more important towns and other features.

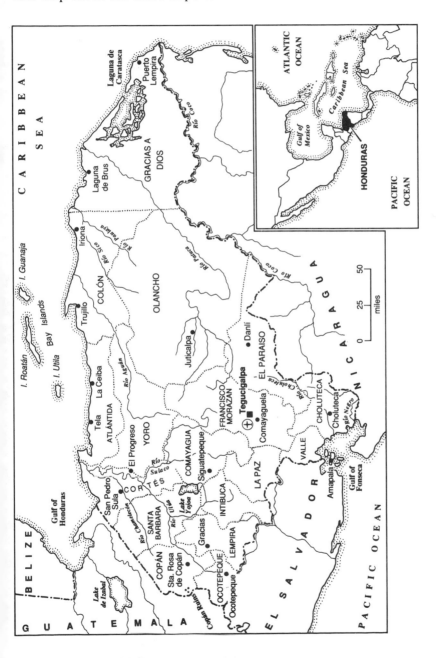